Ralph Engel
Ann Arbor
3-XI-52

CLASSICS AND COMMERCIALS

BOOKS BY EDMUND WILSON

I THOUGHT OF DAISY

POETS, FAREWELL!

AXEL'S CASTLE

THE AMERICAN JITTERS: A YEAR OF THE SLUMP

TRAVELS IN TWO DEMOCRACIES

THIS ROOM AND THIS GIN AND THESE SANDWICHES

THE TRIPLE THINKERS

TO THE FINLAND STATION

THE WOUND AND THE BOW

NOTE-BOOKS OF NIGHT

THE SHOCK OF RECOGNITION

MEMOIRS OF HECATE COUNTY

EUROPE WITHOUT BAEDEKER

THE LITTLE BLUE LIGHT

Classics and Commercials

A LITERARY CHRONICLE OF THE FORTIES

BY EDMUND WILSON

FARRAR, STRAUS AND COMPANY • NEW YORK

CONTENTS

CONTENTS

ACKNOWLEDGMENTS

THIS BOOK contains a selection of my literary articles written during the nineteen-forties. All of them have been revised and some of them considerably rewritten. A few have been brought up to date with postscripts. With the exception of the memoir of Rosenfeld and some of the notes on Connolly and Waugh, they are presented in chronological order. The dates in most cases are those of their first appearance in print; but to *T. K. Whipple, Thoughts on Being Bibliographed* and *Paul Rosenfeld: Three Phases* I have assigned the dates when they were written.

From the article on Harold Nicolson through the article on Ronald Firbank, all the pieces originally appeared in the *New Yorker*. *Archibald MacLeish and the Word, Van Wyck Brooks's Second Phase* and *Max Eastman in 1941* were first printed in the *New Republic*; *The Antrobuses and the Earwickers, Alexander Woollcott of the Phalanx* and *The Poetry of Angelica Balabanoff* in the *Nation*; and *Mr. Joseph E. Davies as a Stylist* in *Partisan Review*. *Thoughts on Being Bibliographed* was written for the *Princeton University Library Chronicle* and appeared in the issue of February, 1944. *T. K. Whipple* was written as an introduction to a volume of Whipple's posthumous papers called *Study Out the Land*, published by the University of California Press in 1943; and *Paul Rosenfeld: Three Phases* was contributed to a memorial volume called *Paul Rosenfeld: Voyager in the Arts,* published by the Creative Age Press in 1947. *The Boys in the Back Room* originally came out as a series in the issues of the *New Republic* of November 11, November 18, December 9 and December 16, 1940, and was republished, with its added *Postscript,* in book-form the following year by the Colt Press of San Francisco.

CLASSICS AND COMMERCIALS

ARCHIBALD MACLEISH AND THE WORD

Mr. Archibald MacLeish, in his new role of Librarian of Congress, has suddenly taken a turn which must be astonishing even to those who have followed his previous career.

In a speech before the American Association for Adult Education, which has been prominently reported in the newspapers and printed by the *New Republic* in its issue of June 10, he has declared that the war novels of such writers as John Dos Passos and Ernest Hemingway (to name only the Americans mentioned), in their railing against "the statements of conviction, of purpose and of belief on which the war of 1914–18 was fought," have left the younger generation "defenseless against an enemy whose cynicism, whose brutality and whose stated intention to enslave present the issue of the future in moral terms—in terms of conviction and belief." Without, says Mr. MacLeish, attempting to "judge these writers," and confessing that he himself at one time indulged a similar impulse, he sternly insists that Dos Passos, Hemingway and Company "must face the fact that the books they wrote in the years just after the War have done more to disarm democracy in the face of fascism than any other single influence."

Now, in the first place, it is obviously absurd for Mr. MacLeish to cite, as he does, two passages describing the feelings of characters in novels by Dos Passos and Hemingway as evidence of the authors' own lack of convictions or

3

of a tendency of their books to "disarm democracy." If anything could be plain to a reader of Dos Passos, it is the fact that moral principles play a more serious part in his work than in that of almost any other important American novelist and that his sympathies are passionately democratic. And if anything could be plain to a reader of Hemingway, it is the fact that he is constantly preoccupied with ideals of gallantry and honor, and is pugnacious almost to the point of madness. Neither Dos Passos nor Henri Barbusse, also cited by Mr. MacLeish, has ever asserted or believed as Mr. MacLeish declares they have, "that nothing men can put into words is worth fighting for"; but the conflict in which Dos Passos and Barbusse were interested during the years of World War I was the fight on the labor front. One of the first things that Barbusse did after the war was to publish an intransigent radical tract called *Le Couteau entre les Dents* which was certainly a "statement of conviction, of purpose and of belief," if any has ever existed. Barbusse became a militant Left journalist and remained one up to his death. But Mr. MacLeish, who is now so eager to fight, takes no account of this kind of militancy. He sounds as if he had never heard of the class war, which has certainly, since the Bolshevist revolution, made itself felt in our world as the fundamental, seismic conflict. Nor can the writers mentioned by Mr. MacLeish be accused, in this connection, of having failed to take fighting slogans seriously: Henri Barbusse, for example, erred in the other direction—by not being critical enough.

It is true that the books of these novelists gave voice to a certain disillusionment with the cause of the Allies in the last war as a struggle for "justice and humanity," as an effort to "save democracy." But it would be necessary for Mr. MacLeish, if he wants to discount what they said, to expound his own view of the last war and to deal with such questions as these: Should not the Allies have put an end to it in January, 1916, by concluding a peace with Austria at the time of the Austrian peace offers? Should the United States have ever gone into it? Did we do anything except prolong it unnecessarily and leave the situation worse than it otherwise might have been? Would not the belligerent nations have made an earlier peace, on a basis less dangerous for the world?— for has it not been precisely the situation of Germany, as she was left by the Allies after their victory, humiliated, dismembered, crushed, mortgaged with an indemnity for generations, that has furnished Hitler his fatal opportunity to figure as a national savior? Did not Wilson, with his enthusiasm for the rights of small nations, derived from the tradition of the Confederacy, simply play into the hands of the Allied statesmen, who wanted to break up Central Europe in order to weaken it and who left it a prey to the first adventurer with the audacity to put it together again? Were there not, in short, very good reasons why anyone who had served in the last war should have considered the Allied slogans an imposture? Mr. MacLeish does concede that the novelists in question were only dramatizing in their fiction "what all of us who were in the war believed." "But," he adds, "they are nevertheless words which have borne bitter and dangerous fruit."

What fruit? Can it really be admitted that the reading of those novels about army life has been the cause of the more general skepticism which seems to be current today as to the value for either Europe or ourselves of the United States' engaging in foreign wars? This skepticism, the skepticism, say, of Charles A. Beard, is surely not the result—save, perhaps, to a very minor degree—of the impression made by disillusioned novelists; it is the result of the same natural causes which also produced their novels and which were as much historical realities at the moment of Mr. MacLeish's writing as the morning after the Versailles Treaty.

But now we come to another point which Mr. Mac-Leish seems to be trying to make in this extraordinarily confused piece. He evidently has some idea that writers should censor themselves in the interests of—it is not clear what; in the interests of some extremely vague idea of what is necessary to "defend ourselves against fascism." This is the author of that poem on the "Social Muse," which appeared only a few years ago in the pages of the same magazine which has published his recent speech —that poem in which Mr. MacLeish depicted the ig- nominious end of writers who went in for causes, and declared that the role of the poet was that of the woman who follows the armies and sleeps with the soldiers of both camps. (*It is also strictly forbidden to mix in ma- neuvers. . . . Is it just to demand of us to bear arms?*) But it will not surprise anyone at this time of day to have it demonstrated that Mr. MacLeish has repudiated an earlier position. He has surely in the course of his career struck a greater variety of attitudes and been ready to repudiate them faster than any other reputable writer of our time; and in the piece under consideration he does not hesitate to tell us that he himself has sinned in the past as Hemingway and Dos Passos have sinned. But today he has been forced to recognize that "perhaps the luxury of the complete confession, the uttermost despair, the farthest doubt, should be denied themselves by writers living in any but the most orderly and settled times." Well, you will not find the farthest doubt or the uttermost despair in the writers whom Mr. MacLeish mentions; they all believe pretty strongly in something. But even if this doubt and despair were there, as they may be in certain other writers, would it really be our duty to dissuade them, as Mr. MacLeish would dissuade them, from uttering their true opinions?

It is hard to see how any person to whom literature was even for a moment real could have written the sentence I have quoted. The farthest doubt and the uttermost despair are, of course, not "luxuries" at all to anyone except a literary "irresponsible," who feels that he can choose his moods, as if they were suits from a well-stocked wardrobe. They are the expressions of the bewilderment or the bitterness imposed on the human spirit by precisely those periods of history which are the reverse of orderly and settled. One would like to ask Mr. MacLeish whether he believes that the dignity of this spirit was lowered by the skepticism of Montaigne or the gloom of the romantic poets, or that any useful end for civilization would have been served by their suppressing what they thought and felt.

But the most remarkable statement in Mr. MacLeish's speech just precedes the one I have quoted. "Perhaps writers," he says, "having so great a responsibility to the future, must not weaken the validity of the Word even when the deceptions of the Word have injured them." That is, if you have ever suffered as a victim to somebody or other's meretricious propaganda, you should not attempt to expose it, but ought to let others go on being duped, for fear of destroying the integrity of "the Word." It is exactly as if a banker were to consider it against his interests to notify the authorities that there was counterfeit money abroad. Mr. MacLeish quotes a statement by John Chamberlain to the effect that the younger generation "distrusts not only slogans and all tags, but even all words—distrusts, that is to say, all statements of principle and conviction, all declarations of moral purpose." Is the logical alternative, then—for fear of impairing "The Word"—to accept all these declarations? Words, for Mr. MacLeish, are apparently ends in themselves—not a technique for understanding, a medium for putting on record, the vicissitudes of human experience, a medium and a technique which must constantly be renewed to meet the requirements of changing experience. The truth is that when the new words come in, the old must be put away; and it is one of the duties of the writer to avoid using outworn words that no longer have any real meaning.

And now let us ask again: in the interests of precisely what has Mr. MacLeish thought it proper to denounce as "disastrous" and "dangerous" the influence of a number of writers whom he characterizes as "honest men," among "the best and most sensitive of my generation"? Mr. MacLeish does not make this clear; but the whole tone of his speech sounds ominously as if he might be trying to prepare us for a new set of political slogans, of "declarations of moral purposes," to be let loose from the same sort of sources as those that launched the publicity of World War I. Mr. MacLeish is today an official, and he strikes us as a little uneasy as to whether the utterances of officials will everywhere be taken quite seriously. He may possibly be haunted by the memory that in the company he sometimes kept before he removed to Washington—*Dos who saw the tyrants in the lime, Ernest that saw the first snow in the fox's feather . . . O living men . . . receive me among you!*—such utterances were not always well received.

Mr. MacLeish is at pains to tell us that he does not want to burn any books or to regiment people's minds; but it is not very reassuring, at this moment of strain and excitement, to find the Librarian of Congress making a fuss about "dangerous" books. He has a good deal to say about liberty in the latter part of his speech, but he makes it perfectly plain that he believes that, as a matter of policy, certain kinds of dissentient writers should be discouraged from expressing their ideas.

There is one passage in this high-principled declaration which plunges it into utter insanity and almost disarms criticism. Mr. MacLeish, in his list of deleterious authors, includes Erich Maria Remarque, the author of *All Quiet on the Western Front,* and Andreas Latzko, the author of *Men in War.* The Librarian has forgotten that Latzko and Remarque, after all, had been soldiering during the war in behalf of "statements of conviction" and "declarations of moral purpose" on the opposite side from those of the Allies—in view of which Mr. MacLeish ought logically to be in favor of there having been more Remarques and Latzkos to demoralize the enemy side. As a matter of fact, the film that was made from *All Quiet on the Western Front* has been violently attacked by the Nazis, who feared its effect on the public. If the books of Remarque and Latzko had really been influential, the Nazis would not now be in France. If this school of writers in general had had the importance which Mr. MacLeish assigns to them, we should have had no second World War at all.

July 1, 1940

VAN WYCK BROOKS'S SECOND PHASE

VAN WYCK BROOKS has now suffered the fate of many a good writer before him. Beginning as an opposition critic, read by a minority of the public, he has lived to become a popular author, read by immense numbers of people and awarded a Pulitzer prize—with the result that the ordinary reviewers are praising him indiscriminately and the highbrows are trying to drop him. One has seen the same sort of thing happen with Eugene O'Neill, with Edna Millay, with Hemingway, with Thornton Wilder—and always to the obscuration of their actual merits and defects.

Let me begin then by stating some of the objections which are being made to Brooks's books on New England by those readers to whom it is most distasteful to see him become the darling of the women's clubs.

1. Brooks's work falls into two distinct divisions, with the break just before his volume on Emerson. The early Brooks was somber and despairing. In the tones of a Jeremiah, he cried out against America for ruining her writers and against the American writers for allowing themselves to be ruined. This period reached its nadir of gloom in the essay on *The Literary Life in America,* contributed to Harold Stearns's symposium *Civilization in the United States,* in which Brooks announced the total extinction of literary genius in America just at the moment when it was again lighting up. But he had already

produced work of great importance in *America's Coming-of-Age* and *The Ordeal of Mark Twain*; and the Brooks of this early period was a searching and original critic, probably, for the writers of those years, the principal source of ideas on the cultural life of the United States. People got from him, not only, as they did also from Mencken, a sense of the second-rateness of recent American writing and a conviction of the need for something better, but also an historical perspective and an analysis of the causes of what was wrong. Though one ended by becoming exasperated with the laments of the early Brooks, one owed him an immense debt, and one associated what one owed him with his sense of the national failure.

It was, then, with something of surprise that we found him, in *The Flowering of New England*, suddenly chortling and crooning in a manner little short of rapturous over those same American household classics—Lowell, Longfellow, Emerson *et al.*—whose deficiencies, in his memorable chapter on *Our Poets* in *America's Coming-of-Age*, he had so unflinchingly forced us to recognize. In the attempt to provide America, as he said, with a "usable" literary past, he seemed to some to have gone too far in the direction of glorification and to have substituted for the bitter insight of *The Ordeal of Mark Twain* the pageant of an historical mural, in which the figures were larger than life and the colors laid on too brightly, and in which the hidden springs of character were not examined at all. One missed the intensity of his early work; he seemed now to be *too much* pleased with everybody; there was no longer any tension of conflict.

2. Moreover, the bold brushwork of these frescoes involved an inordinate development of a feature of Brooks's method which had figured with unhappy results in *The Pilgrimage of Henry James*. Mr. Brooks in

an evil hour had read the books of a Frenchman named Léon Bazalgette, who wrote lives of Thoreau and Whitman, and who adopted the practice of describing his subjects in a medium confected of phrases taken without quotes from their own works. Mr. Brooks has imitated this practice: he has attempted to convey the qualities of the literary personalities he deals with by compounding a kind of paste out of their writings. This paste he spreads on the page and expects it to give us the essence of his author. But, though sometimes, as in the case of an inferior figure like Longfellow, he does succeed in extracting thus a tone and a color which we should not easily catch in dipping into Longfellow himself, since it is necessary to boil down a good deal of such a poet in order to distinguish a flavor—on the other hand, with a first-rate writer like Emerson or Hawthorne or Thoreau, you simply get a sort of predigested sample which seems to have had all the vitamins taken out of it and which causes constant irritation to an admirer of these authors, because it gives the impression of a travesty that is always just off-key and off-color.

This is especially a pity, because Brooks is himself an individual and beautiful writer, whose accent has a fine clarity, and what we get in these confected passages is neither the true Brooks nor his subject. It is a method, furthermore, which involves what amounts to an abdication of the critic, who is here neither speaking about his subject nor allowing his subject to speak for himself. What is the value of all the *as one might call it's* scattered through the pages of Brooks? If it is Brooks who is calling it this or that, the interpolation is totally unnecessary; if, on the other hand, it is someone else, the author ought to tell us who. What is the explanation of the statement, in connection with Charles Eliot Norton, that "his field was of imagination all compact"? If the sentence is Brooks's sentence, he ought not to load it down with this antique cliché; if the opinion is that of some previous critic, the cliché was not worth preserving. Who is it who exclaims of Francis Parkman, "*Eccovi,* this child has been in hell"? Mr. Brooks pointing up his picture with a familiar literary allusion or some Bostonian addicted to Dante? Many phrases which are striking in their contexts lose their significance and seem merely grotesque when they are embedded in the text of someone else. Thus we read in Brooks's account of Louisa M. Alcott that, "She liked to watch the moon. She had good dreams. She had pleasant times with her mind." A footnote explains this last phrase, which turns out to have been taken from a diary written at the age of twelve, in which the words do not sound so grotesque as when sprung on us without preparation. Surely it would have been much more sensible to have quoted the diary in the first place.

3. It has sometimes been said of Mr. Brooks that he is not really a literary critic because he is not interested in literature as an art and lies indeed under serious suspicion of not being able to tell chalk from cheese. There is in this charge this much of truth: Van Wyck Brooks concerns himself with literature mainly from the point of view of its immediate social significance. He is not particularly sensitive to form and style in themselves, and he is not particularly responsive to any other than social morals. Thus, in this latest volume, you find the extraordinary statement that there was "no unity" in Henry Adams' style and that, "except for recurrent conceptions and phrases" his various books "might all have been written by various hands"—whereas a diligent reader of Adams would, I think, be able to recognize a paragraph from any of his books by its rhythm and tone alone. The bland, ironic, weak-backed sentences of *The Education of*

Henry Adams are already in *The History of the United States*. And thus in the charges brought, on page 402, against the later Henry James, we find the strange complaint that James is in the habit of describing his characters "as 'eminent,' as 'wonderful,' 'noble' and 'great'" and then making them perform discreditable actions—an objection which shows a complete incomprehension both of James's all-pervasive irony and of the complexity of his moral vision. And if you look up, among the poems, say, of Lowell, the lyrics recommended by Mr. Brooks, you are likely to be disappointed.

It is perhaps true that Mr. Brooks has to have the status of his authors settled for him before he begins. He seems to accept his subjects as objective facts, as stars of established magnitudes, which he studies in their known relations, their already determined orbits. This assumption is borne out by his extravagant praise of mediocrity among his contemporaries combined with his puzzled indifference to some of the most remarkable writers of his time at the moment of their first emergence. His ineptitude at appraising for himself has become especially conspicuous in connection with this general history. The early Brooks was always comparing our writers with European writers to the disadvantage of the United States. The later Brooks is whooping it up for America's "usable past," but he still leaves in doubt the comparative values of the American writers whose work he describes, in relation to the rest of the world. Doesn't Emerson look meager beside Goethe? Wasn't Thoreau, by any standards, one of the first prose writers of the nineteenth century? Isn't Henry James, for all his shortcomings, a more important novelist than Thackeray? Brooks does not try to answer these questions—of a kind that have been forced on the attention of the expatriate Eliot and James and which they have sometimes discussed acutely.

He has been so far, in his history of our literature, almost exclusively occupied with his subjects in relation to the American scene.

When one has said all this, however, one finds that one has done little more than define the terms themselves on which Van Wyck Brooks has undertaken an immense and difficult task; and what is valid in these objections applies in general less to his new volume than to the one that went before.

Even in *The Flowering of New England* the nature of the task itself partly explains the extravagances. The magnification of the New England poets may be justified on the ground that the author is presenting them as they presented themselves to the audience that thought them great; and it is one of the most striking proofs of Mr. Brooks's possession of the historical imagination that he is able to see the events of the past not merely in retrospect, that he does not merely estimate facts, sum up tendencies, compose obituaries, but that he can show us movements and books as they loomed upon the people to whom they were new. The reader of *The Flowering of New England* beheld the Boston of the first decades of the Republic coming at him, as it were, head-on; and this was what made the book so important. It brought home even to people who had already some acquaintance with the subject as no other book had done what post-revolutionary New England had meant to the America of its day as the cultural spokesman for the new humanity that was to be built in the United States. To get this over to a generation which had known only a shrivelled Boston overlaid with industrial vulgarity and who had probably not very often reopened the New England poets since their schooldays, required some expanse of canvas and some special expenditure of oils.

In his *Indian Summer* of New England, Mr. Brooks is aiming at a different effect: he has here to show us the old virtue passing out of Boston; and it is noticeable that in this second volume the colors are not spread on so thick. Furthermore, he has succeeded in freeing himself, after the first hundred pages or so, from the viscousness produced in *The Flowering* by his stirring into the stream of the story the *ipsissima verba* of his subjects. The presentations of artistic personalities become noticeably more fluent and felicitous with the portraits of the later chapters. This kind of evocation Mr. Brooks has now fully mastered and the Mary L. Wilkins, the Amy Lowell, the E. A. Robinson and the Robert Frost are the best things of the kind he has done.

Indeed, Mr. Brooks has now mastered the whole art of this historical-biographical narrative—an art which has its special difficulties unknown to the teller of invented fables. To reduce this kind of actual material to a story which will carry the reader along, to find a scale and provide a variety which will make it possible to hold his attention, become a species of obstacle race, in which the writer has made a wager to play a graceful and entertaining role while hampered by the necessity of sticking to texts, of assembling scattered data and of organizing a complicated unity.

What, precisely, *is* Mr. Brooks's story? It is not perhaps quite a history of literature. Nor is it—since he somewhat slights philosophy and theology—quite the history of "the New England mind" which he announced in his first volume. It is rather a history of New England society as reflected in its cultural activities. If Mr. Brooks is not always alive to the values of his American subjects in the larger Western setting, he is a master, our only real master since the death of Vernon Parrington, of the social interpretation of literature inside the national frame. To read his *Indian Summer* of New England is, for an American old enough to have been young in the period described, a constantly fascinating and surprising revelation. You will find out in this new book of Mr. Brooks why people went abroad every spring, and why they sometimes went and never came back. See the chapter called *The Post-War Years*, in which he tells how the commercial development that followed the Civil War extinguished the old enthusiasm for culture along with the republican ideals and made cultivated people in general ashamed of the United States—a chapter which perhaps provides the most satisfactory analysis that has yet been made of this situation and which may well become the classical account of it. In the same chapter, you will find out why the ladies in your childhood read the English Kipling and Conan Doyle, and why you were told that Mark Twain was "vulgar." You will find out why your aunt studied botany and why some cousin who had to go West for his health taught you to name the birds without a gun. You will find out the real significance of *The Peterkin Papers*, that monstrous, matter-of-fact comic fantasy that haunts you like a dream of childhood. You will learn who all those people really were whose writings you have never thought to look into since you were old enough to select your own reading and who have remained to you familiar but phantasmal myths, always referred to with their middle names, inseparable from them as Homeric epithets or Russian patronymics: Helen Hunt Jackson, Thomas Bailey Aldrich, Charles Dudley Warner, Edward Rowland Sill. You will learn how Edward Estlin Cummings of Patchin Place, New York, is connected with Ralph Waldo Emerson of Concord.

Mr. Brooks's study of New England is, in short, one of

the three or four prime light-diffusing works on the history of American society—I should include also the Beards' *Rise of American Civilization* and Dos Passos' *U.S.A.*—that have appeared in our own time. It is one of the key books of our period, which places us in time and space and which tells us what to think of ourselves. What Mr. Brooks *used* to tell us to think was depressing, though up to a point also bracing; and his reversal of feeling in *The Flowering of New England* did seem a little overwrought. But in this last volume, he has hit an equilibrium. His account of the decline of Boston is not lugubrious in his early manner: the whole tone is one of pride and confidence. His last pages on the revival of the New England tradition in the writers of the cosmopolitan decade that followed 1914 are among the most eloquent he has written, and among the most impressive. The medium and field he has chosen are justified, as every writer's must be, by his success in producing by means of them an interesting and beautiful book. Mr. Brooks's love of literature is not to be proved or disproved by his habit of evaluating authors in terms of their social implications against the immediate local background any more than the knowledge of humanity of a novelist is to be tested by his setting or his not setting his characters in relation to the rest of the world or by his neglect, in his preoccupation with his own particular scale of values, of someone else's different scale. It is implicit in the purity of his enthusiasms and in his own splendid abilities as an artist.

September 30, 1940

THE BOYS IN THE BACK ROOM

"Set 'em up for the boys in the back room."

1. James M. Cain

RISING from a long submergence in the politics and literature of the nineteenth century, during which I read almost nothing that people were reading, I have just regaled myself with practically the complete works of James M. Cain, Horace McCoy, Richard Hallas, John O'Hara, William Saroyan, John Steinbeck and Hans Otto Storm. These writers are all of fairly recent arrival; they have most of them been influenced by Hemingway; they all live or have lived in California, and they have all, to a greater or lesser extent, written about that State. They thus constitute a sort of group, and they suggest certain generalizations.

Let us begin with Mr. Cain and his school. *The Postman Always Rings Twice* came out in 1934; and Mr. Cain's second novel, *Serenade,* in 1937. They were followed by other similar novels which apparently derived from Mr. Cain. The whole group stemmed originally from Hemingway, but it was Hemingway turned picaresque; and it had its connections also with the new school of mystery writers of the type of Dashiell Hammett.

Mr. Cain remained the best of these novelists. Horace McCoy, the author of *They Shoot Horses, Don't They?* and *I Should Have Stayed Home,* had a subject with possibilities: the miserable situation of movie-struck young men and women who starve and degrade themselves in Hollywood; and the first of his books is worth reading for its description of one of those dance marathons that were among the more grisly symptoms of the early years of the depression. But the faults of Mr. McCoy's first novel— lack of characterization, lack of motivation—show up much more nakedly in the second. *You Play the Black and the Red Comes Up,* by a writer who calls himself Richard Hallas, is a clever pastiche of Cain which is mainly as two-dimensional as a movie. It is indicative of the degree to which this kind of writing has finally become formularized that it should have been possible for a visiting Englishman—the real author is Eric Knight—to tell a story in the Hemingway-Cain vernacular almost without a slip.

The hero of the typical Cain novel is a good-looking down-and-outer, who leads the life of a vagrant and a rogue. He invariably falls under the domination—usually to his ruin—of a vulgar and determined woman from whom he finds it impossible to escape. In the novels of McCoy and Hallas, he holds our sympathy through his essential innocence; but in the novels of Cain himself, the situation is not so simple. Cain's heroes are capable of extraordinary exploits, but they are always treading the edge of a precipice; and they are doomed, like the heroes of Hemingway, for they will eventually fall off the precipice. But whereas in Hemingway's stories, it is simply that these brave and decent men have had a dirty deal from life, the hero of a novel by Cain is an individual of mixed unstable character, who carries his precipice with him like Pascal.

His fate is thus forecast from the beginning; but in the meantime he has fabulous adventures—samples, as it were, from a *Thousand and One Nights* of the screwy Pacific Coast: you have jungle lust in roadside lunch-rooms, family motor-trips that end in murder, careers catastrophically broken by the vagaries of bisexual personality, the fracas created by a Mexican Indian introduced among the phonies of Hollywood.

All these writers are also preëminently the poets of the tabloid murder. Cain himself is particularly ingenious in tracing from their first beginnings the tangles that gradually tighten around the necks of the people involved in those bizarre and brutal crimes that figure in the American papers; and is capable even of tackling—in *Serenade,* at any rate—the larger tangles of social interest from which these deadly little knots derive. Such a subject might provide a great novel: in *An American Tragedy,* such a subject did. But as we follow, in a novel by Mr. Cain, the development of one of his plots, we find ourselves more and more disconcerted at knocking up—to the destruction of illusion—against the blank and hard planes and angles of something we know all too well: the wooden old conventions of Hollywood. Here is the Hollywood gag: the echo of the murdered man's voice reverberating from the mountains when the man himself is dead, and the party in *Serenade,* in which the heroine stabs the villain under cover of acting out a bull-fight; the punctual Hollywood coincidence: the popping-up of the music-loving sea-captain, who is the *deus ex machina* of *Serenade*; the Hollywood reversal of fortune: the singer who loses his voice and then gets it back again, becoming famous and rich in a sequence that lasts about three minutes.

Mr. Cain is actually a writer for the studios (as are also, or have also been, Mr. Hallas and Mr. McCoy). These novels are produced in his off-time; and they are a kind of Devil's parody of the movies. Mr. Cain is the *âme damnée* of Hollywood. All the things that have been excluded by the Catholic censorship: sex, debauchery, unpunished crime, sacrilege against the Church—Mr. Cain has let them loose in these stories with a gusto as of pent-up ferocity that the reader cannot but share. What a pity that it is impossible for such a writer to create and produce his own pictures!

In the meantime, *Serenade* is a definite improvement on *The Postman*. It, too, has its trashy aspect, its movie foreshortenings and its too-well oiled action; but it establishes a surer illusion. *The Postman* was always in danger of becoming unintentionally funny. Yet even there brilliant moments of insight redeemed the unconscious burlesque; and there is enough of the real poet in Cain —both in writing and in imagination—to make one hope for something better than either.

2. John O'Hara

John O'Hara also derives from Hemingway, and his short stories sound superficially like Hemingway's. His longer stories, like Cain's, have it in common with Hemingway that the heroes and heroines are doomed. But O'Hara's main interest in life is of an entirely different kind from Hemingway's, and his writing really belongs to a different category of fiction.

O'Hara is not a poet like Hemingway, but primarily a social commentator; and in this field of social habits and manners, ways of talking and writing letters and dressing, he has done work that is original and interesting. It is essentially the same kind of thing that Henry James and his followers developed, but the center of attention has shifted. The older novelist dealt almost exclusively with a well-to-do upper stratum, and the chief contrast he had to depict was between the American upper classes and the European upper classes, or between the established and cultivated people and the vulgar *nouveaux riches.* John O'Hara subjects to a Proustian scrutiny the tight-knotted social web of a large Pennsylvania town, the potpourri of New York night-life in the twenties, the nondescript fringes of Hollywood. In all this he has explored for the first time from his peculiar semi-snobbish point of view a good deal of interesting territory: the relations between Catholics and Protestants, the relations between college men and non-college men, the relations between the underworld and "legitimate" business, the ratings of café society; and to read him on a fashionable bar or the Gibbsville country club is to be shown on the screen of a fluoroscope gradations of social prestige of which one had not before been aware. There is no longer any hierarchy here, of either cultivation or wealth: the people are all being shuffled about, hardly knowing what they are or where they are headed, but each is clutching some family tradition, some membership in a select organization, some personal association with the famous, from which he tries to derive distinction. But in the meantime, they mostly go under. They are snubbed, they are humiliated, they fail. The cruel side of social snobbery is really Mr. O'Hara's main theme. Only rarely, as in the excellent story called *Price's Always Open,* do the forces of democracy strike back.

This social surface, then, Mr. O'Hara analyzes with delicacy, and usually with remarkable accuracy. His grasp of what lies underneath it is not, however, so sure. His point of view toward his principal characters tends to be rather clinical; but even where his diagnosis is clear, we do not share the experience of the sufferer. The girl in *Butterfield 8* is a straight case of a Freudian complex, somewhat aggravated by social maladjustment; but we don't really know her well. Julian English of *Appointment in Samarra* is apparently the victim of a bad heredity worked upon by demoralizing influences; yet the emotions that drive him to suicide are never really shown. The whole book is in the nature of an explanation of why Julian threw the highball in the face of the Irish climber; yet the explanation doesn't convince us that the inevitable end for Julian would be the suicide to which his creator brings him. As for Mr. O'Hara's latest novel, *Hope of Heaven*, a story of Hollywood, I have not been able to fathom it at all—though here, too, there seems to be discernible a Freudian behavior-pattern. One wonders whether the personality of the script-writer who is telling the story is intended to play some role of which he himself is unaware, in connection with the conduct of the other characters, or whether the author himself does not quite know what he is doing.

One gets the impression—confirmed by a statement which Mr. O'Hara is reported to have made—that he improvises more or less and never reworks or revises. His longer stories always sound like first drafts which ought to be trimmed and tightened up—which might be turned into very fine little novels, but which, as it is, remain rather diffuse and rather blurred as to their general intention. What is the relevance to the story, for example, of the newspaperwoman in *Appointment in Samarra*, whose career is described on such a scale? The account of her beginnings is amusing, but the part she plays in the drama doesn't seem to warrant this full-length introduction. What is the point of the newspaper reporter who suddenly gets into the picture, and more or less between us and it, at the end of *Butterfield 8*? What on earth is the justification—aside from establishing the atmosphere for a drama of general crookedness—of the long story about the man who stole the traveler's checks at the beginning of *Hope of Heaven*? If Mr. O'Hara has definite ideas about the meaning of these characters in his scheme, I can't see that he has brought it out. He seems merely to be indulging his whims. He happens, however, to be gifted with a clean, quick and sure style, which by itself gives an impression of restraint; and the unfaltering neatness of his writing carries him over a good deal of thin ice. But he appears, in perfecting this style, to have been following, from the point of view of architecture, a line of least resistance. Each of his novels has been less successful, less ambitious and less well-disciplined than the one that went before; but while the long stories have been deteriorating, the short stories have been improving: in the most successful of them he has achieved his characteristic effects as he has hardly been able to do in his novels. The best of his work, in my opinion, consists of *Appointment in Samarra,* the admirable long short story called *The Doctor's Son* in the collection of that name, and the short pieces of *Files on Parade* (though there are also a few memorable ones in the early volume—such as *Ella and the Chinee*).

As for *Pal Joey,* his last-published book, it is funny, well-phrased, well-observed; but, heel for heel, Pal Joey is a comedown after Julian English. *Appointment in Samarra* is a memorable picture both of a provincial snob, a disorganized drinking-man of the twenties, and of the complexities of the social organism in which he flourished and perished. But Pal Joey is merely an amoeba of the night-life of the jitter-bug era; and he is a little amoeba-monster. It is not that one objects to O'Hara's creating a monster—*Pal Joey* is successful as

satire precisely because the author is not afraid to go the
whole hog; but that he seems to represent a contraction
of John O'Hara's interests.

The truth is perhaps that O'Hara has never really had
his bearings since he dropped Gibbsville, Pa. He was all
awash in *Butterfield 8* in the night-life of New York—
though he still kept some capacity for judgment; and in
Hope of Heaven he showed serious signs of suffering
from Hollywood lightheadedness. He partly retrieved
himself by becoming the outstanding master of the *New
Yorker* short-story-sketch; but we expected, and still expect, more of him.

3. William Saroyan

The refrain becomes monotonous; but you have to begin by saying that Saroyan, too, derives from Hemingway. The novelists of the older generation—Hemingway
himself, Dos Passos, Faulkner, Wilder—have richer and
more complex origins, they belong to a bigger cultural
world. But if the most you can say of John O'Hara is
that he has evidently read Ring Lardner and F. Scott
Fitzgerald as well as Hemingway, the most you can say
of Saroyan is that he has also read Sherwood Anderson
(though he speaks of having looked into a book which
he bought for a nickel at a bookstore and which was in
Swedish and had pictures of churches). When you remember that Lardner and Anderson were among the
original ingredients in Hemingway, you see how limited
the whole school is.

But what distinguishes Saroyan from his fellow disciples is the fact that he is not what is called hard-boiled.
What was surprising and refreshing about him when he
first attracted notice, was that, although he was telling

the familiar story about the wise-guy who went into the bar, and I said and the bartender said and I said, this story with Saroyan was never cruel, but represented an agreeable mixture of San Francisco bonhomie and Armenian Christianity. The fiction of the school of Hemingway had been full of bad drunks; Saroyan was a novelty: a good drunk. The spell exerted in the theater by his play, *The Time of Your Life,* consisted in its creating the illusion of friendliness and muzzy elation and gentle sentimentality which a certain amount of beer or rye will bring on in a favorite bar. Saroyan takes you to the bar, and he produces for you there a world which is the way the world would be if it conformed to the feelings instilled by drinks. In a word, he achieves the feat of making and keeping us boozy without the use of alcohol and purely by the stimulus of art. It seems natural that the cop and the labor leader should be having a drink together; that the prostitute should prove to be a wistful child, who eventually gets married by someone that loves her; that the tall tales of the bar raconteur should turn out to be perfectly true, that the bar millionaire should be able to make good his munificent philanthropical offers—that they should be really Jack the Giant-Killer and Santa Claus; and that the odious vice-crusader, who is trying to make everybody unhappy, should be bumped off as harmlessly as the comic villain in an old-fashioned children's "extravaganza."

These magical feats are accomplished by the enchantment of Saroyan's temperament, which induces us to take from him a good many things that we should not accept from other people. With Saroyan the whole trick is the temperament; he rarely contrives a machine. The good fairy who was present at his christening thus endowed him with one of the most precious gifts that a literary artist can have, and Saroyan never ceases to explain to us how especially fortunate he is: "As I say, I do not know a great deal about what the words come to, but the presence says, Now don't get funny; just sit down and say something; it'll be all right. Say it wrong; it'll be all right anyway. Half the time I *do* say it wrong, but somehow or other, just as the presence says, it's right anyhow. I am always pleased about this. My God, it's wrong, but it's all right. It's really all right. How did it happen? Well that's how it is. It's the presence, doing everything for me. It's the presence, doing all the hard work while I, always inclined to take things easy, loaf around, not paying much attention to anything, much, just putting down on paper whatever comes my way."

Well, we don't mind Saroyan's saying this, because he is such an engaging fellow; and we don't mind his putting down on paper whatever happens to come his way. It is true that he has been endowed with a natural felicity of touch which prevents him from being offensive or tiresome in any of the more obvious ways; and at their best his soliloquies and stories recall the spontaneous songs of one of those instinctive composers who, with no technical knowledge of music, manage to finger out lovely melodies. Yet Saroyan is entirely in error in supposing that when he "says it wrong," everything is really all right. What is right in such a case is merely this instinctive sense of form which usually saves him—and even when he is clowning—from making a fool of himself. What *is* wrong, and what his charm cannot conceal, is the use to which he is putting his gifts. It is a shock for one who very much enjoyed *The Daring Young Man on the Flying Trapeze* to go back to reading Saroyan in his latest collection, *The Trouble with Tigers*. There is nothing in the book so good as the best things in *The Flying Trapeze*, and there is a good deal that is not above the level of the facility of a daily columnist. A columnist, in fact, is what William Saroyan seems sometimes in danger of becoming—the kind of columnist who depends entirely on a popular personality, the kind who never reads, who does not know anything in particular about anything, who merely turns on the tap every day and lets it run a column.

It is illuminating to compare this inferior stuff with the contents of a less well-known collection published in California. This volume, *Three Times Three*, consists mainly of miscellaneous pieces which the author seems to regard as not having quite come off. The result is something a great deal more interesting than the slick and rather thin stuff of *Tigers*. One of these pieces, *The Living and the Dead*, of which the author rightly says that it is not so good as it ought to be, seems to me, in spite of the fact that it miscarries to some degree, one of the best things Saroyan has written. The scene with the Armenian grandmother after the departure of the money-collecting Communist is of a startling and compelling beauty. This theme of the foreign-born asserting in modern America the virtues of an older society is one of the principal themes in Saroyan; whenever it appears—as in the short story called *70,000 Assyrians*—it takes his work out of the flat dimensions of the guy watching life in the bar; and here he has brought it into play for one of his most poignant effects. This is followed by an admirable scene, in which the young man walks out on the street and sees a child crying at a window, and reflects that for "the children of the world eternally at the window, weeping at the strangeness of this place," where the Communist must always look forward to a perfected society of the future, where his grandmother must always look backward to a world that has gone with her youth and that could never really have been as she remembers it, it is natural enough to escape into the "even more disorderly universe" of drunkenness, a state sad enough in itself. But the conception, with its three motifs, required a little doing; and Saroyan, as he confesses, did not quite bring it off. He would have had to take the whole thing more seriously and to work it out with more care; and he knows that he can get away with an almost infinite number of less pretentious pieces without having their second-rateness complained of.

Rudyard Kipling said one very good thing about writing: "When you know what you can do, do something else." Saroyan *has* tackled in his plays something larger and more complicated than his stories; but these plays seem now to be yielding to a temptation to turn into columns, too. The three that have been acted and printed have many attractive and promising features in a vein a little like J. M. Barrie's; but George Jean Nathan in the *American Mercury* has given a disquieting account of no less than five new plays by Saroyan that have already been unsuccessfully tried out. There was a rumor that Mr. Nathan had been trying to induce Saroyan to take the trouble to acquaint himself with a few of the classics of the theater, but it sounds as if the attempt had come to naught.

In the meantime, Saroyan goes on with his act, which is that of the unappreciated genius who is not afraid to stand up for his merits. This only obscures the issue. Most good artists begin by getting bad reviews; and Saroyan, in this regard, has been rather remarkably fortunate. So let him set his mind at rest. Everybody who is capable of responding to such things appreciates what is fine in his work. The fact that a number of people who do not know good theatrical writing from bad or whose tastes lie in other directions have failed to recognize Saroyan is no excuse for the artist to neglect his craft. He will be judged not by his personality act or by his ability to get produced and published—which he has proved to the point of absurdity; but by work that functions and lasts.

With his triumph there has crept into Saroyan's work an unwelcome suggestion of smugness. One has always had the feeling with his writing that, for all its amiability and charm, it has had behind it the pressure of a hard and hostile environment, which it has required courage to meet, and that this courage has taken the form of a debonair kidding humor and a continual affirmation of the fundamental kindliness of people— a courage which, in moments when it is driven to its last resources and deepest sincerity, is in the habit of invoking a faith in the loyalties of straight and simple people—Armenians, Czechs, Greeks—surviving untouched by the hatreds of an abstract and complex world. In Saroyan the successful playwright, for whom that pressure has been partially relieved, there seems to be appearing an instinct to exploit this theme of lovingkindness and of the goodness and rightness of things; and there is perhaps a just perceptible philistinism. If Saroyan, in *Love's Old Sweet Song*, has hit upon precisely the right way to make fun of *Time* magazine, he has, on the other hand, here, in what sounds like a skit on *The Grapes of Wrath*, at least grazed the familiar complacency which declares the unemployed are all bums. This is the path that leads to Eddie Guest, Professor William Lyon Phelps and Dr. Frank Crane; and let not Mr. Saroyan deceive himself: no writer has a charmed life.

4. Hans Otto Storm

With Hans Otto Storm and John Steinbeck, we get into more ambitious writing.

The work of Mr. Storm has been presented to the public in a curious and probably misleading way. His first two books, *Pity the Tyrant* and *Made in U.S.A.* (the latter published only in a limited edition), attracted relatively little attention. They were both novelettes. *Pity the Tyrant*, one of those stories about an "I" who travels and loves and runs risks and reflects with a sardonic detachment on the things that go on around him, seemed to attach itself to the general school of Hemingway. *Made in U.S.A.* had no "I" and was an exercise in objectivity: a story about people on a ship that ran aground, worked out as a social fable. Both stories had a concentration of form and a kind of conscientiousness in their approach to their material that were rare enough to excite interest in the author.

These books were followed in the fall of 1940 by a very long novel, *Count Ten*, which was enormously advertised by the publishers. To the surprise of Mr. Storm's readers, this book turned out, however, to be very much inferior on the whole to the ones that had gone before and to show what seemed internal evidence of having been written earlier than they. *Count Ten* gives distinctly the impression of being one of those autobiographical novels that young men begin in college and carry around for years in old trunks, keeping them at the back of their minds as refractors for their subsequent experience, but returning to work on them after intervals so long that the texture of the book is always changing, and that the story, when it finally appears, fluctuates between callowness and maturity, literal fact and developing invention. The characters encountered by the hero of *Count Ten* have a sort of goofy unreality which lets us down in an embarrassing way after the pretty well-observed social types of Mr. Storm's other novels; and the book is full of violent incidents which occur, as it were, offstage, in the blank lines between one chapter and the next, and which have no real emotional effect on what follows. The hero preserves a certain consistency; but the story of his adventures rambles on with little proportion, composition or climax. The writing, too, is far below the level of the author's earlier published novels. His style has always been hampered by an uncertainty about idiomatic English and a proclivity for German locutions, and, though his instinct for expressing himself has its own kind of sensitive precision, his language is always here a little cockeyed.

Yet *Count Ten* is not uninteresting to read. Implausible though a good deal of it is, it evidently makes use of actual experience; and the experience of Hans Otto Storm has been of a kind rather unusual among our fiction-writers. In the first place, Mr. Storm, though a radical, is not, like so many other novelists, a radical of the depression vintage. He is—one gathers from *Count Ten*—the descendant of German refugees of the Revolution of 1848 settled in Southern California. The hero of his novel, at any rate, begins by going to jail for resisting the draft in the last war and ends by going to jail again as the result of his activities as campaign manager for a movement evidently drawn from Upton Sinclair's EPIC. He has, in the meantime, had a successful career as an agent of the mining interests. Mr. Storm's perspectives from the Left are obviously a good deal longer than those of the ordinary California Communist: he is both practically more sophisticated and historically better informed.

Mr. Storm is unusual in another way. These youthful autobiographical fictions usually tell the stories of young men who want to be writers, and they do not as a rule get far from the literary life itself. But Mr. Storm is neither a journalist nor a script writer, not a man who has made his living by writing at all: he is a trained engineer; and his hero builds and flies planes, works on a construction gang, sails a ship, runs a furniture business in which he manufactures the furniture himself, and becomes a mining prospector in South America. An engineer who thus goes in for literature is such a novelty that Hans Otto Storm is able to carry us with him because we have never listened to precisely his story before His writing about the sea—in *Made in U. S. A.* and in the episode of the yacht in *Count Ten*—without the parade of technical knowledge which is the betrayal of the layman in Kipling, gives us a much more intimate sense of living the life of the ship than we get from *The Ship That Found Herself* or *The Devil and the Deep Sea*.

Add to this equipment—to this first-hand knowledge of aspects of American life which few American writers know at all—a mentality which is culturally closer to Europe than that of most American writers (there is a suggestion of Conrad about him); and you get something quite unique in our fiction. Mr. Storm has so far, it seems to me, done his best work in *Pity the Tyrant*. Both the earlier published books show an application of engineering aptitude to the technique of constructing novels which is strangely absent in *Count Ten*; but *Pity the Tyrant* has a freshness and vividness which do not appear to the same degree in *Made in U.S.A.*, a more systematic affair. The South American episodes in *Count Ten* sound like mere juvenile sketches for it. Here in this story of an American technician involved in a Peruvian revolution and sorely perplexed between his job, his proletarian political sympathies and a love affair with a South American lady, Mr. Storm does succeed in dramatizing one of those cases of social conscience which do not come off so well in *Count Ten*. Here he really attains intensity; and *Pity the Tyrant*—though not quite in the class with Hemingway and Stephen Crane—belongs among the more distinguished products of this tradition of American storytelling.

5. John Steinbeck

John Steinbeck is also a native Californian, and he has occupied himself more with the life of the State than any of these other writers. His exploration in his novels of the region of the Salinas Valley has been more tenacious and searching than anything else of the kind in our recent fiction, with the exception of Faulkner's exhaustive study of the State of Mississippi.

And what has Mr. Steinbeck found in this country he knows so well? I believe that his virtuosity in a purely technical way has tended to obscure his themes. He has published eight volumes of fiction, which represent a variety of forms and which have thereby produced an illusion of having been written from a variety of points of view. *Tortilla Flat* was a comic idyl, with the simplification almost of a folk tale; *In Dubious Battle* was a strike novel, centering around Communist organizers and following a fairly conventional pattern; *Of Mice and Men* was a compact little drama, contrived with almost too much cleverness, and a parable which criticized humanity from a non-political point of view; *The Long Valley* was a series of short stories, dealing mostly with animals, in which poetic symbols were presented in realistic settings and built up with concrete detail; *The Grapes of Wrath* was a propaganda novel, full of preachments and sociological interludes, and developed on the scale of an epic. Thus attention has been diverted from the content of Mr. Steinbeck's work by the fact that when his curtain goes up, he always puts on a different kind of show.

Yet there is in Mr. Steinbeck's fiction a substratum which remains constant and which gives it a certain weight. What is constant in Mr. Steinbeck is his preoccupation with biology. He is a biologist in the literal sense that he interests himself in biological research. The biological laboratory in the short story called *The Snake* is obviously something which he knows at first hand and for which he has a strong special feeling; and it is one of the peculiarities of his vocabulary that it runs to biological terms. But the laboratory described in *The Snake*, the tight little building above the water, where the scientist feeds white rats to rattlesnakes and fertilizes starfish ova, is also one of the key images of his fiction. It is the symbol of Mr. Steinbeck's tendency to present human life in animal terms.

Mr. Steinbeck almost always in his fiction is dealing either with the lower animals or with humans so rudimentary that they are almost on the animal level; and the relations between animals and people are as intimate as those in the zoöphile fiction of David Garnett and D. H. Lawrence. The idiot in *The Pastures of Heaven*, who is called Little Frog and Coyote, shows his kinship with the animal world by continually making pictures of birds and beasts. In *Tortilla Flat*, there is the Pirate, who lives in a kennel with his dogs and has practically forgotten human companionship. In *In Dubious Battle*, there is another character whose personality is confused with that of his dogs. In *The Grapes of Wrath*, the journey of the Joads is figured at the beginning by the progress of a turtle, and is accompanied and parodied all the way by animals, insects and birds. When the expropriated sharecroppers in Oklahoma are compelled to abandon their farm, we get an extended picture of the invasion of the house by the bats, the weasels, the owls, the mice and the pet cats that have gone back to the wild. Lennie in *Of Mice and Men* likes to carry around pet animals, toward which as well as toward human beings he has murderous animal instincts. The stories in *The Long Valley* are almost entirely about plants and animals; and Mr. Steinbeck does not give the effect, as Lawrence or Kipling does, of romantically raising the animals to the stature of human beings, but rather of assimilating the human beings to animals. *The Chrysanthemums, The White Quail* and *The Snake* deal with women who identify themselves with, respectively, chrysanthemums, a white quail and a snake. In *Flight,* a young Mexican boy, who has killed a man and run away into the mountains, is finally reduced to a state so close to that of the beasts that he is apparently mistaken by a mountain lion for another four-footed animal; and in the fantasy *Saint Katy the Virgin,* in which a vicious pig is made to repent and become a saint, the result is not to dignify the animal as the *Little Flowers of Saint Francis* does, for example, with the wolf of Agubbio, but to make human religion ridiculous.

Nor does Steinbeck love his animals as D. H. Lawrence does. The peculiar point of view is well analyzed in connection with Thomas Wayne in *To a God Unknown:* "He was not kind to animals; at least no kinder than they were to each other, but he must have acted with a consistency beasts could understand, for all creatures trusted him. . . . Thomas liked animals and understood them, and he killed them with no more feeling than they had about killing each other. He was too much an animal himself to be sentimental." And Steinbeck does not even dwell much, as Lawrence likes to do, on the perfections of his various beasts each after its own kind. It is the habits and behavior of the animals, not the impression they make, that interests him.

The chief subject of Mr. Steinbeck's fiction has been thus not those aspects of humanity in which it is most thoughtful, imaginative, constructive, nor even those aspects of animals that seem most attractive to humans, but rather the processes of life itself. In the ordinary course of nature, living organisms are continually being destroyed, and among the principal things that destroy them are the predatory appetite and the competitive instinct that are necessary for the very survival of eating and breeding creatures. This impulse of the killer has been preserved in a simpleton like Lennie of *Of Mice and Men* in a form in which it is almost innocent; and yet Lennie has learned from his more highly developed friend that to yield to it is to do something "bad." In his struggle against the instinct, he loses. Is Lennie bad or good? He is betrayed as, the author implies, all our human intentions are, by the uncertainties of our animal nature. And it is only, as a rule, on this primitive level that Mr. Steinbeck deals with moral questions: the virtues like the crimes, for him, are still a part of these planless and almost aimless, of these almost unconscious, processes. The preacher in *The Grapes of Wrath* is disillusioned with the human moralities, and his sermon at the grave of Grampa Joad, so lecherous and mean during his lifetime, evidently gives expression to Mr. Steinbeck's own point of view: "This here ol' man jus' lived a life an' jus' died out of it. I don't know whether he was good or bad, but that don't matter much. He was alive, an' that's what matters. An' now he's dead, an' that don't matter. Heard a fella tell a poem one time, an' he says, 'All that lives is holy.'"

The subject of *The Grapes of Wrath*, which is supposed to deal with human society, is the same as the subject of *The Red Pony*, which is supposed to deal with horses: loyalty to life itself. The men who feel themselves responsible for having let the red pony die must make up for it by sacrificing the mare in order that a new pony may be brought into the world alive. And so Rose of Sharon Joad, with her undernourished baby born dead, must offer her milk, in the desolate barn which is all she has left for a shelter, to another wretched victim of famine and flood, on the point of death from starvation. To what end should ponies and Oakies continue to live on the earth? "And I wouldn' pray for a ol' fella that's dead," the preacher goes on to say. "He's awright. He got a job to do, but it's all laid out for 'im an' there's on'y one way to do it. But us, we got a job to do, an' they's a thousan' ways, an' we don' know which one to take. An' if I was to pray, it'd be for the folks that don't know which way to turn."

This preacher who has lost his religion does find a way to turn: he becomes a labor agitator; and this theme has already been dealt with more fully in the earlier novel, *In Dubious Battle*. But what differentiates Mr. Steinbeck's picture of a labor movement with radical leadership from most treatments of such subjects of its period is again the biological point of view. The strike leaders, here, are Communists, as they are in many labor novels, but *In Dubious Battle* is not really based on the formulas of Communist ideology. The kind of character produced by the Communist movement and the Communist strategy in strikes (of the Communism of the day before yesterday) is *described* by Mr. Steinbeck, and

it is described with a certain amount of admiration;
yet the party member of *In Dubious Battle* does not
talk like a Marxist of even the Stalinist revision. The
cruelty of these revolutionists, though they are working
for a noble ideal and must immolate themselves in the
struggle, is not palliated by the author any more than
the cruelty of the half-witted Lennie; and we are made
to feel all through the book that, impressive though the
characters may be, they are presented primarily as examples of how life in our age behaves. There is developed
in the course of the story—especially by a fellow-traveler
doctor who seems to come closer than the Communist to
expressing Mr. Steinbeck's own ideas—a whole philosophy of "group-man" as an "animal."

"It might be like this, Mac: When group-man wants
to move, he makes a standard. 'God wills that we re-
capture the Holy Land'; or he says 'We fight to make
the world safe for democracy'; or he says, 'We will wipe
out social injustice with communism.' But the group
doesn't care about the Holy Land, or Democracy, or
Communism. Maybe the group simply wants to move,
to fight, and uses these words simply to reassure the
brains of individual men. . . ."

"How," asks Mac, "do you account for people like
me, directing things, moving things? That puts your
group-man out."

"You might be an effect as well as a cause, Mac. You
might be an expression of group-man, a cell endowed
with a special function, like an eye cell, drawing your
force from group-man, and at the same time directing
him, like an eye. Your eye both takes orders from and
gives orders to your brain."

"This isn't practical," objects Mac. "What's all this
kind of talk got to do with hungry men, with lay-offs
and unemployment?"

"It might have a great deal to do with them. It isn't

a very long time since tetanus and lockjaw were not connected. There are still primitives in the world who don't know children are the result of intercourse. Yes, it might be worth while to know more about group-man, to know his nature, his ends, his desires. They're not the same as ours. The pleasure we get in scratching an itch causes death to a great number of cells. Maybe group-man gets pleasure when individual men are wiped out in a way."

Later, when the mob of striking fruit-pickers begins to get out of hand, the Communists themselves begin to think of them in these infra-human terms:

"They're down there now. God, Mac, you ought to of seen them. It was like all of them disappeared, and it was just one big animal, going down the road. Just all one animal." . . .

"The *animal* don't want the barricade. I don't know what it wants. Trouble is, guys that study people always think it's men, and it isn't men. It's a different kind of animal. It's as different from men as dogs are. Jim, it's swell when we can use it, but we don't know enough. When it gets started it might do anything."

So the old pioneer of *The Leader of the People* describes a westward migration which he himself once led as "a whole bunch of people made into one big crawling beast. . . . Every man wanted something for himself, but the big beast that was all of them wanted only westering."

This tendency on Steinbeck's part to animalize humanity is evidently one of the causes of his relative unsuccess at creating individual humans. The *paisanos* of *Tortilla Flat* are not really quite human beings: they are cunning little living dolls that amuse us as we might be amused by pet guinea-pigs, squirrels or rabbits. They are presented through a special convention which is calculated to keep them cut off from any kinship with the author or the reader. In *The Grapes of Wrath*, on the other hand, Mr. Steinbeck has summoned all his resources to make the reader feel his human relationship with the family of dispossessed farmers; yet the result of this, too, is not quite real. The characters of *The Grapes of Wrath* are animated and put through their paces rather than brought to life; they are like excellent character actors giving very conscientious performances in a fairly well-written play. Their dialect is well managed, but they always sound a little stagy; and, in spite of Mr. Steinbeck's efforts to make them figure as heroic human symbols, one cannot help feeling that these Okies, too, do not exist for him quite seriously as people. It is as if human sentiments and speeches had been assigned to a flock of lemmings on their way to throw themselves into the sea. One remembers the short story called *Johnny Bear*. Johnny Bear is another of Steinbeck's idiots: he has exactly the physique of a bear and seems in almost every way subhuman; but he is endowed with an uncanny gift for reproducing with perfect mimicry the conversations he overhears, though he understands nothing of their human meaning.

It is illuminating to look back from *The Grapes of Wrath* to one of the earliest of Steinbeck's novels, *To a God Unknown*. In this book he is dealing frankly with the destructive and reproductive forces as the cardinal principles of nature. In one passage, the hero is described by one of the other characters as never having "known a person": "You aren't aware of persons, Joseph; only people. You can't see units, Joseph, only the whole." He finds himself, almost unconsciously and in contravention of Christianity, practicing a primitive nature cult, to which, in time of terrible drought, he sacrifices first his wife, then himself, as blood offerings to bring the rain. This story, though absurd, has a certain interest, and it evidently represents, on the part of Steinbeck just turned thirty, an honorably sincere attempt to find expression for his view of the world and his conception of the powers that move it. When you husk away the mawkish verbiage from the people of his later novels, you get down to a similar conception of a humanity not of "units" but lumped in a "whole," to a vision equally grim in its cycles of extinction and renewal.

Not, however, that John Steinbeck's picture of human beings as lemmings, as grass that is left to die, does not have its striking validity for the period in which we are living. In our time, Shakespeare's angry ape, drest in his little brief authority, seems to make of all the rest of mankind angry apes or cowering rodents. The one thing that was imagined with intensity in Aldous Huxley's novel, *After Many a Summer Dies the Swan*, was the eighteenth-century exploiter of the slave-trade degenerating into a fetal anthropoid. Many parts of the world are today being flooded with migrants like the Joads, deprived of the dignity of a human society, forbidden the dignity of human work, and made to flee from their houses like prairie-dogs driven before a prairie fire. Aldous Huxley has a good deal to say, as our American "Humanists" did, about a fundamental moral difference which he believes he is able to discern between a human and an animal level, and the importance of distinguishing between them; and, like the Humanists, he has been frightened back into one of those synthetic cults which do duty for our evaporated religions. The doctor of *In Dubious Battle* is made, on the contrary, to deprecate even such elements of religion as have entered into the labor cause at the same time that he takes no stock in the utopianism of the Marxists. When he is depressed by the barbarity of the conflict and is reminded by the neophyte Jim that he "ought to think only of the end: out of all this struggle a good thing is going to grow," he answers that in his "little experience the end is never very different in its nature from the means . . . It seems to me that man has engaged in a blind and fearful struggle out of a past he can't remember, into a future he can't foresee nor understand. And man has met and defeated every obstacle, every enemy except one. He cannot win over himself. How mankind hates itself." "We don't hate ourselves," says Jim. "We hate the invested capital that keeps us down." "The other side is made of men, Jim, men like you. Man hates himself. Psychologists say a man's self-love is balanced neatly with self-hate. Mankind must be the same. We fight ourselves and we can only win by killing man."

The philosophy of Mr. Steinbeck is obviously not satisfactory in either its earlier or its later form. He has nothing to oppose to this vision of man's hating and destroying himself except an irreducible faith in life; and the very tracts he writes for the underdog let us see through to the biological realism which is his natural habit of mind. Yet I prefer his approach to the animal-man to the mysticism of Mr. Huxley; and I believe that we shall be more likely to find out something of value for the control and ennoblement of life by studying human behavior in this spirit than through the code of self-contemplation that seems to grow so rootlessly and palely in the decay of scientific tradition which this latest of the Huxleys represents.

For the rest, Mr. Steinbeck is equipped with resources of observation and invention which are exceptional and sometimes astonishing, and with color which is all his own but which does not, for some reason, possess what is called magic. It is hard to feel that any of his books, so far, is really first-rate. He has provided a panorama of California farm-life and California landscape which is unique in our literature; and there are passages in some ways so brilliant that we are troubled at being forced to recognize that there is something artistically bad about them. Who has ever caught so well such a West Coast scene as that in *To a God Unknown* in which we visit the exalted old man, with the burros, who has built his hut high on the cliff so that he can look down on the straight pillars of the redwoods and off at the sea far below, and know that he is the last man in the western world to see the sun go down? What is wrong here is the animal sacrifice which the old man performs at this moment and which reminds us of the ever-present paradox of the mixture of seriousness and trashiness in the writing of Mr. Steinbeck. I am not sure that *Tortilla Flat,* by reason of the very limitations imposed by its folk-tale convention, is not artistically his most successful work.

Yet there remains behind the journalism, the theatricalism and the tricks of his other books a mind which does seem first-rate in its unpanicky scrutiny of life.

6. Facing the Pacific

Contemporary California has thus been described by our novelists on a very extensive scale. It has probably had as much attention as any other part of the country. Yet the California writers—and this is true even of Steinbeck, the most gifted of them—do not somehow seem to carry a weight proportionate to the bulk of their work.

Why is this? All visitors from the East know the strange spell of unreality which seems to make human experience on the Coast as hollow as the life of a troll-nest where everything is out in the open instead of being underground. I have heard a highly intelligent Los Angeles lawyer who had come to California from Colorado remark that he had periodically to pinch himself to remind himself of the fact that he was living in an abnormal, a sensational, world which he ought to get down on paper, but that he could never pull out of the trance sufficiently to react and to judge in what he still at the back of his mind considered the normal way. There is in one of these Hollywood novels, *You Play the Black and the Red Comes Up*, a veracious account of the feelings of a man leaving Southern California. The hero has just crossed the mountains after a great career of love and crime. And yet "it was like all I had done in California was just a dream. And at first it felt good, and then it felt worse, because Sheila was only a dream with everything else. And that was bad. I could remember everything about California, but I couldn't feel it. I tried to get my mind to remember something that it could feel, too, but it was no use. It was all gone. All of it. The pink stucco houses and the palm trees and the stores built like cats and dogs and frogs and ice-cream freezers and the neon lights round everything."

This is partly no doubt a matter of climate: the empty sun and the incessant rains; and of landscape: the dry mountains and the void of the vast Pacific; of the hypnotic rhythms of day and night that revolve with unblurred uniformity, and of the surf that rolls up the beach with a beat that seems expressionless and purposeless after the moody assaults of the Atlantic. Add to this the remoteness from the East and the farther remoteness from Europe. New York has its own insubstantiality that is due to the impermanence of its people, of its buildings, of its business, of its thoughts; but all the wires of our western civilization are buzzing and crossing here. California looks away from Europe, and out upon a wider ocean toward an Orient with which as yet any cultural communication is difficult.

This problem of the native Californian to find a language for the reality of his experience is touched upon in Hans Otto Storm's *Count Ten*. "If things now and then did not look real to you; if you were bothered by that particular question, Eric thought, then you ought certainly to keep off the Gulf of California. It hadn't looked real the time they did or did not bathe their feet in it and eat the clams, and it certainly did not look real now, this deadish place where no ships ever came and where the waves move with such an unutterable weariness." The hero is puzzled but his interest is pricked by an Easterner he meets at Berkeley, who misses the New England seasons and tries to explain to him the dramatic character which they impart to the cycle of the year; and when, gazing over San Francisco bay, he quotes Heine to one of his girls, she objects: "'That isn't Heine any more. It's a hakku. It makes me think of tea-cakes without salt.' She shivered a little. 'It's getting cold. No, that doesn't click in California. In California you can't sit and meditate on through the sunset.'" The young man applies himself to learning Chinese.

Add to this that the real cultural center, San Francisco, with its cosmopolitanism and its Bohemian clubs, the city of Bret Harte and Ambrose Bierce, was arrested in its natural development by the earthquake of 1906, and that thereafter the great anti-cultural amusement-producing center, Los Angeles, grew up, gigantic and vulgar, like one of those synthetic California flowers, and tended to drain the soil of the imaginative life of the State. (It is a question how much the movies themselves have been affected by the California atmosphere:

might they not have been a little more interesting under
the stress of affairs in the East?) In this city that
swarms with writers, none yet has really mustered the
gumption to lay bare the heart and bowels of the moving-picture business. The novels I have mentioned
above only trifle with the fringes of Hollywood, as the
stage comedies like *Boy Meets Girl* only kid it in a superficial way. A novel on a higher level of writing than any
of those I have mentioned—*The Day of the Locust* by
Nathanael West—is also mostly occupied with extras
and gives mere glimpses into the upper reaches. Aldous
Huxley's California novel, *After Many a Summer Dies
the Swan*, does not get even so far into the subject as
his compatriot Mr. Eric Knight, the author, under a
pseudonym, of *You Play the Black etc.* Mr. Huxley
here seems well on his way to becoming a second-rate
American novelist. Satirizing in more or less conventional fashion the Hearstian millionaire, the vapid Hollywood beauty and the burlesque pomps of a Los Angeles cemetery, he has succumbed to one of the impostures with which the Golden State deludes her victims:
the Burbankized West Coast religion; and Mr. Huxley
and his ally, Mr. Gerald Heard, will be lucky if they do
not wake up some morning to find themselves transformed
into Yogis and installed in one of those Wizard-of-Oz
temples that puff out their bubble-like domes among the
snack bars and the lion ranches.

The novel about Hollywood with most teeth in it is
still that intrepid satire by Miss Anita Loos called *The
Better Things of Life,* which came out serially in the
Cosmopolitan and was repeatedly announced by her
publishers, but which never appeared between covers.
It seems to be true, in general, of Hollywood as a subject
for fiction that those who write about it are not authentic

insiders and that those who know about it don't write.*

But, as I say, it is not merely in Los Angeles that the purposes and passions of humanity have the appearance of playing their roles in a great open-air amphitheater which lacks not only acoustics to heighten and clarify the speeches but even an attentive audience at whom they may be directed. The paisanos of *Tortilla Flat* also eat, love and die in a golden and boundless sunlight that never becomes charged with their energies; and the rhapsodies of William Saroyan, diffused in this non-vibrant air, pass without repercussions. Even the monstrous, the would-be elemental, the would-be barbaric tragedies which Robinson Jeffers heaps up are a little like amorphous cloud-dramas that eventually fade out to sea, leaving only on our faces a slight moisture and in our ears an echo of hissing. It is probably a good deal too easy to be a nihilist on the coast at Carmel: your very negation is a negation of nothing.

---

* The relation between the movies and prose fiction works in two ways. There are the actual writers for the pictures like Mr. West and Mr. Cain who produce sour novels about Hollywood. And there are the serious novelists who do not write for the films but are influenced by them in their novels. Since the people who control the movies will not go a step of the way to give the script-writer a chance to do a serious script, the novelist seems, consciously or unconsciously, to be going part of the way to meet the producers. John Steinbeck, in *The Grapes of Wrath,* has certainly learned from the films—and not only from such documentary pictures as those of Pare Lorentz, but from the sentimental symbolism of Hollywood. The result is that the *Grapes of Wrath* has poured itself on to the screen as easily as if it had been written in the studios, and that it is probably the sole serious story on record that seems almost equally effective as a book and as a film. Ernest Hemingway's *For Whom the Bell Tolls,* which also has elements of movie romance, was instantly snapped up by Hollywood.

One theme does, however, it must be said, remain serious for the California novelists: the theme of the class war. The men and women of the Cain-O'Hara novels are doomed: they are undone by their own characters or by circumstances. But in time—as in Cain's *Serenade* and O'Hara's *Hope of Heaven**—the socialist diagnosis and the socialist hope begin to appear in the picture. This has been true, of course, during the thirties, of our American fiction in general; but the labor cause has been dramatized with more impact by these writers of the Western coast than it has been, on the whole, in the East, where the formulas of Marxist theory have been likely to take the place of experience. I do not mean the Hollywood Stalinism which is satirized by Mr. McCoy in the swimming-pool scene of *I Should Have Stayed Home*: I mean the tradition of radical writing which Californians like Storm and Steinbeck are carrying on from Frank Norris,† Jack London and Upton Sinclair.

This tradition dates from Henry George, who witnessed, in the sixties and seventies, the swallowing-up of the State—in what must have been record time— by capital; and California has since been the scene

---

* O'Hara is not yet a Californian either by birth or by adoption. Except in *Hope of Heaven,* he had always had the Eastern edge and tension.

† Steinbeck's close relationship with Norris is indicated by what is evidently a borrowing from *McTeague* in *Of Mice and Men.* The conversation that is so often repeated between Norris's Polish junk dealer and the cracked Spanish-American girl, in which he is always begging her to describe for him the gold table service she remembers from her childhood, must have suggested the similar dialogue that recurs between Lennie and George, in which the former is always begging the latter to tell him more about the rabbit farm they are going to have together. Steinbeck's attitude toward his rudimentary characters may, also, owe something to Norris—who, like him, alloys his seriousness with trashiness.

of some of the most naked and savage of American labor wars. The McNamaras, Mooney and Billings, the Wobblies and Vigilantes, the battles of the longshoremen and the fruit-pickers, the San Francisco general strike—these are names and events that have wrung blood and tears in the easy California climate; and it is this conflict that has kept Mr. Storm afloat in the Pacific vacuum, fixed securely in his orientation toward the east of the social world, and that has communicated to Mr. Steinbeck the impetus that has carried the Joad jalopy into the general consciousness of the nation.

Here the novelists of California know what they are talking about, and they have something arresting to say. In describing their special mentality, I do not, of course, in the least, mean to belittle their interest or value. The writing of the Coast, as I say, may seem difficult to bring into focus with the writing that we know in the East. But California, since we took it from the Mexicans, has always presented itself to Americans as one of the strangest and most exotic of their exploits; and it is the function of the literary artist to struggle with new phases of experience, and to try to give them beauty and sense.

Postscript

These notes were first written during the autumn and early winter of 1940. Since then, several events have occurred which require a few words of postscript.

On December 21, 1940, F. Scott Fitzgerald suddenly died in Hollywood; and, the day after, Nathanael West was killed in a motor accident on the Ventura boulevard. Both men had been living on the West Coast; both had spent several years in the studios; both, at the time of their deaths, had been occupied with novels about Hollywood.

The work of Nathanael West derived from a different tradition than that of these other writers. He had been influenced by those post-war Frenchmen who had specialized, with a certain preciosity, in the delirious and diabolic fantasy that descended from Rimbaud and Lautréamont. Beginning with *The Dream Life of Balso Snell*, a not very successful exercise in this vein of phantasmagoria, he published, after many revisions, a remarkable short novel called *Miss Lonelyhearts*. This story of a newspaper hack who conducts an "advice to the lovelorn" department and eventually destroys himself by allowing himself to take too seriously the sorrows and misfortunes of his clients, had a poetic-philosophical point of view and a sense of phrase as well as of chapter that made it seem rather European than American. It was followed by *A Cool Million*, a less ambitious book, which both parodied Horatio Alger and more or less reproduced *Candide* by reversing the American success story. In his fourth book, *The Day of the Locust*, he applied his fantasy and irony to the embarrassment of rich materials offered by the movie community. I wrote a review of this novel in 1939, and I shall venture to append it here—with apologies for some repetition of ideas expressed above—to make the California story complete:

Nathanael West, the author of *Miss Lonelyhearts*, went to Hollywood a few years ago, and his silence had been causing his readers alarm lest he might have faded out on the Coast as so many of his fellows have done. But Mr. West, as this new book happily proves, is still alive beyond the mountains, and quite able to set down what he feels and sees—has still, in short, remained an artist. His new novel, *The Day of the Locust*, deals with the nondescript characters on the edges of the Hollywood studios: an old comic who sells shoe polish and his film-struck daughter; a quarrelsome dwarf; a cock-fighting Mexican; a Hollywood cowboy and a Hollywood Indian; and an undeveloped hotel clerk from Iowa, who has come to the Coast to enjoy his savings—together with a sophisticated screen-writer, who lives in a big house that is "an exact reproduction of the old Dupuy mansion near Biloxi, Mississippi." And these people have been painted as distinctly and polished up as brightly as the figures in Persian miniatures. Their speech has been distilled with a sense of the flavorsome and the characteristic which makes John O'Hara seem pedestrian. Mr. West has footed a precarious way and has not slipped at any point into relying on the Hollywood values in describing the Hollywood people. The landscapes, the architecture and the interior decoration of Beverly Hills and vicinity have been handled with equal distinction. Everyone who has ever been in Los Angeles knows how the mere aspect of things is likely to paralyze the aesthetic faculty by providing no *point d'appui* from which to exercise its discrimination, if it does not actually stun the sensory apparatus itself, so that accurate reporting becomes impossible. But Nathanael West has stalked and caught some fine specimens of these Hollywood lepidoptera and impaled them on fastidious pins. Here are Hollywood restaurants, apartment houses, funeral churches, brothels, evangelical temples and movie sets—in this latter connection, an extremely amusing episode of a man getting nightmarishly lost in the Battle of Waterloo. Mr. West's surrealist beginnings have stood him in good stead on the Coast.

The doings of these people are bizarre, but they are

also sordid and senseless. Mr. West has caught the emptiness of Hollywood; and he is, as far as I know, the first
writer to make this emptiness horrible. The most impressive thing in the book is his picture of the people from
the Middle West who, retiring to sunlit leisure, are trying
to leave behind them the meagerness of their working
lives; who desire something different from what they have
had but do not know what they desire, and have no other
resources for amusement than gaping at movie stars and
listening to Aimee McPherson's sermons. In the last episode, a crowd of these people, who have come out to see
the celebrities at an opening, is set off by an insane act of
violence on the part of the cretinous hotel clerk, and gives
way to an outburst of mob mania. The America of the murders and rapes which fill the Los Angeles papers is only the
obverse side of the America of the inanities of the movies.
Such people—Mr. West seems to say—dissatisfied, yet
with no ideas, no objectives and no interest in anything
vital, may in the mass be capable of anything. The day-
dreams purveyed by Hollywood, the romances that in
movie stories can be counted on to have whisked around
all obstacles and adroitly knocked out all "menaces" by
the time they have run off their reels, romances which
their fascinated audiences have never been able to live
themselves—only cheat them and embitter their frustration. Of such mobs are the followers of fascism made.

I think that the book itself suffers a little from the lack
of a center in the community with which it deals. It has
less concentration than *Miss Lonelyhearts*. Mr. West has
introduced a young Yale man who, as an educated and
healthy human being, is supposed to provide a normal
point of view from which the deformities of Hollywood
may be criticized; but it is also essential to the story that
this young man should find himself swirling around in
the same aimless eddies as the others. I am not sure

that it is really possible to do anything substantial with Hollywood except by making it, as John Dos Passos did in *The Big Money*, a part of a larger picture which has its center in a larger world. But in the meantime Nathanael West has survived to write another distinguished book— in its peculiar combination of amenity of surface and felicity of form and style with ugly subject matter and somber feeling, quite unlike—as *Miss Lonelyhearts* was —the books of anyone else.

Scott Fitzgerald, who at the time of his death had published only short stories about the movies, had been working for some time on a novel* in which he had tackled the key figure of the industry: the successful Hollywood producer. This subject has also been attempted, with sharp observation and much humor, by Mr. Budd Schulberg, Jr.; whose novel *What Makes Sammy Run* has been published since my articles were written. But Mr. Schulberg is still a beginner, and his work in *What Makes Sammy Run* does not rise above the level of a more sincere and sensitive George Kaufman; whereas Scott Fitzgerald, an accomplished artist, had written a considerable part of what promised to be by all odds the best novel ever devoted to Hollywood. Here you are shown the society and the business of the movies, no longer through the eyes of the visitor to whom everything is glamorous or ridiculous, but from the point of view of people who have grown up or lived with the industry and to whom its values and laws are their natural habit of life. These are criticized by higher standards and in the knowledge of wider horizons, but the criticism is implicit in the story; and in the meantime, Scott Fitzgerald, by putting us inside their group and making us take

---

* Later published as *The Last Tycoon*.

things for granted, is able to excite an interest in the mixed destiny of his Jewish producer of a kind that lifts the novel quite out of the class of this specialized Hollywood fiction and relates it to the story of man in all times and all places.

Both West and Fitzgerald were writers of a conscience and with natural gifts rare enough in America or anywhere; and their failure to get the best out of their best years may certainly be laid partly to Hollywood, with its already appalling record of talent depraved and wasted.

1940–41

MAX EASTMAN IN 1941

MAX EASTMAN, during the year just past, has published two remarkable books: *Stalin's Russia and The Crisis in Socialism* and *Marxism: Is It Science?* There is perhaps no contemporary figure whose importance is so difficult to estimate.

From 1913 to 1922, as editor of *Masses* and the *Liberator,* Max Eastman was one of the dominant figures of the intellectual life of New York. After 1922, his reputation was in relative eclipse. In that year he went to Europe and remained there for five years. In the course of a sojourn in Russia, he became identified with the Trotskyist side of the Stalin-Trotsky split; and as a result, he was subjected after his return to a systematic vilification and boycott which was continued through the thirties when so many of the intelligentsia fell under the influence of the Stalinists. Today he is emerging again, and it is time some attempt was made to appreciate his real role and stature.

It is not the purpose of this article, however, to attempt a complete account of his career. In order to do that, it would be necessary to write a good deal of history, political and journalistic, and to trace his extensive influence through the channels of his personal relations. For four years an instructor in Philosophy at Columbia, he continued to figure as a teacher even after he became editor of the *Masses*. He is one of those men who have a natural genius for stimulating trains of thinking and suggesting ideas to others, whose thought, instead of having its complete development inside his own head and being completely contained in his own books, interfuses and interchanges in its processes with the minds of those around him, supplying lights and starting impulses for personalities quite different from the teacher's own. This is not to say that there has ever been anything that could be called an Eastman school of thought: on the contrary, it is characteristic of this type of suggestive mind that it does not turn out disciples. This is a quite different kind of teaching from that of an Irving Babbitt, who must either overpower his pupil or goad him into rebellion. Yet of the many kinds of intellectuals who were young enough to learn anything at all during the decade of 1910-20, it is probable that an enormous number owe a special debt to Max Eastman— from the artist who was encouraged to draw pictures, the poet who was encouraged to write poems, for the *Liberator* and the *Masses,* to the journalist whom a conversation with Max first induced to follow out the implications of the emotions aroused by a strike. The writer of this article well remembers his having had his first introduction to psychoanalysis in a magazine article by Max— the quiet and common-sense explanation with the drawl that carried over into print and that exerted so different a persuasive power from that of the ordinary professor. The editors of the *Masses* themselves, whose boss behind the Kremlin walls was recently denouncing Max Eastman as a "notorious gangster" and "crook," would not now have their magazine, with whatever is individual in its format and its tone, if Max had not created it for them.

In 1922, Max Eastman went abroad to study the Russian Revolution, and did not return till 1927. He had, as I have said, during his absence become partially forgotten in New York, and from the time of the banishment of Trotsky in 1925, the partisans of Stalin applied their pressure to make this oblivion as complete as possible. When his presence among us again began to make itself felt, he seemed to wear a different aspect. This aspect was partly the invention of those political enemies of Max, who at that time ruled the radical roost. It was in the days before the Moscow frame-ups had discredited the verdicts of Communists and when it was possible to seem to back with the austere authority of Lenin the condemnation of a revolutionist who was supposed to have gone soft. And this treatment—together perhaps with the difficulties of readjustment to an American scene which had very much changed during the middle twenties—had the result of engendering in Max himself, always excessively sensitive to atmosphere, a less generous and outgoing attitude.

The Max Eastman of the *Masses* and the *Liberator*, who had appreciated and encouraged and aroused, and who had stood at the center of things, had turned into a critic on the sidelines who girded and jeered and complained, and whose preachments seemed mainly negative. *The Enjoyment of Poetry* of 1913 had communicated the exhilaration of a lover of lyric verse, and it naturally went into the hands of every teacher of English in the country who cared enough about literature to know that he had to give his students something more than the right answers to the examination questions. *The Literary Mind* of 1931, obscured by a premature old-fogeyism, made itself disagreeable at the expense of precisely the boldest and most serious of those writers who were working to carry on the great tradition of literature, and it succeeded in irritating everybody who was trying to fight the battle of Joyce and Eliot against the Philistines who were yapping at them. In the same way, the friend of John Reed, the inspirer of Mike Gold, the unsuppressible editor of the *Masses* claimed attention with a critique of Marxism which demonstrated by relentless analysis the Marxist inconsistencies and superstitions without conveying the revolutionary ardor which had animated Marx and Lenin and which had taken Max Eastman himself to Russia. Moreover, this man who had lent to his cause a gift of grace and charm and a power of dealing straight with threatening issues, now developed controversial manners which disquieted his admirers and which weakened the force of certain very sound things that he was trying at this time to say. In arguing with Sidney Hook or in criticizing Ernest Hemingway, he adopted a bitter or a malicious tone which the situation did not seem to warrant, and he went in for a modern variation of the old device of imputing motives by gratuitously psychoanalyzing his subjects and attempting to undermine their philosophical positions or the products of their artistic activity, by showing that they were suffering from adolescent fixations or infantile illusions of inferiority. This whole period of Max Eastman's writings was damaged by a peculiar disgruntled tone. In dealing even with those contemporary figures—Trotsky and Freud, for example—whose ideas he has courageously defended, he sounded as if he were airing a grievance, the nature of which was never made plain.

Now for a fighter, for a worker in ideas, it is dangerous, it may prove fatal to one's effectiveness, to betray that one's feelings have been hurt. The critic must remain invulnerable. When goaded, he should show himself not peevish, but indignant, with a background of scorn. This Max Eastman at his best knows how to do; and he has written a few superb polemics. But up

until about the middle of the thirties he was tending to
fall into the querulousness of the partisan whose side has
had reverses, of the prophet who has lost his public.
The isolation in which Max found himself was at
this time all the more complete because he did not belong even to a minority. He was as incapable of submit-
ting politically to the imperious dictatorship of Trotsky
as of subscribing to the Marxist Dialectic, and he had to
forego even the support of the leader whose obloquy
and defeat he had shared.

In 1934 the murder of Sergei Kirov announced the
doom of those liberalizing elements in Russia which had
still made it possible for liberals abroad to give Stalin
the benefit of the doubt, and precipitated the wholesale
purge of the revolutionary generations which covered
up the official rejection of the original Stalinist aims.
The American intellectuals who had been depending
for their ideas about Russia on the wonderfully dramatized photographs of *USSR in Construction* and who
had been kept slightly boozy by the flattery of the
League of American Writers now commenced to sober
up, and the news of the Hitler-Stalin pact nipped the
illusions of all but the dullest. In the scene of devastation
that followed, Max Eastman, who had first published
the Testament of Lenin and who had been warning
people since 1925 against the tendencies that had now
triumphed, was seen standing like a stout if slightly
twisted lone pine. He began to reacquire credit; people
quoted him with respect again. The young no longer
shrank from his contact as from a damned soul who had
blasphemed the Kremlin. And Max himself seemed to
muster new forces. *Stalin's Russia and the Crisis in Socialism* and *Marxism: Is It Science?* have presented
what is, so far as I know, the most intelligent and search-

ing as well as the best informed discussion of the implications of the Marxist movement and the development
of the Revolution in Russia that has yet appeared in
English.

Let us, however, for a moment look back over the
whole sequence of Max Eastman's books during this
period of his partial eclipse. A glance into *The Literary Mind* today reveals, rather surprisingly to one who
was prejudiced against the book when it first appeared,
that it was distinguished by a deeper comprehension of
the real issues raised by contemporary literature than
almost anything else that had been written during the
twenties. The end of the twenties was marked by a
hullabaloo of aesthetic crankery, philosophical pedantry
and academic moralizing; and Max Eastman was almost
alone in his attempt to work out as an enlightened
modern man the larger relations of art and science to one
another, and of both to the society behind them. It is
significant of Max's demand for clarity of understanding
that, though rather unsympathetic with Joyce, he should
have interviewed him in Paris and brought back the
only straight story of what he was trying to do in *Finnegans Wake*. The account of this interview in *The Literary Mind* is more valuable to the student of Joyce than
much of the stuff that was written by his admirers.

When we go back to Max Eastman's own poetry, published that same year in a collected edition, we decide
that he had a much better right than the young people
of that era allowed him to talk to them about what
poetry ought to be. His verse has perhaps never been
brought to the high pitch of craftsmanship and intensity that produces the perfect poem; and it indulges
certain deplorable vices. Max has never quite got away
from the sentimental and amateurish verse that dominated the field in America during the nineties of the

last century and the first decade of this. He still tends to
hover around the precincts of the magazine mausoleum
of Stedman's *American Anthology,* and he has never
really understood the housecleaning, the raising of artistic standards, effected by Eliot and Pound. Moreover,
it is true that when Max tries to talk about the emotions
directly, he is likely to become rhetorical and turbid.
Yet there *is* a lyric poet in Max Eastman, a personal
voice, an original imagery, a temperament volatile and
fugitive, glistening in delightful sun or vibrating from
moments of feeling, that is particularly felicitous in those
of his poems that get their images from birds or water—
from the tranquil pools of the forest, from the shots of
silver spray, from the drops on the window-pane casting
a silver shadow, from the ferns, from the wet-petaled
lilies, from the delicate-leaved bamboo, from the king-
bird with quivering tiny wings, from the slender wild
egret, from the breath-taking realization of the beauty of
a woman, when the mind flickers electrically with bright
perceptions.

As for his writings on the politics of the Left, one who
has recently worked in this field and who has been
through the whole series of Max Eastman's books inspired by the Russian Revolution will testify that he has
found them the most valuable of the commentaries in
English on this subject so inflammatory to prejudice. Who-
ever wants to understand the real (as distinguished from
the artificial) exchange during the period after the War
between Soviet Russia and the United States will have to
read Max Eastman as well as John Reed: *Since Lenin
Died, Leon Trotsky, Marx and Lenin, and the Science of
Revolution* (now incorporated for the most part in
Marxism: Is it Science?), *Venture, Artists in Uniform,*
and the two newest books which I have mentioned.

John Reed and Max Eastman both observed the Russian Revolution at first hand. John Reed, American adventurer and democratic idealist, gave Lenin to America as an American, and died for what he believed to be the purposes of the Revolution. Max Eastman, with his cooler spirit and his better intellectual equipment, carefully studied its texts, analyzed its fundamental ideas, watched its politics, assessed its personalities; and he lived to see its betrayal and burial. Through all this, he remained as American as Reed. Mark Twain, the friend of his parents, had had his influence on Eastman's youth in Elmira: Max's manner as a public speaker is in the tradition of Mark Twain: the dead-pan drollery and the casual drawl that disguises perfect timing. With a considerable cosmopolitan culture, Max Eastman brought to Moscow the Yankee skepticism and the humane common sense of Mark Twain's *Innocents Abroad*. And no power on earth could prevail upon him to succumb to the Marxist jargon, which has concealed so much confusion, so much intellectual insincerity and so much deliberate fraud. When Max has got the Marxist ideas into English, the historical mythology of Marxism is seen to have disappeared: nothing remains but what is intelligible to American modes of thought and applicable to American actualities.

Max Eastman's great contribution to the study of this subject in English has been to go to the mat with the fundamental conceptions of Marxism. It has usually been true that the professional philosophers have left Marxism disdainfully alone, while the political adherents of the Marxist sects have failed to examine the Marxist philosophy. Max Eastman, a trained philosopher, showed the inadequacy of the Marxist system, which Marx, in his preoccupation with politics, had never found the time to work out; and he dragged out the theological delusions, carried over from the old religion by way of German idealistic philosophy, which were concealed by the scientific pretensions of Marx. For the pragmatical American mind, the ideas and literature of Marxism are peculiarly difficult to grapple with; and the American, when converted, tends to accept them, as he does Methodism or Christian Science, as a simple divine revelation. The fact that Marx and Engels combined an unexamined idealism with real and great intellectual genius has made it possible for American intellectuals to whoop it up for the Marxist religion, under the impression that they were applying to the contemporary world a relentless intellectual analysis; and, strong in the assurance of standing right with the irresistible forces of History, the Marxist substitute for the old-fashioned Providence, they have felt confident that History would see them through without further intellectual effort on their part, and swallowed all the absurd policies and the expedient lies that the Stalinist agents fed them just as the obedient Catholic swallows the priest's doctrine.

Max Eastman has differed from these thinkers turned gapers in being an intellectual who really works at it. The thing that strikes one today in reviewing the work of the last twenty years by this radical who is supposed to have wilted is not the softness of his mind but its toughness. He went to study in the Soviet Union the implications and the possibilities of the socialist doctrine he had been preaching, and he proceeded to formulate his conclusions in a series of writings on which he continued to labor when the fashion had quite turned against radicalism, which he had in some instances to publish at his own expense and which received almost no attention. One cannot see that movements and fashions have affected in any way—except to make him at times a little irritable—Max's testimony to what he thought true. The child of a mother and father both ordained Congregational ministers, with a long ancestry of parsons behind him, he has been upheld perhaps by a vocation neither political nor artistic, a conviction that there is an indispensable part to be played in human society by persons who make it their business to keep clear of the standards of the world and to stick by certain instincts of thinking and feeling whose value is not measured by their wages, and which it is always to the immediate interest of some group to mutilate, imprison or suppress. I know that I have produced in this paragraph a strange blend of the intellectual and the spiritual callings, as they are commonly understood, but it is only in some such special terms that it is possible to describe the role of Max Eastman.

This role has its weaknesses, of course; and in these weaknesses are to be located perhaps the ultimate reasons for Max Eastman's eclipse. There is probably something basic in common between the charges brought against him, respectively, by the politicos and by the poets. Both have felt that he was criticizing them severely, and even on occasion ill-naturedly, without sharing the rigors of their tasks. After all, Max Eastman was a poet who had not accepted the last discipline of his craft; a revolutionist who had stepped out of the battle to explain that the outcome was uncertain; a philosopher who held no chair; a journalist who had allowed his magazine to be captured by an opposition that parodied it in the interests of everything that Eastman most desired to fight. Above all, he was continually going on about something he called "science"—though he himself was no species of scientist and had had, so far as one could discover, no scientific training at all—with which he was always laying about him at philosophers, partisans and poets alike. I do not know how it happened that Max Eastman became so obsessed by the idea of science: he has erected it into a totem, about which it is as if he has talked too much because he has not known what clan he belonged to. So, also, the continual emphasis on what he calls "living" may have compensated his failure to cultivate intensively the several departments in which he has worked. Certainly Max has written with eloquence, as a non-scientific essayist can—for example, in the essay on *What Science Is* in his *Marxism: Is it Science?*—about the spirit and objectives of the scientist; and he has conveyed his conviction that "living," in a world where abstraction and specialization have been resulting in wholesale destruction, has an importance and rights of its own. But it is true that one has sometimes felt that these words were being waved in one's face at moments when Max himself might well have been more scientific about, as well as more alive to, certain things that were happening in the world about him.

This said, and it has already been said often, we must recognize that Max Eastman, after all, has justified his anomalous role of preacher-teacher-critic-poet. He has justified it in a way quite distinct from the way in which he first attracted attention—that is, as a public figure; he presents himself to his contemporaries today *as primarily a writer to be read.* The public figure in Max—by a process probably not very congenial to him—has, in his lecturing and popularizing, become to some extent disassociated from the independent student and thinker who sometimes had to publish at his own expense and could rarely hope to sell. This is the Eastman of *The Enjoyment of Laughter* and of the *Anthology for the Enjoyment of Poetry*—entertaining and readable books appropriate for bringing in money.

But, on the other hand, his serious writing has been

growing a good deal more interesting. One remembers his *Liberator* articles as having seemed a little diffuse and lacking in bony structure. But the prose of these recent books has a clarity and terseness of form, an intellectual edge, which would be hard to match elsewhere today in the American literature of ideas. This prose is not primarily an instrument for polemics but the medium for a point of view. The writings of Max Eastman make a commentary, imaginative, witty, sharp, uncompromising in its adherence to the line of its own conscience, not unlike that of André Gide; and the audience of intellectuals which has surely overrated Gide has underrated Max Eastman. His novel *Venture,* for example, which passed almost unnoticed in 1927, before the torrent of strike novels had started, is an idea-novel of the type of Gide's, which deals with the problems of industry in a most unconventional way. The Platonic-Nietzschean capitalist, who talks his young disciple into Bolshevism by expounding his ideals of a superior caste without perceiving that a superior caste may pursue anti-capitalist aims, is one of Eastman's best inspirations; and the book is full of his characteristic aphorisms, finely phrased and often acute, on the various aspects of experience.

Max Eastman's comprehension of the modern world is limited in certain respects, and this is probably another reason for the recent neglect of his work. As his novel is quite non-naturalistic, so his discussion of the Soviet Union and of the general situation of the West does not include an adequate picture of economic and social conditions. It is strange that this student of Marxism should never have learned from Marx what is certainly most valid in his system: the class analysis of historical happenings. Max Eastman, as Philip Rahv has pointed out, tends to talk as if the fallacies of Marxism had by themselves wrecked the Leninist revolution, and is not interested in finding out how the development of social forces has affected the application of ideas. But though it is true that he thinks mainly in terms of psychological motivations, of philosophical and moral positions, his criticism along these lines has, nevertheless, proved extremely salutary at a time when people were trusting to arrangements of statistical figures to demonstrate the rights and wrongs of History without being able to smell the corpses in the Lubyanka or to take stock of what was healthy at home. Max Eastman has continued to perform for us the same function that he did in the first World War: that of the winter log that floats in the swimming-pool and prevents the concrete from cracking by itself taking the pressure of the ice.

He is also the unpopular foreigner who opens the window on the Russian train; the indiscreet guest who saves the banquet by making fun of the guest of honor; the rude and ill-regarded professor whose courses the brighter students all find out they have to take. And these courses are now available in their definitive and polished form in *Stalin's Russia* and *Marxism: Is It Science?*

February 10, 1941

T. K. WHIPPLE

I FIRST KNEW T. K. Whipple in the winter of 1912–13. He was a senior at Princeton then and editor of the *Nassau Literary Magazine,* and I was a freshman contributor. The *Lit* had been rather in eclipse up to the time that T. K. (whom the campus called "Teek") had taken command of it the year before. Robert Shafer, since known as a critic and a follower of Paul Elmer More, was, I believe, the first editor in a series that represented a new period of literary activity at Princeton—the first since the early nineties, the days of Booth Tarkington and Jesse Lynch Williams. Whipple took over from Shafer, and the succeeding boards included John Peale Bishop, Hamilton Fish Armstrong, Isador Kaufman, W. Stanley Dell, Raymond Holden, F. Scott Fitzgerald, John Biggs, Jr., and myself. Among the contributors were Keene Wallis and A. O'Brien-Moore. Up to the time of Whipple's editorship the *Lit* had had the existence of a mouse that lurked timidly in a crevice of the college life. I remember Teek telling me of the hopelessness with which he and the other editors had canvassed the college rooms for subscriptions. The freshmen would buy tiger pictures, but they knew from the lack of confidence with which the salesmen for the *Lit* approached them that the magazine was not taken seriously.

In the new era the *Lit* came to life. It made connections with the other college activities: the *Princetonian* and the Triangle Club; and at the same time it defended with boldness positions that were antagonistic to both official and undergraduate opinion. We engaged in sharp controversies with the *Princetonian* over the problems of the curriculum and academic freedom, and there was a moment, under the editorship of John Bishop, when Bishop's poetry—which seemed very "modern"—created an issue on the campus almost comparable to the fight over the eating-club system. We had an awfully good time out of the *Lit* and got some excellent practice in writing and being read—for which courses in "creative writing" had not yet at that date become necessary; and we were usually able to cut, at the end of the year, a melon which yielded each of us a slice of about fifty dollars. Teek Whipple, who had stayed on at the Graduate School after his graduation in 1913, had been with us through all this period. He had helped and advised, and he had written for the *Lit* in his limpid and witty prose; and he had thus given the whole evolution a continuity it would not otherwise have had. He had somehow established the atmosphere in which the *Lit* was flourishing, and he continued to water its roots.

Not that he was in the least a promoter or the kind of man who likes to pull strings. He was a long-legged, loose-jointed fellow, with pale blond hair and a Missouri drawl, whose expression, with its wide grin, seemed at once sad and droll. His movements and manner were languid when he was lounging on a window seat or Morris chair; but when one saw him striding the campus, hump-shouldered and hands in pockets, one felt in him a purposive independence. All that he did he did unobtrusively, but definitely and with conviction. In some ways he was remarkably mature for an American undergraduate. His enthusiasm for our Princeton humanism—by which I mean the tradition of, say, Lionel Johnson, a great favorite of T. K.'s at this time, not the Humanism of Babbitt and More—burned in an air that was dryer than the rather humid and dreamy atmosphere that tended to beglamor our minds: an air of disillusioned common sense; and he seemed sure in the decisions of his judgment and taste as few men at college do. I remember it as characteristic of him that when I told him I was reading *Marius the Epicurean* and began to grope for phrases to express my mixed feelings about it, he said at once that it "would be a good book if it were not so badly written." And his devotion to literature was never dilettante-ish, as it is likely to be with undergraduates, nor did it ever become a matter of routine, as it is likely to do with professors: it was something fundamental to his life. He presented an unusual combination of Princetonian and Middle Westerner—of pleasantry, casualness and elegance with homeliness, simplicity and directness. Though he was not intellectually the most energetic or imaginatively the most brilliant of the group, he had something that is very rare and a little hard to define. He diffused a quiet kind of light that accompanied him like a nimbus. You were always glad to see him; you always knew the glow was there; and in that medium the *Lit* revived.

T. K. and I, when I got to be editor for the year 1915–16, worked together in renovating the magazine and laying for it a firmer base. We changed the type and format, as new editors are likely to do, and we gave it a permanent cover, with an owl and the motto from Horace so often invoked by Poe: *Omne tulit punctum, qui miscuit utile dulci*; we reorganized the magazine and established an editorial procedure; and we refurnished and redecorated the *Lit* offices. One of the features of this latter transformation was a large wooden settle, painted black, in the back of which we sawed diamond-shaped holes and which we set against the long front windows in such a way that, though we were screened from the campus, we were able to watch all that went on there—a device that we regarded as at once a symbol and a facilitation of the semi-godlike role of the critic. These activities of ours, of course—though at that time we did not know it—were a reflection, perhaps, rather, a part, of the general revival of literary activity that was going on all through the United States, and they were paralleled in the other colleges. We amused ourselves by sending one day for two little volumes of verse which had been printed by the author himself in Rutherford, New Jersey, and which had been advertised in the local paper. We had a library of bad poetry in the *Lit* office, and we hoped they would turn out to be funny; but we were puzzled by what we got. The poems *were* some of them quite funny, regarded from the conventional point of view; but they had also a kind of spare dignity, and were they wholly without merit? The poet was William Carlos Williams. A volume of plays called *Thirst* which reached us in 1914 was reviewed in the *Lit* as follows: "This volume, by Eugene G. O'Neill, contains five one-act plays which, if it were not for the author's manifest intention of making them something else, we should call very trashy."

I had begun to have hopes of America's producing some first-rate writers. It was true that the only contemporaries (Henry James was already a classic) that I could read with any genuine enthusiasm were Edith Wharton and E. A. Robinson; but the year before I came to college I had discovered H. L. Mencken, and I could see that there were possibilities for a kind of American literature which would not necessarily be published, as Mrs.

Wharton and Robinson were, under the auspices of W. C. Brownell, at that time chief editor at Scribner's. Mr. Brownell, as I was afterwards to learn, was rejecting at that very moment—admitting that the book was able but declaring that such a packet of blasphemies could never be published by Scribner's—Van Wyck Brooks's important essay, *America's Coming-of-Age,* which complained rather impatiently of our national classics and demanded something better. But between our generation and the Civil War there had extended a kind of weedy or arid waste where people with an appreciation of literature had hardly hoped to find anything of value growing and where they had tended to be suspicious of anything that did manage to bloom; and T. K., a few years older than I, had grown up with the outlook of this period. Not only was there no interest at that time on the part of the conventional academic world in anything that American writers were doing or might do; there was not even any real interest in our classics. I remember my surprise at hearing that Professor T. R. Lounsbury of Yale was occupying himself with American subjects. At Princeton, Duncan Spaeth was a permanent scandal by reason of his admiration for Whitman: "Born on Long Island, died in Camden—found life beautiful!" Dr. Spaeth used to roar in defiance of people who, living close to Camden, assumed that it was too far away from the localities mentioned in *The Scholar Gypsy* to inspire the right kind of poetry. Thus, though T. K. read Mencken, too, with evident appetite, he used to confront me with incomprehension when I talked to him about working our own field. "You mean," I remember his saying to me one day at the Graduate School, when I was telling him that I'd rather stay at home than do as James and the rest had done, "that you'd rather be a big toad in a small puddle?"

I believe that those years at the Graduate School were,

apart from his interest in the *Lit,* rather a barren time
for T. K. I think of him always as enmeshed in two interminable Ph.D. theses: one on the influence of the
Greek orator Isocrates on Milton's prose style, the other
on the seventeenth-century epigram. There was something rather nightmarish about it: at first there had
been only one thesis, which he was never able to finish,
and then presently there were two, and I felt that the
whole thing was hopeless. I used to go over to see him in
the Graduate School, a sumptuous Gothic creation which
had just been erected by Ralph Adams Cram in the middle of the Princeton golf links and which was then being broken in. T. K. would invite me to a dreary enough
dinner in the immense medieval dining hall, where the
faculty sat on a dais and the students filed in in black
gowns to the boom of a fugue of Bach from a hand-
carved organ loft. The Graduate School was a luxurious
affair, and there was something about that life he liked.
But, as a man from Kansas City, he couldn't help being
funny about the suits of armor in the halls; and I never
went over to see him without a feeling of desolation. I
would traverse the enclosed court, where the new gray
stone in its rawness did not in the least remind you of the
stone of Oxford or Cambridge. I would ascend the
monastic stair, knock at the oaken door, and find T. K.
inert in his Morris chair, imprisoned amid the leaded
windows, unable to bring himself to get through any
more volumes of seventeenth-century epigrams and un-
willing or without any appetite to read anything more
stimulating. It was as if he had succumbed to some terrible
doom from which he was powerless to save himself and
from which nobody else could save him. The whole
spectacle gave me a horror of Ph.D. theses from which
I have never recovered.

Then the United States entered the War, and the

board of the *Lit* were dispersed. T. K. somehow managed to finish his thesis and get his Ph.D. degree, and he enlisted in the Marines and went to France. There he came down with sarcoma of the bladder and spent many miserable months in hospital. After the war, he taught English for a time at Union College, Schenectady—a town of which he wrote me that the inhabitants were "devoid of the attractive qualities alike of men and of animals."

I felt even more depressed about him than I had when he was studying at the Graduate School, so I was very much surprised and cheered when I suddenly found him emerging in an entirely new role. I began to come upon articles by him on contemporary American subjects—articles of a quality which set them apart from anything else of the kind being done; and when I would see him on his rare trips to New York I would find him full of something more than even his old enthusiasm of the *Lit* days about what was being written in America. In 1928 he published a volume called *Spokesmen,* which contained essays on Henry Adams, E. A. Robinson, Dreiser, Frost, Anderson, Cather, Sandburg, Lindsay, Lewis and O'Neill—the whole literary world of the twenties, in which I did not know he had been interested. He said in his foreword that Van Wyck Brooks had "first awakened" in him "the desire to try to understand the United States." There was no ballyhoo in *Spokesmen;* there was not even the patriotic leniency that lets its subjects off from damaging questions and comparisons; but there was the definite recognition that a new cultural era had opened. "Americans," he wrote, "for the first time in their history are seeking honest self-knowledge instead of self-glorification. The nation is self-conscious, with an eager curiosity as to all that concerns itself past or present, with a genuine desire to get acquainted with itself. It is willing to be told bitter truth, so long as it is told something about itself. If anyone is skeptical as to the awakening in the United States, I invite him to revert in his mind to the year 1910 or thereabouts, and ask himself whether the United States is not more alive now than then. . . . All over the United States there is a stirring and a striving —after no one knows what. But the new life has already by its achievements established a claim to respect. It has produced buildings and books and plays and pictures which entitle it to admiration."

In the meantime he had gone to teach at Berkeley, where his courses became extremely popular. He had sometimes a nostalgia for Princeton, and he used to complain of the vacuity of California; but he found there an eager audience and security in his academic position, and he seems to have felt behind him the life of the whole country as I had never known him to do in the East. His field was lying right there before him, though he hadn't been able to see it from the Princeton Graduate School, and as soon as he began to work it, it was plain that this was the thing he should do. The Middle Westerner in T. K. came forward to meet the Middle Western writers who were playing such a conspicuous part in the American literature of the period; but he met them with the cultivated intelligence which was supposed to be characteristic of the East. He was, I think, the first of our critics to study the new novelists and dramatists and poets at the same time appreciatively and calmly, to try to see the work of each as a whole and to make some sort of summary of it. Mencken and Rascoe and the rest had induced people to read the new writers; and now the process of understanding them and appraising them was beginning with T. K. Whipple.

These essays of T. K.'s, to one who had known him, were a special cause of satisfaction. When one is ten years out of college, one has already seen so many gifted friends fail to do any of the things one had hoped of them, and it was stimulating to find a man who had never made pretensions or been petted accomplishing something excellent. His writing had certain characteristics excessively rare in the twenties: he knew precisely what he wanted to say, and he said it with equanimity. He somehow—what seems to me unique among the men of my acquaintance of our generation—got through not only the twenties but even the thirties without being thrown off his base. The good sense and good taste which had distinguished him at college in the placid days before the war somehow survived all those years when other people were going to pieces and finding themselves bent into unexpected shapes. I had felt in him already at college a stoicism, a kind of resignation, which was not at all characteristic of the American undergraduate. I had been struck by his quoting to me from *Rasselas,* seriously and not merely for the phrase, the characterization of human life as a state (I may not have it quite right) "where much is to be suffered and little known." Now the malady which had disabled him in the army was menacing him with painful recurrences, which continued through the whole last twenty years of his life; and it may be that a conscious or unconscious awareness of the fate that was always following him contributed to make him indifferent to many things through which others became demoralized.

It was all the more remarkable, then, that a new social-political interest should have begun to show itself in his work. I was surprised again in the thirties at the force of the democratic instincts which were aroused in him by the literature of the Left and which caused him to declare himself a socialist. This was a common enough phenomenon at that period, but it was not common to find criticism from the Left so unhysterical and un-stampeded as Whipple's. One sees in his later essays how the fine discriminations and pressures of his mind had managed to digest even a considerable dose of Marxism without absorbing from it anything but nourishment; and, looking back on his career at college, with its em-phases that were so quiet yet so definite, his atti-tude toward the eating-club system and his policy with contributors to the *Lit,* I could see now that these equal-itarian instincts were not getting out of hand because they had always been there and had always been reck-oned with. I imagine that his experience of the War, in which he had served without a commission, had wak-ened, as it did in most such cases, a sympathy with the common man that remained with him ever after. He had shared the solidarity of the Marine Corps, and he always felt the special pride in it which is characteristic of that branch of the service.

He responded at any rate to the times with a liveliness and youthfulness that seemed amazing—though I have found that those men and women who really live in close contact with the arts remain young when the people who live with the ups and downs of business, of the stock market or of current politics, become stale with middle age. I last saw him in 1938 when he had got a sabbatical year from Berkeley and come East to write a new book. He could hardly have been fuller of projects if he had just graduated from college. He had come out to see me in the country, and it was quite like the old *Nassau Lit* days when he had used to drop over from the Graduate School. But now he was no longer blocked by the style of Isocrates. He was going to write about things that excited him and about which he had something to say, and he knew that there were people who would read him.

He died suddenly of an attack of his malady in the spring of the following year, June 3, 1939. The pieces he had left completed were published after his death by the University of California Press, under the title *Study Out the Land,* a phrase from a poem of Whitman's; and they show how the glow of that light which had survived days of dullness and days of pain was intensified to a special brightness just before it went out.

December, 1942

THE ANTROBUSES AND
THE EARWICKERS

THE *Saturday Review of Literature* of December 19, 1942, published an article by Joseph Campbell and Henry Morton Robinson asserting that Thornton Wilder's play *The Skin of Our Teeth* derives from James Joyce's *Finnegans Wake*. At the time this article appeared I had been concocting the following little parody, based on Book I, Chapter 6, of Joyce's book. I had had some correspondence with Wilder on the subject of *Finnegans Wake*, and I had intended to send him this as a joke. I did not, however, send it because I was afraid it might look as if it had been inspired by the invidious *Saturday Review* article. I did not approve of the tone of that article, but its principal contentions were true, and since they have generally been received with incredulity, I may as well produce my burlesque:

What pyorrheotechnical edent and end of the whirled in comet stirp (a) brings dionysaurus to Boredway yet manages to remain good bronx orpheus; (b) gave Jed harrors but made Mike meyerbold; (c) was voted a tallulahpalooza and triumpet allakazan by the waitups of the dramatical dimout; (d) stamps them bump, backs them bim, oils them in the bowels and rowels them in the aisles, causes them to beep buckups and sends them hope sobhappy; (e) adds a dash of the commedia deadhearty and a flicker of Fleerandello to the whoopfs of

81

Hellzapiaffin; (f) sidesteps coprofoolya but seminates heimatophilia; (G!) translimitates polyglint prosematics into plain symbol words of one syrupull; (H——!!!) disinfects Anna Livia and amenicanizes H. C. Earwicker?

Answer: Skinnegone Sleek.

The Messrs. Campbell and Robinson are, then, quite correct in their assertion that Wilder owes something to Joyce. *The Skin of Our Teeth* is based on *Finnegans Wake*—as Mr. Carl Ballett, Jr., another writer in the *Saturday Review,* has pointed out—in very much the same way *The Woman of Andros* was based on Terence's *Andria.* It would certainly have amused Joyce to know that a Broadway play inspired by *Finnegans Wake* had been praised by critics who were under the impression that his book was unintelligible gibberish. People like Mr. Wolcott Gibbs, who has ridiculed, in a skit in the *New Yorker,* the discoveries of the Campbell-Robinson article, make a very naïve mistake when they assume that situations presented in the straight English of Thornton Wilder's play can have nothing to do with situations presented in the "kinks english" of sleep in which *Finnegans Wake* is written. It is precisely the same mistake that they would make if they insisted that *The Woman of Andros* could have nothing to do with Terence because Terence wrote in Latin. In Mr. Gibbs's case, it is clear that he has looked at the first page of *Finnegans Wake,* one of the relatively few passages in the book which present a real appearance of opacity, and emitted a hoot of derision. That he has not explored Joyce for himself is proved by his invoking a passage which is not in *Finnegans Wake* at all but which was printed in an article by Robert McAlmon before Joyce had removed it from his manuscript.

Mr. Gibbs's readiness to scoff at the borrowings indicated by Campbell and Robinson is due to his not understanding the peculiar kind of close attention to phrases, words and rhythms which the reader of *Finnegans Wake* must cultivate. Words and rhythms here have been given a different value from their value in ordinary books: they do not merely describe, they *represent,* the characters and the elements of the plot; and any real addict of *Finnegans Wake* recognizes in Wilder's play— though these may sometimes have been brought into it unconsciously—cadences and words to which Joyce has given a life of their own. The general indebtedness to Joyce in the conception and plan of the play is as plain as anything of the kind can be; it must have been conscious on Wilder's part. He has written and lectured on *Finnegans Wake*; is evidently one of the persons who has most felt its fascination and most patiently explored its text.

This derivation would not necessarily affect one way or the other the merits of Wilder's play. Joyce is a great quarry, like Flaubert, out of which a variety of writers have been getting and will continue to get a variety of different things; and Wilder is a genuine poet with a form and imagination of his own who may find his themes where he pleases without incurring the charge of imitation. I do not think that *The Skin of Our Teeth* is one of Wilder's very best things, but it is certainly an adroit and amusing play on a plane to which we have not been accustomed in the American theater lately, with some passages of Wilder's best. It deserves a good deal of the praise it has had, and all of the success.

It is probably true, however—though what Wilder is trying to do is quite distinct from what Joyce is doing— that the state of saturation with Joyce in which the play was written has harmed it in certain ways: precisely, in distracting Wilder from his own ideas and effects; and that it suffers, as a serious work, from the comparison suggested with Joyce.

In the first act, you get, for example, the following line spoken by Sabina in her description of Mr. Antrobus: "Of course, every muscle goes tight every time he passes a policeman; but what I think is that there are certain charges that ought not to be made, and I think I may add, ought not to be allowed to be made; we're all human; who isn't?" This has obviously been caught over from the first book of *Finnegans Wake*, in which Earwicker, in his fallen role of Lucifer-Napoleon-Finnegan-Humpty Dumpty-Adam, is arrested for obscure offenses. But this theme of apprehensive guilt, developed by Joyce at length, gets no further attention from Wilder. Antrobus, in the second act, becomes self-important and careless, falls for the hussy Sabina and is ready to divorce his wife; but we do not hear anything about him which makes us see why he should fear the police. The scene in the third act between Antrobus and Cain, which seems to have great possibilities, falls flat for the reason that the father is not made to share the son's guilt. It is as if *The Skin of Our Teeth* needed something which can only be found in *Finnegans Wake*. Again, the letter which, in the second act, Mrs. Antrobus throws into the sea is Wilder's echo of the letter which plays such a conspicuous part in Joyce. But this scene is rather pointless in the play because it is simply something caught over and has no connection with anything else; and rather irritating to readers of Joyce because the letter (pp. 623-624) is one of the main themes of *Finnegans Wake*, in which it represents the mystery of life itself, whereas Wilder has merely exploited—and in a rather sentimental way—Mrs. Earwicker's feminine version of it.

Again, the character of Sabina-Lilith seems conven-

tional and even a little philistine in comparison with
the corresponding characters both in *Finnegans Wake*
and in Bernard Shaw's *Back to Methuselah,* another
work of which *The Skin of Our Teeth,* in certain of its
aspects, reminds us. The Lilith of Joyce is Lily Kinsella,
who plays the remote and minor role of a woman who
is odious to Mrs. Earwicker for having once had de-
signs on Earwicker; but the conception of the Woman
as Seductress is impossible to identify with any of the
individual women of either the Earwicker family or
the dream-myth. You cannot put your finger on her
or isolate her, because she may under appropriate circumstances be incorporated in any one of them: by
the wife in her younger phase, by the daughter in her
adolescence, by the niece who figures as the "prank-
quean." She is something that any woman may be, at
some period or moment in her life. The Lilith of Shaw is
the principle of change that always breaks up the pattern
and leads on to something different and higher. But the
Lilith of Wilder is a hussy: parlor-maid, gold-digger,
camp-follower—a familiar enough comic type, perhaps a
little bit too close to Mrs. Antrobus' disapproving notion
of her.

Finally, I believe that Wilder has been somewhat
embarrassed and impeded by the model of the Earwicker family. He has taken over the Earwicker daughter—in *The Skin of Our Teeth,* Gladys—and done with
her practically nothing; and he seems to have tried to
avoid taking over the twin Earwicker brothers, who give
Joyce a Shaun as well as a Shem, an Abel as well as a
Cain, and who figure in their duality the conflict inside
the personality of their father. Wilder has got rid of Abel
by having him killed by Cain in the Ice Age phase of
the Antrobuses before the play begins; and in the subsequent phases he does not show us or hardly shows us

the people whom Cain attacks. Thus we never see Cain confronted, as Joyce's Shem always is, by his inevitable complementary opponent—with the result that there is no real dramatization of the "war in the members" in humanity. Even the scene between Cain and Antrobus fails, as I have noted above, to get this conflict into the play. The pages of *Finnegans Wake,* with their words that take on malign meanings, produce a queer effect of uncertainty. The Antrobuses are a little too cozy, even when ruined by war.

January 30, 1943

ALEXANDER WOOLLCOTT OF
THE PHALANX

ALEXANDER WOOLLCOTT is dead; and a hostile obituary in the New York *Herald Tribune*, which dwelt on his disagreeable traits, has prompted me to try to pay some tribute to his more attractive ones.

I knew Woollcott only slightly, but my relations with him were based on an aspect of him which may not have been very well known. He was born at the North American Phalanx near Red Bank, New Jersey, and I was born at Red Bank. The North American Phalanx was one of the longest-lived of the socialist communities that flourished in the middle of the last century, and Woollcott's grandfather was for many years the head of it. My family knew all his family, and my grandfather, who was a doctor at Eatontown, brought Woollcott into the world.

When I first came to New York and met Woollcott, I did not connect him with the Woollcotts of Red Bank or the curious old Fourierist building, half barracks and half hotel, to which I had been taken, as a child, to call. At that time, when I had just started working in the office of *Vanity Fair,* to which he was a distinguished contributor, I saw his more erinaceous side. I provoked him to ferocity one day by asking him who the Father Duffy was to whom he was in the habit of referring as if he were the Apostle Paul. I had spent a year and a half in France during the war but had not been aware of Father Duffy; and I had not grasped the fact that Woollcott had created for himself a calendar of saints whose glory must not be questioned. But one day at the Algonquin he asked me whether I was the son of Lawyer Wilson of Red Bank, and we talked about the Phalanx. He told me about a Fourierist uncle who had devoted himself to painting with so much single-mindedness and so little material success that he had finally had to go into bankruptcy. My father had extricated him from his troubles; and I presently discovered that a picture that hung in my mother's house—the old phalanstery building itself dimly looming behind the fresh green of the straight-stemmed New Jersey forest—was one of this uncle's productions, which at that time he had given my father. I had been struck, when Woollcott told me of this incident, by the evident admiration he felt for the completeness of his uncle's unworldliness: not only for the immense number of pictures he had painted but for the enormous sum of money he had failed for.

From then on our relations were cordial. When a play of mine was done at the Provincetown Playhouse in the early nineteen twenties, Alec, then the dramatic critic of the *Times*, wrote a rather sympathetic review of it, but ended by explaining that his judgment might possibly have been somewhat softened by the fact that thirty-odd years before a certain kindly old country doctor had been called on a snowy night to attend Mrs. Woollcott of the Phalanx, etc. When he found out later on that the kindly old doctor had gone to Hamilton College, of which Alec was one of the most loyal alumni, my grandfather came to figure, from his connection with Alec's birth, as a species of Angel of the

Annunciation; and I was surprised to find myself involved in one of those sentimental myths on which he fed the unsatisfied affections that had for objects only his heroes, his friends and the memories of his family.

This myth would occasionally crop up in his writings, and even after I ceased to see him, I would hear from him from time to time. One day I ran into him in New York in the street somewhere in the West Forties. He was going very fast, but stopped a second and said brusquely, "I'm having a play produced!" I asked him what it was called. *"The Crime in the Whistler Room,"* he snapped and passed on. *The Crime in the Whistler Room* had been the title of my play at the Provincetown. Later on, when I published a study of Kipling, he wrote me several long letters on the subject, about which he had some sober and shrewd ideas. I had also, however, been writing about Dickens and praising his gloomy later novels; and this elicited from Alec a sulky "I do not care to discuss Dickens with you." He did, nevertheless, indicate his preferences; and I could see him as a child in the phalanstery lying in the hammock on a summer day with *Pickwick* or *David Copperfield.* His point of view was perfectly infantile. It turned out that he did not like *Bleak House* simply because it was the only one of the novels which he had not read as a child.

In the meantime, however, in the years of the depression, I had had with him a curious interview. I had been travelling around the country doing articles on labor and economic conditions, and he wrote me that he had been reading these articles and said he would like to talk to me. I invited him to dinner, but he answered that he was a much older man than I and that I ought to come to him. So I called on him at Sutton Place, where he occupied a splendid apartment looking out on the East River. As soon as I entered the room, he cried out,

without any other greeting: "You've gotten very fat!"
It was his way of disarming, I thought, any horror I
might have felt at his own pudding-like rotundity,
which had trebled since I had seen him last. He did not
rise and was wearing a dressing-gown, so I asked whether
he had been ill. He shortly replied that he hadn't; and
wanted to know whether I thought he was ill because he
was wearing a dressing-gown. There were other guests,
and they kept coming and going. Drinks were brought
by a butler: Woollcott never stirred from his chair; and
there was a backgammon board, at which people were
playing. A secretary in a room beyond was typing an
article for him; and he would rap out from time to time
peremptory orders to the butler, who was feeding a
phonograph in a neighboring room with Gilbert and
Sullivan records.

He made no attempt to talk to me, and I wondered
why he had wanted to see me. At last there came a
moment, however, when all the guests had gone and
there was nobody but him and me. His demeanor changed
entirely. He began to speak naturally and frankly: a note
of uncertainty came into his voice, and a look of distress-
ful anxiety tightened his brows above his spectacles. He
asked me about the Communist movement in America.
I told him a little, and he went on to talk about the North
American Phalanx—on which he had been collecting
material and about which he meant some day to write. He
said that he had always known that labor was going to be
the great force in the modern world; and he told me about
the Labor Day rites at the Phalanx, over which his grandfather had presided. He said that the kind of reporting
that I had been doing for the *New Republic* was the kind
of thing he should like to do himself: he should like to go
around the country and see what was going on—he had
friends in the West and the South whom it would be easy

for him to visit; and the only consideration that had prevented him from carrying out this project was the fact that, reduced as his income was, he had difficulty in finding a chauffeur who could also do dictation and typing.

Then another batch of guests came in, and Woollcott resumed his role in that theatrical-journalistic world in which he was both a "personality" of print and a "star" in an eccentric part. I wasn't sure that anybody but me could recognize in his anagrams and croquet, his Dickens and Gilbert and Sullivan, his idealization of the stars of the early nineteen hundreds such as the Barrymores and Mrs. Fiske, and his general wide-eyed excitement of the semi-suburban Jerseyman over all that was going on in New York—could recognize in this the persistence of the atmosphere and the habits of an old-fashioned childhood, but seemed quite exotic, a pose, in the modern New York of the thirties.

When *The Man Who Came to Dinner* was done on the stage, I was rather depressed to hear that Alec was acting in the West the character drawn from himself. But when I saw the play in New York, I ceased to be troubled by this. Kaufman's comedy was stupid enough; and it was slightly offensive, like most of his things, because it was an exploitation by an expert contriver of curtains and exploder of firecracker laughs of an idea that had better possibilities. But its very comic-supplement mechanics made Woollcott's participation in it a relatively innocent matter. Kaufman had put on the stage some of Woollcott's superficial idiosyncrasies without ever even attempting to do anything with his real personality. The bad side of the Kaufman character was simply a combination of fiendishness and childishness, while the better side was simply a stage Santa Claus, straight out of the last act of a George Arliss play. A portrayer of the actual Woollcott would have had to show how his arrogance and venom arose from the vulnerability of an excessively sensitive man rather badly favored by nature and afflicted by glandular disorders. When Woollcott addressed his friends as "Repulsive," it was like his receiving me with a hoot at my increasing weight: he was afraid you were going to find him so. And a serious portrait of Woollcott would have had to show the lifelong inspiration for him of the Fourierist background of the Phalanx.

His interest in communism, so far as I know, did not have any practical upshot; but a certain queer moral authority which he exerted throughout his career was derived from the idealism that had bankrupted the Phalanx; and what made him seem impossible to editors, to producers whose plays he reviewed and to the arrangers of radio programs, were not entirely his fits of bad temper but also a boldness and an independence, learned in the same school, that made him intolerant of other people's policies when they conflicted with his own judgment, and prevented him from hesitating a moment about throwing up any job, no matter how fraught with prestige, when principle demanded a choice between submission and resignation. The idea that "social betterment" and the "elevating" effects of the arts were the most important things in the world and causes to be served gratuitously was always alive in his mind; and one might be very far from sharing a good many of his enthusiasms and very much dislike his way of expressing them, and yet feel that his lights were not vulgar ones and that Alec had not betrayed them.

He had it, moreover, in common with the older American radicalism that, in the days of totalitarian states and commercial standardization, he did not hesitate to assert himself as a single unique human being: he was not afraid to be Alexander Woollcott; and even when Alexander Woollcott was horrid, this somehow commanded respect. In *The Man Who Came to Dinner*, it made him a kind of folk-hero.

February 6, 1943

THE POETRY OF
ANGELICA BALABANOFF

ANGELICA BALABANOFF is a once well-known Russian Socialist, who has been living of recent years in this country. The career of Comrade Balabanoff has involved her in political defeats which have brought her, also, much disillusion in regard to personalities and movements. She played an energetic and a high-hearted role in the campaigns of the Italian Socialists of the period before the first world war, and was a friend and confidante of Mussolini in his early pseudo-Socialist phase; she was a member of the Socialist minority who kept alive the Zimmerwald peace movement in Europe in the teeth of the belligerent nations; she joined the Bolsheviks in 1917, returned to Russia after the Revolution and became the first secretary of the Comintern. In those early days of the Soviet Union, she remained on good terms with Lenin, but was unable to reconcile herself to the splintering tactics of the Comintern leaders and the provocative methods of the Cheka, and was eventually eliminated in a way that today seems gentle, at the end of 1921, in the days before critics of the official line were forced to appear at public trials and confess themselves guilty of treason.

On her departure from the Soviet Union, as she was crossing the sea to Sweden, she found herself ill and depressed; and to fortify herself against seasickness, in the midst of a storm that came up, she resorted to reciting to herself and to translating into other languages some poems that she had learned in her girlhood. Later, as she tells us in her autobiography *My Life as a Rebel*, too ill for political activity and "so weakened by work and undernourishment that I had felt like an old woman at forty-three," she began to compose poetry of her own "in various languages with the greatest facility. I seemed to be overwhelmed, carried away by a flood of rhythm." She wrote poems in all the languages she knew: Russian, German, French, Italian and English. It was her method of recovering from collapse, and it has proved one of the consolations of her years of disappointment and retirement.

These poems have now been published in a volume which, though hardly a first-rate work of literature, must be unique as a literary curiosity and has its place in the revolutionary record. It is also a symptom of the pressure, in our time, of the need for an international language. We have lost medieval Latin and eighteenth-century French, and have not yet arrived at Basic English; and in the meantime we have to do the best we can talking all the languages at once, like Marx and Engels in their correspondence, like Joyce in *Finnegans Wake*, like Eugene Jolas in his polyglot poetry, and like Angelica Balabanoff in these poems. She developed a habit of writing the same poem in each of her five languages, and these pieces are not translations because there is no original: they are quite distinct treatments of the same theme. They are all written in the same kind of meter, very irregular, a little vague. The author is so completely internationalized that the versions in her native Russian do not even seem much different from or better than the others. She has relatively little sense of the metrical differences of the various languages, and it is hard to tell whether or not she even allows for the metrical value of the silent final *e* in French.

Such pieces are better adapted for platform than for private reading. They become unexpectedly impressive when the author herself recites them; and their usefulness as perorations before audiences of different nationalities seems to have given her a special inducement to multiply her polyglot versions. In any case, they constitute a document that has at the moment a peculiar pathos. If anybody has been wondering, in this era of spy-infested police-states, of hideous mechanical warfare and of streamlined political pressure groups—if anybody has been wondering what has become of humanitarianism, of socialist internationalism and of militant intellectual courage—well, here they all are in this book. Defeated and driven underground, in the case of Angelica Balabanoff, by fascism, by Communist chicanery, by nationalistic wars, they have burst out through another channel. It is a relief as well as a surprise to find someone, at the present time, who has never doubted the dignity of the working "masses" and who still wants to educate and lead them rather than to manipulate and drive them, who feels sympathy with their human sufferings instead of contempt for their animal helplessness. And here you have, also, the recent emotions of one who has given her life to the more generous socialist ideals and has not been discouraged in her loyalty. In one of the most touching of her poems Comrade Balabanoff writes:

> *J'ai cherché la vérité*
> *Et je l'ai adorée,*
> *C'est à elle que j'ai immolé*
> *Ce que je suis et ce que j'ai été*
> *Et je meurs oubliée . . .*

Courbés sous le joug invisible
   De leur misère,
Je les vois tous les jours résignés et paisibles
   Gravir leur calvaire . . .
Tandis que mon coeur embrasse
   Leur souffrance infinie
Il se serre avec une atroce angoisse
   Et ne bat plus . . .
Je meurs saluant la mort,
Comme un voyageur arrivé au port
Après une longue traversée
Qu'il n'a ni voulue, ni aimée . . .

November 27, 1943

MR. JOSEPH E. DAVIES AS A STYLIST

I HAVE JUST been reading *Mission to Moscow,* Mr. Joseph E. Davies' book, after seeing the film of the same title. The picture, I find, coincides with the book in almost no respect. The real Mr. Joseph Davies, for example, is a shrewd corporation lawyer who contributed to the Roosevelt campaign fund and was appropriately rewarded with an ambassadorship. The Davies of the Warner Brothers picture is a plain rugged American business man, played by Mr. Walter Huston rather like a more elderly version of Sinclair Lewis's Dodsworth, who demurs with a touching humility when the President asks him to go to Russia, and protests that he is really not qualified because he has had no diplomatic training. The real Mr. Davies was sent for the perfectly specific purpose of discussing a trade agreement and arranging for the settlement of debts contracted by the Kerensky government. But these objectives do not figure in the film. The Hollywood Mr. Davies is simply entrusted with a mission of reporting on the Soviet Union. The real Mr. Davies was troubled by the tyrannies of the Stalinist police state. "No physical betterment of living standards," he wrote in *Mission to Moscow,* "could possibly compensate for the utter destruction of liberty of thought or speech and the sanctity of the individual . . . The government is a dictatorship not 'of the proletariat,' as professed, but 'over the proletariat.' It is completely dominated by one man." One could quote him in this sense at length.

There is one point, however, in which the film is quite faithful to the real Mr. Davies. When the Davies of Walter Huston is made to attend the Moscow trials, he enunciates the following statement: "Based on twenty years of trial practice, I'd be inclined to believe these men's testimony." The trials themselves, it is true, are represented falsely, and this is not precisely the kind of thing that Mr. Davies was saying about them at the time; but the undependable syntax of the Warner Brothers' Davies is absolutely true to life. I should say, indeed, from reading the book, that the author of *Mission to Moscow* is, so far as my knowledge extends, the greatest master of bad official English since the late President Harding.

The prose style of President Harding has been analyzed by H. L. Mencken in his admirable little paper, *A Short View of Gamalielese;* and this piece, which I have lately been rereading, has stimulated me to try to do some justice to the beauties of Mr. Davies' writing.

Let me begin with one of the cultural notes with which Davies the connoisseur and man of taste diversifies his record of affairs of state, a passage which illustrates brilliantly his skill in producing the effect of surprise:

"For weeks there have been celebrations of the centenary of Pushkin's death all over the country. He is a combination of Byron and Shakespeare for the Russian people. He was a liberal in thought and married to a noblewoman who, it is alleged, was a mistress of the tsar. He was killed in a duel, which, as the story goes, was a frame-up. Both the opera and the ballet were based on Pushkin's works and the music was by the great Tchai-

kovsky. The opera was *Eugen Onegin,* a romantic story
of two young men of position whose friendship was
broken up over a misunderstanding and lovers' quarrel
which resulted in a duel in which the poet was killed.
It was significant of Pushkin's own end and oddly
enough was written by him."

The sequence of relative pronouns here in the sentence before the last, each one depending on the one
before, is a very fine bit of writing, but it only prepares
for the climax. It drags us, by a series of hitches, up an
incline like the hump on a roller-coaster, from the top of
which we suddenly dip into a dizzying and breath-de-
priving excitement. What is it that makes the next
sentence so startling? Not syntax, for the syntax is normal. Not logic: no mere fallacy is involved. We cannot
assign this sleight to any of the familiar categories of
rhetorical or logical error. The device is original and
daring; it takes us a moment to grasp it; but then we
become aware that the trick consists of first explaining
that the opera which Mr. Davies calls *Eugen Onegin*
(though this is neither the Russian nor the English form
of the title) is based on Pushkin's poem; then of indi-
cating a striking parallel between the circumstances of
Pushkin's death and the poem; and then of suddenly
making the point that, by some scarcely believable coincidence, the poem was written by Pushkin. But to
paraphrase the passage thus is to rob it of all its thrill.
The whole effect depends on the quickness of the shift
in the sense and on the simple phrase *oddly enough,* at
once arresting and casual. Only a bad writer of special
gifts could have hit upon and placed this phrase. It is as
if a long red carpet upon which we had been walking,
on our way to some ceremony of state, had suddenly
been pulled out from under us.

There is, however, one example even bolder of Mr. Davies' ability to baffle and to dazzle:

"The peace of Europe, if maintained, is in imminent danger of being a peace imposed by the dictators, under conditions where all of the smaller countries will speedily rush in to get under the shield of the German aegis, and under conditions where, even though there be a concert of power, as I have predicted to you two years ago, with 'Hitler leading the band.'"

Here the opening is weighty and portentous: a veteran man of affairs with a large experience of Europe is about to deliver a considered opinion. The first indication of anything queer comes with *the shield of the German aegis;* but although this gives us pause for a moment, we immediately reassure ourselves by concluding that Mr. Davies surely knows that a shield is an aegis, and has allowed himself the little tautology, in the exuberance of his enjoyment of his official position, as a mere rhetorical flourish. But then we come to the *as I have predicted to you two years ago.* The tense here is incorrect: it should be *as I predicted to you two years ago.* We conclude that Mr. Davies does not know this, but that, even though he does not know it, the instinct of his genius has guided him to hit upon the perfect deviation which, by adding to the solemnity of the tone at the same time as to the absurdity of the writing, will lead the way to the final effect. And what an effect it is! The sentence never comes to a conclusion. It is a new sort of aposiopesis—an aposiopesis with a full-stop at the end. Yet the grammatical impossibility has with wonderful art been half-concealed. The writer has first given us an adverbial clause beginning with *under conditions where,* which completes itself in the logical way, but then he has gone on to another clause, which begins in the same way: *and under conditions where.* Since we have just seen the first one brought off, we are prepared for the fulfilment of the second. But this second clause is never completed. Mr. Davies, by a rare stroke of art, starts another subordinate clause, *even though there be,* etc., and at the end of this clause he stops. On first reading, we fail to grasp it; we go back and read the sentence again. The use of the subjunctive here, *even though there be,* is another of his fine manipulations to give us confidence in the structure of his thought. We find it very hard to believe that a man who can use the subjunctive in this noble traditional way would be capable of leaving his sentence with one end sticking out in the air, like the rope in the Indian rope trick. And yet Mr. Davies *has* left it so, and we can only accept and wonder, just as we can only accept and wonder at his giving the public his word for the authenticity of all the testimony that is supposed to be quoted, in his film, from the records of the Moscow trials and that includes a confession by Tukhachevsky imagined and written by Hollywood; at his flying back from Moscow on his second mission with the advertisement *Mission to Moscow* painted, in English and Russian, in large yellow letters on his plane; and at his watching with gratification, in the company of Stalin and his retinue, while this film was shown in the Kremlin.

Let me finally quote a passage less distinguished by brilliance of language than by the felicity with which it mirrors the qualities of the man himself. Mr. Davies is reporting an interview with a representative of the Soviet Foreign Office, at which the trade agreement and the debts were discussed:

"He stated that they were having difficulty, in connection with guaranteeing $4,000,000 of purchases in the United States. . . . I stated quite frankly, however, that while, personally, I made these admissions to him 'and against interest,' that [sic] quite frankly I had absolutely no tolerance for a position that would haggle over an increase of $10,000,000 in purchases (from $30,000,000 to $40,000,000) in view of both the equities and the practicalities of this situation; that in my opinion it was not an evidence of approaching the matter in a broad-minded and appreciative attitude of the position which Secretary Hull had taken so fairly and in such a large-minded way on this particular problem."

The style here, of course, is remarkable, as Mr. Davies' style always is. The superfluous *that* is good. The *broad-minded* and *large-minded* are like the flourish of persuasive hands brushing doubts and inhibitions aside; and in the next sentence but one we already see the spell that is cast by the verbal incantation, taking effect on the Soviet department head:

"Mr. Neymann manifested a very fair-minded attitude in reply and stated in conclusion that he would not be disposed to quarrel with that point of view . . ."

But there glints through in this passage, when the figures are named, the relentless *fortiter in re*—to resort to a kind of ornament much relished by Mr. Davies— which always lurks behind his *suaviter in modo*. Mr. Davies is of Welsh blood, he tells us, and, like a Welshman, he knows how to combine an elevated and shimmering eloquence with a certain subtlety of practical shrewdness. The glint is half lost in the mist; the purpose is half obscured by the shower of flattering words that, meaningless though most of them are, rather soothe us and please us as we read. These words may perhaps have made it easier for Mr. Davies, at the time of his embassy, to further the interests of the United States; but there are moments when the metallic gleam that pierces from time to time the shifting lights of Mr. Davies' language, has the look of an eye fixed intently on opportunities for conspicuous self-dramatization.

Winter, 1944

THOUGHTS ON BEING BIBLIOGRAPHED*

THERE HAS come a sort of break in the literary movement that was beginning to feel its first strength in the years 1912-16, at the time I was in college at Princeton: the movement on which I grew up and with which I afterwards worked. The first prophets of that movement are patriarchs now—classics or pseudo-classics. Of the writers in their late forties or their fifties, some go on rather somniferously bringing out just the same kind of books that they were writing with more energy twenty years ago; and others, who have practised an intenser art and seemed to promise self-renewal, are in a state of suspended animation. Two of the best of our poets of fiction, Sherwood Anderson and F. Scott Fitzgerald, have died prematurely, depriving us of a freshening and an exhilarating influence that had been felt by us as principles of life, and leaving a sad sense of work uncompleted (though Anderson was in his sixties, it was impossible to think of him as aging, and though he had published a score of books, he seemed always still making his way toward some further self-realization). Certain others of our top rank of writers have disconcertingly abandoned their own standards and published work so outrageously awful that it suggests premature

---

* Written for the *Princeton University Library Chronicle* of February, 1944, in which a bibliography of my work appeared.

senility. Others yet, whom we might have been regarding as men of still-maturing abilities, on the verge of more important things, have turned up suddenly in the role of old masters with the best of their achievement behind them, and are attempting to pass on the torch, with paternal and hieratic gestures, to a war-driven younger generation which has obviously no idea what to do with it.

These "classes" who have come on since the depression —it is a better word here than the vague "generations"— have found themselves involved in very different conditions from the ones into which we emerged at the end of the last war. For us, a variety of elements seemed to contribute to produce an atmosphere that was liberating and stimulating. The shadow of Big Business that had oppressed American culture in our childhood seemed finally to be passing away. Woodrow Wilson, for all his shortcomings, had something of the qualities of the presidents of the earlier years of the Republic: he was a writer and thinker of a kind, and, though most of his reforms were aborted, he did succeed, on the plane of ideas at least, in dissociating the government of the United States from financial and industrial interests, and presided with some moral dignity over the entry of the United States out of its complacent provinciality on to the larger stage of the world. Later, a livid spark seemed to flash from the American labor movement in the direction of the Russian Revolution. And then the period of "prosperity" began, and there was no end of money around, which publishers and editors and foundations could dispose of as well as brokers. The American writer at this moment seemed at last to be getting all the breaks, and it was not always obvious to him that he was in danger of becoming debauched by an atmosphere of fantastic speculation. In the last years of the century before, a "straight" writer like Stephen Crane or Dreiser had found that it demanded all his stubbornness and courage even to get his novels published, and that he then had to be prepared to face public suppression and private slander, while the quieter kind of artist was left simply to die of chill. In that era, it was possible for Theodore Roosevelt to acquire a reputation as a great patron of the national letters by procuring for E. A. Robinson a job in the custom-house. But now in our day it was altogether different. The young man or young woman was scarcely out of college when his first novel was seized on by a publisher who exploited instead of censoring whatever in it was improper or disturbing, and he soon found himself a figure of glamor in the world between the Algonquin and Greenwich Village, at a kind of fancy-dress party of frantic self-advertisement. Even the older and more sober writers who had survived the inhospitable period suffered sometimes from the dazzling Klieg lights and the forcing of immediate profits—as Anderson was persuaded, I feel, to write a spurious bestseller in *Dark Laughter* before his always reliable instincts led him back to his small towns and obscurity. The less mature writers, in that period, often gambled, without quite being aware of it, on values that had been overinflated, like those of the Boom days of the stock market.

In any case, at the end of the twenties, a kind of demoralization set in, and this was followed by a shrinkage of those values, and for the writer the conditions became different again. There was suddenly very little money around, and the literary delirium seemed clearing. The sexual taboos of the age before had been dismissed both from books and from life, and there was no need to be feverish about them; liquor was legal again, and the stock market lay gasping its last. The new "classes" of intellectuals—it was a feature of the post-Boom period

that they tended to think of themselves as "intellectuals" rather than as "writers"—were in general sober and
poor, and they applied the analysis of Marxism to the
scene of wreckage they faced. This at least offered a discipline for the mind, gave a coherent picture of history
and promised not only employment but the triumph of
the constructive intellect. But then, within the decade
that followed, the young journalists and novelists and
poets who had tried to base their dreams on bedrock, had
the spectacle, not of the advent of "the first truly human culture," the ideal of Lenin and Trotsky, but of
the rapid domination of Europe by the state socialism
of Hitler and Stalin, with its strangling of political discussion and its contemptuous extermination of art; and
they no longer knew what to think. In some cases, under
the illusion that the bureaucracy that ran Russia was still
Lenin and that they were serving the cause of a better
world by calling themselves Communists in secret, they
fell a pathetically easy prey to the two great enemies of
literary talent in our time: Hollywood and Henry Luce,
who reduced them to a condition where they appeared
to have been subjected to druggings and secret opera-
tions and converted into creatures so radically deprived
of any kind of personal self-confidence that they had
hardly the moral conviction that gives a dignity to
genuine unhappiness. Those who have not lent themselves to this fate have for the most part fallen back on
teaching, a profession where they are at least in a position to keep in touch with the great work of the past instead of degrading the taste of the present. Though we
are left now with very little journalism of the literary
and liberal kind that flourished just after the last war,
we are witnessing the curious phenomenon—which
would have been quite inconceivable in my college days
—of young men teaching English or French in the

most venerable schools and universities at the same time that they hold radical political opinions and contribute to "advanced" magazines. The youngest classes of all, the ones not yet out of or just out of school, emerge into manhood on the contemporary stage at the moment when the curtain is down and the scenery is being shifted, and find themselves dispatched into the services with no chance to think seriously of literary careers.

It is thus, as I have said, rather difficult for the veteran of letters of the earlier crop who is retiring a little before his time, to find an appropriate young master on whom to bestow the accolade. On their side, the younger people want precisely to thrust him into a throne and have him available as an object of veneration. The literary worker of the twenties who had recently thought of himself as merely—to change the figure—attempting to keep alive a small fire while the cold night was closing down, is surprised and even further disquieted to find himself surrounded by animals, attracted or amazed by the light, some of which want to get into the warmth but others of which are afraid of him and would feel safer if they could eat him. What is wonderful to both these groups is that the man should have fire at all. What is strange is that he should seem to belong to a kind of professional group, now becoming extinct and a legend, in which the practice of letters was a common craft and the belief in its value a common motivation. The journalist of the later era is troubled at the thought of a writer who works up his own notions and signs his own name; and for the literary man in a college, incorporated in that quite different organism, the academic profession, with its quite other hierarchies of value and competitions for status, the literary man of the twenties presents himself as the distant inhabitant of another intellectual world; and he figures as the final installment of the body of material to be studied. The young men of our earlier classes saw in literature a sphere of activity in which they hoped themselves to play a part. You read Shakespeare, Shelley, George Meredith, Dostoevsky, Ibsen, and you wanted, however imperfectly and on however infinitesimal a scale, to learn their trade and have the freedom of their company. I remember Scott Fitzgerald's saying to me, not long after we had got out of college: "I want to be one of the greatest writers who have ever lived, don't you?" I had not myself quite entertained this fantasy because I had been reading Plato and Dante. Scott had been reading Booth Tarkington, Compton Mackenzie, H. G. Wells and Swinburne; but when he later got to better writers, his standards and his achievement went sharply up, and he would always have pitted himself against the best in his own line that he knew. I thought his remark rather foolish at the time, yet it was one of the things that made me respect him; and I am sure that his intoxicated ardor represented a healthy way for a young man of talent to feel. The young men of the later classes have too often seemed inhibited from these impulses. The good fortune of the college faculties in acquiring some of the ablest of them has, I fear, been offset by the curbs thus imposed on the writers themselves. But it had been true from the beginning of many of these men that they were resigned to classify and to analyze: it was the case with the Marxist critics as well as with the teachers who read Eliot. Marxism, as Trotsky said, had produced a new political culture but no distinctive artistic culture. The young intellectuals of the thirties *did* want to join Marx and Lenin in their great field of intellectual historical action; but when the problems of historical action seemed to have been removed in Europe to a less intellectual plane, they could only take sanctuary in learned research. The scholar-

ship of Marxism in some cases shaded easily into the
scholarship of the English Department; and the inquest
on literary culture from the social-economic point of
view was contracted to a simple ambition to get the
whole thing under glass. And this is where this bibliography comes in.

I visited Princeton last spring, and one evening, at
the house of a professor, I uneasily became aware that
this all-absorbing scholarship was after me. I had already
been slightly troubled by the efforts of the Princeton
Librarian to collect the letters of Mencken and by his
project of bringing out a volume of them while the
writer was still alive. I still thought of Mencken as a
contemporary, whose faculties showed no signs of failing; I still looked forward to reading what he should
write. That the librarian should have been able to induce
him to accept this semi-posthumous status seemed to me
an ominous sign that the movement was folding back on
itself before having finished its work. And now they
were creeping up on me, who was fifteen years younger
than Mencken and had arrived at middle age under
the illusion that I had not yet really begun to write. I
had even a chilling impression that the forces of bibliography would prefer me already to be dead, since the
record could then be completed.

I have lent myself, however, to their dubious design
under the persuasion of Arthur Mizener (who of course
ought to be writing his own essays and poems instead of
cataloguing Archibald MacLeish's and mine). My scholarly instincts were tempted as well as my literary
vanity, and I have ended by scraping up items of nauseat-
ing puerilia and insignificant reviews and paragraphs
which the Library might never have found for itself
and which might better perhaps have been left un-

identified. Having thus, to this extent, fallen a victim to the folding-back process myself, I may as well complete my lapse by playing the patriarch, too, and performing a brief obituary on my work as it is bibliographed here—a process which will lead me again to the general questions with which I began.

This list, then, is the record of a journalist, and the only real interest it can have is that of showing how a journalist works. When I speak of myself as a journalist, I do not of course mean that I have always dealt with current events or that I have not put into my books something more than can be found in my articles; I mean that I have made my living mainly by writing in periodicals. There is a serious profession of journalism, and it involves its own special problems. To write what you are interested in writing and to succeed in getting editors to pay for it, is a feat that may require pretty close calculation and a good deal of ingenuity. You have to learn to load solid matter into notices of ephemeral happenings; you have to develop a resourcefulness at pursuing a line of thought through pieces on miscellaneous and more or less fortuitous subjects; and you have to acquire a technique of slipping over on the routine of editors the deeper independent work which their over-anxious intentness on the fashions of the month or the week have conditioned them automatically to reject, as the machines that make motor parts automatically reject outsizes. My principal heroes among journalists in English have been DeQuincey, Poe and Shaw, and they have all, in their various manners, shown themselves masters of these arts. Poe in particular—though at the cost of an effort which was one of the pressures that shattered him —succeeded in selling almost all he wrote to the insipid periodicals of his day, studying the forms that were effective with the public, passing off his most anguished visions in the guise of mystery stories, and, be getting the editors, in some cases, to print pieces that had been published before but of which he had prepared new versions, scoring the triumph of thus making them pay him for the gratuitous labor of rewriting demanded by his artistic conscience. The masterpieces excreted like precious stones by the subterranean chemistry of his mind were sprinkled into a rapid stream of news letters and daily reviewing that was itself made to feed his interests and contribute to his higher aims. And Bernard Shaw, when he was doing for the *Saturday Review* the weekly chronicle of the London theaters, succeeded, without ever being dull, in gradually impressing on his readers his artistic and moral principles. My own strategy —to make an anti-climax—has usually been, first to get books for review or reporting assignments to cover on subjects in which I happened to be interested; then, later, to use the scattered articles for writing general studies of these subjects; then, finally, to bring out a book in which groups of these essays were revised and combined. There are usually to be distinguished in the writings listed here at least two or three stages; and it is of course by the books that I want to stand, since the preliminary sketches quite often show my subjects in a different light and in some cases, perhaps, are contradicted by my final conclusions about them. This method of working out in print one's treatment of something one is studying involves a certain amount of extra writing and consequently of energy wasted; but it does have the advantage of allowing one's ideas first to appear in a tentative form, so that they are exposed to correction and criticism. My non-critical and non-reportorial productions I have also to some extent smuggled in, and their forms may have been sometimes affected by the importunate consideration of the usefulness of detachable units of the right size for magazines.

As for the content of all these articles, I see that I was more or less consciously trying to follow a definite tradition. I had been stimulated at boarding-school and college by the examples of Shaw and Mencken, and, to a lesser extent, by that of James Huneker. All these men were exciting in their day because they had news to bring and unconventional causes to serve. In Huneker's case, it was simply a matter of communicating to the United States, then backward to what seems an incredible degree in its assimilation of cultural movements abroad, the musical and literary happenings of the preceding half-century in Europe. But Mencken and Shaw were the prophets of new eras in their national cultures to which they were also important contributors; and, though their conceptions of their social aims differed, both were carrying on that work of "Enlightenment" of which the flame had been so fanned by Voltaire. I suppose that I, too, wanted to prove myself a "soldier in the Liberation War of humanity" and to speak for the "younger generation" who were "knocking at the door": such phrases were often in my head. But for American writing, when I came upon the scene, the battle had mostly been won: I was myself a beneficiary of the work that had been done by Mencken and others. There remained for the young journalist, however, two roads that had still to be broken: the road to the understanding of the most recent literary events in the larger international world—Joyce, Eliot, Proust, etc.—which were already out of the range of readers the limits of whose taste had been fixed by *Egoists* and *The Quintessence of Ibsenism*; and to bring home to the "bourgeois" intellectual world the most recent developments of Marxism in connection with the

Russian Revolution. I was of course far from being either alone or first in popularizing either of these subjects; but they were the matters with which I was mostly concerned, and I felt that what I was doing had some logical connection with the work of the older men I admired.

And now what is the next logical step? I am today past the age for this kind of activity; but I have been wondering in the last few years, and especially going back over my work in this list, what the next phase of literature will be and what is to become of the "Enlightenment." Well, in the literary field, it does look as if the movements for which people have been fighting had, if not actually run their courses, at least completed certain phases of their development. Two of the tendencies that have stimulated most controversy, both *vis-à-vis* traditional methods and in conflict with one another: naturalism and symbolism—culminated and fused in the work of Joyce at the time that he wrote *Ulysses*. And there was also embodied in *Ulysses* an exploitation or a parallel exploration of the Freudian tendencies in psychology which had themselves had to fight for their lives and which could still seem sensational in fiction. *The Waste Land* came out the same year as *Ulysses*: 1922; and the result was one of those blood-heating crises that have been occurring periodically in literature since the first night of *Hernani* in 1830: howls of denunciation, defiant applause and defense, final vindication and triumph. But when the successor to *Ulysses* arrived, even more daring and equally great though it was, its reception was completely different; and the difference is significant and perhaps marks the drop of a trajectory in modern literature. Such occasions had never been deprived in the past either of evening clothes to hiss from the boxes or of young men to wear the red vest of Gautier; but the appearance of *Finnegans Wake,* instead of detonating a battle, was received with incurious calm. No exalted young journalists defended it; no old fogeys attacked it with fury. The reviewers spoke respectfully of Joyce while deprecating an aberration, and detoured around the book without giving it the smallest attention; and among the older writers who had been interested in *Ulysses,* now comfortably ensconced in their niches, a few read it, but most ignored. The only group of intellectuals that gave a serious hearing to this work turned out, by a curious reversal of the traditional situation, to be made up, precisely, of members of the profession which had become proverbial as the enemies of anything new. *Finnegans Wake* went straight from the hands of Joyce into the hands of the college professors, and is today not a literary issue but a subject of academic research. Nor is this, in my opinion, entirely due to the complex erudition of the book itself or to the abstruseness of some of its meanings: *Finnegans Wake* gives a scope to Joyce's *lyric* gift in a way that *Ulysses* did not, and it makes a new departure in the merging of the techniques of the novel and verse that ought to be of special interest to poets and fiction-writers both. The fate of *Finnegans Wake* is partly, I believe, the result of the process which I have mentioned above: the inevitable gravitation toward teaching jobs of able young literary men who can find no decent work outside them. In the twenties, Mr. Harry Levin, who has written so brilliantly on Joyce, would undoubtedly have been editing the *Dial* and going to bat for *Ulysses* in its pages: today he teaches English at Harvard, while an old-red-waistcoat-wearer like me who made a move to get the garment out of moth-balls at the time *Finnegans Wake* was published, is being treated to a quiet bibliography under the auspices of the Princeton

Library, where, as I remember, in 1912, Ernest Dowson and Oscar Wilde were the latest sensational writers who had got in past the stained-glass windows.

As for the Marxist or social-economic branch of the naturalistic school—John Dos Passos and André Malraux—it has definitely passed into eclipse, either perplexed or suppressed by the war. The reaction against all forms of naturalism in the direction of universalizing mythologies which had already been a vital element in Yeats and Eliot and Joyce and Mann, and which has lately taken the form of a cult for the psychological fantasies of Kafka, natural and useful though this shift may be, hardly constitutes, as some of its partisans insist, a great renovating subversive movement for which its champions must still contend. An attempt to get back to the pure fairy-tale would certainly be retrograde if it ever became formidable; and in the meantime, what, from the artistic point of view, have Kafka and his emulators done—though they reflect a different moral atmosphere—that had not already been done in the nightmares of Gogol and Melville and Poe?

In the case of political journalism, something similar has taken place. The exponents of the various traditions of radical and liberal writing have mostly been stunned or flattened out by Hitler's bombs and tanks. The socialists are now for the most part simply patriots, as they inevitably become in time of war; the Communists are Russian nationalists who would not recognize a thought of Lenin's if they happened by some mistake to see one; the liberal weeklies are not merely dull shades of the luminous spirits they once were, but false phantoms whose non-incandescence is partly due to an alien mixture of the gases of propaganda injected by the Stalinists and the British. All this press of the Left had been losing its best talent, through its own mediocrity and timidity, to the Curtis and Luce organizations. But the *Saturday Evening Post,* our old enemy, seems itself to have passed into a decline, and to have abandoned the talent-wrecking field to *Fortune* and *Time* and *Life,* whose success during the last fifteen years has been one of the main events of our journalism. The method of summarizing the news which has been characteristic of these magazines has had of course its considerable value. It is a logical result of the need to survey and to articulate the happenings which wireless and airplane can bring us so much quicker and in so much greater abundance than was possible in the past. The kind of reports that you find in *Time,* factual, lucid and terse, give you something that you cannot get from the newspapers or the liberal weeklies; and they compensate by compactness and relative perspective for the shredding and dilution of the radio. But the competence of presentation tends to mask the ineptitude and the cynicism of the mentality behind the report; and the effect on the public consciousness may be almost as demoralizing in its more noncommittal way as the tirades of the old Yellow Press. For you cannot have a presentation of facts without implying also an attitude; and the attitude of the Luce publications has been infectious though it is mainly negative. The occasional statements of policy signed by Mr. Luce and others which appear in these magazines are on the level of Sixth Form orations or themes: they confirm the impression one gets from the rest of a complete absence of serious interpretation on the part of the editorial director; and the various points of view of the men who put *Time* together, appear to have been mashed down and to figure in what they print only as blurred streaks of coloration that blot the machine-finished surface. Their picture of the world gives us sometimes simply the effect of schoolboy mentalities in a position to avail themselves of a gigantic research equipment; but it is almost always tinged with a peculiar kind of jeering rancor. There is a tendency to exhibit the persons whose activities are chronicled, not as more or less able or noble or amusing or intelligent human beings, who have various ways of being right or wrong, but—because they are presented by writers who are allowed no points of view themselves—as manikins, sometimes cocky, sometimes busy, sometimes zealous, sometimes silly, sometimes gruesome, but in most cases quite infra-human, who make speeches before guinea-pig parliaments, issue commands and move armies of beetles back and forth on bas-relief battle-maps, indulge themselves maniacally in queer little games of sport, science, art, beer-bottle-top collecting or what-not, squeak absurd little boasts and complaints, and pop up their absurd little faces in front of the lenses of the Luce photographers—adding up to a general impression that the pursuits, past and present, of the human race are rather an absurd little scandal about which you might find out some even nastier details if you met the editors of *Time* over cocktails. This habit of mind must have been prompted in the beginning by a natural reaction from the habit of the period just before, when Charley Schwab, Charley Mitchell and Herbert Hoover had all been celebrated as great public figures; but it has turned into purely gratuitous caricature —that is, caricature without a purpose. The journalism of the age of Voltaire was a journalism that was mainly purpose with a selection of relevant facts, and its inadequacies have often been noted; but a journalism which aims merely at facts, with no political or moral intent, ends by dispensing with even the conviction that the human race ought to go on, and so cannot help making it hateful. Who would drive a plane or man a ship or write a sentence or perform an experiment, or even build a factory or organize a business, to perpetuate the race shown in *Time?* It is the part of an educated man—and the employees of Henry Luce are far from the old-fashioned illiterate reporters—to try to give life some value and point; but these papers which were started on the assumption, to quote an early statement of Luce's "that most people are not well-informed, and that something ought to be done," have ended by having nothing to tell them that appears to be worth the telling.

In all this, it is very hard to know whether tendencies are coming or going, whether movements are running down or merely being interrupted. But certainly, as I said at the beginning, a definite break has occurred. It is the moment, perhaps, failing anything better, for an innocent bibliography. Tomorrow the cessation of the war will be turning loose again those forces that are in conflict within all our nations, and setting free, with the end of the slaughter, the creative instincts again. We must hope that the men who will come out of the services will do again as they did in 1919: both demand and provide better work. But, in the meantime, in spite of bibliographies and their effect of well-ordered finality, we must apply ourselves to bridging a gap; and the risks of the civilian writer which he is bound to accept in war-time are poor remuneration or complete lack of market, public disapproval, self-doubt.

1943

THROUGH THE EMBASSY WINDOW:
HAROLD NICOLSON

The Desire to Please is the second installment of Harold Nicolson's memoirs of his family and his childhood, of which the first installment was the volume called *Helen's Tower*. The general title *In Search of the Past* evidently echoes Proust; but the purpose of Mr. Nicolson's own chronicle seems a little vague.

Mr. Nicolson's ancestry is varied and distinguished: it has included a viceroy of India, a celebrated Irish patriot and a veteran diplomat, his father. His childhood, as he tells us in this book, was spent mostly out of England in the embassies. From Persia, where he was born, his father, he says, "went to Constantinople; from Constantinople to Budapest; from Hungary to Sofia; from Bulgaria to Morocco; from Morocco to Madrid and from Madrid to Russia"; and the son in his earlier years continued the diplomatic tradition: he was present at the Peace Conference, in the British delegation, and he accompanied Lord Curzon to Locarno. His experience has thus been unusual, and one would expect of him a story more interesting than these volumes and his studies in diplomacy have yet turned out to be. He is often engaging and sometimes brilliant—he has a genuine literary gift; and it is only after we have been reading him a little that we begin to feel his limitations.

There is a passage in the present volume which is significant in this connection. Harold Nicolson tells us how wistfully he longed in his childhood for a permanent home; how much he "wanted to be localized and concentrated." But he had never any home except the Embassy, always in a new country, but always the same official world. And this is a part of the explanation both of the unsatisfactoriness of his writing and of the fact that we should find this unsatisfactoriness surprising. We were expecting from so cosmopolitan a figure, who has read such a variety of books and met so many famous people, something a little more exciting. We did not realize that throughout his travels he has only resided in one country: the British Foreign Office; and that he has approached the prime ministers and kings as members of the special caste to which he himself belongs: the caste of professional officials. If he is not able to make their activity ever seem quite real, it is partly because he has never been in contact with any other kind of life, and so has no real means of judging them. When you set out to read, say, his account of the Peace Conference or his recent article on Boris of Bulgaria, you may be prepared to be taken behind the scenes; but what you find are merely pictures of persons and places which, neat and bright though they are, leave you with the conviction that, whatever was happening, Harold Nicolson did not know much about it. The great social groups and movements of which the pressures are felt and reflected in the embassies, the parliaments, the palaces, seem to exist for him only remotely: they are merely the armies and mobs—"mob" is a favorite word of his for any kind of popular demonstration—that make the background of dim figures in his picture book. And this picture book, for all the cleverness which the author has

brought to his drawings, tells in general a schoolboy
story in which England is always St. George. Mr.
Nicolson has been quite uncontaminated by the more
cynical aspects of foreign policy. He is still the good little
governing-class boy who accepts the version of things
supplied by his English governess. This governess is a
feature of all the books in which he writes of his childhood experience, and though she is treated with affectionate humor, her influence seems to pervade them.
Harold Nicolson gives us the impression of standing, well-
brushed and well-bred, a credit to this admirable woman's care, looking out through the Embassy window at
the streets of strange non-English cities which he knows
that he mustn't explore.

Not that the life beyond the window doesn't interest
him. He has a lively enthusiasm for poetry, and he used
in his younger days to like to write on literary subjects.
Some of his books about poets were excellent—but here,
too, the glass intervened. He could never really drop the
idea that literary people were freaks and essentially disreputable characters. There was some merit in his opinion that the failure of Verlaine—Nicolson is a real connoisseur of verse—to achieve the highest intensity of poetry was due to the moral instability of the poet; but it
was priggish to be shocked by Verlaine, as Nicolson obviously was, and to dismiss him with a sharp tone of rep-
rimand; and it was priggish to be so prim about the
harmless enough vices of Swinburne. As for his book on
the last phase of Byron, readable and vivid though it is,
admirable though it is in its circumstantial tracing of the
events of the expedition to Greece, it is made irritating
by a tone of irony, evidently caught over from Strachey
—a tone which implies with Strachey a definite line of
criticism but in the prissy and invidious form in which it

is applied by Nicolson seems rarely to have any point. The biographer must have had some real sympathy with Byron to write this book on his last desperate days; he seems in fact to feel a kind of fascination with the more scandalous type of poets; but when he comes to look into their histories, he is forced in a reflex action to detach himself socially from their company by a quiet but well-placed accent of amusement, disapproval, disdain.

This new book, which deals with the adventures of Nicolson's ancestor Hamilton Rowan, has the same kind of faults as the Byron, but is a great deal worse in this way. It is as if the anxieties of the war and perhaps his recent term in Parliament had stimulated Nicolson's sense of his official responsibility at the expense of his literary intelligence. It may be noted in passing as a characteristic touch that, in explaining his interest in Rowan and asserting that he himself, if he had happened to grow up in Ireland, might have found himself "at variance with kith and class and creed," he should remark that he might "have been lost in the mists of the Abbey Theatre"—an easy and inaccurate banality of which I believe he would have been ashamed in the days when he was writing about Verlaine. But the whole book shows a worried solicitude to maintain a correct official attitude which, given the character of the hero and the fact that he was the biographer's great-great-grandfather, becomes comic and seems almost perverse.

Hamilton Rowan was an eighteenth-century gentleman of property of the "Protestant Ascendancy" in Ireland, who, stimulated by the French and the American Revolutions, took the side of the Irish against the English, got sent to jail for circulating a pamphlet that advocated suffrage for Catholics, incurred a more serious

penalty by associating himself with a project of Wolfe
Tone's for a French invasion of Ireland, succeeded in
escaping to France, was in Paris at the fall of Robes-
pierre and became disgusted with the Terror, came to
America and earned a poor living as hired man, print-
maker and brewer, and ultimately asked for a pardon,
obtained it and returned to his property amidst a tumul-
tuous welcome by the Irish. Hamilton Rowan, on his
descendant's own showing, seems rather a noble fellow.
Certainly he behaved with imprudence in allowing
Wolfe Tone's proposal to be circulated in his own handwriting; but such mistakes seem easily attributable to a
certain natural recklessness and arrogance often displayed
by eighteenth-century gentlemen. It would not seem to
deserve the wringing of hands, the anguished cry of
"Why? Why? Why?" with which the great-great-grand-
son of Rowan is continually interrupting his story in per-
plexity over his ancestor's wrongheadedness. Mr. Nicolson is even unable to tell of one of those eighteenth-
century carouses at which Liberty and Equality were
toasted, without shrugging his shoulders to indicate that
that is not the sort of thing that is countenanced by the
Foreign Office; and he dwells with what sounds like an
unpleasant satisfaction on the poverty and humiliation
into which his ancestor's mad courses brought him. He
apologizes for his story in advance by speaking of Hamilton Rowan's "really deplorable career"; but when we
have read this story, we see that it can be described as
deplorable only on the assumption—which Hamilton
Rowan certainly did not share—that the most praise-
worthy object in life is always to remain clean and correct, and never to get into trouble. There is an element
of coy and sly humor in this attitude of Mr. Nicolson's;
but it is a humor that almost always works in the con-

ventional direction, and it is plain that the heroic ro-
manticism and the humanitarian enthusiasm of that age
simply make Mr. Nicolson nervous.

On the subject of the Irish he surpasses himself: "It
seems strange to me that more than a century after his
death Hamilton Rowan should still be classed among the
heroes. I quite see that the Irish memory is different in
quality from the English memory. . . . Much as I like
the Irish, deeply though I wish them well, I regret
that the proportions between their memory and their
forgetfulness, between their forgiveness and their rancor, should be so disarranged." These are phrases appropriate for a public speech; in their context here they
only suggest that Mr. Nicolson is rather frightened by
his whole Irish family connection.

I don't, however, want to leave the subject without
offsetting my account of this biography by mentioning
what seems to me the one very good book that Harold
Nicolson has written. *Some People* is a series of stories
about types that Mr. Nicolson has known: a French
snob, a Ronald Firbank aesthete, a phony expert on
foreign affairs, an English lord and his valet. It is at
once his most candidly personal and his most irresponsible
production, and it succeeds in touching off as none of
his other books does the memories of his diplomatic experience into something like artistic ignition—because
he has here turned *in* on this experience instead of trying
to see the rest of the world *through* it. The fantastic
characters of *Some People* are as funny and as well observed as anything in Max Beerbohm or Evelyn Waugh,
and Mr. Nicolson has managed to present himself as a
kind of comic character, too, in a way that illustrates
much more delicately than I have been able to do his
relationship both to politics and to literature. I am not

much of a rereader of fiction, but I can never look into *Some People* without reading several of the stories through, and I have been opening every new book of Nicolson's with an eagerness which, though gradually diminished, is still always stirred by the hope of finding something else as good.

January 1, 1944

KAY BOYLE AND
THE *SATURDAY EVENING POST*

I PICKED UP Kay Boyle's *Avalanche* in the hope of finding a novel worth reading, and have been somewhat
taken aback to get nothing but a piece of pure rubbish.

Aside from a few literary devices such as italicized
"interior monologues," *Avalanche* is simply the usual
kind of thing that is turned out by women writers for
the popular magazines. A blond heroine, half French,
half American, who fled France when the Germans
came, returns to work with a relief committee and becomes involved in the underground movement in the
mountains of the Haute-Savoie. The villain is a Gestapo
agent masquerading as a Swiss clock manufacturer, who
sneers at the French so openly and makes himself in general so provocatively unpleasant that the reader is at first
led to think that this character must himself be a French
patriot masquerading as a German spy, and is later impelled to wonder how he has ever held down his job.
The hero, Bastineau, leader of the mountain resistance,
combines the glamor of Charles Boyer with the locomo-
tive proficiency of Superman. Adored by his followers
almost as a god, he constantly outwits the Germans, performs prodigies of fidelity to the Girl and, like the
Frankenstein monster of the movies, is always pretending to be killed and then sensationally coming to life.

The Girl herself keeps the story going only by exercising so stubborn a stupidity that it becomes difficult to understand how any underground movement could have trusted her: she is thoroughly mystified by the snarling Gestapo agent and is puzzled at finding that her old friends of the village avoid her when they see her in his company; and it takes her the greater part of the book to grasp the facts of the secret opposition, which one would think must have been perfectly plain to her from the things she has seen and heard even if she had not just come from America and so shared with the reader the advantage of having read the American papers.

The climax is terrific: just at the instant when the Gestapo man is about to shoot the Girl, the hero leaps down through a large open chimney "easily, gracefully as a jumper on skis. . . . his arms spread like a diver's, his eyes and teeth pure white and savage in his face," singing *"L'Infant'rie Alpin-e, voilà mes amours!"* "And then he was on de Vaudois' head and shoulders, his knees locked around him, the heel of one boot cracking the right wrist so that the shot went wild across the kitchen." It is the work of a moment to dispatch the Nazi and to ask the Girl to be his wife. " 'Yes,' said Fenton, 'yes,' and her eyes moved on his face before her, touching the silky brows, and the hair springing back from his forehead; seeing the clear white teeth, and the deep sweet lines of the sun and the weather at his eyes and mouth. 'Yes, Bastineau. Yes, Bastineau,' she said." *"Monsieur le curé"* has just popped in, and he marries them that very night.

I have heard Miss Boyle praised as a stylist, but, though there are in *Avalanche* a few fine images and gray and white mountain landscapes, I cannot see how a writer with a really sound sense of style could have produced this book even as a potboiler. One recognizes the idiom of a feminized Hemingway: "There was one winter when the blizzard got us part way up . . . If you looked in the direction the wind was coming from, your breath stopped suddenly as if someone took you by the throat"; and a sobbing Irish lilt: "He touches my hand as if it were a child's hand, and his promise of love is given to a woman. To him it is nothing to walk into a mountain refuge and find me, and to me it's the three years without him that have stopped crying their hearts out at last." And, for the rest, there are several tricks that Miss Boyle overworks with exasperating effect. She is always giving possessives to inanimate objects, so that you have "the weather's break," "the balcony's rail," and "the mitten's pattern" all within a space of sixteen lines; and there is a formula that recurs so often in the passages of conversation that one can almost say the whole book is built of it: " 'They're fiercer, more relentless,' he said, and the sound of threat was there:" " 'And there is de Vaudois,' he said, and he put the mittens on;" " 'You're French, partly French,' he said, and his eyes were asking the promise of her"—these are quoted from a space of less than two pages. Sometimes you get both these devices together: " 'What is the story of that?' said de Vaudois, and his eye went suddenly shrewd beneath his hat's crisp brim."

Miss Boyle has indulged herself, also, in the bad romantic habit of making foreign conversation sound translated. It is perhaps a part of her Hemingway heritage. A Spaniard, Arturo Barea, has demonstrated in an essay in *Horizon*, that the dialogue of *For Whom the Bell Tolls* is not really a translation of Spanish but a language of Hemingway's own. So Miss Boyle—to take her at her simplest, where there is no question of special eloquence involved—will have her characters make speeches like the following:

"And Bastineau? What of Bastineau?"
"One by one they've gone from us."
"A friend come back from America is here."

Now this is certainly not colloquial English; but when you try putting it into French, you have:

"*Et Bastineau? Quoi de Bastineau?*"
"*L'un après l'autre, ils s'en sont allés de nous.*"
"*Une amie revenue de l'Amérique est ici.*"

—which is even more impossible as French. My best guess at the kind of thing you would get if the last of these thoughts, for example, were naturally expressed in French would be "*Voici une amie revenue de l'Amérique*"—of which the natural English would be "Here's a friend of ours who's come back from America." But Miss Boyle needs the false solemnity, the slow-motion portentousness, that this Never Never language gives in order to carry off her story.

It is easy to be funny about *Avalanche* but it has its depressing aspect. I have not read much else by Kay Boyle since her very early work, so that I do not have a definite opinion about the value of her writing as a whole; but I know from those early stories, written when she lived abroad and printed in the "little" magazines of the American *émigrés,* that she was at least making an effort at that time to produce something of serious interest. Today she is back at home, and *Avalanche* was written for the *Saturday Evening Post.* I did not see it there, but I have been haunted since I read it by a vision of *Saturday Evening Post* illustrations, in which the ideal physical types of the skin-lotion and shaving-soap ads are seen posing on snowy slopes. Nor do I doubt that this novel was constructed with an eye to the demands of Hollywood, that intractable magnetic mountain which has been twisting our fiction askew and on which so many writers have been flattened. I have been thinking, since I finished this book, about the alloy of dubious metal that already existed in *For Whom the Bell Tolls* and was naturally drawn to the Hollywood magnet, and of how Hemingway's novel of the Spanish war came back in its pancake form as one of the stupidest films on record. I have been thinking, also, of *The Moon Is Down,* and of Steinbeck's remarkable innovation: a novel contrived in such a way that it was convertible almost without change into a play for the stage or a movie —perhaps into a comic strip. And I think about the days of *This Quarter* and *Transition,* full of nonsense though those magazines were, with a wistfulness it would have surprised me in that period to be told I should ever feel.

January 15, 1944

THE LIFE AND TIMES OF
JOHN BARRYMORE

If you merely take a glance at *Good Night, Sweet Prince,* Gene Fowler's biography of John Barrymore, you may suppose that it is a cheap journalistic job.

Certainly the style couldn't be more journalistic in a flowery old-fashioned way, which has sometimes a tinge of O. Henry, sometimes a tinge of Woollcott ("A block to the east of the Arch Street Theatre lay the wise bones of Benjamin Franklin"). For Mr. Fowler, Broadway is inevitably "this street of fickle lustre," a distiller a "maker of spirituous delicacies," and Shakespeare "Stratford's first gentleman"; cigarette-smoking is "bronchial debauchery," hair on the chest "torsorial upholstery" and the men's washroom "ammoniac grottos" equipped with "cracked and homely porcelains." When he wants to convey the idea that some white mice were multiplying rapidly, he says that the "snowy rodents were fruitful"; and when Barrymore sets out to play Hamlet, or take on "the Danish assignment," Mr. Fowler says that he "announced . . . his decision to draw on the black tights of the classic Scandinavian." His notion of syntax and the meaning of words is also of the vaguest. When it is a question of anybody's conduct, the word "behaviorism" is always summoned: "After the passing of his grandmother he entered upon a bouncing behaviorism"; and when, in reporting an interview with Alexander Woollcott, he seems to feel that he should make an effort to have this celebrator of Hamilton College talk like an educated man, he produces the following tribute to grammar: "'And when you write of him, as I fear you shall, for heaven's sake remember one thing.'"

The language of Mr. Fowler has no structure and no harmonics. It is something that is exhaled like breath or exuded like perspiration. And yet the fuzzy raffish style of this book has its special appropriateness to the subject: it is a literary equivalent for the atmosphere in which the events take place. What we get here is the folklore of the Barrymores; and, as you read, you can smell the aroma of the Manhattans and highballs and cigars of the old Hoffman House and the Knickerbocker bar, you seem to drift on the long late conversations at the Players club and the Lambs on which the Barrymore mythology was nourished. John Barrymore did in a sense live his legend; but you cannot really feel its validity unless you see it presented in terms of the smoking room, the city room, the green room, of the mirrors behind the bar and the shaded lamps at the club, all elements of urban life themselves rather remotely associated with the realities of common day. In this world of nocturnal fancy, Jack Barrymore was a fabulous character: a great drinker, a great man with women, a great comedian of public and private life, and finally a great maker of money. Gene Fowler, with his word-slinging jargon and his husky-throated sports-writer humor, is the right person to tell this story which might otherwise never have been told; and his book contains a most entertaining collection of funny theatrical anecdotes, phantasmagoric binges and what would in the days of the Knickerbocker bar have been described as "gorgeous yarns."

Yet this *Life and Times of John Barrymore* is absorbing for another reason, too; and the author has put into it something more than the favorite tales of a raconteur. The truth is that you get from this chronicle a much more convincing picture of its subject than you usually expect to find in either a fan or an official biography. Gene Fowler shows both insight into Barrymore and delicacy in handling his difficult case; and the piecing together of the record becomes fascinating because it is directed by a definite conception, always sympathetic but also quite realistic, of the man inside the reputation.

To begin with: the evidence of this book establishes indubitably a fact which the more fanatical admirers of the Barrymores are sometimes rather loath to admit. The generation of the Barrymore family that included John, Lionel and Ethel never really wanted to be on the stage. Their father, an Englishman named Blythe, who had assumed the stage name of Barrymore, was the son of an officer in India and had been educated at Harrow and Oxford. It was expected that he would read for the law, and his taking to the stage was a kind of a lapse, which, in spite of the long theater tradition on the mother's side of the family, the children seemed anxious to retrieve. "We became actors," says Ethel Barrymore, as reported by Mr. Fowler, "not because we wanted to go on the stage but because it was the thing we could do best." And Lionel corroborates this: "Neither Jack nor myself preferred the stage. We both wanted to become painters. Yet it seemed that we had to be actors. It was as if our father had been a street-cleaner and had dropped dead near a fire hydrant, and we went to pick up his shovel and broom to continue his work. Perhaps we didn't clean the corners well, but we did a better job at it than someone who never had been in the environment. What other thing could we have done better?"

This covers the case precisely. The Barrymores have occupied a position which has been at least as much social as theatrical. Seeing them on the stage was not always so very much different from meeting them in private life; and there was a tendency on the part of the public to imagine that the events of the play were happening to John or Ethel. They were none of them, even John, great actors, because they never had the actor's vocation. You see it very clearly if you compare them with their uncle John Drew, who, glass of fashion and mold of form though he was, took the theater with professional seriousness, and even in his later years, at his blindest and most arthritic, kept his cast and himself up to scratch with the rigor of an old general at maneuvers; whereas, as Gene Fowler tells us, the father of the three, Maurice Barrymore, used to neglect to memorize his lines and "contrive amazing excursions from the text," and John carried this cavalier treatment of the conventions and discipline of the stage to what must have been unprecedented lengths—breaking up his fellow-actors with elaborate and cruel jokes, stepping out of his character to denounce the audience and, in general, doing everything possible to sabotage an occupation he scorned.

The artistic deficiencies of the Barrymores were thrown into striking relief at the time—the season of 1922–23—when the Moscow Art Theater first visited America. That was also the season when the Barrymores were attempting their most ambitious roles: that fall John had opened in *Hamlet* and Ethel in Hauptmann's *Rose Bernd;* but when one compared these productions with the Russian ones, they had almost the aspect of private theatricals. Kachalov, of the Moscow Art Theater, was by way of being the Russian John Barrymore—that is, he was a good-looking and popular actor with a romantic reputation, who was supposed to do a good deal of drinking. But, if you went to see Kachalov in a play, you would find the dilapidated baron of Gorky's *The Lower Depths* or the elderly and bourgeois Stockmann of Ibsens's *An Enemy of the People*. If you had failed to look at the program, you might sit through a couple of acts before you recognized Kachalov at all: you had absolutely had the illusion that you were watching the creation of the dramatist. When you went to see John Barrymore in *Hamlet*, however, what you found was John Barrymore in *Hamlet*. His voice was better-trained than it had been and he had cultivated a new kind of vehemence; but he was obviously the same engaging fellow who had been playing around with the stage for years; and as the run of the show continued—one story Mr. Fowler does not tell—he would kid with the audiences at Shakespeare's expense by substituting, in the play scene, "Hollywood, Hollywood!" for "Wormwood, wormwood!" So Ethel, as Rose Bernd, a part in which a Russian actress would completely have incorporated herself, made a conscientious effort for a scene or two to impersonate a country girl who had been gotten with child by her master, then would drop the whole thing and smile graciously and become her delightful self.

Yet John Barrymore was a gifted person, and he counted for something in the life of his time. The extracts from his letters and diaries which Mr. Fowler has included in this book show his wit and his sensibility, and a refractory integrity of character which has nothing in common with the temperament of the ordinary popular actor. He belonged to an American tradition of the high-strung man of talent who makes hay of the Ameri-

can standards—runs amuck, takes to dissipation and is
broken down young. But poor Barrymore never realized
himself in either his painting or his acting as, say, Poe or
Stephen Crane did in his writing, and he never found
the right thing to do or be. It was only when some aspect
of a character he was playing coincided with some aspect
of his own personality that he was really creative on the
stage: the scenes in which Hamlet takes his bitterness
out in baiting the various figures of the Court, the opening of *Richard III*—one of the moments he came closest
to greatness—in which the young Richard, full of envy as
he sees how his deformities must cripple his life, vows himself, with a young man's spirit that moves us for the moment with its passion, to revenge upon normal humanity. Though I saw John Barrymore, through the years,
in most of his important parts, from *The Fortune Hunter* to *Hamlet,* I can remember, leaving aside the light
comedies, only one in which he seemed indistinguishable
from the character he was impersonating: the bank
clerk in Galsworthy's *Justice,* who commits a forgery out
of love for a woman and is sentenced to solitary confine-
ment. This came at the beginning of the period when
Barrymore's friends were trying to persuade him to take
his dramatic abilities more seriously, and it gave him a
chance, I suppose, to identify with the character he was
playing all that shrinking and uncertainty of his nature
which, according to Mr. Fowler, made a lady who knew
him well call him "a confused child."

He tried hard to find some role in life itself that he
could count on and that would express him; and this biography is the story of his successive attempts. A disturbing and saddening story; for whenever, through exercise
of will, he had achieved a high point of intensity by im-
posing on life his personal dream, the role always failed
and let him down with a crash. First there was the effort

of hard training that raised him to his Shakespearean roles, which he tired of and discarded so soon; then there was the quite different effort, inspired, when he was forty-three, by his idealization of Dolores Costello, to find at last some high and enduring ground as lover, husband, father. John Barrymore's solitary voyage on his yacht, as recorded by himself in his diary, when he is exalted by his vision of his love, yet living with his own thoughts and obviously happier alone with them than he is ever likely to be in his relations with other people, makes an attractive episode in his story but contains its tragic implications. The dream went to pieces when he tried to embrace it, as he had evidently the premonition it would do, and he had lost forever now the fine dignity of his independence, which had been partly sustained by the dream. It is quite plain from Mr. Fowler's account that the débâcle of John Barrymore's final years was almost as much the result of an actual loss of his faculties as the complete mental breakdown which his father had had at about the same age; yet in this hideous self-parody and self-ruination there was also perhaps a kind of arrogance, a paroxysm of contempt for the stage, and a last desperate effort in an inverted form to achieve that extreme intensity that enables one to realize oneself.

January 22, 1944

"NEVER APOLOGIZE, NEVER EXPLAIN":
THE ART OF EVELYN WAUGH

I DID NOT READ Evelyn Waugh at the time when he was first attracting attention. I never got started on him till a year ago, when I picked up a reprint of *Decline and Fall* and was so much exhilarated by it that I went on to *Vile Bodies,* and then read his four other novels in the order in which they were written. I may thus lay claim to a fresh impression of Evelyn Waugh's work—an impression, I believe, not much influenced by any journalistic interest that work may have had, appearing at the end of the twenties, as a picture of the delirium of that period. Nothing can taste staler today than some of the stuff that seemed to mean something then, that gave us twinges of bitter romance and thrills of vertiginous drinking. But *The Great Gatsby* and *The Sun Also Rises* hold up; and my feeling is that these novels of Waugh's are the only things written in England that are comparable to Fitzgerald and Hemingway. They are not so poetic; they are perhaps less intense; they belong to a more classical tradition. But I think that they are likely to last and that Waugh, in fact, is likely to figure as the only first-rate comic genius that has appeared in English since Bernard Shaw.

The great thing about *Decline and Fall,* written when the author was twenty-five, was its breath-taking spontaneity. The latter part of the book leans a little too heavily on Voltaire's *Candide,* but the early part, that hair-raising harlequinade in a brazenly bad boys' school, has an audacity that is altogether Waugh's and that was to prove the great principle of his art. This audacity is personified here by an hilarious character called Grimes. Though a schoolmaster and a "public-school man," Grimes is frankly and even exultantly everything that is most contrary to the British code of good behavior: he is a bounder, a rotter, a scoundrel, but he never has a moment of compunction. He is supplemented by Philbrick, the butler, a graduate of the underworld, who likes to tell about revolting crimes. This audacity in Waugh's next book, *Vile Bodies,* is the property of the infantile young people who, at a time "in the near future, when existing social tendencies have become more marked," are shown drinking themselves into beggary, entangling themselves in absurd sexual relationships, and getting their heads cracked in motor accidents. The story has the same wild effect of reckless improvisation, which perfectly suits the spirit of the characters; but it is better sustained than *Decline and Fall,* and in one passage it sounds a motif which for the first time suggests a standard by which the behavior of these characters is judged: the picture of Anchorage House with its "grace and dignity and other-worldliness," and its memories of "people who had represented their country in foreign places and sent their sons to die for her in battle, people of decent and temperate life, uncultured, unaffected, unembarrassed, unassuming, unambitious people, of independent judgment and marked eccentricities."

In *Black Mischief* there is a more coherent story and a good deal of careful planning to bring off the surprises and shocks. There are descriptions of the imaginary black kingdom of Azania, which is the principal scene of the action, that are based on the author's own travels and would not be out of place in a straight novel. We note that with each successive book Evelyn Waugh is approaching closer to the conventions of ordinary fiction: with each one—and the process will continue—we are made to take the characters more seriously as recognizable human beings living in the world we know. Yet the author never reaches this norm: he keeps his grasp on the comic convention of which he is becoming a master—the convention which makes it possible for him to combine the outrageous with the plausible without offending our sense of truth. It is a triumph for him to carry from book to book the monsters of *Decline and Fall* and to make us continue to accept them as elements in later novels that touch us or stir us with values quite different from those of the earlier ones. There are two important points to be noted in connection with *Black Mischief*. The theme of the decline of society is here not presented merely in terms of night-club London: it is symbolized by the submergence of the white man in the black savagery he is trying to exploit. The theme of audacity is incarnated here, not in a Philbrick or a Grimes, but in a bad-egg aristocrat, who steals his mother's emeralds to run away from England, manipulates the politics of Azania by talking modern ideas to the native king and, forced at last to flee the jungle, eats his sweetheart unawares at a cannibal feast.

A Handful of Dust, which followed, is, it seems to me, the author's masterpiece. Here he has perfected his method to a point which must command the admiration of another writer even more perhaps than that of the ordinary non-literary reader—for the latter may be carried from scene to scene of the swift and smooth-running story without being aware of the skill with which the author creates by implication an atmosphere and a set of relations upon which almost any other novelist would spend pages of description and analysis. The title comes from T. S. Eliot's line, "I will show you fear in a handful of dust," but, except on the title page, the author nowhere mentions this fear. Yet he manages to convey from beginning to end, from the comfortable country house to the clearing in the Brazilian jungle, the impression of a terror, of a feeling that the bottom is just about to drop out of things, which is the whole motivation of the book but of which the characters are not shown to be conscious and upon which one cannot put one's finger in any specific passage. A charming woman of the aristocracy deserts a solid county husband and a high-spirited little boy to have a love affair with the underbred and uninteresting son of a lady interior decorator; the child is killed at a hunt; the husband runs away to Brazil and ends as the captive of an illiterate halfbreed, who keeps him for years in the jungle reading the novels of Dickens aloud. The audacity here is the wife's: her behavior has no justification from any accepted point of view, whether conventional or romantic. Nor does the author help out with a word of explicit illumination. He has himself made of audacity a literary technique. He exemplifies, like so many of his characters, the great precept of Benjamin Jowett to young Englishmen just starting their careers: "Never apologize, never explain."

The next novel *Scoop* is not quite so good as the ones just before and just after it, but it has in it some wonderful things. A quiet country gentleman, who writes nature notes for a big London paper called the *Daily Beast*, gets railroaded, through a confusion of identities, to another of Waugh's Negro countries, where he is supposed to act as war correspondent. The story is simpler than

usual, and it brings very clearly to light a lineup of opposing forces which has always lurked in Evelyn
Waugh's fiction and which is now even beginning to
give it a certain melodramatic force. He has come to see
English life as a conflict between, on the one hand, the
qualities of the English upper classes, whether arrogant,
bold and outrageous or stubborn, unassuming and eccentric, and, on the other, the qualities of the climbers,
the careerists and the commercial millionaires who dominate contemporary society. The story of William Boot
comes to its climax when the grown-up public-school boy
faces down the Communist boss of Ishmaelia, who is
trying to get him off the scene while a revolution takes
place: " 'Look here, Dr. Benito,' said William. 'You're
being a bore. I'm not going.' " And the book has a more
cheerful moral than any of its predecessors: William
succeeds in holding his own against the barbarisms both
of Africa and of London, and in the end he returns to
the country, where they cannot get him again and
where he continues to write his notes about the habits of
the local fauna—though "outside the owls hunted mater-
nal rodents and their furry broods." If this book is less
exciting than the others, it is perhaps because the theme
of audacity appears mainly in connection with the *Daily
Beast*, with which the author cannot feel any sympathy.

Waugh's most recent novel, *Put Out More Flags*,
written during and about the war, has an even more
positive moral. Basil Seal, the aristocratic scoundrel who
has already figured in *Black Mischief*, exploits the war
to his own advantage by informing against his friends
and shaking down his sister's county neighbors with
threats of making them take in objectionable refugees,
but finally he enlists in the Commandos, who give him
for the first time a legitimate field for the exercise of his
resourcefulness and nerve. Evelyn Waugh's other well-

born wastrels are already in the "corps d'élite," somewhat sobered after years of "having fun." "There's a new spirit abroad. I see it on every side," says stupid old Sir Joseph Mainwaring. "And, poor booby," says the author, "he was bang right." We see now that not only has the spirit of audacity migrated from the lower to the upper classes, but that the whole local emphasis has shifted. The hero of *Decline and Fall* was a poor student reading for the church, whose career at Oxford was wrecked by the brutality of a party of aristocratic drunks: "A shriller note could now be heard rising from Sir Alastair's rooms; any who have heard that sound will shrink at the recollection of it; it is the sound of the English county families baying for broken glass." And at the end he is addressed as follows by another and more considerate young nobleman: "You know, Paul, I think it was a mistake you ever got mixed up with us; don't you? We're different somehow. Don't quite know how. Don't think that's rude, do you, Paul?" But it is now this young man, Percy Pastmaster, and Sir Alastair Digby-Vaine-Trumpington and the English county families generally who are the heroes of *Put Out More Flags.* Evelyn Waugh has completely come over to them, and the curious thing is that his snobbery carries us with it. In writing about Harold Nicolson, I remarked on his fatal inability to escape from the psychology of the governing class, which was imposed on him by birth and office. The case of Waugh is the opposite of this: he has evidently approached this class, like his first hero, from somewhere outside, and he has had to invent it for himself. The result is that everything is created in his work, nothing is taken for granted. The art of this last novel is marvellous. See the episode in which Basil Seal blackmails the young married woman: the attractiveness of the girl, which is to prompt him to try a conquest, and her softness, which will permit his success (Evelyn Waugh is perhaps the only male writer of his generation in England who is able to make his women attractive), are sketched in with a few physical details and a few brief passages of dialogue that produce an impression as clear and fresh as an eighteenth-century painting.

Evelyn Waugh is today a declared Tory and a Roman Catholic convert; he believes in the permanence of the social classes and, presumably, in the permanence of evil. It has been pointed out by Mr. Nigel Dennis in an article in the *Partisan Review* that this would make him rather a dubious guide for England after the war. But, after all, he does not set up as a guide; and his opinions do not damage his fiction. About this fiction there is nothing schematic and nothing doctrinaire; and, though the characters are often stock types—the silly ass, the vulgar parvenu, the old clubman, etc.—everything in it has grown out of experience and everything has emotional value. *Put Out More Flags* leaves you glowing over the products of public schools and country houses as examples of the English character; but it is not a piece of propaganda: it is the satisfying expression of an artist, whose personal pattern of feeling no formula will ever fit, whether political, social or moral. For the savagery he is afraid of is somehow the same thing as the audacity that so delights him.

March 4, 1944

JOHN MULHOLLAND AND
THE ART OF ILLUSION

JOHN MULHOLLAND is a top-notch magician, the editor of the magicians' magazine, the *Sphinx,* and one of the world's leading authorities on professional magic. He is also probably the best writer in the field since the Englishman who called himself Louis Hoffmann. "Hoffmann" was a barrister named Lewis, who led a kind of second life as a conjuror and produced, in his *Modern Magic, More Magic, Later Magic* and *Latest Magic,* which began coming out in the seventies, a series of treatises in the soundest tradition of British expository writing: dense, comprehensive, exact and ornamented with Latin quotations. These books became classics and some of them are still in print. Though in certain respects out of date, they are, I believe, the only works on their subject which have long remained in circulation.

The literature of magic is now immense, but it mostly consists of technical writings intended for professional magicians. The articles on conjuring in the *Encyclopaedia Britannica* have always been unsatisfactory. The best-known one was written by Maskelyne, the proprietor of the Egyptian Hall, a famous theater of magic in London, and it is mainly in the nature of an encomium on the wonders of the Egyptian Hall. The late Harry Houdini, a great student of the subject, succeeded in getting this article cut down—it had, besides, been rather snooty about American magicians—when the new edition of the *Britannica* was prepared under American auspices, and had a paragraph on himself added, but it is still incomplete and out of date. Houdini had a voracious curiosity about everything connected with the miraculous and a desire to master all its arts. He read enormously and wrote several books, and he marks the emergence in his field of a spirit of scientific inquiry. But it was not till Mr. Mulholland appeared that this department of human activity was explored in all its aspects and branches by a scholarly and critical intelligence which knew how to express itself. When further encyclopedia articles have to be written, Mr. Mulholland ought to write them.

Mr. Mulholland's new book—*The Art of Illusion: Magic for Men to Do*—is not one of his most important works, but it is perfect for its limited purpose: to teach the beginner a few primary principles and to provide him with an effective repertoire which requires neither sleight of hand nor difficult apparatus. Mr. Mulholland makes some very shrewd remarks on the general psychology of magic, and he has selected his tricks with care. If he has not given us an up-to-date Hoffmann, this is partly the fault of the times. From the directions and diagrams of Hoffmann it was possible to learn the rudiments of sleight of hand and how to build your own apparatus; but magic has, it seems, fallen a victim to the same pressures that produce outlines of philosophy and digests of famous novels. A growth in interest in non-professional conjuring has been accompanied by an increasing reluctance to take any trouble about it, so that the amateur is likely to satisfy himself with devices that require no more skill to operate than the jokes on sale at novelty shops. Mr. Mulholland has at least tried to show him that the chief pride of the magician is derived not from exploiting mechanical toys but from putting something over on his audience, and that you can be far more amazing with an ordinary coin, a piece of string or a pack of cards than with a pocketful of gadgets.

This whole matter of mystifying people is more interesting than may be supposed. A little acquaintance with the subject will afford a startling revelation of the common human incapacity to observe or report correctly; and anyone who has deluded an audience into believing that he was doing something which he had merely suggested to their minds, while he was actually doing something else that they were perfectly in a position to notice, will always have a more skeptical opinion of the value of ordinary evidence. Mr. Mulholland has written three fascinating books, from which a great deal may be learned: two on the history of professional conjuring, *The Story of Magic* and *Quicker than the Eye,* and one, perhaps the best that has been done, on the history of spiritualism, *Beware Familiar Spirits.* With the advance of the scientific method, the field of thaumaturgy has come to be split between two groups of miracle-workers who grow more and more antagonistic. On the one hand, you have the magicians, who want to be admired for their skill; on the other, the mind-readers and the mediums, who claim to possess supernatural powers. When magicians like Houdini and Mulholland try to show people, in the interests of truth, that there is not a single feat on record as having been performed by a mind-reader or a medium that a magician would accept as genuine, they find themselves confronted with a will to believe against which they are utterly helpless. Mr. Mulholland points out that, though the Fox sisters confessed to the fraudulence of their manifestations, and though one of them actually went on tour exposing her own tricks, they are still venerated as authentic by spiritualists; that the late Sir Arthur Conan Doyle gave a gratuitous endorsement to a mind-reader named Zancig who had never pretended to be genuine and was a member of the Society of American Magicians; and that the faithful of the spiritualist cult even insisted that Houdini himself, though for some reason he chose to deny it, performed his feats through supernatural agency.

One aspect of the subject on which, so far as I know, Mr. Mulholland has not written but on which one would like to hear him is the special psychology of magicians and of the people who like to see them perform. That the attraction of magic may be felt as irresistible by certain kinds of people seems indicated by Lewis-Hoffmann and by the late Dr. Samuel C. Hooker, who had one of the strangest of American careers. Dr. Hooker was an able chemist, who made a fortune in sugar refining and was known as "the father of the beet-sugar industry," but he retired from business in his forties and occupied the rest of his life with magic. His aim was to astonish the magicians themselves, and the great triumph of his later years was to baffle Houdini and Thurston with a Teddy-bear's head that floated in the air and playing cards that stood on end and answered questions. The function of the magician has characteristics in common with those of the criminal, of the actor and of the priest (it was quite natural that Charles Dickens, who had affinities with all three, should become an enthusiastic magician); and he enjoys certain special advantages impossible for these professions. Unlike the criminal, he has nothing to fear from the police; unlike the actor, he can always have the stage to himself; unlike the priest, he need not trouble about questions of faith in connection with the mysteries at which he presides. This is perhaps one of the reasons that magicians, though sometimes rather egoistic, usually appear to be happy in their work. I have never met or heard of an accomplished magician who did not seem to be delighted with himself and to enjoy amazing people with tricks off the stage as well as on.

There is, besides, more to these feats and to our pleasure in them than we are likely to be conscious of. Some of the tricks that have lasted longest and become fixed in the popular imagination must be the remnants of fertility rites. The wand is an obvious symbol, and has its kinship with Aaron's rod and the Pope's staff that puts forth leaves in *Tannhäuser*. Its production of rabbits and flowers from a hat has become the accepted type-trick of conjuring. And the magician who escapes from the box: what is he but Adonis and Attis and all the rest of the corn gods that are buried and rise? This was quite plain in the case of Houdini, who was continually inventing new ways, each more challenging than the last, to get himself buried and bound, and who seemed to experience, in breaking away, an actual exaltation. The ordeals to which he subjected himself were dangerous and sometimes nearly cost him his life: he had himself sunk in a river, immersed in a can of milk, frozen in a cake of ice, hung upside down to a bridge and confined by every possible kind of shackle and rope in every possible kind of trunk and sack; and he was evidently not driven merely by motives of fame and money, but gave the impression of obeying some private compulsion to enact again and again a drama of death and resurrection. These old type-tricks can still create excitement and give both audience and magician satisfaction; and it is significant both that conjuring should never have died out, though people no longer take it for real, and that, recovering today from a period when it followed the tendency of the age by going in very heavily for machinery, it should have reverted—like painting after its photographic phase—to something both more primitive and more impressive; so that the conjuror's public today asks for nothing better than to watch the incomparable Cardini stand silent in an opera cloak and impassively produce from bare hands an endless quantity of cards and cigarettes.

March 11, 1944

WHAT BECAME OF LOUIS BROMFIELD

In the days of *The Green Bay Tree* and *The Strange Case of Miss Annie Spragg*, Mr. Louis Bromfield used to be spoken of as one of the younger writers of promise. By the time he had brought out *Twenty-four Hours*, it was more or less generally said of him that he was definitely second-rate. Since then, by unremitting industry and a kind of stubborn integrity that seems to make it impossible for him to turn out his rubbish without thoroughly believing in it, he has gradually made his way into the fourth rank, where his place is now secure.

His new novel, *What Became of Anna Bolton*, is one of his most remarkable achievements. The story begins in the London season of 1937, and in a succession of brilliant scenes which, for the density of the social picture, recall the opening of *War and Peace*, Mr. Bromfield makes us acquainted with a vivid and varied company from that international haut monde about which he writes with authority. As we pass among these glittering worldlings, Mr. Bromfield characterizes each one with a magically evocative phrase. There are fading Lady Kernogan, "quite simply a tart, with certain superior qualities"; Major von Kleist from the German Embassy, "with the peculiar erect stiff carriage of Prussian military men"; Lady Haddonfield, "whom the years had turned into a rather handsome bony mare" and who at fifty "loved politics and intrigue and was considered the greatest hostess of the Tory Party." But cynosure of all smart London is the American Anna Bolton, of unknown origins but immense wealth, who stands at the top of the staircase of the great Georgian house she has rented, "triumphant and handsome and hard," welcoming "a gaudy, dying world." "There, side by side," thinks a young American guest, as he sees Lady Haddonfield and Mrs. Bolton, "receiving half of Europe, stand the two hardest, most ambitious bitches in the world!" And yet, he notes, Anna Bolton looks "like a fine race horse in training."

This young American, a foreign correspondent—it is he who tells Anna's story—is the only person present who knows who Anna Bolton is, for he comes from her home town of Lewisburg, Ohio, and went to school with her years ago. Mr. Bromfield, at this point, by a deft device, takes us back to Anna Bolton's childhood; and, brilliant social observer that he is, as much at home among the stratifications of a small American town as among the nuances of rank in a London drawing-room, he shows us the unbridgeable difference between the well-to-do classes of Lewisburg and those who, in a racy colloquial phrase which becomes one of the leit-motifs of the story, live "on the wrong side of the tracks." Anna Bolton, we are startled to hear, was once simply Annie Scanlon, the daughter of an Irish cleaning woman and a drunken Irish brakeman, who lived just beyond the railroad crossing. When little Annie first went to high school, the other children couldn't help noticing her "because of her bold looks and coloring—her red hair and blue eyes and a figure developed beyond her years. It was a figure like that of a young Venus Genetrix, made for love, made for bearing children." "Even the high-school boys who didn't understand such things felt them by instinct," Mr. Bromfield tells us shrewdly, with one of his revealing insights into the psychology of adolescence.

Annie fell in love with Tom Harrigan, "the very core" of whose attraction "was a kind of healthy animal magnetism," "as good-looking a boy as I have ever seen—the Irish kind with black curly hair and blue eyes and high color, with big heavy shoulders and long straight legs. . . . I suppose he fell in love the same way he did everything else. He knew what it was all about without being told. He knew with the sure instinct of a young male animal what it was he wanted and went for it." He seduced Annie and made her pregnant, but when she told him, "he was not puzzled at all. He said quite simply, with a curious mature wisdom, 'We'll get married. After all that's why we love each other. That's the way things are. That's why people fall in love—to have babies. That's the way it was meant to be.'" But Annie is "shanty Irish" and Tom "lace-curtain Irish," a further shade of social distinction of which Mr. Bromfield makes us aware. Tom's rich parents object, but he marries her, and Tom gets himself a job as an automobile salesman in Pittsburgh, and there their baby is born. They are ideally happy together till one day Tom is killed in a motor accident, and that same year the baby catches measles, develops pneumonia and dies. In the hands of a less skillful artist, the death of Annie's husband and her baby might seem rather impromptu and meaningless, a gratuitous visitation of tragedy, but Mr. Bromfield has taken care to make Tom Harrigan so completely unconvincing a character that we do not complain of or notice any lack of plausibility in his death. Since we have never for a moment believed in him, we are not touched by what happens to him. The important thing is the effect on Anna. "I met her on the street," the narrator says, "the day she came back from the funeral of the baby. Something had happened to her eyes. They were like stone, as if there were no more tears in them." There seems to be an assumption in all this and through the whole of Anna's story that she is the victim of the "intricate, senseless pettiness and wornout traditions" of the town where she was born; yet she had obviously done pretty well for herself, and, though Tom had had his fatal accident while hurrying in answer to a telegram, apparently a pretext to lure him home, announcing that his father was dangerously ill, the disastrous end of her marriage can hardly be charged to small-town snobbery. That Mr. Bromfield should have arranged this accident and have made Anna feel this grievance is of the essence of his tragic conviction, somewhat akin to Thomas Hardy's, of the unpredictability of human events.

And then Anna turns up in Europe with a fortune that a rich second husband has left her, riding the high tide of social success and as if "sitting perpetually in a theater box watching a corrupt but breathless play." For Mr. Bromfield, with his epic sense of social forces, paints around her the larger background of the disintegration of Europe. "It was a world dominated by too many intriguers, by too many small people, a world lost for lack of decency and leadership, with scarcely a statesman in it . . . Vienna was like an old whore who had once been very pretty. . . . In France the people were on the brink of revolt against the corruption and intrigue of their own government. But Rome was worst of all. . . . Rome was the mad carnival of Europe at its worst. . . . And strangest of all there was a mad, sinister, vagrant who took the name of Hitler."

But Anna is too vital a creature to fall a victim to this decadence of the Old World, and how she fares when war comes to France makes the chief drama of Mr. Bromfield's story. Leaving the Ritz, which has become her home, she flees Paris before the Nazi invasion, but her escape is held up by an air raid, in which she sees a woman killed. The husband of this woman, though Anna protests, makes her drive him to the nearest town. "He said, in a very quiet voice, 'You're going where I tell you. I know your kind. You're the cause of everything.' And suddenly he slapped her hard on the side of the face." This is the beginning of awakening for Anna. She has recognized already in this arrogant young fellow a resemblance to the man she once loved: "She felt suddenly faint and leaned against the car, letting the torch fall to the ground at her side. For what she had seen was Tom Harrigan—a big man with blue eyes and dark, curly hair." Here again we might be tempted to feel, in the case of a less adroit novelist, that the appearance in Anna's life of a second man who is virtually a replica of the first, with a child who closely resembles her own child, strains a little the legitimate license which we are accustomed to accord to fiction; but since the character of the first Tom Harrigan has the two-dimensional quality of a paper doll, it is not difficult to accept an exact duplicate cut out of the same piece of paper.

This second Tom Harrigan is a Russian, perhaps a better man than the first Tom, for he possesses the simple courage, perfect honesty and vast humanity characteristic of his race. In the love between him and Anna, Mr. Bromfield seems to give us a symbol of the union between Russia and the United States which was cemented at Teheran. Not that the author necessarily accepts the Soviet experiment in toto; for, in spite of Tom II's rude behavior on the occasion of his first meeting with Anna, he turns out to be very well-born, the son of a White Russian émigré, and thus keeps up the high social tone which Mr. Bromfield has taught us to expect in his fiction.

Anna takes in his motherless child and she sets up a canteen for refugees in a town just over the line in then still unoccupied France. She works her high connections in Paris and her acquaintance with the Prussian von Kleist, to get supplies for the despoiled population, but she refuses to marry von Kleist, who wants her, as he tells her, "because I am tired and sick and corrupt and you are strong and healthy and young"—a decision from which, also, it is possible for the politically minded reader to draw a significant moral. She finds that she loves this young Russian, who is active in the underground movement, and for the first time, after many arid years of pleasure-seeking and worldly notoriety, Anna Bolton at last finds herself. Her companion, Harriet Godwin, puts it eloquently in the memorable scene in which Harriet is dying: "I've seen something happen to you, my dear, something miraculous. . . . I think I've seen you grow a soul." "That is really what this story is about," Mr. Bromfield has already told us, "how Anna changed and came to be born at last as a whole person, without deformity, how Anna learned understanding and humanity, and the value of things of life."

When the United States declares war, Anna's position in France becomes impossible, and she escapes to Algiers with the second Tom. There the narrator meets her again "She turned toward me and I knew at once the woman was Anna Bolton, yet as I saw her in full face there was something about her that was not Annie Scanlon, at least not the Annie I had known. The hard look was no longer in the eyes. There was no hardness about the mouth. The experience was an extraordinary one." She is married and thoroughly happy. When this old friend sees her Russian husband, "it seemed to me that Tom Harrigan was looking at me. . . . I heard Anna saying, 'You see?' And then softly in English in that

warm new voice of hers, she said, 'I am very grateful.
God gave me another chance.'"

Mr. Bromfield, in *What Became of Anna Bolton,* has
accomplished something in the nature of a miracle. In
hardly more than sixty thousand words—a story that recalls, by its length, *A Lost Lady* and *Ethan Frome*—he
has produced, by severe compression, a small masterpiece
of pointlessness and banality. Most novelists of Mr.
Bromfield's rank have some hobby about which they become interesting, some corner of life which they know
and about which they have something to tell, some
humor or infectious sentimentality or capacity for creating suspense; and it must have cost Louis Bromfield a
rigorous labor of exclusion to achieve this smooth and
limpid little novel in which there is not a single stroke
of wit, not a scene of effective drama, not a phrase of
clean-minted expression, and hardly a moment of credible human behavior.

I have been trying to describe this production in the
manner appropriate to it—that is, as far as possible, in
the language of the ladies who admire Louis Bromfield
and who write enthusiastic reviews in the *Times* and
the *Herald Tribune.* But the truth is that the book reviewer is baffled when he attempts to give an account
of a work which has already turned its back on literature
and embarrasses him on every page by stretching out
its arms to Hollywood. He comes to feel that what he
ought to have done was simply to pass it along to the
movie department. For the characters of Louis Bromfield are hardly even precisely stock fiction characters:
they are blank spaces like the figures on billboards before the faces have been painted in. When their features
are finally supplied, they will be the features of popular actors. Mr. Bromfield seems to have made it easy, by

giving Anna a similar name, for his heroine to wear the face of Ann Sheridan, who, not so very far back, in *Kings Row,* was playing just such an Irish girl from the other side of the tracks, in love with a rich young man; and in the same way Eric von Kleist can merge readily into Erich von Stroheim. No doubt the public will see them soon and will not mind if what they are and do has no logic and no motivation, no likeness of any kind to life. But the book reviewer is rather up against it, since he has to have something to take hold of, even to say that a book ought to be better, and *Anna Bolton* completely eludes him because it is really sub-literary and proto-film.

April 8, 1944

A review by Mary Ross published in the *New York Herald Tribune* after the above article was written, closed with the following paragraph:

"This is a simply told and unassuming story, centered in the figure of a proud Irish girl from an American town, rather than the decadent glitter of pre-war Europe or the contrast of gluttony and misery which followed the fall of France. Mr. Bromfield brings the war close, as the story is told in the first person by David Sorrell, but it will be Anna herself that you will remember. This is an appealing novel which it is hard to lay down, and I think it will be hard to forget."

J. DOVER WILSON ON FALSTAFF

I DARE SAY that no other national poet presents quite the same problem as Shakespeare to the academic critics who study him. Goethe and Dante were great writers by vocation: they were responsible and always serious; they were conscious of everything they did, and everything they did was done with intention; they were great students and scholars themselves, and so always had something in common with the professional scholars who were to work over them. And this was hardly less true of Pushkin. But Shakespeare was not a scholar or self-consciously a spokesman for his age as Dante and Goethe were; he was not even an "intellectual." He was what the sports-writers call a "natural," and his career was the career of a playwright who had to appeal to the popular taste. He began by feeding the market with pot-boilers and patching up other people's plays, and he returned to these trades at the end. In the meantime, he had followed his personal bent by producing some extraordinary tragedies which seem to have got rather beyond the range of the Elizabethan theater and by allowing even his potboiling comedies to turn sour to such a degree as apparently to become unpalatable to his public. But he displayed all along toward his craft a rather superior and cavalier attitude which at moments even verged on the cynical—a kind of attitude which a

Dante, or a Dostoevsky, could hardly have understood. He retires as a serious artist—in *Cymbeline* and *The Winter's Tale*—before he has stopped writing and says farewell to his audience, in *The Tempest*, through a delightful and rather thoughtful masque.

It would perhaps be an exaggeration to say, as John Jay Chapman did, that Shakespeare regarded the writing of plays as a harmless kind of nonsense. He had certainly, by the end of his life, come to see himself in the role of Prospero: a powerful and splendid enchanter. But it is difficult for the professional scholar to understand the professional playwright; and there is always the danger that a pedant who does come to direct his attention upon the theatrical tradition behind Shakespeare may end by attempting to resolve him into terms of mere stage conventions. It is equally difficult for the scholarly critic who has been nourished on the moralistic literature of the English or American nineteenth century to understand a pure enchanter for whom life is not real and earnest but a dream that must finally fade like the dramas in which he reflects it. Mr. J. Dover Wilson, the English scholar, whose books on *Hamlet* are well known and who has just published a study of *Henry IV* called *The Fortunes of Falstaff*, is an exception to both these limitations, and he has criticized them with much common sense. A good deal of his recent book is occupied, in fact, with exposing various errors that derive from these sources; and, though always pleasant to read, it is thus not always of especial interest to the ordinary reader or playgoer who is accustomed to getting Shakespeare at first hand and has never been bemused by the atmosphere, so curiously un-Shakespearean, engendered by the dramatist's commentators. It does not occur to us today to try, as was at one time a critical fashion, to examine the creations of Shakespeare as if they were actual persons about whom it would be possible to assemble complete and consistent biographies. Mr. Wilson shows how very different the development of Falstaff is from even the kind of presentation of character that one gets in a modern novelist who has worked out a dossier in advance. He makes us see how the personality of Falstaff is created as the long play progresses, and how it exists only in terms of this play. Nor is the ordinary admirer of Shakespeare very likely to have been misled by the theory of certain critics who cannot bear to admit that Falstaff is a rascal and who have attempted to prove, for example, that he never behaved like a coward: a school of opinion not hard to confute.

Mr. Wilson does occasionally himself fall into another kind of error. He belongs to the rarer group of critics—of whom A. W. Verrall, the Greek scholar, is one of the most conspicuous examples—who have themselves a touch of the creative artist, whose virtue is that they seem to wake the text to a new dynamic life by force of their own imaginations and whose fault is that they sometimes read into it new dramas of their own invention. This last is what has happened, I think, in the case of Mr. Wilson's version of the scene after the Gad's Hill robbery, in which Falstaff boasts of having put to rout a group of assailants whose number increases in the course of the conversation as the boastful mood carries him away. Mr. Wilson has convinced himself that this passage is not merely a comic "gag" of Shakespeare's not quite top vintage—in spite of the fact that these plays, especially Henry V, are full of crude and implausible jokes—but a particularly subtle bit of comedy only to be grasped by the most intelligent spectators: Falstaff has been aware all the time, according to Mr. Wilson, that the two men who chased him were the Prince and Poins, and, in boasting to them now of his boldness, he is merely playing up to their joke for reasons which Mr. Wilson leaves rather unclear. If Falstaff really knew all the time that his antagonists were the Prince and Poins, then he must also have been merely pretending when at Gad's Hill he ran away from them roaring—a supposition which is surely absurd and which it seems to me that Mr. Wilson rather slips out of facing. And, as it proceeds, Mr. Wilson's story of the affair of Prince Henry and Falstaff gets slightly at a tangent to Shakespeare's. He is excellent in tracing the phases through which Prince Hal and his companion pass in the two parts of *Henry IV* (the growing sense of responsibility of Hal under pressure of his father's impending death and the simultaneously increasing impudence of Falstaff, what Mr. Wilson calls his "comic *hubris*," which has been stimulated by the undeserved glory that he has acquired at the Battle of Shrewsbury); and in pointing out that the dramatist has been plotting these curves all along for the moment when they shall intersect, with the inevitable disastrous result. He is contending against the disposition to become sentimental over Falstaff and to denounce the crowned Hal as mean-spirited and harsh when he turns him off at the end so firmly. But I think that Mr. Wilson overdoes his case in trying to reduce the pathos when he talks about the "wicked smile" of Falstaff just after the repudiation, as he says, "Master Shallow, I owe you a thousand pound." The old man has been completely discredited; he must accept his humiliation, and he is sportsmanlike and hence pathetic. It is perhaps Falstaff's greatest line, the first stroke that makes us sympathize with him completely. It prepares the way in turn for the report of Falstaff's death in *Henry V*. And I think that Mr. Wilson goes entirely off the track—since he has already shown the close continuity between the two parts of *Henry IV*—in trying to rule out this deathbed as irrelevant. It is true that in the epilogue to *Henry IV* Shakespeare had announced to his audience an intention of making Falstaff play in *Henry V* a more considerable and more comic role than he does in the play which he actually wrote. But we do not know what Shakespeare may have then thought of writing; we only know what he did write; and he certainly shows Falstaff crushed. This is not a made-to-order sequel like *The Merry Wives of Windsor*: it is the true end of Falstaff's story.

I want to suggest another kind of view of the relation between Falstaff and Hal which has not occurred to Mr. Wilson and which—though my reading in this field is not great—I have never seen expressed. Certainly it is true, as Mr. Wilson insists, that *Henry IV* is not open to criticism on the ground that Prince Hal is the hero and that he is made to behave like a prig. As is usual with Shakespeare, the two main personalities are played off against one another with the full dramatic effectiveness that results from his making us feel that each is fulfilling the laws of his nature and that there is no easy escape from a conflict in which one of them has to break. Mr. Wilson has shown us, furthermore, that the adventures of Prince Hal with Falstaff run true to a traditional formula derived from the "morality" of Everyman or Youth and his temptation by Vanity and Riot, at the end of which the Elizabethan audience would expect to see virtue triumphant. But there is surely something more to this problem. Mr. Wilson, who much invokes Dr. Johnson as a witness to the worthiness of Henry, fails to take account of his remark to the effect that the reader's interest suffers a fatal slump from the moment when Falstaff and his friends fall victims to the new Henry's reforms. Most people probably do feel this. Most people probably feel that *Henry V* is, for

Shakespeare, relatively thin and relatively journalistic. But if the dramatist really meant Henry V to be taken as a model of a prince, why should this be the case?

I believe that in Shakespeare's more conventional plays, we must always, in order to understand them, look for a personal pattern behind the ostensible plot. In saying, as I did above, that Shakespeare was a fabricator of potboilers both at the beginning and at the end of his life, I did not of course mean to imply that these pieces, even aside from their magnificent poetry, had nothing in them of serious interest. On the contrary, he could hardly write anything without projecting real emotional conflicts in the form of imagined personalities. Now, these Henry plays just precede *Julius Caesar*, and *Julius Caesar* just precedes *Hamlet*. The great salient patterns of Shakespeare that give us symbols for what is most personal and most profound are beginning to take shape in these chronicles. The reader finds his sympathy weighted (as no doubt the Elizabethans did, since Falstaff became so tremendously popular) for Falstaff as against Hal, because Shakespeare, though he can give us both sides and holds the dramatic balance, is identifying himself with Falstaff in a way he cannot do with the Prince. He has already made us sympathize queerly with those of his characters who have been bent out of line by deformities or social pressures, whose morality is twisted, whose motives are mixed. Faulconbridge runs away with *King John*, and Shylock, the villain of *The Merchant of Venice*, becomes by a single speech a great deal more interesting than Antonio. Has not even Richard III in his horrid way a fascination—as of a Quilp or a Punch whose motives we have been made to understand—which the author could not possibly give Richmond? Falstaff is not deformed in quite the same obvious way as these others, but he is both physically and morally monstrous.

and his nature is also mixed. And from Falstaff through Brutus to Hamlet is not such a great step. Hamlet is also complex and also out of tune, though what is wrong with him is less obvious still; like Falstaff, he is at once quick-witted and extremely inept at action, a brilliant and constant talker and a man always at odds with his social group. The opposition between Falstaff and Henry unmistakably reappears in the contrast between Hamlet and Fortinbras; and "Master Shallow, I owe you a thousand pound," with the deathbed scene that follows, is to flower into the tragic eloquence of that series of final scenes in which Shakespeare is to make us feel that Hamlet and Othello and Lear and Antony and Coriolanus, for all their confusion and failure, have been rarer and nobler souls than the opponents, unworthy or worthy, who have brought their destruction about. In *Hamlet,* the Falstaff figure, with changed mask but a similar voice, holds the undisputed center of the stage; Prince Henry has dwindled to Fortinbras, who is felt mainly as an offstage force, but still represents the straight man of action who is destined to take over in the end. But later we shall have Antony and Octavius, Coriolanus and Aufidius. Here, too, the balance will be evenly held, and we shall never get melodrama. We are not allowed to sentimentalize over Antony any more than we are over Falstaff. Octavius is perfectly right: he does his duty as Henry does; but we shall always like Antony better, just as we did poor old Falstaff. Falstaff and Richard II are the two most conspicuous prototypes of Shakespeare's tragic heroes.

April 29, 1944

A TOAST AND A TEAR FOR
DOROTHY PARKER

REREADING DOROTHY PARKER—in the Viking Portable Library—has affected me, rather unexpectedly, with a distinct attack of nostalgia. Her poems do seem a little dated. At their best, they are witty light verse, but when they try to be something more serious, they tend to become a kind of dilution of A. E. Housman and Edna Millay. Her prose, however, is still alive. It seems to me as sharp and as funny as in the years when it was first coming out. If Ring Lardner outlasts our day, as I do not doubt that he will, it is possible that Dorothy Parker will, too.

But the thing that I have particularly felt is the difference between the general tone, the psychological and literary atmosphere, of the period—the twenties and the earlier thirties—when most of these pieces of Mrs. Parker's were written, and the atmosphere of the present time. It was suddenly brought home to me how much freer people were—in their emotions, in their ideas and in expressing themselves. In the twenties they could love, they could travel, they could stay up late at night as extravagantly as they pleased; they could think or say or write whatever seemed to them amusing or interesting. There was a good deal of irresponsibility, and a lot of money and energy wasted, and the artistic activities of the time suffered somewhat from its general vices, but it was a much more favorable climate for writing than the period we are in now.

The depression put a crimp in incomes, and people began to have to watch their pockets. Then they began to watch their politics. The whole artistic and intellectual world became anxiously preoccupied with making sure that their positions were correct in relation to the capitalist system and the imminence or the non-imminence of a social revolution; they spent a good deal of time and print arguing with one another about it. Some writers who had been basing their work on the uproar and glamor of the boom grew discouraged and more or less stopped. The young writers who came out of college were likely to be short of cash and have no prospect of easy jobs; they were obliged to be circumspect. The tougher ones tried to work with the Communists or other radical groups; the more conventional became professors. Some tried to do both at the same time, with uncomfortable and unsatisfactory results, for they found themselves in the situation of being obliged to worry about both their standing with the academic authorities and the purity of their political line.

With the writings of Dorothy Parker you are still as far away from all this as you are with those of Scott Fitzgerald. It is a relief and a reassurance, in reading her soliloquies and dialogues—her straight short stories, which are sometimes sentimental, do not always wear quite so well—to realize how recklessly clever it used to be possible for people to be, and how personal and how direct. All her books had funereal titles, but the eye was always wide open and the tongue always quick to retort. Even those titles were sardonic exclamations on the part of an individual at the idea of her own demise. The idea of the death of a society had not yet begun working on people to paralyze their response to experience.

But the literary movement of the twenties showed a tendency to break down and peter out which we never should have expected at that time, when it seemed to us that American writing had just had a brilliant rebirth. It was a shock to know that Scott Fitzgerald, who had seemed to be still on his way to fulfilling the promise of imperfect books, was suddenly and prematurely dead; and we soon found that this imperfect work had almost the look of a classic: its value had been heightened by its rarity, since there was not going to be any more of it either by him or by anyone else. And we find when we take up this new volume, which contains Dorothy Parker's complete published works, that a similar shift of feeling occurs. Mrs. Parker is not yet dead nor has she altogether ceased writing: there are several new stories in this volume, and they hold up with the earlier ones. But she nowadays produces little, and she has suffered, to our disappointment, one of the dooms of her generation. A decade or more ago she went out to Hollywood and more or less steadily stayed there, and, once away from her natural habitat, New York, she succumbed to the expiatory mania that has become epidemic with film-writers and was presently making earnest appeals on behalf of those organizations which talked about being "progressive" and succeeded in convincing their followers that they were working for the social revolution, though they had really no other purpose than to promote the foreign policy of the Soviet Union. She ought, of course, to have been satirizing Hollywood and sticking pins into fellow-travellers; but she has not, so far as I know, ever written a word about either. There are among the new pieces here a couple that deal with the war—*The Lovely Leave* and

Song of the Shirt, 1941—but this collection mostly makes you feel that you are reliving a vanished era. Except for one sketch of the Spanish War, the record seems to break off abruptly sometime in the early thirties.

Yet it, too, this collected volume, has a value derived from rarity—a rarity like that of steel penknives, good erasers and real canned sardines, articles of which the supply has almost given out and of which one is only now beginning to be aware of how excellent the quality was. It seems to me, though I shall name no names, that it has been one of the features of this later time that it produces imitation books. There are things of which one cannot really say that they are either good books or bad books; they are really not books at all. When one has bought them, one has only got paper and print. When one has bought Dorothy Parker, however, one has really got a book. She is not Emily Brontë or Jane Austen, but she has been at some pains to write well, and she has put into what she has written a voice, a state of mind, an era, a few moments of human experience that nobody else has conveyed. And the format of this volume, as is not always the case, is appropriate to and worthy of the contents. It is compact, well printed, and small, easy to carry and handle: the kind of thing that ought to be encouraged, as distinguished from the more ponderous type of omnibus. The title is simply *Dorothy Parker*.

May 20, 1944

A TREATISE ON TALES OF HORROR

THERE HAS lately been a sudden revival of the appetite for tales of horror. First, Pocket Books published *The Pocket Mystery Reader* and *The Pocket Book of Mystery Stories*. Then came *Tales of Terror*, with an introduction by Boris Karloff; *Creeps by Night*, with an introduction by Dashiell Hammett; and *Best Ghost Stories of M. R. James* (all three brought out by World). Finally, Random House has produced a prodigious anthology called *Great Tales of Terror and the Supernatural*, edited by Herbert A. Wise and Phyllis Fraser.

One had supposed that the ghost story itself was already an obsolete form; that it had been killed by the electric light. It was only during the ages of candlelight that the race of ghosts really flourished, though they survived through the era of gas. A candle can always burn low and be blown out by a gust of air, and it is a certain amount of trouble to relight it, as is also the case with a gas-jet. But if you can reach out and press a button and flood every corner of the room, leaving the specter quite naked in his vapor, or if you can transfix him out of doors with a flashlight, his opportunities for haunting are limited. It is true that one of the most famous of ghost stories, Defoe's *Apparition of Mrs. Veal*, takes place in the afternoon; that it is a part of the effectiveness of *The Turn of the Screw* that its phantoms appear out-

doors in broad daylight as well as indoors at night; and
that that eeriest of all ghost stories supposed to be true,
the anonymous book called *An Adventure*, purports to
give the experiences of two English ladies visiting Versailles in the afternoon; but these are all in the nature of
tours de force on the part of the apparitions or the authors. The common run of ghost needed darkness. It
will be noticed in all these anthologies that most of the
writers belong by training to the last decades of the nineteenth century, even though a few of their stories have
been written in the first years of this.

What is the reason, then—in these days when a lonely
country house is likely to be equipped with electric light,
radio and telephone—for our returning to these antiquated tales? There are, I believe, two reasons: first, the
longing for mystic experience which seems always to
manifest itself in periods of social confusion, when political progress is blocked: as soon as we feel that our own
world has failed us, we try to find evidence for another
world; second, the instinct to inoculate ourselves against
panic at the real horrors loose on the earth—Gestapo and
G.P.U., tank attacks and airplane bombings, houses rigged
with booby-traps—by injections of imaginary horror,
which soothe us with the momentary illusion that the
forces of madness and murder may be tamed and compelled to provide us with a mere dramatic entertainment.
We even try to make them cozy and droll, as in *Arsenic
and Old Lace*, which could hardly have become popular
or even been produced on the stage at any other period
of our history. This craving for homeopathic horror first
began to appear some years ago in the movies—with the
Frankenstein monsters, the werewolves, the vampires and
the insane sadistic scientists, of whom such a varied assort-
ment are now to be seen along West Forty-second Street;
and recently, in such films as *The Uninvited*, the pictures,

too, have been reaching back to pull toward us the phantom fringe which has been exploited by these anthologies.

The best of these volumes is the new Random House one, because it is the most comprehensive (though the book itself has the fault of so many American omnibuses and anthologies of being too cumbersome to handle comfortably in bed, the only place where one is likely to read ghost stories), and not unintelligently edited. The two collections in the Pocket Book series, both edited by Miss Lee Wright, are, however, quite well selected, and have the merit of costing only a quarter each. And yet one cannot read a large number of pieces in any of these compilations without feeling rather let down. The editors are always building up their authors: "Certain of these stories, like *Lost Hearts* and *The Ash-Tree*," says the foreword to the *Best Ghost Stories of M. R. James*, ". . . should, we think, be skipped altogether by the squeamish and faint of heart"; a story by Robert Hichens is "unsurpassed for its subtle unfolding of a particularly loathsome horror"; and *Caterpillars*, by E. F. Benson, is "brilliantly told, and without doubt . . . one of the most horrifying stories in this collection." Now, I find it very hard to imagine that any of these particular tales could scare anybody over ten. Two of them simply play on the gooseflesh that is stimulated in certain people by the idea of caterpillars or spiders, and demon caterpillars and demon spiders very easily seem absurd. Other stories much esteemed by these anthologists, such as the one mentioned above, by Robert Hichens—*How Love Came to Professor Guildea*—or Helen R. Hull's *Clay-Shuttered Doors*, have promising macabre ideas—a great scientist who has cut himself off from all human relationships but is driven to desperation by an invisible imbecile who loves him; the wife of an ambitious New

Yorker, who regalvanizes her decaying body and goes on playing her social role several months after she has been killed in a motor accident—but they are trashily or weakly done and do not realize their full possibilities. In either case, the authors content themselves with suggesting unpleasant sensations. They fail to lay hold on the terrors that lie deep in the human psyche and that cause man to fear himself.

These collections, of course, aim primarily at popular entertainment; they do not pretend to a literary standard. But I should like to suggest that an anthology of considerable interest and power could be compiled by assembling horror stories by really first-rate modern writers, in which they have achieved their effects not merely by attempting to transpose into terms of contemporary life the old fairy-tales of goblins and phantoms but by probing psychological caverns where the constraints of that life itself have engendered disquieting obsessions.

I should start off with Hawthorne and Poe, who are represented in these collections, but I should include, also, Melville and Gogol, who are not. The first really great short stories of horror came in the early or middle nineteenth century, when the school of Gothic romance had achieved some sophistication and was adopting the methods of realism. All four of these authors wrote stories that were at the same time tales of horror and psychological or moral fables. They were not interested in spooks for their own sake; they knew that their demons were symbols, and they knew what they were doing with these symbols. We read the tales of Poe in our childhood, when all that we are likely to get out of them is shudders, yet these stories are also poems that express the most intense emotions. *The Fall of the House of Usher* is not merely an ordinary ghost story: the house—see the opening paragraph—is an image for a human personality, and its fate—see the fissure that runs through the wall—is the fate of a disrupted mind. And as for Gogol, he probably remains the very greatest master in this genre. I should put in at least *Viy* and *The Nose*—the former, a vampire story, one of the most terrific things of its kind ever written, and the latter, though it purports to be comic, almost equally a tale of horror, for it is charged with the disguised lurking meaning of a fear that has taken shape as a nightmare. I should include, also, *Bartleby the Scrivener* of Melville, which oddly resembles Gogol in this vein of the somber-grotesque, as well as *Benito Cereno*, a more plausible yet still nightmarish affair, which ought to be matched farther on by Conrad's *Heart of Darkness*.

In the latter part of the century, however, the period to which Conrad belongs, these fables tend to become impure. There was by that time much more pressure on the artist to report the material and social facts of the nineteenth-century world, and it seems difficult to combine symbolism with the inventories of naturalistic fiction or the discussion of public affairs. You have Stevenson, Kipling, Henry James. In Stevenson's case alone, this pressure did not inhibit his fancy, for he rarely wrote anything but fairy-tales, but he has much less intensity and substance than Conrad or Kipling or James. Nevertheless, though I might do without Jekyll and Hyde, I think I should have to have *Olalla* and *Thrawn Janet* (it is queer that a writer so popular in his time should be represented in none of these collections). But with Kipling you run into the cramping effects of a technical and practical period. I should include a couple of stories of Kipling's—say, *At the End of the Passage* and *Mrs. Bathurst*—as examples of borderline cases of the genuinely imaginative story which is nevertheless not first-rate. In such an early tale of Kipling's as *At the End of the Passage* or *The Phantom Rickshaw,* he is trying to write a mere vulgar ghost story, but something else that is authentic gets in. If we have carefully studied Kipling, we can recognize in the horrors of these tales—the blinded phantom, the wronged woman—obsessions that recur in his work and to which we can find the key in his life. But a story of this kind should convey its effect without our having to track down its symbols. We need nothing but the story itself to tell us that the author of *Viy* has put all the combined fascination and fear with which he was inspired by women into the vigil of the young student in the little wooden church beside the coffin of the farmer's daughter. When Kipling sets out later on to work up a more complex technique and attempts several layers of meaning, he gives us a piece like *Mrs. Bathurst*—the pursuit by a wronged woman, again —in which, however, the main character's sense of guilt is tied up through the symbol of the woman with his duty to the British Empire in connection with the Boer War, and he introduces a political element which seems clumsy and out of place in a ghost story and somehow gives Mrs. Bathurst a slight tinge of the newspaper cartoon. Henry James, a more serious writer, produced a strange special case in *The Turn of the Screw.* He asserted that he, too, had aimed merely at a conventional ghost story intended for a more knowing audience than that susceptible to the ordinary kind; but readers familiar with his work and conscious of his preoccupations have tended to see in the tale something more: the governess is not really, as she tells us, defending the children in her charge against the influence of malevolent spirits, she is frightening them herself with the projections of her own repressed emotions. There are, however, points in the story which are difficult to explain on this theory, and it is probable that James, like Kipling, was unconscious of having raised something more frightening than the ghosts he had contemplated. At any rate, I should put in *The Turn of the Screw,* and also *The Jolly Corner,* which seems to me James's other best ghost story. In this latter case, the author is of course quite conscious of what he is doing, but there is here, as in *Mrs. Bathurst,* an element rather difficult to assimilate (though Henry James does make us accept it) in the issue between England and the United States, a social and historical problem, which provides the moral of the fable.

During this period there were some very good ghost stories done by popular writers of distinction like Conan Doyle and W. W. Jacobs, but, capital fairy-tales though *The Monkey's Paw* and *Playing With Fire* are, I should not admit them to my ideal collection. Nor should I—on the basis of the specimens I have read—include anything from a different school, which grew up in the late years of the century and which was stimulated perhaps by the encroachments of the spread of the new methods of lighting on the old-fashioned kind of ghost. This school, which is represented abundantly in the Random House collection, derives, I take it, from Arthur Machen, and features, instead of resurrected bodies and insubstantial phantoms, a demonology of ancient cults driven underground by Christianity but persisting into our own day, and exploits the identification of the Devil with the pagan god Pan. Machen's story on this theme called *The Great God Pan* (in the Random House collection) seems to me to sum up in a fatal way everything that was most "ham" in the aesthetic satanism of the *fin de siècle.* M. R. James, a great favorite of these anthologists, played countless variations on this theme and had some really fiendish flashes of fancy, but he never took any trouble to make his stories seem even halfway plausible, so his hobgoblins are always verging on parody.

A better writer is Algernon Blackwood, who belongs to this same general group and has an even greater reputation than M. R. James. He, too, tends to lean on anti-human creatures that embody the forces of nature, but he is interesting for another reason: you can see in him very clearly the shift from a belief in evil spirits as things that come to plague us from outside to a consciousness of terrors inside us that merely take possession of our minds. But where Kipling or Henry James knew how to dramatize these terrors in solid images that command our credence, Blackwood, beginning as a rule with a locale which he has actually observed and which he more or less convincingly describes, invariably transposes the story, from the moment when the supernatural element appears, onto a plane of melting, gliding nightmare where nothing seems really to be taking place. Now, a story of this kind, to impress us, must *never* seem to be a dream. The tales of Poe, for all the wildness of their fantasy, are as circumstantial as Swift or Defoe; when Gogol retells a Ukrainian legend, he so stiffens its texture with authentic detail that we seem to hear the voices of the peasants and smell the countryside.

I should, therefore, decline to pass Algernon Blackwood, but I should certainly admit Walter de la Mare, who sometimes errs in the direction of the too dreamlike but makes up for it through poetic imagination. His story called *Seaton's Aunt* comes close to being a masterpiece in this genre, and I should include also *Out of the Deep*, which is equally good in conception though not quite so good in execution. (The first of these has been included in *The Pocket Book of Mystery Stories* and the second in the Random House anthology.) De la Mare, a great admirer of Poe, has done work that is quite his own in this field of supernatural fiction; it is in my opinion superior to his verse. His stories at their best are poetic, psychologically subtle and creepy to a high degree.

And, finally, I should include Franz Kafka, also absent from any of these collections. Stories like *The Metamorphosis* and *Blumfeld, an Elderly Bachelor* are among the best things of their kind. The first of these unpleasant pieces deals with a young travelling salesman who suddenly wakes up one morning to find that he has turned into an enormous roach, to the horror of his parents, with whom he lives and who have been counting on him to pay off their debts; the second tells of an office worker, a selfish and bureaucratic upper clerk, who is haunted by two little bouncing balls that represent his niggardly consciousness of two children that help him in his office. The stories that Kafka has written on these two unconventional subjects are at the same time satires on the bourgeoisie and visions of moral horror; narratives that are logical and compel our attention, and fantasies that generate more shudders than the whole of Algernon Blackwood and M. R. James combined. A master can make it seem more horrible to be pursued by two little balls than by the spirit of a malignant Knight Templar, and more natural to turn into a cockroach than to be bitten by a diabolic spider. Kafka, who was writing these stories at the time of the last World War, had brought back the tale of terror to the true vein of Gogol and Poe. In his realm of imagination no social or political problems intrude in such a way as to spoil the show. The modern bourgeoisie and the Central European bureaucracy have turned into the enchanted denizens of a world in which, prosaic though it is, we can find no firm foothold in reality and in which we can never even be certain whether souls are being saved or damned. As an artist in this field of horror, Kafka is among the greatest. Living in the era of Freud, he went straight for the morbidities of the psyche with none of the puppetry of specters and devils that earlier writers still carried with them. Whether his making out of these subjects at that time of day the Hoffmannesque fantasies that he did make, and whether the rapt admiration for them in *our* time represents a retrogression or a progress in the development of modern literature in general, I shall not attempt to decide.

May 27, 1944

A GUIDE TO *FINNEGANS WAKE*

A Skeleton Key to Finnegans Wake, by Joseph Campbell and Henry Morton Robinson, is an indispensable book for anyone interested in Joyce and should make many new readers for *Finnegans Wake.*

This last book of James Joyce is a very great poem, one of the top works of literature of our time. It is in some ways, in fact, a more extraordinary production than *Ulysses*—digging deeper into human psychology, breaking new intellectual ground and exhibiting Joyce's musical genius as perhaps none of his other books does. Yet *Finnegans Wake* has acquired the reputation of being inordinately difficult to read, and Joyce has even been accused in some quarters of having perpetrated an insolent hoax or excreted an insane mess of gibberish. Even readers who have admired *Ulysses* have been reluctant to tackle its successor. But the book has now been out five years, and it is time that these doubts and inhibitions were dispelled. The appearance of the Campbell-Robinson key should open a new era in the acceptance and currency of *Finnegans Wake.* In recommending this guide, however, I want to make a few suggestions of my own which are, it seems to me, needed to supplement this introduction.

In the first place, it is an excellent thing, though perhaps not absolutely required, for the reader to be fairly familiar with the other writings of Joyce. Then, it will help this reader immensely if he comes to *Finnegans Wake* with some acquaintance with Virgil, Dante and Milton. It is a better equipment for Joyce to know something of the most accomplished masters of the writing of fiction in verse than to have formed one's ideas of literary art from the reading of modern novels. The art of narrative literature was brought by the great epic poets of the past to a point from which it later declined with the rise of the prose novel. A man like Dante has a command of language, a power to make it render the nuances of atmosphere, color, sound, phases of feeling and traits of personality, in comparison with which the writing of even a respectable novelist of the infancy of the novel, like Fielding, seems quite wooden, hardly writing at all. It was only with the Romantics that the language of prose fiction began to be flexible and sensitive enough to represent directly—by the sound and the look and the connotations of words—the things that it was describing. Flaubert was the first writer of prose fiction to challenge the ancients on this ground, and Flaubert had his limitations: his effects, like his mood, are monotonous. But he was studied and emulated by Joyce, whose range was enormously wider and who turned out to be, in fact, as T. S. Eliot said, the greatest master of language in English since Milton. *Ulysses* and *Finnegans Wake* are epics which not only perform feats of style hitherto unknown in the novel but also, like the *Æneid* and *The Divine Comedy*, deal with national myths and the destiny of man in a way that is unexpected for the ordinary novel reader. *Ulysses* had still enough of the framework of conventional fiction so that this ordinary reader could navigate it at the cost of a little effort. *Finnegans Wake*, however, though it was more "realistic" than it looked at first sight, seemed completely to have cast off the conventions.

The epic of *Ulysses* consisted of a day in the lives of certain characters; that of *Finnegans Wake* covers the sleeping life of a man during a single night. The next difficulty is to grasp this design. We may understand the purpose of Dante to construct an all-comprehensive poem out of a vision of Hell, Purgatory and Heaven; and we may not be baffled in the least by such literary renderings of dream or trance as De Quincey's opium rhapsodies, Flaubert's *Tentation de Saint Antoine,* Lewis Carroll's Alice books or the dreams in Dostoevsky's novels. Yet we may not be prepared for a book of more than six hundred pages which plunges us into a man's sleeping mind and keeps us there till he is about to wake up. Nor is it easy at first to realize that Joyce is using the resources of a poet not only to present the billowing emotions and the kaleidoscopic imagery of a dream but also to render with accuracy all the physical states of sleep. I may give a simple example, since the authors of the *Skeleton Key* have not emphasized this aspect of *Finnegans Wake.* The heavy breathing and the snoring of the hero run all through the book and are exploited for poetic effects which it might well be thought that no great poet would be so bold or so absurd as to attempt and which yet are made to contribute triumphantly to some of Joyce's most lyrical writing. The heaving of the four deep breaths which always marks the hero's subsidence into a deeper stratum of sleep provides much grotesque humor, such as the "What a hauhauhauhaudibble thing, to be cause! How, Mutt?" of the inarticulate conversation between the loutish prehistoric men; but it also gives the fall of darkness and the widening of the river at the close of the "Anna Livia Plurabelle" chapter, one of the incomparably beautiful things in the book: "Dark hawks hear us. Night! Night! My ho head halls. I feel as heavy as yonder stone," etc.

The sleeper in *Finnegans Wake* is a man named H. C. Earwicker, who keeps a pub on the Liffey and has a family consisting of a wife, one daughter and twin sons. The nexus of his family relations and Earwicker's career in Dublin are the immediate materials of his dream, but Joyce, with his epic intentions and a kind of modern Jungian conception of a myth-creating mind of the race, has contrived to make his dream universal. How he has done this I need not explain in detail because Campbell and Robinson have explained it better than anybody else has yet done. The dream itself is a myth, with characters and a plot of its own, and though its main elements multiply their aspects with all the shifting metamorphosis of a dream, they are constant and perfectly plain. Do not be put off by the opening pages, which have mysteries for even the adept at Joyce. Earwicker has fallen asleep: he has lost consciousness, but he is not yet dreaming. The moment seems dark and blank, but it is a blur of all his being holds. Joyce has resorted to the device, in *Finnegans Wake,* of conveying the ambiguities and vagueness of the visions and sensations of sleep by the invention of punning portmanteau words like the language of *Jabberwocky,* and these words have here been crammed with meanings to a point where all the many symbols appear hopelessly jumbled and mashed. Messrs. Campbell and Robinson, however, have unpacked a good many of these meanings, so that we can see what was in the portmanteaux of the first paragraphs of *Finnegans Wake,* and thus have eliminated one of the obstacles which have been baffling the willing reader. When you get through this choked defile and the action of the dream begins, you will find yourself among recognizable presences that flicker but speak and move, and the powerful current of language will continue to carry you along even through queer interruptions and eclipses. If you will read the Campbell-Robinson synopsis at the beginning of their *Skeleton Key*, you will see that the large architecture of *Finnegans Wake*, in spite of the complication of detail, is solid, precise and simple, as the principal themes of the book are matters of obvious universal experience, so utterly commonplace that the difficulty in grasping them comes sometimes from the sophisticated reader's unreadiness to accept anything so little esoteric as the basic facts of family life, the mixed moral nature of man and the phenomena of birth, growth and death rather than from the dense psychological web which Joyce has spun among them or the variegated legendry and language with which they have been embroidered.

The great thing is to get the hang and to follow the line of the myth, and this Campbell and Robinson will help you to do. They have provided a paraphrase of Joyce which disentangles and tightens this line. One may not approve every step of their trail, every abridgment, selection or reading, and they have sometimes made actual errors, but they have opened up the book to the public at the cost of much patience and care, and they deserve a citation from the Republic of Letters for having succeeded in bringing it out at this time. Mr. Campbell is a folklore scholar, with considerable knowledge of Ireland, who is particularly qualified to interpret Joyce on his mythological and historical sides; Mr. Robinson, who is an editor of *Reader's Digest*, here applies a special skill acquired in whittling down magazine articles to condensing a masterpiece.

This condensation, of course, is compelled to leave a great deal out. The authors' paraphrase of Joyce necessarily strips away most of the master's magnificent poetry, and thus transmits no idea at all of the *emotional* power of the original, since, where everything is not merely described but represented directly, the style is involved with the content to a degree which is not common with contemporary writers. In the Campbell-Robinson key, you will find almost no indication of the infinite variation in the texture and tone of the writing which reflects the various phases of the night.

Another matter which the authors neglect, in holding on to the sequence of the myth, is the family situation, which has its grip on the whole fantasia. The real story behind the dream story is something that we have to guess at and which it becomes one of the fascinations of reading *Finnegans Wake* to work out. There are moments when it breaks through the myth with its insistent and naked facts, and it is at all times the hidden director which determines the shape of the dream by its alternate impulsions and checks, its quick blendings and its sudden reversals. The sleeper, who passes from fatigue to refreshment, from death to resurrection, is enacting a universal drama which is enacted every night by every man in the world; but every man is a particular man, and this man is a particular Dubliner, asleep on a certain night in a room above a certain pub in the bosom of a certain family. The authors of the *Skeleton Key* have pretty nearly combed the real family away in presenting their simplification of the myth; they tend to disregard the indications which Joyce is very careful to plant about Earwicker's real situation; and they do not always seem quite clear about the author's technique in dealing with the connection between the dream and these realities. They, for example, simply follow the language of the dream in the question-and-answer chapter, which is intended, though the real questions and answers are always just around the corner from the dreamed ones, to give the reader a very definite statement of the location and personnel of the household; and they seem to think that Earwicker, through part of the book, has been lying drunk on the floor of the pub and that he goes upstairs to bed at some point, and, later, in the scene before dawn, when one of the twins wakes the mother and she goes into his room to calm him, that the husband gets up and goes in with her and afterwards has intercourse with her; whereas it is plain that, in the first case, the falling on the floor and the going upstairs themselves take place in the dream, and that, in the second, he has hardly awakened but, half aware of what his wife is doing, has sunk back into fitful slumber. It is an essential feature of the plan of the book, it makes its artistic unity, that Earwicker shall be always in bed and that he shall never wake up till morning—just the moment after the book ends. The later chapters of the *Skeleton Key* are thus definitely unsatisfactory. The authors prove themselves heroically strong in the cracking of such formidable nuts as the colloquy between St. Patrick and the Archdruid, but they are weak and even misleading on the more obvious human elements which make the end of *Finnegans Wake* one of the greatest things Joyce ever wrote.

In any case, if you have not tried *Finnegans Wake*, you cannot do better than get it and get the Campbell-Robinson key and prepare to have them around for years. A few more last words of guidance. The conditions for reading this book are different, so far as I know, from those for reading any other ever written. You have to take it rather slowly, a section at a time, and you have to keep on rereading it. Joyce worked on it through seventeen years, and it is equivalent to about seventeen books by the ordinary gifted writer. You may think it too much that Joyce should ask you to strain your wits over solving his elaborate puzzles, but the fact is that a good deal of the book, once you see the general pattern, is readable and comprehensible even when the language is queer. Joyce counts on a certain dimness to give the effect of a dream; and for people who do like to solve puzzles, the puzzles are fun to solve. Today, when we are getting so many books in which the style is perfectly clear but the meaning nonexistent or equivocal, it affords a certain satisfaction to read something that looks like nonsense on the surface but underneath makes perfect sense. Admirers of Balzac and Trollope think nothing of devoting years to reading their favorites through, and why should we grudge time to Joyce? The demands that he makes are considerable, but the rewards he provides are astounding. I do not deny that he is tedious at times: I am bored by the relentless *longueurs* of some of the middle chapters of *Finnegans Wake* just as I am bored by those of the latter part of *Ulysses,* and I have found it puts me straight to sleep to try to follow the charting of these wastes which has intrepidly been carried out by the authors of the *Skeleton Key,* just as it did to read Joyce's original. But it is an exciting, a unique experience to find pages that have seemed to us meaningless start into vivid life, full of energy, brilliance, passion. The chance to be among the first to explore the wonders of *Finnegans Wake* is one of the few great intellectual and aesthetic treats that these last bad years have yielded.

August 5, 1944

A NOVEL BY SALVADOR DALI

SALVADOR DALI has published a novel, and it is startling, but not at all in the same way as his famous deliquescent pianos and ladies full of bureau drawers. It is one of the most old-fashioned novels that anybody has written in years, for it consists almost exclusively of a potpourri of the properties, the figures and the attitudes of the later and gamier phases of French romantic writing. The preposterous Lesbian boudoir of Balzac's *Fille aux Yeux d'Or;* the proud and perverse aristocrats of Barbey d'Aurevilly's *Diaboliques,* with their grandiose duels of sex; the exalted erotic mysticism of Villiers de l'Isle-Adam's *Axel;* the cultivation of artificial sensations of Huysmans' Des Esseintes and the demonological researches of his Durtal—all these have been disinterred by Mr. Dali in *Hidden Faces* and put through their old routines to the tune of an improvised style which makes the whole thing seem to verge on parody. The only relatively up-to-date elements are a superficial injection of Freudianism and an overlay of surrealist rhetoric—when, if you follow me, Mr. Dali allows the milliped and Boschesque crustaceans of his hermetic imagination to caress the tentacular algae of his subaqueous and electrified impudicity or the nacreous and colubrine doves of a psychosomatic idealism to circle in shimmering syndromes the façades of a palladian narcissism. But this modernism is more than offset by the uncontrollable tendency of his characters to write one another long letters that sound like a burlesque of *Werther* or *La Nouvelle Héloïse:* "Dear Hervé—my beloved—is it a dream to be able to call you thus? Know, my beloved, that of your letter I have retained only your first words of love, which will remain engraved in my heart till after I am dead. Even when the worms shall have gnawed this heart away they will have to perish and be consumed in turn at the bottom of my coffin, curled up in the form of the letters of the inscription they have devoured, so true it is that this inscription must be and shall be the last reality that can be effaced from my existence!"

In an atmosphere of ringing aristocratic names, men and women of resplendent beauty, and balls and banquets of incredible luxury, which will take the English-speaking reader back to Disraeli, Bulwer-Lytton and Ouida, it is a surprise to hear suddenly about Hitler, the Communists or the Maginot Line. But the war does descend on Mr. Dali's world (though the truth is that, for all the grasp that Mr. Dali displays of his time, it might almost as well be the Crimean War or the fall of the Second Empire). And what do they all do then —these iridescent Comtes de Grandsailles and Vicomtes d'Angerville and Princes d'Orminy and Solanges de Cléda, with their Byzantine bouquets made of jewels, their elegant and daring toilettes, their opium-smoking and their cold, depraved passions? Why, their versatile creator drops at once the preciosity in which he has been clothing them and makes them behave almost exactly like so many characters by Louis Bromfield—with whom, I fear, Salvador Dali has something fundamentally in common. When they realize the plight of France, they gallantly pull themselves together and begin performing prodigies of heroism—proving, by their readiness to sacrifice themselves, the stuff of which the French nobility, even in its decadence, is made. The truth is, in fact, that the point of view of the Catalonian Dali is, to all intents and purposes, that of some trashy old French royalist snob such as Barbey d'Aurevilly, who, as I say, seems to haunt *Hidden Faces*. It is touching to find Mr. Haakon M. Chevalier, who has translated Dali's novel, attempting to reassure us in a foreword by implying that the author has been favorably impressed by the Russian Revolution and pointing out his sympathy with the peasant. Mr. Dali's attitude toward the peasant is that of a romantic *grand seigneur*, or, rather, of one who has read a good deal about the attitudes of *grand seigneurs*, and his attitude toward Communists and Anarchists and all that they try to do is one of perkily-mustachioed disdain.

One element appears in his novel which had not entered the cosmos of Barbey: the role of the United States as a power to be reckoned with by Europe. But this power is represented for Dali by a *richissime* American girl distinguished by the selfishness, arrogance, frigidity and long-limbed blond beauty which had already become the standard attributes for such characters in French fiction, and a dashing and indomitable young aviator bearing the fine Virginian name of John Randolph, who repudiates the "revolutionary illusions" that had led him to aid the Loyalists in the Spanish Civil War, and declares, "I, too, believe once more in the ineradicable forces of tradition and aristocracy." When he and the Comte de Grandsailles (great noble and upholder of the feudal ideal) come to confront one another through their oxygen masks, just before taking off on a perilous flight, "their eyes appeared alike, equally pure, and in neither case could one tell whether it was exaltation or coldness that gave them their greater luster. With a single impulse the two men removed their gloves, and their hands clasped for a moment, like those of wrestlers." Yet the moment will later arrive when they must come to blows in America over the *richissime* Veronica, and here there is something flattering for the land in which Mr. Dali is sojourning, if not something for its great moving-picture industry: "'A curious country, America, don't you think, Randolph?' said the Count of Grandsailles, making a face after biting into a piece of pear impaled on his fork, and putting down his implement on the edge of the plate. 'Its fruit has no flavor, its women have no shame, and its men are without honor!' . . . 'The fruit of our country,' said Randolph, measuring each syllable, 'have the flavor of liberty and hospitality, which you have basely taken advantage of to feed yourself and your secrets; our women are those whom you try unsuccessfully to corrupt, to pervert and make sterile, and our men are those who have the honor of sacrificing their lives in that Europe of yours to redeem the honor which you weren't men enough to defend and shamefully lost to the enemy.'"

Yet, in spite of this concession to current events, it is always the Comte de Grandsailles, with his eccentric and faultless taste and his satanic and devious temperament, who enchants his creator, Dali. The war, from the author's point of view, is being fought to save the honor of old France—betrayed by ignoble politicians—against the upstart and ill-bred Nazis.

All this is not, of course, to say that the painter of *Debris of an Automobile Giving Birth to a Blind Horse Biting a Telephone* is not a very clever fellow, or that his novel may not afford entertainment. I have been quoting from the later part, which is more or less unadorned balderdash; but the earlier chapters, which the author has been at more pains to embroider and dramatize, have passages, images, ideas that lend them at moments an illusion of brilliance. There is the theory, not entirely implausible, put forward by one of the characters about Hitler: that he is really an heroic masochist, whose true hope and goal is defeat, though he has pledged himself to play the game according to all the rules and make every effort to win, before he will be able to fulfill himself by provoking his own annihilation. There is the satire on pre-war French culture implicit in the relation between the Comte de Grandsailles and his factotum, the local notary. The notary is rude and provincial but has a gift of pungent wit; the Count, who lacks originality, is always stopping the conversation to write down the other's good things, and he then sorts them into various categories, reduces them to polished form, and passes in Paris for a witty talker. And there is also a long gruesome account of an opium and heroin jag which has something of the same kind of fascination as Charles Jackson's *The Lost Weekend* (it may be that the epic of drugging is a genre which has arrived in our era).

But, on the evidence of *Hidden Faces*, I should say that Mr. Dali was no writer. I cannot believe that the translator has betrayed him. Mr. Haakon M. Chevalier certainly knows French perfectly, and when he is doing his own work, he can command a very sound English prose. He complains in his foreword here of the redundancies and mixed metaphors of Dali, and explains that he has done what he could to trim his language and straighten out his style. I think he might still have spared the reader a certain amount of stumbling by the exercise of a little more care about not carrying over French tenses; and not inflicted on him such sentences as "His face . . . gave witness that the emotions of his heart with their weakness had no right to cloud the clean limpidness of his diction" (where the more correct word "limpidity" would have saved him at least from one of the endings in "ness"); or such English as "she saw a figure approaching her . . . without scarcely noticing it" and "Cécile and I will arrive only in the last moment." He might even, one might think, have told Dali that *"nemo"* does not mean "nothing," and that the man who made the clock with glass works was not "Oudin" but Robert-Houdin. Yet I definitely get the impression that Mr. Chevalier has been somewhat demoralized by his original's Hispanic French and orgies of loose-squandered verbiage, and that he has here not been quite himself.

On Dali's side, one finds in this novel none of the qualities that are good in his pictures, which are certainly not deficient in craftsmanship: there is no clarity, no sharp-focussed vividness, no delicacy or firmness of line. We are far from the beneficent influences that have presided over his development as a painter: Picasso and Chirico, Velásquez and Vermeer. Dali's literary models have been bad ones, and, from the moment that he abandoned his real métier, they have swept him into a retrogression that affords one of the most curious examples of the contemporary stoppage and lapse of the arts in collision with the political crisis.

July 1, 1944

A LONG TALK ABOUT JANE AUSTEN

THERE HAVE BEEN several revolutions of taste during the last century and a quarter of English literature, and through them all perhaps only two reputations have never been affected by the shifts of fashion: Shakespeare's and Jane Austen's. We still agree with Scott about Jane Austen, just as we agree with Ben Jonson about Shakespeare. From Scott, Southey, Coleridge and Macaulay (to say nothing of the Prince Regent, who kept a set of her works "in every one of his residences") to Kipling and George Moore, Virginia Woolf and E. M. Forster, she has compelled the amazed admiration of writers of the most diverse kinds, and I should say that Jane Austen and Dickens rather queerly present themselves today as the only two English novelists (though not quite the only novelists in English) who belong in the very top rank with the great fiction writers of Russia and France. Jane Austen, as Mr. Stark Young once said, is perhaps the only English example of that spirit of classical comedy that is more natural to the Latin people than to ours and that Molière represents for the French. That this spirit should have embodied itself in England in the mind of a well-bred spinster, the daughter of a country clergyman, who never saw any more of the world than was made possible by short visits to London and a residence of a few years in Bath and who found her subjects mainly in the problems of young provincial girls looking for husbands, seems one of the most freakish of the many anomalies of English literary history.

In *Speaking of Jane Austen*, by G. B. Stern and Sheila Kaye-Smith, two of Jane Austen's sister novelists have collaborated to pay her homage. Both Miss Stern and Miss Kaye-Smith have read the six novels again and again, and they have at their fingers' ends every trait, every speech, every gesture of every one of Jane Austen's people. Here they discuss, in alternate chapters, which give the effect of a conversation, a variety of aspects of their subject. Miss Kaye-Smith is especially concerned with the historical background of the novels: she turns up a good deal that is interesting about the costume and food of the period and the social position of clergymen, and she traces the reflection, so meager and dim, of the cataclysmic political events that took place during Miss Austen's lifetime. Miss Stern is more preoccupied with the characters, whom she sometimes treats as actual people, classifying them on principles of her own and speculating about their lives beyond the story; sometimes criticizes from the point of view of a novelist who would see the situation in some cases a little differently, modifying or filling out a character or assigning a heroine to a different mate. The two ladies debate together the relative merits of the novels, agreeing that *Pride and Prejudice* belongs not at the top but toward the bottom of the list, and partly agreeing and partly not as to which of the characters are least successful. They have notes on Miss Austen's language and they underline some of her fine inconspicuous strokes. They make an effort to evoke the personalities of characters who are mentioned but never appear, and they have concocted a terrific quiz, which few readers, I imagine, could pass.

The book thus contains a good deal that will be interesting to those interested in Jane Austen, though neither Miss Stern nor Miss Kaye-Smith, it seems to me, really goes into the subject so deeply as might be done. My impression is that the long study of Jane Austen which has lately been published by Queenie Leavis in the English magazine called *Scrutiny* gets to grips with her artistic development in a way that the present authors, who do not mention Mrs. Leavis' essay, have scarcely even attempted to do. Yet *Speaking of Jane Austen*, as an informal symposium, revives the enthusiasm of the reader and stimulates him to think about the questions suggested by Miss Kaye-Smith and Miss Stern. Let me contribute a few comments of my own which will bring certain of these matters to attention:

1. The half-dozen novels of Jane Austen were written in two sets of three each, with an interval of about ten years between the two: *Pride and Prejudice, Sense and Sensibility* and *Northanger Abbey; Mansfield Park, Emma* and *Persuasion.* The first of these lots, both in its satiric comedy and in the pathos of *Sense and Sensibility,* is quite close to the eighteenth century, whereas the second, with its psychological subtlety and such realism as the episode in *Mansfield Park* in which Fanny goes back to her vulgar home, is much closer to what we call "modern." In the second lot, the set comic character of the type of Lady Catherine de Bourgh, who at moments, as Miss Stern points out, falls into the tone of an old-fashioned play, tends to give way to another kind of portraiture—as in the small country community of *Emma*—which is farther from caricature and more recognizable as a picture of everyday life, and in *Persuasion,* a sensitivity to landscape and a tenderness of feeling appear that have definitely a tinge of the romantic. It is not

true, as has been sometimes complained, that Miss Austen took no interest in nature, though this last novel is the only one of her books of which one clearly remembers the setting. Miss Kaye-Smith does note of *Persuasion* that "the weather and scenery have taken on some of the emotional force that permeates the whole book." But both authors seem to treat the novels as if they have always coëxisted in time, instead of forming a sequence. What I miss in *Speaking of Jane Austen* is any account of the successive gradations, literary and psychological, which lead from *Pride and Prejudice* to *Persuasion*.

2. The authors of this book both believe that there is something wrong with *Mansfield Park*, and they have a great deal to say about it. They feel that the chief figure, Fanny Price, a poor relation who immolates herself to the family of a great country house, is too meaching—too "creep-mouse," Miss Kaye-Smith says— to be an altogether sympathetic heroine, and that in this case the author herself, in a way that is not characteristic, adopts a rather pharisaical attitude toward the more fun-loving and sophisticated characters. Miss Kaye-Smith tries to explain this attitude by suggesting that Jane Austen at this period may have come under the influence of the Evangelical Movement, to which two references are to be found in the book.

To the reviewer, this line of criticism in regard to *Mansfield Park* is already very familiar—it seems to represent a reaction which is invariable with feminine readers; yet I have never felt particularly the importance of the objections that are made on these grounds nor been shaken in my conviction that *Mansfield Park* is artistically the most nearly perfect of the novels. It is true that I have not read it for thirty years, so that I have had time to forget the moralizings that bother Miss Kaye-Smith and Miss Stern, but the sensations I remember to have had were purely aesthetic ones: a delight in the focussing of the complex group through the ingenuous eyes of Fanny, the balance and harmony of the handling of the contrasting timbres of the characters, which are now heard in combination, now set off against one another. I believe that, in respect to Jane Austen's heroines, the point of view of men readers is somewhat different from that of women ones. The woman reader wants to identify herself with the heroine, and she rebels at the idea of being Fanny. The male reader neither puts himself in Fanny's place nor imagines himself marrying Fanny any more than he does the nice little girl in Henry James's *What Maisie Knew*, a novel which *Mansfield Park* in some ways quite closely resembles. What interests him in Miss Austen's heroines is the marvellous portraiture of a gallery of different types of women, and Fanny, with her humility, her priggishness and her innocent and touching good faith, is a perfect picture of one kind of woman.

Whatever tone Jane Austen may sometimes take, what emerge and give the book its value are characters objectively seen, form and movement conceived aesthetically. It is this that sets Jane Austen apart from so many other women novelists—whether, like the author of *Wuthering Heights* or the author of *Gone With the Wind,* of the kind that make their power felt by a projection of their feminine day-dreams, or of the kind, from *Evelina* to *Gentlemen Prefer Blondes,* that amuse us by mimicking people. Miss Austen is almost unique among the novelists of her sex in being deeply and steadily concerned, not with the vicarious satisfaction of emotion (though the Cinderella theme, of course, does figure in several of her novels) nor with the skillful exploitation of gossip, but, as the great masculine novelists are, with the novel as a work of art.

3. *Emma,* which both these critics adore, is with Jane Austen what *Hamlet* is with Shakespeare. It is the book of hers about which her readers are likely to disagree most; they tend either to praise it extravagantly or to find it dull, formless and puzzling. The reason for this, I believe, is that, just as in the case of *Hamlet,* there is something outside the picture which is never made explicit in the story but which has to be recognized by the reader before it is possible for him to appreciate the book. Many women readers feel instinctively the psychological rightness of the behavior attributed to Emma, and they are the ones who admire the novel. Some male readers, like Justice Holmes, who was certainly a connoisseur of fiction yet who wrote to Sir Frederick Pollock that, "bar Miss Bates," he was "bored by *Emma,*" never succeed in getting into the story because they cannot see what it is all about. Why does Emma take up her two protégées? Why does she become so much obsessed by her plans for them? Why does she mistake the realities so and go so ludicrously wrong about them? Why does it take her so unconscionably long to reach the obvious rapprochement with Knightley?

The answer is that Emma is not interested in men except in the paternal relation. Her actual father is a silly old woman: in their household it is Emma herself who, motherless as she is, assumes the functions of head of the family; it is she who takes the place of the parent and Mr. Woodhouse who becomes the child. It is Knightley who has checked and rebuked her, who has presided over her social development, and she accepts him as a substitute father; she finally marries him and

brings him into her own household, where his role is
to reinforce Mr. Woodhouse. Miss Stern sees the difficulties of this odd situation. "Oh, Miss Austen," she
cries, "it was *not* a good solution; it was a bad solution,
an unhappy ending, could we see beyond the last
pages of the book." But among the contretemps she fore-
sees she does not mention what would surely have been
the worst. Emma, who was relatively indifferent to men,
was inclined to infatuations with women; and what
reason is there to believe that her marriage with Knightley would prevent her from going on as she had done
before: from discovering a new young lady as appealing
as Harriet Smith, dominating her personality and situ-
ating her in a dream-world of Emma's own in which
Emma would be able to confer on her all kinds of imaginary benefits but which would have no connection
whatever with her condition or her real possibilities?
This would worry and exasperate Knightley and be hard
for him to do anything about. He would be lucky if he
did not presently find himself saddled, along with the
other awkward features of the arrangement, with one
of Emma's young protégées as an actual member of the
household.

I do not mean to suggest for *Emma* any specific Freudian formula, but I feel sure that it is the one of her
novels in which the author's own peculiar "condition-
ing" is most curiously and clearly seen. Jane Austen spent
all her life with persons related to her by blood—her
parents, her five brothers, her single unmarried sister—
and the experience behind the relationships imagined
by her in her novels is always an experience of relationships of blood, of which that between sisters is certainly the most deeply felt. Miss Stern and Miss Kaye-
Smith are agreed with George Moore that Marianne's love
for Willoughby in *Sense and Sensibility* is the most

passionate thing in Jane Austen; but isn't it rather the emotion of Elinor as she witnesses her sister's disaster than Marianne's emotion over Willoughby of which the poignancy is communicated to the reader? The involvement with one another of the sisters is the real central theme of the book, just as the relation of Elizabeth to her sisters is so vital a part of *Pride and Prejudice*. For, though Miss Austen's intelligence was free to follow and understand other women when they were flirting or comfortably married, hunting husbands or breaking their hearts, she seems always to have been held suspended by the web of her original family ties. To some special equilibrium of the kind, which she never felt the necessity of upsetting, she must partly have owed the coolness, the patience, the poise, the leisure of mind to work at writing for its own sake, that made it possible for her to become a great artist. The solicitude of the sober Elinor Dashwood watching her giddy sister Marianne becomes in time the detached interest of the author looking on at the adventures of her heroines. In the last of her novels, *Persuasion*, one does find a different element and feel a personal emotion of the author's—a tinge of sadness at a woman's self-fulfilment missed—but the pattern is still much the same. Anne Elliot is herself a young sister: she, too, has a big sister, Lady Russell, who, like Emma, has misled her protégée—in this case, by discouraging her from marrying and nearly spoiling her life. Miss Stern and Miss Kaye-Smith do not care much for Lady Russell as a character; but she is worth thinking seriously about as a very important motif in Jane Austen. The comedy of the false sister-relationship of *Emma* has turned into something almost tragic.

June 24, 1944

"YOU CAN'T DO THIS TO ME!"

SHRILLED CELIA

The Robe, by Lloyd C. Douglas, has become, from the
point of view of sales, one of the greatest successes of publishing history. Published in October, 1942, it stood at one
time at the head of the best-seller list for fiction for
eleven consecutive months, and is still well up toward
the top. It has sold, in less than two years, one million,
four hundred and fifty thousand copies, and the publishers estimate that it has been read by five times that
number of people. Houghton Mifflin, with their re-
stricted supply of paper, have twice had the book reset
in order to reduce the number of pages, and have had to
resort to other special economies to meet the demand at
all. They have announced, in the *Publishers' Weekly,* a
vast new advertising campaign for August, and one
sometimes gets the impression that they have ceased to
bring out any other books. One of their publicity releases
reports that a copy of *The Robe,* auctioned off at the
opening of the Fifth War Loan Drive, brought $525,-
000 in War Bonds.

Never having looked into this book, I lately decided
that it was time for me to take cognizance of it. I have
procured a copy of *The Robe,* and what I have found in
it has been rather surprising. Instead of the usual trash
aimed at Hollywood and streamlined for the popular

magazines, one is confronted with something that resembles an old-fashioned historical novel for young people. Here is the tone of the opening page: "Because she was only fifteen and busy with her growing up, Lucia's periods of reflection were brief and infrequent, but this morning she felt weighted with responsibility. Last night her mother, who rarely talked to her about anything more perplexing than the advantages of clean hands and a pure heart, had privately discussed the possible outcome of Father's reckless remarks yesterday in the Senate, and Lucia, flattered by this confidence, had declared maturely that Prince Gaius wasn't in a position to do anything about it. But after she had gone to bed, Lucia began to fret. . . . They would all have to be careful now or they might get into serious trouble. The birds had awakened her early. She was not yet used to their flutterings and twitterings; for they had returned much sooner than usual, Spring having arrived and unpacked before February's lease was up. Lucia roused to a consciousness of the fret that she had taken to bed with her. It was still there, like a toothache. . . . For the past year or more, Lucia had been acutely conscious of her increasing height and rapid development into womanhood, but here on this expanse of tessellated tiling she always felt very insignificant. . . . No matter how old she became, she would be ever a child here."

There are five hundred and fifty-six pages of this. It is a story of the Roman Empire in the days of early Christianity, and its appeal is exactly the same as that of *The Last Days of Pompeii, Quo Vadis?* and *Ben-Hur.* The surface has been brought up to date by diluting the old grandiose language of the novel of ancient Rome with a jargon which sounds as if Dr. Douglas had picked it up during the years when, as the publishers' leaflet tells us, he was a counsellor of college students at the Universities of Michigan and Illinois. The aristocratic Romans are always saying things like "You're definitely drunk," "But what's the matter with idols? They're usually quite artistic!," "Indeed! Well—she'd better be good!," "I wouldn't know," "What do you mean—'a Christian'?" At one point a lady of Tiberius' court addresses her noble lover as follows: "You liked me well enough until you came here and noticed this Gallus girl's curves! And it's plain to see she despises you! . . You can't do this to me! Where will *you* stand with Sejanus when I tell him you have treated me like an ordinary trollop?" But, for the rest, it is as leisurely, as formless and as careful of all the maidenly proprieties as any novel of the nineteenth century. It differs from Bulwer-Lytton only in being written worse. Dr. Douglas has woven, in *The Robe,* an almost unrivalled fabric of old clichés, in which one of the only attempts at a literary heightening of effect is the substitution for the simple "said" of other more pretentious verbs—so that the characters are always shrilling, barking, speculating, parrying, wailing, wheedling or grunting whatever they have to say.

It is so difficult, when one first glances into *The Robe,* to imagine that any literate person with even the faintest trace of literary taste could ever get through more than two pages of it for pleasure that one is astounded and terrified at the thought that seven million Americans have found something in it to hold their attention. What is the explanation of this? Dr. Douglas himself, in an article distinguished by both modesty and good sense (*Why I Wrote "The Robe,"* in the June *Cosmopolitan*), has indicated a part of the answer. In the first place, he says, you can always score a success by writing a novel about Jesus, if you take care to avoid the controversies which have split the later Christians into sects. He cites *Ben-Hur,* which "sold more than a million copies during one of the most placid decades in American history," and a novel called *In His Steps*, by a clergyman in Kansas. But there is also, perhaps, he adds, a special reason why a novel about Jesus should be widely read at this time. It is quite natural that people should find it a relief to hear about somebody who was interested in healing the blind and the crippled rather than in blinding and crippling people, and in comforting the persecuted rather than in outlawing large groups of human beings. This must certainly be true, and there are also special reasons why Dr. Douglas' picture of Jesus should particularly command attention. Dr. Douglas, who is a Congregational minister and the son of a country parson, has an asset which can only be described as old-time Christian feeling. He is a genuine man of God of the type that used to do his best in the American small-town pulpit and that the community felt it could rely on. He is an anachronism, but he represents something that a good many Americans must feel to be reassuring. And, besides this, he has given to *The Robe* one virtue which can make a good bad novel, just as it constitutes a *sine qua non* for every really excellent one: he has imagined the whole thing for himself. *The Robe* has not been made out of other books: Dr. Douglas has lived the story —he has attempted to see for himself how the Christians would look to the Romans and how the Romans would look to the Jews. The fact that this has been done many times before does not deter Dr. Douglas or prevent him from creating in his story a certain atmosphere of suspense and adventure. He has set out to track down a conceivable Jesus in an alien but conceivable world; and his book, on its lower level, has the same kind of dramatic effectiveness as Bernard Shaw's *Saint Joan*. Finally, we must count it to him for righteousness that Dr. Douglas has had the courage to let his hero and heroine, at the end of the story, be executed as martyrs to the new religion instead of leaving them on the threshold of a comfortable marriage with a starry-eyed kiss and a fadeout.

When, therefore, one compares *The Robe* with the frankly faked publishers' goods with which the public are usually fed, one sees that Dr. Douglas' novel is a work of a certain purity and that the author deserves a certain respect. It is rather to the credit of the millions who have been buying or borrowing *The Robe* that they should prefer a long and tedious novel about the influence of the power of Jesus on the Roman who carried out the crucifixion to the livelier and easier productions which have been specially flavored to please them. It demonstrates that the ordinary reader, even in our ghastly time, does long for moral light, that he cannot live by bilge alone. But that seven and a half million Americans should not find it in the least distasteful to devour five hundred and fifty pages of Dr. Douglas' five-and-ten-cent-store writing is something to give pause to anyone who may have supposed that the generation of Mencken had lifted American taste a little above the level of Gene Stratton-Porter and Harold Bell Wright.

August 26, 1944

ALDOUS HUXLEY IN
THE WORLD BEYOND TIME

ALDOUS HUXLEY'S NEW NOVEL, *Time Must Have a Stop*, is a good deal better than his last one, *After Many a Summer Dies the Swan*. For one thing, he has returned to Europe for his characters and his settings, and he is much more successful with the English intellectuals in the London and Florence of the twenties than he was, in the earlier book, with an American millionaire and his hangers-on. His people, in many cases, are still conventional figures of satire: the disgusting voluptuary who lives in Italy and talks about the art of life, the rude rich old lady who has a pet Pomeranian and raps out imperious orders, and an up-to-date version of the hard Gradgrind parent, who is a socialist instead of a utilitarian; but Huxley does not run here the same risk of an obvious and purely external caricature that he did in his California fantasia. Here there is much more that is piquant in the social observation, much more wit in the talk and the unspoken thoughts of the characters, much more novelty of invention in the action. And along with this there goes an improvement in his handling of the religious element which has lately come to figure in his fiction. Huxley's peculiar version of the life of contemplation and revelation was expounded in *After Many a Summer* by a boring non-satirical character who read homilies to the other characters with an insufferable air of quiet authority and who constantly made the reader feel that it would have been better if he, too, had been satirically treated as a typical California crank. But in this new novel these matters have been dramatized and incorporated in the story on the same level as the other material. The voluptuary dies of a stroke, and we follow him into the non-sensual world. We see him drift about the fringes of the Divine within its gravitational field; return at moments to communicate with his friends through the agency of an extremely stupid medium, who garbles what he is trying to say; and finally, shrinking from absorption in God, get himself born back into humanity in the body of a baby expected by the wife of one of the other characters. Now, one may not be prepared to accept Huxley's views about spiritualistic phenomena and the Platonic rebirth of souls, but the whole thing has been given plausibility —though queer, it is never creepy—by treating the disembodied vicissitudes of Eustace Barnack's soul in the same dry or droll way as the adventures of his consciousness while still in the flesh. The result of threading this in with the doings of the characters who are still alive is an effect which must be new in fiction. In its essentially rather dismal and dark-brown way, *Time Must Have a Stop* is quite a brilliant performance.

It is difficult, however, for Huxley to celebrate convincingly in a novel his present ideals of abnegation and withdrawal from the things of the world, just as it was for T. S. Eliot, in *Murder in the Cathedral*, to celebrate the ideal of humility. These are virtues which— unlike some others: courage and brotherly love, for example—do not lend themselves to being illustrated in public by clever and accomplished writers, long admired and much in view. Just as Eliot's Thomas Becket becomes superior to the verge of snobbery in his perfect achievement of meekness, so Bruno Rontini, the contemporary saint of Huxley's latest novel, seems sometimes attainted by the smart virtuosity of so many of Huxley's other characters in his insight into other people's states of mind, his power to forecast what they are going to do and an ability to outmaneuver them morally which gives almost the impression of scoring off them—all talents that have something in common with those of the infallible detective that figures in so much mystery fiction. Aldous Huxley sharply criticizes Dante for carrying up into Heaven his partisan antagonisms and his pride, but the danger with Huxley himself is that he will turn Buddha, Pascal and St. John of the Cross into another neat performance for the salon. It must, however, be said that his descriptions of the dissociated trancelike states in which his characters sometimes feel or seem about to feel a super-corporeal union with God have a certain sound of authenticity and convince one that they are based on experience.

One's objection to what, at this point in his career, can only be called the moral teaching of Huxley is not that it is not derived from real states of exaltation, but that these states of exaltation themselves imply an incomplete experience of the earthly possibilities of human life. Huxley's satire has always been founded not only upon a distaste for humanity but also upon a real incapacity for understanding most of the things that seemed to other people important and exciting. It used to be fashionable to call him "intelligent," but he was never particularly intelligent. His habit of reading the *Encyclopaedia Britannica* gives the quality of his appetite for facts and ideas; his interest in the great intellectual movements that were bringing most light in his own time was on exactly the same level as his interest in a twelfth-century heresy, a queer species of carnivorous plant, a special variety of Romanesque architecture or a Greek poet surviving in fragments. Freud, Lenin, Einstein, Joyce—he sometimes expressed about them, in his casual essays, opinions as obtuse and philistine as those of the ordinary Fleet Street journalist. The new paths that they opened, the new hopes that they woke, were not opened or awakened for Huxley. For Huxley, in his satirical novels, the man whose imagination was aroused by, say, the quantum theory did not appear any more interesting than the old-fashioned pre-quantum mechanist, or the connoisseur of abstract painting than the fancier of Victorian bric-a-brac.

For the satirist, of course, this attitude may provide a basis for valid work. The Lilliputians of Swift seem too little, no matter what they do; the Bouvard and Pécuchet of Flaubert (invoked by one of the characters of *Time Must Have a Stop*) remain numskulls no matter what sciences or arts they think they are experimenting with. But Huxley is not, like Swift or Flaubert, complete and self-sufficient as a satirist. He has not even had the real love of writing, the power to express himself through art, of Evelyn Waugh or Ronald Firbank, the novels of both of whom may very well last longer than Huxley's. Merely a manipulator of Punch-and-Judy figures, he has inevitably to shake them off his hands and to use these hands in pulpit gestures as he comes forward to preach his way of life; and in this role his defects of intelligence again become fatally clear. We realize that his readiness to reject the world is due to his not knowing what is in it. That mixed and immature humanity which has been handled by the great artists and the great thinkers of his time—Huxley was not impressed by what they had been able to create from it because he had never had the full sense of what that humanity was like and, hence, of what it might become. His whole ascetic system, for example, is arrived at by way of the conclusion that "the flesh," though theoretically to be tolerated as a device for perpetuating the species, can never, through sexual selection or through the idealizations of love, become a part of our higher activities. In this novel, sex is never represented as anything but cold or perverse. There is nothing beyond momentary pleasure in any of the amorous relations of *Time Must Have a Stop*. Of the fact that the relations between men and women are involved in everything humanity builds—in the forms of art, in the structure of thought, in the incitement to achievement and leadership —you will get no inkling from Huxley. This would be perfectly all right in a satire which did not purport to be anything else—the satirist has always the license to turn down the flame of life in order to let us take account more grimly of the mechanical aspect of the fixtures and the sordidness of the surrounding room; but it is very misleading in a fable which pretends to bring us solemnly to consider the fundamental problems of human behavior and destiny.

Aldous Huxley would probably say, in reply to the objection above, that it does not really matter what we build on this earth. Our retort would be: How does he know?, since he has taken little part in the building. His inability to build solidly in his novels is itself an evidence of this. You cannot live in them; the author himself has not lived in them. He has always found it easy to drop them in order to report on his spiritual progress. The epilogue to *Time Must Have a Stop* consists mostly of a series of *pensées,* the journal of the central character, a poet who is schooling himself in the discipline of self-renunciation. These last pages have a terseness of writing and an accent of moral sincerity that one has hardly found before in Huxley. But what sort of general validity can be expected of a set of principles derived from the diminished and distorted world invented by the author of this novel? Since the story is admittedly a satire, it should follow that a religious system deduced from the conduct of its characters is either not wholly serious or not susceptible of wide application.

September 2, 1944

VLADIMIR NABOKOV ON GOGOL

IF YOU READ E.-M. de Vogüé's *Le Roman Russe,* you will learn that Nikolai Gogol was a pioneer of Russian realism; if you read Mérimée's essay on him, you will be told that he was first of all a satirist, who, if he had written in a more widely read language, might well have "acquired a reputation equal to that of the best English humorists"; and these two notions have remained the chief elements in the Western conception of Gogol. If we set out to read Gogol himself, we may be puzzled to find he does not fit them. We soon recognize that we are a long way here from the familiar Russian realism, of which the purest example is Tolstoy. Gogol's characters are social types, but they are also mythical monsters; his backgrounds are vulgar in a way that was new in Russian fiction, but the sordid detail is intensified, thrown into a dramatic relief which does not allow any illusion that we are watching the lives of ordinary people; and both characters and backgrounds, by a strange Homeric growth, are continually putting forth gigantic similes involving characters and scenes of their own, which give the whole thing a queer other dimension. And though we may laugh at *The Inspector General,* we shall find that Gogol's stories inspire more horror than mirth, and a horror rather tragic than satiric. We shall also find long passages of prose lyricism that probably— for richness of texture combined with emotional power

—beat anything else of the kind written by anyone in the nineteenth century.

The truth is, in fact, that Gogol, who called his *Dead Souls* a poem, is primarily a great *poet*, in a sense that sets him rather apart from the other most-read Russian novelists, though there is a side of Dostoevsky which has something in common with him. Gogol's characters and his grotesque details are symbols for states of the soul; his meanings and his moods are complex. Writing in the same period as Melville and Poe, he is much closer to them than to the later realists. He worked on a far bigger scale than Poe and he realized himself as an artist more completely than Melville did, but the St. Petersburg petty officials of Gogol's short stories of the supernatural belong to the same world as the damned Virginia gentlemen of Poe's, and one of the books that *Dead Souls* most resembles, for all the differences between the ostensible subjects, is certainly *Moby Dick*, in which Ahab's pursuit of the white whale is no more merely a fishing expedition than Chichikov's journey through Russia to buy up titles to deceased serfs is merely a swindling trip.

This is the great point that Vladimir Nabokov makes in his new book on Gogol—*Nikolai Gogol*—one of the best volumes so far in the interesting series called *Makers of Modern Literature*. Mr. Nabokov is himself a poet who has developed a complicated imagery and a novelist of the non-realistic sort, and he has written the kind of book which can only be written by one artist about another—an essay which takes its place with the very small body of first-rate criticism of Russian literature in English. Nobokov's *Gogol* must be henceforth read by anybody who has any serious interest in finding out about Russian culture. Not only has he shifted the lighting on the conventional picture of Gogol in such a way as to bring out his real genius as no other writer in English has done, but he has labored to give the reader some accurate impression of Gogol's style—a feature of his art which has come off badly in most of the English translations. The author of *Dead Souls,* a Ukrainian who wrote in Russian, had a peculiar interest in language of a kind that was somewhat akin to Joyce's. All the main characters in *Dead Souls* are collectors, and Gogol collected words. He liked the jargons of special occupations and special social strata; he liked to use unexpected verbs; he liked to invent words of his own; and he worked at making elaborate set-pieces as tangled and full of hidden implications as the jungle of the cracked landowner Plushkin's estate, as compelling in their rhythm and their cumulative power as Chichikov's departure in his carriage, that takes him through the little country towns and finally out into the steppe—"crows like flies, a limitless horizon"—and culminates later in the vision of Russia hurtling through the world like a troika while the other nations look on amazed. Mr. Nabokov has here described some of the devices of Gogol's style, and he has translated some famous passages into an English that attempts to reproduce their effects and that will give the reader some idea of why Russians sometimes know them by heart.

The chief faults of Mr. Nabokov's book are due to the fact that he is fundamentally a fiction writer and that Gogol, having been a real man, does not lend himself to the author's accomplished technique of sudden sidelights and juxtaposed glimpses quite so readily as if he had been a character invented by Nabokov himself. The effort to apply to Gogol the usual methods of the Nabokov portraiture has resulted in a certain amount of violence to the subject's career and work: large areas of both are skipped over, and the aspects that have been

treated at length seem sometimes rather capriciously chosen. The reader is also annoyed by the frequent self-
indulgence of the author in poses, perversities and van-
ities that sound as if he had brought them away from the
St. Petersburg of the early nineteen-hundreds and piously
preserved them in exile; and, along with them, a kind of
snapping and snarling on principle at everything connected with the Russian Revolution that sometimes throws
the baby out with the blood bath—to be guilty of a species
of witticism to which Mr. Nabokov is much addicted and
which tends, also, a little to disfigure his book. His puns
are particularly awful. In writing English, he has not yet
acquired the sense of how horribly "the government specter" and "Gogol's spas were not really spatial" are calculated to grate on English-speaking readers. Aside from
this, in spite of some errors, Mr. Nabokov's mastery of
English almost rivals Joseph Conrad's.

September 9, 1944

KATHERINE ANNE PORTER

Miss KATHERINE ANNE PORTER has published a new book of stories, her third: *The Leaning Tower and Other Stories*. To the reviewer, Miss Porter is baffling because one cannot take hold of her work in any of the obvious ways. She makes none of the melodramatic or ironic points that are the stock in trade of ordinary short story writers; she falls into none of the usual patterns and she does not show anyone's influence. She does not exploit her personality either inside or outside her work, and her writing itself makes a surface so smooth that the critic has little opportunity to point out peculiarities of color or weave. If he is tempted to say that the effect is pale, he is prevented by the realization that Miss Porter writes English of a purity and precision almost unique in contemporary American fiction. If he tries to demur that some given piece fails to mount with the accelerating pace or arrive at the final intensity that he is in the habit of expecting in short stories, he is deterred by a nibbling suspicion that he may not have grasped its meaning and have it hit him with a sudden impact some minutes after he has closed the book.

Not that this meaning is simple to formulate even after one has felt its emotional force. The limpidity of the sentence, the exactitude of the phrase, are deceptive in that the thing they convey continues to seem elusive even after it has been communicated. These stories are not illustrations of anything that is reducible to a moral law or a political or social analysis or even a principle of human behavior. What they show us are human relations in their constantly shifting phases and in the moments of which their existence is made. There is no place for general reflections; you are to live through the experience as the characters do. And yet the writer has managed to say something about the values involved in the experience. But what is it? I shall try to suggest, though I am afraid I shall land in ineptitude.

Miss Porter's short stories lend themselves to being sorted into three fairly distinct groups. There are the studies of family life in working-class or middle-class households (there are two of these in *The Leaning Tower*), which, in spite of the fact that the author is technically sympathetic with her people, tend to be rather bitter and bleak, and, remarkable though they are, seem to me less satisfactory than the best of her other stories. The impression we get from these pieces is that the qualities that are most amiable in human life are being gradually done to death in the milieux she is presenting, but Miss Porter does not really much like these people or feel comfortable in their dismal homes, and so we, in turn, don't really much care. Another section of her work, however, contains what may be called pictures of foreign parts, and here Miss Porter is much more successful. The story which gives its name to her new collection and which takes up two-fifths of the volume belongs to this category. It is a study of Germany between the two wars in terms of a travelling American and his landlady and fellow-lodgers in a Berlin rooming house. By its material and its point of view, it rather recalls Christopher Isherwood's *Goodbye to Berlin,* but it is more poetic in treatment and more general in implication. The little plaster leaning tower of Pisa which has been cherished by the Viennese landlady but gets broken by her American tenant stands for something in the destruction of which not merely the Germans but also the Americans have somehow taken a criminal part (though the American is himself an artist, he finds that he can mean nothing to the Germans but the power of American money). So, in a fine earlier story, *Hacienda*, a Mexican peon is somehow destroyed—with no direct responsibility on the part of any of the elements concerned—by a combination of Soviet Russians intent on making a Communist movie, their American business manager and a family of Mexican landowners.

In both cases, we are left with the feeling that, caught in the meshes of interwoven forces, some important human value has been crushed. These stories especially, one gathers, are examples of what Miss Porter means when she says, in her foreword to *Flowering Judas* in the Modern Library edition, that most of her "energies of mind and spirit have been spent in the effort to grasp the meaning" of the threats of world catastrophe in her time, "to trace them to their sources and to understand the logic of this majestic and terrible failure of the life of man in the Western world."

But perhaps the most interesting section of Katherine Anne Porter's work is composed of her stories about women—particularly her heroine Miranda, who figured in two of the three novelettes that made up her previous volume, *Pale Horse, Pale Rider*. The first six pieces of *The Leaning Tower* deal with Miranda's childhood and her family background of Louisianians living in southern Texas. This is the setting in which Miss Porter is most at home, and one finds in it the origins of that spirit of which the starvation and violation elsewhere make the subjects of her other stories. One recognizes it in the firm little sketches that show the relations between Miranda's grandmother and her lifelong colored companion, the relations between the members of the family and the relations between the family and the Negro servants in general. Somewhere behind Miss Porter's stories there is a conception of a natural human spirit in terms of their bearing on which all the other forces of society are appraised. This spirit is never really idealized, it is not even sentimentalized; it can be generous and loving and charming, but it can also be indifferent and careless, inconsequent, irresponsible and silly. If the meaning of these stories is elusive, it is because this essential spirit is so hard to isolate or pin down. It is peculiar to Louisianians in Texas, yet one misses it in a boarding house in Berlin. It is the special personality of a woman, yet it is involved with international issues. It evades all the most admirable moralities, it escapes through the social net, and it resists the tremendous oppressions of national bankruptcies and national wars. It is outlawed, driven underground, exiled; it becomes rather unsure of itself and may be able, as in *Pale Horse, Pale Rider*, to assert itself only in the delirium that lights up at the edge of death to save Miranda from extinction by war flu. It suffers often from a guilty conscience, knowing too well its moral weakness; but it can also rally bravely if vaguely in vindication of some instinct of its being which seems to point toward justice and truth.

But I said that this review would be clumsy. I am spoiling Miss Porter's stories by attempting to find a formula for them when I ought simply to be telling you to read them (and not merely the last volume but also its two predecessors). She is absolutely a first-rate artist, and what she wants other people to know she imparts to them by creating an object, the self-developing organism of a work of prose. The only general opinion on anything which, in her books, she has put on record has been a statement about her craft of prose fiction, and I may quote it—from the foreword to which I have referred—as more to the purpose than anything that the present critic could say. Here is the manifesto of the builder of this solid little sanctuary, so beautifully proportioned and finished, for the queer uncontrollable spirit that it seems to her important to save:

"In the face of such shape and weight of present misfortune, the voice of the individual artist may seem perhaps of no more consequence than the whirring of a cricket in the grass, but the arts do live continuously, and they live literally by faith; their names and their shapes and their uses and their basic meanings survive unchanged in all that matters through times of interruption, diminishment, neglect; they outlive governments and creeds and the societies, even the very civilizations that produced them. They cannot be destroyed altogether because they represent the substance of faith and the only reality. They are what we find again when the ruins are cleared away. And even the smallest and most incomplete offering at this time can be a proud act in defense of that faith."

September 30, 1944

A PICTURE TO HANG IN THE LIBRARY:

BROOKS'S AGE OF IRVING

THE NEW VOLUME of Van Wyck Brooks's literary history of the United States, *The World of Washington Irving,* though the third in order of publication, is the first in chronological order. It covers the ground from 1800 to the early years of the forties, and treats at length Jefferson, Audubon, Cooper, Irving, Simms, Poe, Bryant and Willis. It treats also dozens of minor figures and deals not only with literature proper but with political oratory, the reports of explorers and naturalists, the folklore of Davy Crockett and Mike Fink, and ethnological and archeological study; and it contains so much information about painting, music, landscape-gardening, architecture, mechanical invention and social manners that it might almost be more appropriately described as a history of American culture.

These decades were enormously lively: the country was still uncommercialized; the Americans were still exhilarated by the success of the Revolution and the adventure of the new country; the great intellectual figures were many-sided in their interests and talents, and men of the great worlds of society, geography and nature. There was a splendor of the Renaissance about figures like Jefferson and Audubon; Joel Barlow, diplomat, promoter and poet; Samuel F. B. Morse, who was a painter as well as a mechanical genius; William Dunlap, who was a painter, a historian of painting, a dramatist and a theatrical producer; and even Cooper, sailor, landowner, novelist, historian and critic of society—though we remember only his Indian tales. Poe—whom we greatly slight by reading him mainly for his tales of horror—was also typical of the period in the variety of his curiosities and his virtuosity in literary form. It is a wonderful period to go back to, and Mr. Brooks has written about it what seems to me so far the most attractive volume of the series that began with *The Flowering of New England*. The book is quite free from the cloggedness and overpainting that sometimes appeared in the earlier volumes. He has mastered his method so completely that we never get the effect of labor: style, narrative and organization have been brought to a point of perfection seldom reached in our historical and critical writing. Yet he has had to assimilate vast masses of print, surveying the whole field afresh and reading all the books for himself, and he has accepted none of the conventional limits by which scholars simplify their tasks: his light overflows these limits and seems to penetrate every crevice, reveal every in-between phase, of the observing and imagining American mind of the early years of the Republic. For the reader who is curious about cultural phenomena, there is not a dull page or dull footnote in the book. Mr. Brooks has the answers to all the questions with which the academic historians of literature will not usually help you much. Why did the South—apart from the political writing that accompanied the Revolution— produce so little in the way of literature? Why did people set so much store by Bryant? Why did they devour Washington Irving? How and when did the piety and prudery which have so tended to stunt the national art and thought close down on the free-thinking plain-speaking tradition of the realistic and cosmopolitan minds that presided at the birth of the Republic? What was the effect of the actual experience of the putting into practice of social equality and of the career open to the talents on the classically educated men of property who had defended the democratic ideal against the political tradition of Europe? How did they meet the age of Andrew Jackson?

To explain and dramatize all these matters is what Mr. Brooks can do as no one else in the United States has done it. Rarely, in fact, outside France has the appetite for learning been united with intelligence and literary ability to the degree that we find it here. He has put on the whole picture a color, a finish, a glaze like those of the best paintings of the period: the portraits of the pupils of Benjamin West, the genre studies of Mount and Bingham, the landscapes of the Hudson River school. You can hang this new volume in your library uninhibited by any embarrassment such as you may have felt in connection with his New England portraits, over a sometimes too fulsome treatment and a sometimes too pink-and-blue palette. You may occasionally pull yourself up with the reflection that the ripe and harmonious picture must still, to some extent, represent an idealization; but, after all, what Mr. Brooks is engaged on is not a sociological report but a presentation of the early eighteen-hundreds through the eyes of imaginative writers who brought to it their own color and excitement, and an account of these writers from the point of view of how they looked and what they meant to their contemporaries. (It is curious to contrast this volume with the bleak surveys of American civilization in 1800 and 1817 of Henry Adams' history. Though Adams is telling the same story of the birth of a national character and culture, an American intellectual, in the trust-ridden eighties and nineties, was not able to believe in these with such certainty as a man of Mr. Brooks's generation, and could not, therefore, find in our past so much to be cheerful about.)

In this reliving of the visions of our fathers, the question of absolute values becomes, for Mr. Brooks's purpose, unimportant and almost irrelevant. But there is a common complaint against this series that, in neglecting to deal with such values, in failing to measure the American writers by the best that has been done in the world, Mr. Brooks has been shirking the true business of the critic. This complaint has less force in the present case than it had in connection with the previous volumes, because the author does not here overinflate the men of mediocre ability as he did in the earlier books. He does not mislead us by creating the impression that Cooper and Washington Irving, the two dominant writers of the era, were men of greater talent than they were. Yet the question has still to be dealt with. Between *The World of Washington Irving* and its immediate predecessor in the series, *New England: Indian Summer,* Mr. Brooks has published a more personal book, *Opinions of Oliver Allston,* in which he has stigmatized as "coterie-literature" the work of some of the greatest of his contemporaries, and revealed that his own standards of excellence are still more or less those of an enthusiastic young man in his twenties in the heyday of H. G. Wells, a young man for whom Tolstoy and Ibsen, on the one hand, and Victor Hugo and Browning, on the other, all inhabit the same empyrean of greatness. But the paradox of Brooks's career is that he has himself been able to develop into one of the first-rate American writers of his time without achieving any commensurate development of his appreciation of other writers save as material for cultural history. He has, in the present vol-

ume, one case of an artist—Poe—who takes his place in
a company far higher than that of his literary companions in the book. One looked forward with interest to
his handling of Poe as a test case of his literary judgment,
and since Poe is a great favorite of mine, I watched
Mr. Brooks like a hawk during the chapters in which he
deals with this subject, so peculiarly fraught with pit-
falls—moral, social, aesthetic and regional—which has
probably given rise to more rubbishy and vulgar writing,
both romantic and denunciatory, than any other American career with the exception of Abraham Lincoln's.
Now Mr. Brooks has walked right through all these pit-
falls with perfect delicacy, coolness and sense, and he
has brought to his presentation of Poe's pathological
personality a touch of that psychological insight which,
I believe, has not appeared in his work since *The Ordeal
of Mark Twain*. Van Wyck Brooks's interest in Poe is
not the interest of Baudelaire or of Walter de la Mare,
but from his own entirely different point of view he
can indicate correctly Poe's importance: "With Poe another age had opened," he says, "intenser, profounder
than [Washington Irving's]"; and this makes us see Poe
in his historical perspective as we may not have done before.

In his attempts to evaluate literature, Mr. Brooks is
still likely to fall back on rather vague and conventional
phrases. He says of Bryant's poem *To a Waterfowl* that it
is "the most intense of all his poems, in which for a moment he entered the realm of magic." Well, I know that
Mr. Yvor Winters admires this poem of Bryant's, but I
doubt whether it would be possible to find many modern poets who would agree with Mr. Brooks. If the
magic he means is the magic that Matthew Arnold introduced into literary criticism with a famous discussion
of such passages as Shakespeare's "daffodils, That come

before the swallow dares, and take The winds of
March with beauty," then Bryant's poor old waterfowl
that guides through the boundless air his certain flight
and brings to the poet the conviction that God will lead
his steps aright can scarcely deserve that description.

And here is a passage on the prose of Cooper: "With
his marked feeling for the sublime, he rose moreover
now and then to moments of the noblest and most eloquent prose. Such were the descriptions of the icefields
in *The Sea Lions*—a tale of American sealers in antarctic
waters—the vast mass of floating mountains, generally of
a spectral white, through which the mariners moved in
an unknown sea. The walls, like ridges of the Alps,
bowed and rocked and ground one another, stirred by
the restless ocean, with a rushing sound, and sometimes
a prodigious plunge as of a planet falling tossed the
water over the heaving ramparts. The cliffs, half a league
in length, with their arches and pinnacles and towers
and columns, suggested the streets of some fantastic city
that was floating in the sunlight in the sea, black here
and there in certain lights and orange on the summits,
throwing out gleams and hues of emerald and gold."
Now if someone were to speak to you suddenly of "the
noblest and most eloquent prose," in connection with a
work of fiction, you might think of Melville, you might
think of Flaubert, you might think of D. H. Lawrence;
but you would not be at all likely to think of anything
you had ever read in Cooper, where an occasional poetry
of atmosphere seems barely to manage to seep through
the verbose and clumsy writing. If there is something in
Cooper as good as Mr. Brooks seems here to suggest, then
you feel that you ought to know about it. But when you
look up the icebergs in *The Sea Lions*, you find that
Van Wyck Brooks has not merely been reflecting the
glory of something that is much better in the original:

he has put together his very pretty passage out of more or less undistinguished bits scattered through a great number of pages: "Each time, however, the sun's rays soon came to undeceive him; and that which had so lately been black and frowning, was, as by the touch of magic, suddenly illuminated, and became bright and gorgeous, throwing out its emerald hues, or perhaps a virgin white, that filled the beholder with delight, even amid the terrors and dangers by which, in very truth, he was surrounded. The glorious Alps themselves, those wonders of the earth, could scarcely compete in scenery with the views that nature lavished, in that remote sea, on a seeming void. . . . The passages between the bergs, or what might be termed the streets and lanes of this mysterious-looking, fantastical, yet sublime city of the ocean, were numerous, and of every variety," etc., etc.

The creation is not Cooper's but Brooks's: he has sifted out the images from *The Sea Lions* and made out of them something quite new. With the work of a Thoreau or a Hawthorne, this method does not succeed, because you cannot rewrite a good writer: you can only discolor and weaken. But with somebody like Cooper, Mr. Brooks has a field almost like that of the artist who deals directly with crude experience. And how many inferior or tedious writers he must have transmuted in this book! We cannot compare the art with the phenomena themselves so readily as we can in the novelist's case; but when we go to the trouble of doing so, we are amazed at the skill with which Brooks has been turning the old carriage springs, spectacle frames and pickaxes of 1800–1840 into a fine-beaten kind of white gold.

October 7, 1944

WHY DO PEOPLE READ DETECTIVE
STORIES?

FOR YEARS I have been hearing about detective stories. Almost everybody I know seems to read them, and they have long conversations about them in which I am unable to take part. I am always being reminded that the most serious public figures of our time, from Woodrow Wilson to W. B. Yeats, have been addicts of this form of fiction. Now, except for a few stories by Chesterton, for which I did not much care, I have not read any detective stories since one of the earliest, if not the earliest, of the imitators of Sherlock Holmes—a writer named Jacques Futrelle, now dead, who invented a character called the Thinking Machine and published his first volume of stories about him in 1907. Enchanted though I had been with Sherlock Holmes, I got bored with the Thinking Machine and dropped him, beginning to feel, at the age of twelve, that I was outgrowing that form of literature.

Since, however, I have recently been sampling the various types of popular merchandise, I have decided that I ought to take a look at some specimens of this kind of fiction, which has grown so tremendously popular and which is now being produced on such a scale that the book departments of magazines have had to employ special editors to cope with it. To be sure of getting something above the average, I waited for new novels by writers who are particularly esteemed by connoisseurs. I started in with the latest volume of Rex Stout's Nero Wolfe stories: *Not Quite Dead Enough*.

What I found rather surprised me and discouraged my curiosity. Here was simply the old Sherlock Holmes formula reproduced with a fidelity even more complete than it had been by Jacques Futrelle almost forty years ago. Here was the incomparable private detective, ironic and ceremonious, with a superior mind and eccentric habits, addicted to overeating and orchid-raising, as Holmes had his enervated indulgence in his cocaine and his violin, yet always prepared to revive for prodigies of intellectual alertness; and here were the admiring stooge, adoring and slightly dense, and Inspector Lestrade of Scotland Yard, energetic but entirely at sea, under the new name of Inspector Cramer of Police Headquarters. Almost the only difference was that Nero Wolfe was fat and lethargic instead of lean and active like Holmes, and that he liked to make the villains commit suicide instead of handing them over to justice. But I rather enjoyed Wolfe himself, with his rich dinners and quiet evenings in his house in farthest West Thirty-fifth Street, where he savors an armchair sadism that is always accompanied by beer. The two stories that made up this new book—*Not Quite Dead Enough* and *Booby Trap*—I found rather disappointing; but, as they were both under the usual length and presented the great detective partly distracted from his regular profession by a rigorous course of training for the Army, I concluded that they might not be first-rate examples of what the author could do in this line and read also *The Nero Wolfe Omnibus*, which contains two earlier book-length stories: *The Red Box* and *The League of Frightened Men*. But neither did these supply the excitement I was hoping for. If the later stories were sketchy and skimpy, these seemed to have been somewhat padded, for they were full of long episodes that led nowhere and had no real business in the story. It was only when I looked up Sherlock Holmes that I realized how much Nero Wolfe was a dim and distant copy of an original. The old stories of Conan Doyle had a wit and a fairy-tale poetry of hansom cabs, gloomy London lodgings and lonely country estates that Rex Stout could hardly dupli-cate with his backgrounds of modern New York; and the surprises were much more entertaining: you at least got a room with a descending ceiling or a snake trained to climb down the bellrope, whereas with Nero Wolfe—though *The League of Frightened Men* makes use of a clever psychological idea—the solution of the mystery was not usually either fanciful or unexpected. I finally got to feel that I had to unpack large crates by swallow-ing the excelsior in order to find at the bottom a few bent and rusty nails, and I began to nurse a rankling con-viction that detective stories in general are able to profit by an unfair advantage in the code which forbids the reviewer to give away the secret to the public—a cus-tom which results in the concealment of the pointless-ness of a good deal of this fiction and affords a protection to the authors which no other department of writing enjoys. It is not difficult to create suspense by making people await a revelation, but it does demand a certain talent to come through with a criminal device which is ingenious or picturesque or amusing enough to make the reader feel that the waiting has been worth while. I even began to mutter that the real secret that Author Rex Stout had been screening by his false scents and interminable divagations was a meagerness of im-agination of which one only came to realize the full ghastliness when the last chapter had left one blank.

I have been told by the experts, however, that this endless carrying on of the Doyle tradition does not represent all or the best that has been done with the detective story during the decades of its proliferation. There has been also the puzzle mystery, and this, I was assured, had been brought to a high pitch of ingenuity in the stories of Agatha Christie. So I have read also the new Agatha Christie, *Death Comes as the End*, and I confess that I have been had by Mrs. Christie. I did not guess who the murderer was, I was incited to keep on and find out, and when I did finally find out, I was surprised. Yet I did not care for Agatha Christie and I hope never to read another of her books. I ought, perhaps, to discount the fact that *Death Comes as the End* is supposed to take place in Egypt two thousand years before Christ, so that the book has a flavor of Lloyd C. Douglas not, I understand, quite typical of the author. ("No more Khay in this world to sail on the Nile and catch fish and laugh up into the sun whilst she, stretched out in the boat with little Teti on her lap, laughed back at him"); but her writing is of a mawkishness and banality which seem to me literally impossible to read. You cannot *read* such a book, you run through it to see the problem worked out; and you cannot become interested in the characters, because they never can be allowed an existence of their own even in a flat two dimensions but have always to be contrived so that they can seem either reliable or sinister, depending on which quarter, at the moment, is to be baited for the reader's suspicion. This I had found also a source of annoyance in the case of Mr. Stout, who, however, has created, after a fashion, Nero Wolfe and Archie Goodwin and has made some attempt at characterization of the people that figure in the crimes; but Mrs. Christie, in proportion as she is more expert and concentrates more narrowly on the puzzle, has to eliminate human interest completely, or, rather, fill in the picture with what seems to me a distasteful parody of it. In this new novel, she has to provide herself with puppets who will be good for three stages of suspense: you must first wonder who is going to be murdered, you must then wonder who is committing the murders, and you must finally be unable to foresee which of two men the heroine will marry. It is all like a sleight-of-hand trick, in which the magician diverts your attention from the awkward or irrelevant movements that conceal the manipulation of the cards, and it may mildly entertain and astonish you, as such a sleight-of-hand performance may. But in a performance like *Death Comes as the End*, the patter is a constant bore and the properties lack the elegance of playing cards.

Still fearing that I might be unjust to a department of literature that seemed to be found so absorbing by many, I went back and read *The Maltese Falcon*, which I assumed to be a classic in the field, since it had been called by Alexander Woollcott "the best detective story America has yet produced" and since, at the time of its publication, it had immediately caused Dashiell Hammett to become—in Jimmy Durante's phrase, referring to himself—"duh toast of duh intellectuals." But it was difficult for me to understand what they had thought —in 1930—they were toasting. Mr. Hammett did have the advantage of real experience as a Pinkerton detective, and he infused the old formula of Sherlock Holmes with a certain cold underworld brutality which gave readers a new shudder in the days when it was fashionable to be interested in gangsters; but, beyond this, he lacked the ability to bring the story to imaginative life. As a writer, he is surely almost as far below the rank of Rex Stout as Rex Stout is below that of James

Cain. *The Maltese Falcon* today seems not much above those newspaper picture-strips in which you follow from day to day the ups and downs of a strong-jawed hero and a hardboiled but beautiful adventuress.

What, then, is the spell of the detective story that has been felt by T. S. Eliot and Paul Elmer More but which I seem incapable of feeling? As a department of imaginative writing, it looks to me completely dead. The spy story may perhaps only now be realizing its poetic possibilities, as the admirers of Graham Greene contend; and the murder story that exploits psychological horror is an entirely different matter. But the detective story proper had borne all its finest fruits by the end of the nineteenth century, having only declined from the point where Edgar Allan Poe had been able to communicate to M. Dupin something of his own ratiocinative intensity and where Dickens had invested his plots with a social and moral significance that made the final solution of the mystery a revelatory symbol of something that the author wanted seriously to say. Yet the detective story has kept its hold; had even, in the two decades between the great wars, become more popular than ever before; and there is, I believe, a deep reason for this. The world during those years was ridden by an all-pervasive feeling of guilt and by a fear of impending disaster which it seemed hopeless to try to avert because it never seemed conclusively possible to pin down the responsibility. Who had committed the original crime and who was going to commit the next one?—that second murder which always, in the novels, occurs at an unexpected moment when the investigation is well under way; which, as in one of the Nero Wolfe stories, may take place right in the great detective's office. Everybody is suspected in turn, and the streets are full of lurking agents whose allegiances we cannot know. Nobody seems guiltless, nobody seems safe; and then, suddenly, the murderer is spotted, and—relief!—he is not, after all, a person like you or me. He is a villain—known to the trade as George Gruesome—and he has been caught by an infallible Power, the supercilious and omniscient detective, who knows exactly where to fix the guilt.

October 14, 1944

BERNARD SHAW ON THE TRAINING
OF A STATESMAN

Everybody's Political What's What?, by Bernard Shaw, is a supplement rather than a companion piece to *The Intelligent Woman's Guide to Socialism and Capitalism*. The *Guide* came out in 1928 when the author was seventy-two and his mind was still in perfectly good working order; the *What's What?* appears sixteen years later, when Bernard Shaw is eighty-eight and his powers show signs of failing. There is nothing in this new book like the clear line of thought that made the *Guide* a great piece of exposition, and nothing so eloquent as its magnificent peroration on the evils of capitalism. The *What's What?* is not, in fact, an expository work at all in the same sense that the earlier book was. It is a treatise on a classical model that was popular in the Renaissance, when Castiglione wrote his *Courtier* and Machiavelli his *Prince*. Shaw might have called his book *The Statesman*, because its subject is the education of the ideal statesman of the future.

The old-fashioned ideal of democracy—one man, one vote—says Shaw, must today be regarded as discredited. It was inevitable that the modern dictators, who wanted to get something done, should sweep aside the impotent parliaments. But what we need—i.e., what England needs—are a new class of public servants, specially trained and tested as lawyers and doctors are, and registered as "mentally capable of functioning efficiently" in municipal or national office. (There should be not merely one Cabinet but several—"for cultural questions, industrial questions, agricultural questions," etc.) There would be plenty of such candidates available, since the opportunity for higher education would be thrown open to the whole population by a system of state-endowed schools, and it would be possible for able individuals from all classes of society to qualify; and these candidates would represent conflicting opinions and interests. The larger questions of public policy could thus still be determined by a popular vote that would select among these qualified candidates (though the voters themselves, one gathers, would have to be qualified for the franchise by something more than a literacy test). Now, given this state of things, how much should such an official have to learn of the various departments of knowledge and precisely how far should he allow himself to go in controlling the activities of society? The whole book is hung on this imaginary statesman and a variety of subjects are discussed—political, economic, social, religious, aesthetic, hygienic—in relation to his probable point of view. This discussion is rather informal and not particularly systematic; as Shaw says, he has "omitted much that has been dealt with by other writers" and aimed "rather at reminders of the overloooked, and views from new or neglected angles." The result is something unexpectedly close, for Shaw, to such ancient and garrulous works as Montaigne's *Essays* and Burton's *Anatomy*. The book runs much to personal anecdotes and curious historical examples, and contains many reminiscences of the author's long and full career, as well as stories about his father, his uncles, his grandfather and even his great-grandfather.

In comparison with Shaw's other productions—even with the work of his seventies—the *What's What?* is, thus, rather relaxed. Bernard Shaw is still earnest and still self-assertive, but he can ruminate now on the years he has known, the many subjects in which he has been interested, and can even gossip about them. He is sometimes betrayed by the lapses of a longevity that is rivalling Voltaire's. He frequently repeats his examples and makes the same point several times, and in his chapter on *Law and Tyranny* he reiterates almost unaltered, from fifty pages before, a whole mass of material on the history of medicine—anecdotes, instances and all. There are passages where he seems to be losing the thread and led astray by obsessive associations, so that they make on us a little the impression of the dream explanations in *Finnegans Wake* that are always changing the subject, and we feel that these pages are hardly real, that we are reading Bernard Shaw in our sleep. He has always had the habit—rather confusing in his prefaces, though essential to his genius as a dramatist—of presenting the different aspects of a subject all with a kind of biting overemphasis, as if they were not parts of a general survey, but actually contradictory attitudes; and this habit gives sometimes here a certain effect of disintegration. You may find, for example, on the same page, two apparently irreconcilable statements: "I, an artist-philosopher, mistrust laboratory methods because what happens in a laboratory is contrived and dictated . . . but the artist's workshop is the whole universe as far as he can comprehend it; and he can neither contrive nor dictate what happens there: he can only observe and interpret events that are beyond his control"; "But let no statesman or elector imagine that an artist cannot be as dangerous a fool as a laboratory researcher. The painting, the statue, the symphony, the fable, whether narrative or dramatic, is as completely contrived, selected, dictated and controlled by the artist as the laboratory experiment by the scientist." And his egoism seems to have increased instead of fading out with age. Once the panache of the young critic and dramatist, which he carried with defiance and dash, it now droops and looks out of place: today it makes you rather uncomfortable to find on every fourth or fifth page the recurrent "Take my case" or its equivalent, and you eventually learn to wince at his familiar enumerations of the names of great men of genius as you wait for the inevitable inclusion of his own.

And yet, for all this, the *Political What's What?* is one of the new books that are worth reading this year. Shaw's faculties still remain active to a perfectly amazing degree. There are stretches—such as the chapter on Pavlov and the sections that immediately follow—in which he writes with an incisive directness that seems hardly to have been dulled by age. And it is fascinating to see into the mind of a man who can look back over so long a life and who retains his capacity to compare and judge. We have glimpses into his school days in Dublin, his activity as a clerk for an estate agent, his experience in London as a municipal councillor, as a speaker for the Fabian Society, as a critic of painting, music and the theater; and there are expert observations on politics and society by one who has been scrutinizing public affairs since his conversion to socialism in the eighties. Here are all the main principles of his thought—creative evolution, hero worship, the inevitability of state control, equality of income, the need for religion and the religious character of works of art; and here is, also, a certain amount of old furniture—favorite authorities and fashionable attitudes—that, if we remember the early nineteen hundreds, the days when *Man and Superman* was shocking, we may associate with golfing pictures and Gibson girls.

But Shaw's mind has never really stopped functioning; he has been able, as few old men are, to adapt his fundamental ideas to the demands of the changing reality and to criticize acutely the most recent events. It is an advantage to a social historian to begin with a long view of history, as Shaw did by studying Marx; the great displacements of prestige and power that are the results of revolution and war have thrown many excellent writers off their bases and caused them to die disillusioned, but these do not dismay Bernard Shaw. Here is his diagnosis of World War II: "This is the great corruption of Socialism which threatens us at present. It calls itself Fascism in Italy, National Socialism (Nazi for short) in Germany, New Deal in the United States, and is clever enough to remain nameless in England; but everywhere it means the same thing: Socialist production and Unsocialist distribution. So far, out of the frying pan into the fire. For though Fascism (to call State Capitalism by its shortest name) has doled out some substantial benefits to the proletariat and given bureaucratic status to functionaries who were formerly only casual employees, besides tightening up the public services and preaching a worship of the State (called Totalitarianism) which will lead logically to genuine Socialism, it has produced a world war in which Anglo-American Fascism fights German and Italian Fascism because Fascism is international whilst the capitalists are still intensely national; for when Germany proposes to fashify the whole earth under the Führership of Adolf Hitler, and Italy the same under Benito Mussolini, the Anglo-American Fascists will see Germany damned before they will accept any Fascism that is not of their own making under their own Führers."

He, however, makes an exception for the Soviet Union, where, he says, they have "Democratic Communism." He talks as if the new Russian Constitution had actually been put into practice and he seems to express approval of Stalin's political purges, with a kind of vague fee-faw-fum about the need, in the society of the future, for "liquidating" the socially noxious. (It is a characteristic inconsistency that he should tell us we must concede to the state the right to decree the execution of people who fall into this category at the same time that he indignantly declines to submit to compulsory vaccination and inoculation.)

But even at the points where Shaw's thinking conspicuously fails in coherence, there is still a kind of general wisdom that soaks through the cracks of his argument. It is as if the effect of old age had been at last to break up his rigidities and allow him to arrive at a state of mind where he sees men and institutions a little more under the aspect of eternity: all appropriate developments from their milieux, each performing some natural function. I do not know whether this is what he means when he speaks of having now lived so long that he is beginning to see the dawn of a new way of looking at things; but even this, his latest phase, at an age when most men would be helplessly senile, is full of interest and not without surprises for those who have admired him and followed his work.

October 28, 1944

REËXAMINING DR. JOHNSON

IT IS A PITY that Boswell's *Life of Johnson* should so largely have supplanted for the general reader the writings of Johnson himself. If we know nothing but Boswell and Macaulay's essay, which is read in so many schools, we are likely to have a picture of a great eccentric who was even a bit of a clown. Boswell, in spite of his great respect and of the filial role he assumed, could not help making Johnson a character in an eighteenth-century comedy of manners; Macaulay pointed him up as a monster, at once grotesque and banal, in a bright-colored Victorian novel. And lately the figure of Boswell has become even more prominent at Johnson's expense through the discovery of the Boswell papers and the work of Mr. Chauncey Tinker. That Johnson himself was really one of the best English writers of his time, that he deserved his great reputation, is a fact that we are likely to lose sight of.

Mr. Joseph Wood Krutch, in a new biography called *Samuel Johnson*, has at last provided a study that is designed to restore to Johnson his real literary interest and importance. With all the work that has been done on Johnson and his friends, there has, as he says, been no such biography. "The very intensity of this specialization," he explains in his introduction, "(as well, of course, as the tremendous reputation of Boswell's *Life*) has tended to discourage any attempt in recent times to produce a large inclusive book which would serve to give the general reader a running account of Johnson's life, character and work as they appear in the light of contemporary knowledge and contemporary judgment." Mr. Krutch follows this announcement with some entirely unnecessary apologies for having played down the figure of Boswell. The truth is that he has devoted quite enough attention and given a quite favorable enough account of Boswell, and his nervously apprehensive glances in the direction of the Boswell fans are simply a part of that continued tribute which one dislikes to see exacted to that point by the vain and pushing diarist.

Mr. Krutch, then, has taken on a job which very much needed to be done, and has acquitted himself with honor. This biography is by far the best book that I have ever read by Joseph Wood Krutch. His *Poe*, written back in the twenties, was a rather half-baked performance: incomplete, depending too much on a Freudian oversimplification, insufficiently sympathetic with its subject and somewhat distracted in its judgments by what one might call the despair-hysteria of the period. The *Johnson* is quite another affair. It is scrupulous and comprehensive, and it makes use of the insights of modern psychology in a careful and moderate way—in fact, perhaps leans a little too much over backward in the attempt not to press them too far (since Mr. Krutch has been through Boswell's diary, which is scandalous and has been printed only privately, and since he tells us that Boswell was "neurotic" and has evidently a theory about him, we regret that he has not let us know what this theory is). This new book also shows a capacity for steady and independent judgment, as well as a flexible intelligence, in the discussion both of Johnson's work and of the problems of his personality, that constitute a striking advance in Mr. Krutch's development as a critic.

The only serious general objection that can be brought against Mr. Krutch's treatment is that, in one sense, he does not seem especially close to his subject. Johnson was so solid a man, who saw the world in such concrete terms, and the give-and-take of his age was so lively, direct and brusque, that Mr. Krutch's presentation of them seems, by comparison, attenuated and pallid. His book a little bit lacks *impact*. But he compensates us for this and more or less leads us to forget it by the subtlety, lucidity and sureness of the analysis which he has made his method. And his style—though it has nothing in common with the stout-knotted texture of Johnson, the phrases, the sentences, the paragraphs, that one can feel between one's teeth, though it does sometimes run a little to repetition, to an old-fashioned Southern verbosity and the old-fashioned Southern eloquence of such phrases as "a devotee of Bacchus"—his style has become, on the whole, an admirable instrument for this kind of analysis. Except for an occasional balled-up sentence, the book reads easily and carries you rapidly; and, though it isolates to some extent from the immediate background of their period the principal actors of the Johnson legend, it surrounds them with an even luminosity which, though gentle, is always revealing.

The chapters on Johnson's chief works are not, as so often happens with the products of academic research, merely studies of their historical significance, though Mr. Krutch covers this, too, but—except in the case of Johnson's poems, which Mr. Krutch rather underrates—sound critical appreciations. One hopes that they will stimulate the reading of Johnson. The romantics and their successors have created, by exaggerating Johnson's limitations, an unfair prejudice against him as a critic. Actually, *The Lives of the Poets* and the preface and commentary on Shakespeare are among the most brilliant and the most acute documents in the whole range of English criticism, and the products of a mind which, so far from being parochially local and hopelessly cramped by the taste of its age, saw literature in a long perspective and could respond to the humanity of Shakespeare as well as to the wit of Pope.

One feature of Mr. Krutch's biography I feel moved to dwell upon here a little more than it perhaps deserves from its importance in the whole scale of his book.

There is a tendency in the scholarly writing done by professors and composers of theses that sometimes becomes rather exasperating to the reader outside the college world. This tendency may be briefly described as an impulse on the part of the professors to undermine their subjects or explain them away. An expert on Byron, say, will prove, on purely documentary grounds, that there is no reason to believe that Byron ever had anything to do with women; an authority on Whitman will attempt to show that Whitman had no originality, since everything to be found in his work was already to be found in someone else, and will thereby seem to try to create the impression that there is no real merit in Whitman's poetry. To the outsider, this sounds perverse; but, since these scholars are apparently not the men for perversity, he may be baffled for an explanation. In order to understand this peculiar phenomenon, which it seems to me has been growing more formidable, one must understand, first of all, the relation of the professor to his subjects. This relation is, nine times out of ten, a strained and embarrassing one. The professor would be made most uncomfortable if he had to meet Whitman or Byron; he would not like him—he does not, in fact, like him. But he has gone in for studying literature and he must try to do something to advance himself in that field. His demonstration of Byron's chastity or of the nullity of Whitman's achievement may have no relevance whatever to his author, may indeed amount to an effort to annihilate him, but it *does* constitute a tangible evidence of the scholar's assiduous reading, his checking of dates and texts, and his long hours getting something written out. It is also an act of self-assertion which may produce the illusion that a dent has been left in the author, though it may not add anything to our knowledge of him; and it does raise the status of the scholar in the hierarchy of the academic world.

But to the non-academic reader, this, as I say, can only seem rather stupid. Now, there are just a moment or two when Mr. Krutch, who has been teaching at Columbia, gives some evidence of being attainted with this tendency. He creates the impression that he is trying to show, in his discussion of Johnson's early years in London, that since there is no real documentary proof that Johnson ever missed many dinners, there is no genuine reason for believing that he was as poor as he has been thought to have been; and later, in appraising Johnson's two long poems, Mr. Krutch takes the disheartening line of arguing that the first of these fine pieces, *London*, is merely a monument to the bad old habit of stupidly imitating classical models, and the second, *The Vanity of Human Wishes*, mostly a conventional exercise which hardly rises above the level of commonplace eighteenth-century verse. Yet if anything is plain in Johnson's writings and in his attitude toward the destitute and helpless—as Mr. Krutch's own account clearly shows—it is some intimate and scarifying experience of hardship in these undocumented early years. This is one of the elements in the ground-tone, dolorous, steadfast and somber, that gives emotional depth to his work; and one feels it especially in these poems, which owe certain of their most effective passages to Johnson's first-hand acquaintance with all but the last of his melancholy catalogue of the miseries of a writer's life: "Toil, envy, want, the patron and the jail."

Mr. Krutch does not often depress us thus, but it is regrettable that he should do so at all. He has not been a professor for long and he should be wary of the dangers of the academic air. As a critic, he has been trained in the best tradition of contemporary literary journalism; but it may be that not only the symptoms just noted, but also a feeling one gets that Johnson has been presented in a vacuum, with no general implications, should be charged to the habitual blankness of the outlook of academic scholarship. When Mr. Krutch wrote *The Modern Temper*, he had a much more definite point of view as a critic of literature in relation to life and of life in relation to history.

November 18, 1944

LEONID LEONOV:

THE SOPHISTICATION OF A FORMULA

Road to the Ocean is a long novel about Soviet Russia
by a prominent Soviet novelist. It centers around "socialist construction": the operation of a Russian railroad;
but the author, Leonid Leonov, has genuine literary
gifts which do not lend themselves readily to propaganda, and he has tried to do something subtler, more
complex and more humanly plausible than the ordinary
Communist Sunday-school story. Leonov has a novelist's interest in the crude mixed materials of life and a
literary sophistication very rare in Soviet fiction. His
novel, which is extremely intricate, with a great multiplication of characters, involves elements of the land-
owning class dispossessed by the Revolution, of the bourgeois professional class trying to function in the new socialist economy, of the original generation of devoted
and intrepid revolutionists who established the Soviet society and of the younger generation of the Komsomol
who are helping to get it running in the spirit of Boy
and Girl Scouts.

The presentation of all this is quite skillful: the inter-
dependence of the various individuals is gradually
brought out in a dramatic but usually not obvious way.
Episode leads to episode by transitions apparently meaningless: a character who seems unimportant in one chap-

ter will be shown at full length in the next; till, later
a new nexus of relationships which gives the whole picture a new significance is unexpectedly established
either by continuing the story in the present or by exploring its earlier phases in the past. For example, the
discovery by a Communist historian of a set of old papers in a country house makes a number of the characters fall together into a Chekhovian drama of the old
regime and connects them with the original flotation,
seen as a typical capitalist swindle, of that railroad which
is now the arena of the entirely different exploits of
Soviet industrial effort; then the same house, now turned
into a "rest home" for vacationing Soviet workers, is
made to produce a new grouping of characters and exert
a new kind of influence, when the railroad's Politbureau chief goes for a sojourn there. And there are even
long-distance projections into the future of the Soviet
world which, though sometimes a little tedious, are also
handled in a novel way. Through old documents,
through the memories of the characters, we have been
shown the Russian past; what is the world that they are
working for to be? Leonov is much too clever to bore
us with a socialist utopia. He gives us the visions of Kurilov, the veteran Politbureau chief who is the central
figure of the story, and these visions are conditioned by
Kurilov's mood, and thus by his personal situation at the
moment, just as the visions of Tsarist Russia are conditioned by the outlook of the Communist historian who
has found the old papers and is making out a case against
capitalist enterprise, or by the failing and romantic
memories of the survivors of the gentry and the merchant class. Moreover, the efforts of Kurilov to imagine
the world that is coming—the great wars, the displacements of civilization, the navigation of interplanetary
space—are not in the nature of blueprints but merely

imperfect, sometimes comic dreams which provide not so much a prophecy as a picture of our own state of mind when we try to prefigure the future.

What Leonov is attempting to do is, therefore, ambitious and interesting, and he has been able to fill in his project with so much lively observation of life, so much entertaining invention of incident, that he carries us quite through his elaborate book. We are conscious from the beginning that the characters are types, but we do not at first sight take them for the conventional types of Soviet fiction. They do not seem to be doing the regulation things or striking the regulation attitudes: the bourgeois who has buried his past is evidently working in all good faith at his Soviet railroad job; the Komsomol engine crew make a mess of their first difficult run. And the internal life of these people is presented with as much circumstantiality as the external detail of their homes and work, so that the author half creates the illusion that he is on intimate terms with his characters. We give him the benefit of the doubt: we assume that he knows what he is doing and that he has something astonishing and revealing in store. It is not till we come to the end that we are definitely let down by Leonov, but then we are badly let down. The *ci-devant* bourgeois yardmaster, with whom we have been led rather to sympathize, is shown as, after all, incapable of going along with the new society: incurably egoistic and cold, he is doomed to plot a dastardly crime against the noble Communist Kurilov, and he must be publicly denounced by his brother, an upright and hardworking surgeon. The bad actress and bitchy little wife is transfigured by her contact with Kurilov and becomes not merely a worker for socialist construction but also, apparently, an excellent artist. Looking back, we become aware that these people have never been real in the first place and that we have simply been distracted from minding it by the technical agility of the author, his succession of diverting anecdotes and his air of being up to something intelligent.

Leonov himself, we conclude, must be somewhat more intelligent than his book. He is extraordinarily resourceful and adroit in evading dangerous issues—either by simply omitting things from his picture or by treating them in an objective way which enables him to remain noncommittal. *Road to the Ocean* was published in 1936, and the story is supposed to take place somewhere around 1932. The class stratification of the Soviet society and the tyranny of Moscow officialdom through the agencies of the propaganda press and the terror of the G.P.U. were well under way by that time. But Leonov has contrived a story all in terms of old revolutionists, struggling intelligentsia and earnest young Komsomols. And, by unobtrusively causing his characters to say or think certain things, he manages to indicate an attitude which is distinctly humane and liberal. He says, for example, of Kurilov's sister, an austere saint of the heroic generation, that "it did not occur to her to take revenge on an enemy's offspring for the crimes of a whole political system." It is true that a few years in the middle thirties, the period when this book must have been written, saw a relative relaxation, in cultural and political matters, of the rigors of the Kremlin dictatorship. But after the murder of the liberal Kirov, in December, 1934, the aspiration behind this was rapidly stifled. The political terror began, and millions of men and women were shot or sent to prison. People who knew one another well were afraid to comment aloud on anything they read in the paper, because denunciations to the authorities like that of Leonov's villain by his brother had now become the order of the day; and tried party workers like Kurilov and his sister were vanishing overnight into the dungeons of the G.P.U., till there was hardly an old Bolshevik left. It was so far from occurring to the rulers of Russia that one ought not to revenge oneself on the children for the political crimes of the fathers that the children of liquidated officials were left orphaned and without support, to be ostracized at school, avoided by their neighbors and sometimes driven to suicide. The forces that Leonov seems to deprecate, that have produced the distortions of his story itself, were the forces that were to dominate in Russia.

The net effect, therefore, of Leonov's book is a peculiarly depressing one. In reading a book by a Frenchman written under the Nazi oppression—such as the *Imaginary Interviews* of André Gide—we share his humiliation in being reduced to guarded statements and riddles. A Russian novel like *Road to the Ocean* embarrasses us in a similar way. I should not say, on the evidence of this book—though Gorky highly praised Leonov—that the author was a first-rate novelist; but, among Soviet writers, he is talented, he does have some serious idea of what literature ought to be, and it is painful to see him working to produce a real social novel that would stand up with Malraux or Dos Passos, only to have to surrender his project to the requirements of the Soviet formula.

It is curious to compare Leonov, almost an official Soviet writer, with another Russian novelist, Mark Aldanov, a non-fellow-travelling émigré. I do not know whether they have influenced one another or whether they have been influenced separately by some general literary tendency, but they are in some respects surprisingly similar. Both like to make their stories out of episodes in the careers of assorted characters whose orbits compose a larger pattern but who may barely intersect one another's; and both have taken for their principal figures old men bred in Tsarist Russia who have survived into the new society but who are now very close to death. Leonov has the great advantage over the author of *The Fifth Seal* that he himself has lived the new society: his material is all first-hand; whereas a weakness of Aldanov's novel is the vagueness, if not sometimes the blankness, of the Soviet backgrounds of the characters whom he sees so clearly in their context as visitors to Western Europe. Yet Aldanov has the advantage of freedom: he can write what he observes and feels; and if we want to see how important that advantage is, we may consider the two books side by side. To do so is to put to ourselves problems about which it is rather difficult to arrive at any definite conclusions. Is Aldanov "better" than Leonov because he is so much more satisfactory from this point of view—because he can choose his effect and achieve it? Would Leonov have been more like Aldanov, more impartial and independent, if he had written his book abroad? Or is Leonov "better" than Aldanov, both because of his more abundant material and because he has been able to associate himself with a great creative social purpose? Assuming that abilities are equal—something of which one can by no means be sure—I am afraid that it is Aldanov, the exile, who enjoys the more important advantage. The Leninist idealism which was stimulating in the Soviet literature of the twenties, which struck a kind of moral vitality into some even of the relatively crude melodramas of the earlier Soviet stage, is perceptibly flagging in *Road to the Ocean*. We are continually being shown the miracles wrought upon human nature by the magic of the revolutionary morality, but we no longer really feel its virtue. Instead, we feel the Soviet state, present not in its habit as it lives, as the old Tsarist officialdom was in Gogol, but in a much more powerful and damaging way: by the mold into which it has crushed the book.

December 9, 1944

WHO CARES WHO KILLED
ROGER ACKROYD?

THREE MONTHS AGO I wrote an article on some recent detective stories. I had not read any fiction of this kind since the days of Sherlock Holmes, and, since I constantly heard animated discussions of the merits of the mystery writers, I was curious to see what they were like today. The specimens I tried I found disappointing, and I made some rather derogatory remarks in connection with my impressions of the genre in general. To my surprise, this brought me letters of protest in a volume and of a passionate earnestness which had hardly been elicited even by my occasional criticisms of the Soviet Union. Of the thirty-nine letters that have reached me, only seven approve my strictures. The writers of almost all the others seem deeply offended and shocked, and they all say almost exactly the same thing: that I had simply not read the right novels and that I would surely have a different opinion if I would only try this or that author recommended by the correspondent. In many of these letters there was a note of asperity, and one lady went so far as to declare that she would never read my articles again unless I were prepared to reconsider my position. In the meantime, furthermore, a number of other writers have published articles defending the detective story: Jacques Barzun, Joseph Wood Krutch,

Raymond Chandler and Somerset Maugham have all had something to say on the subject—nor has the umbrageous Bernard De Voto failed to raise his voice.

Overwhelmed by so much insistence, I at last wrote my correspondents that I would try to correct any injustice by undertaking to read some of the authors that had received the most recommendations and taking the whole matter up again. The preferences of these readers, however, when I had a tabulation of them made, turned out to be extremely divergent. They ranged over fifty-two writers and sixty-seven books, most of which got only one or two votes each. The only writers who got as many as five or over were Dorothy L. Sayers, Margery Allingham, Ngaio Marsh, Michael Innes, Raymond Chandler and the author who writes under the names of Carter Dickson and John Dickson Carr.

The writer that my correspondents were most nearly unanimous in putting at the top was Miss Dorothy L. Sayers, who was pressed upon me by eighteen people, and the book of hers that eight of them were sure I could not fail to enjoy was a story called *The Nine Tailors*. Well, I set out to read *The Nine Tailors* in the hope of tasting some novel excitement, and I declare that it seems to me one of the dullest books I have ever encountered in any field. The first part of it is all about bell-ringing as it is practised in English churches and contains a lot of information of the kind that you might expect to find in an encyclopedia article on campanology. I skipped a good deal of this, and found myself skipping, also, a large section of the conversations between conventional English village characters: "Oh, here's Hinkins with the aspidistras. People may say what they like about aspidistras, but they do go on all the year round and make a background," etc. There was also a dreadful stock English nobleman of the casual and debonair kind, with the embarrassing name of Lord Peter Wimsey, and, although he was the focal character in the novel, being Miss Dorothy Sayers's version of the inevitable Sherlock Holmes detective, I had to skip a good deal of him, too. In the meantime, I was losing the story, which had not got a firm grip on my attention, but I went back and picked it up and steadfastly pushed through to the end, and there I discovered that the whole point was that if a man was shut up in a belfry while a heavy peal of chimes was being rung, the vibrations of the bells might kill him. Not a bad idea for a murder, and Conan Doyle would have known how to dramatize it in an entertaining tale of thirty pages, but Miss Sayers had not hesitated to pad it out to a book of three hundred and thirty, contriving one of those hackneyed cock-and-bull stories about a woman who commits bigamy without knowing it, and larding the whole thing with details of church architecture, bits of quaint lore from books about bell-ringing and the awful whimsical patter of Lord Peter.

I had often heard people say that Dorothy Sayers wrote well, and I felt that my correspondents had been playing her as their literary ace. But, really, she does not write very well: it is simply that she is more consciously literary than most of the other detective-story writers and that she thus attracts attention in a field which is mostly on a sub-literary level. In any serious department of fiction, her writing would not appear to have any distinction at all. Yet, commonplace in this respect though she is, she gives an impression of brilliant talent if we put her beside Miss Ngaio Marsh, whose *Overture to Death* was also suggested by several correspondents. Mr. De Voto has put himself on record as believing that Miss Marsh, as well as Miss Sayers and Miss Allingham, writes her novels in "excellent prose," and this throws for me a good deal of light on Mr. De Voto's opinions as a critic. I hadn't quite realized before, though I had noted his own rather messy style, to what degree he was insensitive to writing. I do not see how it is possible for anyone with a feeling for words to describe the unappetizing sawdust which Miss Marsh has poured into her pages as "excellent prose" or as prose at all except in the sense that distinguishes prose from verse. And here again the book is mostly padding. There is the notion that you could commit a murder by rigging up a gun in a piano in such a way that the victim will shoot himself when he presses down the pedal, but this is embedded in the dialogue and doings of a lot of faked-up English county people who are even more tedious than those of *The Nine Tailors*.

The enthusiastic reader of detective stories will indignantly object at this point that I am reading for the wrong things: that I ought not to be expecting good writing, characterization, human interest or even atmosphere. He is right, of course, though I was not fully aware of it till I attempted *Flowers for the Judge*, considered by connoisseurs one of the best books of one of the masters of this school, Miss Margery Allingham. This tale I found completely unreadable. The story and the writing both showed a surface so wooden and dead that I could not keep my mind on the page. How can you care who committed a murder which has never really been made to take place, because the writer hasn't any ability of even the most ordinary kind to persuade you to see it or feel it? How can you probe the possibilities of guilt among characters who all seem alike, because they are all simply names on the page? It was then that I understood that a true connoisseur of this fiction must be able to suspend the demands of his imagination and literary taste and take the thing as an intellectual problem. But how you arrive at that state of mind is what I do not understand.

In the light of this revelation, I feel that it is probably irrelevant to mention that I enjoyed *The Burning Court,* by John Dickson Carr, more than the novels of any of these ladies. There is a tinge of black magic that gives it a little of the interest of a horror story, and the author has a virtuosity at playing with alternative hypotheses that makes this trick of detective fiction more amusing than it usually is.

I want, however, to take up certain points made by the writers of the above-mentioned articles.

Mr. Barzun informs the non-expert that the detective novel is a kind of game in which the reader of a given story, in order to play properly his hand, should be familiar with all the devices that have already been used in other stories. These devices, it seems, are now barred: the reader must challenge the writer to solve his problem in some novel way, and the writer puts it up to the reader to guess the new solution. This may be true, but I shall never qualify. I would rather play Twenty Questions, which at least does not involve the consumption of hundreds of ill-written books.

A point made by three of these writers, Mr. Maugham, Mr. De Voto and Mr. Krutch, is that the novel has become so philosophical, so psychological and so symbolic that the public have had to take to the detective story as the only department of fiction where pure story-telling survives.

This seems to me to involve two fallacies. On the one hand, it is surely not true that "the serious novelists of today"—to quote Mr. Maugham's assertion—"have often," in contrast to the novelists of the past, "little or no story to tell," that "they have allowed themselves to be persuaded that to tell a story is a negligible form of art." It is true, of course, that Joyce and Proust—who, I suppose, must be accounted the heaviest going—have their various modern ways of boring and playing tricks on the reader. But how about the dreadful bogs and obstacles that one has to get over in Scott? the interpolated essays in Hugo? the leaking tap of Thackeray's reflections on life, in which the story is always trickling away? Is there anything in first-rate modern fiction quite so gratuitous as these *longueurs*? Even Proust and Joyce and Virginia Woolf do certainly have stories to tell, and they have organized their books with an intensity which has been relatively rare in the novel and which, to my mind, more than makes up for the occasional viscosity of their narrative.

On the other hand, it seems to me—for reasons suggested above—a fantastic misrepresentation to say that the average detective novel is an example of good storytelling. The gift for telling stories is uncommon, like other artistic gifts, and the only one of this group of writers—the writers my correspondents have praised—who seems to me to possess it to any degree is Mr. Raymond Chandler. His *Farewell, My Lovely* is the only one of these books that I have read all of and read with enjoyment. But Chandler, though in his recent article he seems to claim Hammett as his master, does not really belong to this school of the old-fashioned detective novel. What he writes is a novel of adventure which has less in common with Hammett than with Alfred Hitchcock and Graham Greene—the modern spy story which has substituted the jitters of the Gestapo and the G.P.U. for the luxury world of E. Phillips Oppenheim. It is not simply a question here of a puzzle which has been put together but of a malaise conveyed to the reader, the horror of a hidden conspiracy that is continually turning up in the most varied and unlikely forms. To write such a novel successfully you must be able to invent character and incident and to generate atmosphere, and all this Mr. Chandler can do, though he is a long way below Graham Greene. It was only when I got to the end that I felt my old crime-story depression descending upon me again—because here again, as is so often the case, the explanation of the mysteries, when it comes, is neither interesting nor plausible enough. It fails to justify the excitement produced by the elaborate build-up of picturesque and sinister happenings, and one cannot help feeling cheated.

My experience with this second batch of novels has, therefore, been even more disillusioning than my experience with the first, and my final conclusion is that the reading of detective stories is simply a kind of vice that, for silliness and minor harmfulness, ranks somewhere between smoking and crossword puzzles. This conclusion seems borne out by the violence of the letters I have been receiving. Detective-story readers feel guilty, they are habitually on the defensive, and all their talk about "well-written" mysteries is simply an excuse for their vice, like the reasons that the alcoholic can always produce for a drink. One of the letters I have had shows the addict in his frankest and most shameless phase. This lady begins by pretending, like the others, to guide me in my choice, but she breaks down and tells the whole dreadful truth. Though she has read, she says, hundreds of detective stories, "it is surprising," she finally confesses, "how few I would recommend to another. However, a poor detective story is better than none at all. Try again. With a little better luck, you'll find one you admire and enjoy. Then you, too, may be

A MYSTERY FIEND."

This letter has made my blood run cold: so the opium smoker tells the novice not to mind if the first pipe makes him sick; and I fall back for reassurance on the valiant little band of my readers who sympathize with my views on the subject. One of these tells me that I have underestimated both the badness of detective stories themselves and the lax mental habits of those who enjoy them. The worst of it is, he says, that the true addict, half the time, never even finds out who has committed the murder. The addict reads not to find anything out but merely to get the mild stimulation of the succession of unexpected incidents and of the suspense itself of *looking forward* to learning a sensational secret. That this secret is nothing at all and does not really account for the incidents does not matter to such a reader. He has learned from his long indulgence how to connive with the author in the swindle: he does not pay any real attention when the disappointing dénouement occurs, he does not think back and check the events, he simply shuts the book and starts another.

To detective-story addicts, then, I say: Please do not write me any more letters telling me that I have not read the right books. And to the seven correspondents who are with me and who in some cases have thanked me for helping them to liberate themselves from a habit which they recognized as wasteful of time and degrading to the intellect but into which they had been bullied by convention and the portentously invoked examples of Woodrow Wilson and André Gide—to these staunch and pure spirits I say: Friends, we represent a minority, but Literature is on our side. With so many fine books to be read, so much to be studied and known, there is no need to bore ourselves with this rubbish. And with the paper shortage pressing on all publication and many first-rate writers forced out of print, we shall do well to discourage the squandering of this paper that might be put to better use.

January 20, 1945

"MR. HOLMES, THEY WERE THE
FOOTPRINTS OF A GIGANTIC HOUND!"

My ARTICLE of four weeks ago on detective stories has
called forth a burst of correspondence even more over-
whelming than that provoked by my earlier piece—well
over a hundred letters. But in this case the people who
write me mostly agree with my adverse attitude. Among
the few letters from those who do not, some, however,
are excessively bitter. One lady adds a postscript in
which she declares that she has never liked men named
Edmund, and another asks me jeeringly how much I
have been paid by "the non-detective fiction publishers."
The furious reaction of these readers confirms me in my
conclusion that detective stories are actually a habit-form-
ing drug for which its addicts will fight like tigers—an
opinion that is explicitly corroborated by many of the
approving letters. The evangelical note at the end of
my piece was intended to have a burlesque flavor, but
some of my correspondents seem to have taken it more
seriously than it was meant, and write to tell me that,
though they have long been addicts, they have made a
vow, since reading my article, never to touch another
detective story. An old friend, a classical scholar and ar-
cheologist, has rather horrified me by writing to confess
that he, too, has been a victim of this form of narcotic

and that he had already had the intention of doing for
it in literature what De Quincey has done for opium-eat-
ing.

I will now confess, in my turn, that, since my first
looking into this subject last fall, I have myself become
addicted, in spells, to reading myself to sleep with Sherlock Holmes, which I had gone back to, not having
looked at it since childhood, in order to see how it compared with Conan Doyle's latest imitators. I propose,
however, to justify my pleasure in rereading Sherlock
Holmes on grounds entirely different from those on
which the consumers of the current product ordinarily
defend their taste. My contention is that Sherlock
Holmes *is* literature on a humble but not ignoble level,
whereas the mystery writers most in vogue now are not.
The old stories are literature, not because of the conjuring tricks and the puzzles, not because of the lively melodrama, which they have in common with many other
detective stories, but by virtue of imagination and style.
These are fairy-tales, as Conan Doyle intimated in his
preface to his last collection, and they are among the
most amusing of fairy-tales and not among the least distinguished.

The Sherlock Holmes stories, almost as much as the
Alice books or as Edward Lear's nonsense, were the casual products of a life the main purpose of which was
something else, but creations that in some sense got detached from their author and flew away and had a life
of their own. Conan Doyle, it seems, worked conscientiously to document his historical romances, which he
considered his serious work, but he regarded Holmes
and Watson as the paper dolls of rather ridiculous and
undignified potboilers, and he paid so little attention to
what he wrote about them that the stories are full of inconsistencies, which Doyle never bothered to cor-

rect. He forgot Watson's Christian name and later on gave him a new one; he shifted the location of his wound; he began by making an ignorance of literature an essential trait of Holmes's personality and then had him talk about Petrarch and Meredith; and he even, on one occasion, changed the season abruptly from July to September. (It is an odd evidence of Holmes's vitality that some of his admirers should have gone to the trouble of attempting to account for these discrepancies, as if Watson and Holmes had been real men, and that they should actually have published their conjectures in a volume called *Profile by Gaslight.*) Doyle had become so impatient with his hero by the end of the second series in the *Strand Magazine* that he got rid of him by killing him off, totally without preparation, in a manner that was little short of frivolous. But Sherlock Holmes was like a genie let out of a bottle; there was no way of getting him back and, once at large, he was always available to minister to his master's wants. Doyle eventually brought Holmes back to life and wrote five more volumes about him. For perhaps the only time in his life, he had hit upon a genuine spell.

Whence had he mustered this spell and what elements had been mixed to make it? Well, there was Poe, of course, and there was also unquestionably R. L. Stevenson's *New Arabian Nights. The Adventure of the Hansom Cab* and *The Adventure of the Superfluous Mansion* must have suggested both the Sherlock Holmes titles and the formula of taking people to unexpected places and having them witness mysterious happenings. But Doyle, though much less "literary" than Stevenson, somehow got solider results, which depended on quite different qualities from Stevenson's suave Oriental tone and the limpid iridescence of his fantasy. For one thing, Stevenson was weak on character, whereas Doyle had produced two real personalities. And, for another, Conan Doyle had created his own vein of fantasy, which was vivider, if rather less fine, than Stevenson's. You see the force of his imagination exemplified in a curious way in some of those stories in which the dénouement is inadequate or disappointing. A young woman goes to work in a country house where she will be extravagantly overpaid if she will consent to have her hair cut short, to wear a dress of electric blue, to sit in certain places at certain times and to allow herself to be made to laugh uproariously at a succession of funny stories told by the master of the house; a professional interpreter of Greek finds himself suddenly shanghaied in a cab and taken to a stuffy London house with velvet furniture, a high white marble mantelpiece and a suit of Japanese armor, where a man who wears glasses and has a giggling laugh compels him to put questions in Greek to a pale and emaciated captive, whose face is all crisscrossed with sticking plaster. Neither of these stories—*The Copper Beeches* or *The Greek Interpreter*—quite lives up to its opening evocation. The way of accounting for the sticking plaster seems, indeed, entirely unsatisfactory, and since Watson tells us that this "singular case" is "still involved in some mystery," we are almost inclined to suspect that the affair concealed something else which the detective had failed to penetrate; but the images have exercised their power—a power that is partly due to their contrast with, their startling emergence from, the dull surface of Victorian London.

Here Doyle is exploiting a device quite remote from the suave story-spinning of Stevenson: he is working in the familiar tradition—in which the English art of fiction has excelled since the days of *Robinson Crusoe*—of the commonplace and common-sense narrative which arouses excitement and wonder. He can make us feel

the presence of the "sinister"—to use one of his favorite
words—even in a situation which does not include any
fantastic ingredient. Take the story of *The Naval
Treaty*, which follows *The Greek Interpreter* in Doyle's
carefully varied program. A young man in the Foreign
Office has been entrusted with an important document,
which he has been copying at night in his office. He is
alone and there is no entrance to the room save by a cor-
ridor that leads to the street. No one except the Foreign
Minister knows that he has the treaty. At last he rings for
the doorman to bring him some coffee, but an unknown
woman answers the bell, large and coarse-faced and
wearing an apron. She says that she is the doorman's wife
and promises to send the coffee, but some time passes and
the coffee does not come, and he goes downstairs to see
what is the matter. He finds the doorman asleep, but the
man is immediately awakened by a bell that rings loudly
overhead.

" 'I was boiling the kettle when I fell asleep, sir.' He
looked at me and then up at the still quivering bell with
an ever-growing astonishment upon his face.
" 'If you was here, sir, then who rang the bell?' he
asked.
" 'The bell!' I cried. 'What bell is it?'
" 'It's the bell of the room you were working in.' "

Both these incidents, so soberly told, the appearance
of the woman and the ringing of the bell, give us shocks
that reverberate. Of course there is no one upstairs in the
room and the naval treaty has been taken.

The stories have also both form and style of a kind
very much superior to what one finds in our padded
novels, though sometimes, it seems to me, the requirements of length for short stories in the *Strand Magazine*
compelled Doyle somewhat to skimp his endings. There

is wit, not mere tricks, in the "deductions" of Holmes and wit in the dialogue, and not only in the interchanges between Watson and Holmes but even in some of the stagy lines which Doyle's very sure sense of point save from being merely absurd. Take for example, the conclusion of *The Second Stain*:

"'Come, sir,' said he. 'There is more in this than meets the eye. How came the letter back in the box?'

"Holmes turned away smiling from the keen scrutiny of those wonderful eyes.

"'We also have our diplomatic secrets,' said he and, picking up his hat, he turned to the door."

The writing, of course, is full of clichés, but these clichés are dealt out with a ring which gives them a kind of value, while the author makes speed and saves space so effectively that we are rarely in danger of getting bogged down in anything boring. And the clichés of situation and character are somehow made to function, too, for the success of the general effect. This effect owes its real originality not only to the queer collocations of elements, such as those I have mentioned above, but also to the admirable settings: the somber overcarpeted interiors or the musty empty houses of London, the remote old or new country places, always with shrubbery along the drives; and the characters—the choleric big-game hunters and the high-spirited noble ladies—have been imbued with the atmosphere of the settings and charged with an energy sufficient—like the fierce puppets of a Punch-and-Judy show—to make an impression in their simple roles.

But over the whole epic there hangs an air of irresponsible comedy, like that of some father's rigmarole for children, like that of, say, Albert Bigelow Paine in his stories about the Coon, the Possum and the Old Black

Crow who all lived together in a Hollow Tree. The story-teller can make anything happen that will entertain his nightly audience and that will admit some kind of break at bedtime. The invention of Professor Moriarty, that scientific master-mind of crime who was to checkmate the great scientific detective, is simply an improvisation to bring to an end an overlong story, and the duel in which each is straining to outthink and outtrick the other is exhilarating because totally impossible. I do not share the prejudice of some Holmes experts against the two latest series of stories. Inferior though these often are in plot, Doyle amuses himself here in a way which makes them extremely funny. I am delighted by *The Adventure of the Dying Detective*, in which Holmes feigns a tropical disease and refuses to let Watson treat him: "Facts are facts, Watson, and after all, you are only a general practitioner with very limited experience and mediocre qualifications. It is painful to have to say these things, but you leave me no choice." "I was bitterly hurt," says Watson. And it was a capital idea to have Watson himself sometimes undertake the inquiry and bungle it, or, conversely, in other cases, to have Holmes tell the stories instead of Watson, in an attempt to divest them of the fortuitous glamor which he insists that his friend has added. (I have discovered, by the way—though I see that it had already been hinted by Christopher Morley—that Rex Stout's great detective, Nero Wolfe, has the look of having been inspired by one of the most diverting of Doyle's variations: Sherlock's brother Mycroft, who is also a master-mind but who has grown so stout and inert that he is unable to work on a problem till all the data have been dug out and brought him.)

And it all takes place in the Hollow Tree—in that

atmosphere of "cozy peril," to quote a phrase from, I think, Mr. Morley, who, in his prefaces to the Sherlock Holmes omnibus and an anthology called *Sherlock Holmes and Dr. Watson,* has written so well on this subject. They will, of course, get safely back to Baker Street, after their vigils and raids and arrests, to discuss the case comfortably in their rooms and have their landlady bring them breakfast the next morning. Law and Order have not tottered a moment; the British police are well in control: they are the stoutest, most faithful fellows in the world if they can only be properly directed by Intellect in the form of a romantic personality possessed by the scientific spirit. All the loose ends of every episode are tidily picked up and tucked in, and even Holmes, though once addicted to cocaine, has been reformed by the excellent Watson. In this world, one can count on the client to arrive at the very moment when his case has just been explained, and Holmes and Watson always find it possible to get anywhere they want to go without a moment's delay or confusion. Here is an incident from *The Greek Interpreter* which illustrates this unfailing punctuality. The interpreter, after his visit to the mysterious house, has been driven away and dropped.

"The carriage which had brought me was already out of sight. I stood gazing round and wondering where on earth I might be, when I saw someone coming towards me in the darkness. As he came up to me I made out that he was a railway porter.

" 'Can you tell me what place this is?' I asked.

" 'Wandsworth Common,' said he.

" 'Can I get a train into town?'

" 'If you walk on a mile or so to Clapham Junction,' said he, 'you'll just be in time for the last to Victoria.' "

So, no matter what those queer Greeks do in London, there will always be a British porter and he will always help you to get your train. In the newer kind of mystery novel, this porter would not have been a real porter; he would have had some unintelligible connection with the men in the upholstered house, and, far from helping the poor interpreter to catch the train, he would have involved him in endless further trouble—just as the man who wanted a young woman in an electric blue dress to cut her hair and laugh at his jokes would have turned out to be suffering from some form of derangement suggested by Krafft-Ebing or Freud. One rarely finds the word "sinister" even in mystery fiction today; it implies that a spy or a murder, a piece of treachery or an insane neurosis, is something of exceptional occurrence.

February 17, 1945

GLENWAY WESCOTT'S WAR WORK

THE HANDWRITING of Glenway Wescott is unusual and rather arresting. It looks somewhat like the elegant and rigorous script that one finds cut on the copper of sundials of the seventeenth and eighteenth centuries: the same clarity, the same heavy shadings, the same inflexibly maintained slant. It always seems to have been engraved in metal rather than merely written on paper. There is in it a certain element of boyishness—big round capitals and rounded "m"s and "n"s—but it is always a copybook boyishness, inseparable from a self-imposed discipline.

Mr. Wescott's style makes a similar impression. One is struck by the firm vigor and the craftman's precision with which the short phrases are cut. Here is a personal and handmade product, the achievement of an individual skill. It, too, may have begun with a copybook, with exercises on classical models, but it is hard to put one's finger on these models. Terse and sharp though the language is as English, the form may be based on French. In any case, this style is as far from the colloquialism of Hemingway as from the literary clichés of Louis Bromfield. When one starts reading anything by Wescott, one always feels a satisfaction which comes as something unexpected.

His new novel, *Apartment in Athens,* has these qualities of style at their best, and, as a work of imagination, it is a longer and better sustained performance than the book just before it, *The Pilgrim Hawk.* It is the story of a Greek middle-class family upon whom a German officer is quartered, and it suggests an obvious comparison with that widely known and overrated story *Le Silence de la Mer* by Vercors, which deals with a similar situation in France. But it constitutes a curious proof of the superior advantage of possessing imagination to that of being on the spot that Wescott, who has never been in Greece and has seen nothing of occupied Europe, should give us an effect of reality so much more convincing than that produced by a patriotic Frenchman who knows the German occupation at first hand. Two-thirds, at least, of Mr. Wescott's novel compels us to share, in a way that is at once fascinating and painful, the constrained and suffocated life of a little city apartment in the first months after the Greek defeat. The cramped physical and moral conditions, the readjustments in the relationships of the family, the whole distortion of the social organism by the unassimilable presence of the foreigner—all this is most successfully created. I did have the impression—though without knowing much about either Germans or Greeks—that the Greeks have been allowed to become perhaps a little too servile toward the Germans and that the German, in view of what has gone before, has been made to behave, at the end, a little too basely toward the Greeks. Yet the author—up, at least, to this final turn—makes us accept what he tells us as true, and I have not read any other book—either of fiction or of direct documentation—that has given me the feeling of starving and stifling, of falling back on interior positions, constructing interior defenses, reorganizing and redirecting, behind a mask of submission, the whole structure and aim of one's life, as *Apartment in Athens* does.

It is only at the end of the book that we find the illusion failing. This is a common fault in Wescott's fiction. The incisive beginnings are sometimes betrayed by a tendency to blur at the close; the sure hand, with its deliberate strokes, seems to falter when it comes to the point of drawing the action to a head and driving the meaning home. In the case of *Apartment in Athens*, the line for the story to follow would seem to be clear enough, yet the incidents cease to be vivid, and the psychological atmosphere is violated by the intrusion of a passage of propaganda which throws the whole story out. The Greek father, sent to jail by the Nazi, smuggles out to his wife a long letter, in which he not only preaches resistance to Germany but also urges that his brother-in-law in the underground shall immediately betake himself to the United States and devote himself to a rather vague project of soliciting support for the Greeks—and this in spite of the fact that the prisoner knows little about America and little about what his brother-in-law is doing at home. He states his message to the Americans as follows: "It is important for them to be told what we have learned from the German rule and misrule. I want Petros to tell them. For if we all continue to take our cue in world politics from the Germans as we have done—in reckless appreciation of them when they are on their good behavior, only fighting when they choose to fight, and pitying them whenever they ask for pity— sooner or later they will get what they want: a world at their mercy."

Glenway Wescott has called this book his "war work," but I don't think that ought to let him out of a strict accountability to ideals which he himself has certainly tried to serve. After all, *Apartment in Athens* is the most ambitious piece of fiction that he has published in many years, and we expect of it some revelation of deeper insight and longer range than the mere admonition that the Germans should be restrained from making any more wars. Opposition to the encroachments of the Nazis is now part of the daily business of life, like keeping the house warm and wearing a coat, in order to escape pneumonia; we do not need Glenway Wescott to remind us. But we do need the Glenway Wescotts to tell us what is going on inside ourselves and the Nazis. Through the greater part of this book, Mr. Wescott *is* trying to tell us, and though the story itself carries us on with a skillfully created suspense, it is the explanation of human relations that holds our serious interest. Yet the author does seem rather to drop, or at least to relax, this effort when he consigns his Greek citizen to jail, where we no longer share his intimate life, and sets him to editorializing.

In general, it has been disappointing to find so many writers of serious talent turning away from the study of human behavior to reassure themselves and their readers by invoking some immediate political program or reviving some obsolete religion. Glenway Wescott, like Kay Boyle in *Avalanche*—though the two books have nothing else in common—has, as it were, passed on to characters who disappear in the European underground, problems which he ought to be tackling right out in the open of the United States. The result of this propagandizing is simply to land the writer in melodrama: Wescott not so abjectly as Miss Boyle, but still with some slight loss of caste. It is too easy an evasion of the difficulties of the present situation of man to try to meet them with the symbols of a mythology—whether religious or patriotic. For a writer to pretend today that it is enough for the reader to know that the Germans must be defeated is as much to stake one's art on a childish faith —in a sense, in the very myth which the Nazis themselves have created—as to pretend, as other writers are doing, that it is enough for a writer to believe in the civilizing role of the United States or in the triumph—or, for that matter, in the curbing, if that is regarded as an ultimate goal—of the power of Soviet Russia.

March 3, 1945

A CRY FROM THE UNQUIET GRAVE

CYRIL CONNOLLY founded in 1939 the English literary monthly *Horizon*, and has been publishing it ever since. *Horizon* has been a fine magazine and Mr. Connolly an exceptional editor. It seemed to me a proof of his merit, when I was in London at the end of the war, that, in the literary and Left political worlds, almost everybody complained about him and it, but that everybody, at the same time, seemed in some degree dependent on them. The danger of such magazines is that they are likely to fall into the hands of a group and reflect its limitations and smugness, or that they try, without exercising taste, systematically to proceed on some policy in the interests of which they feel obliged to print mediocre or boring stuff. Mr. Connolly appears to have published only things that he himself has found interesting, and to have been constrained as little as possible by preconceptions—the worst handicaps for a magazine—of what *Horizon's* clientele would like to read. He would print papers on Benjamin Constant or the minor French romantics which irritated both the Left and the people who thought that it was immoral to disregard the war, and he brought out, in several installments, an orthodox Communist tract which annoyed both the littérateurs and the more emancipated Leftists. He published some of the best reporting—of an unofficial and personal

kind—that was written about the war, and he elicited
from Augustus John his delightful discursive memoirs,
in which history is unimportant and chronology does
not exist. One feature, I imagine, pleased nobody: a
goose-flesh-producing document called *Naughty Mans*,
in which a father reported in baby-talk the reactions of
his son to the war, between the ages of three and five.

Mr. Connolly also showed his special gifts in thinking up some really happy ideas for series to be written to
order. There is in general, for a literary man, nothing
more disheartening in the world than an editor's idea
for a series, but Mr. Connolly has got up some good ones,
such as the articles on *Where Shall John Go?*, in which
people who know various countries intimately have been
sending in informal reports on what it is like to live in
them. It is characteristic of Mr. Connolly that he
will not admit to this series any article that praises a country too lavishly. *Horizon*, in its political outlook, has stood
against the current in Europe by being quietly anti-
nationalistic, and it has tried, in the cultural field, to re-
establish the wrecked communications between different
parts of the world.

Though *Horizon*, to the occasional reader, may have
appeared rather relaxed and casual, you came to feel, if
you followed it month by month, that the magazine
must have behind it a personality of some courage and
distinction. In Mr. Connolly's new book, *The Unquiet
Grave*, that personality reveals itself. This book is a
sort of journal, kept through the years of the war—a
collection of what the French call *pensées*, that invokes
and to some extent imitates Pascal, La Rochefoucauld
and Chamfort. But the writer has made a form of his
own. There are themes that weave in and out in a fashion rather symphonic than aphoristic: the memories of

a love affair, alternately nostalgic and aggrieved; the fluctuation between a physical well-being that seems always to involve self-indulgence and a reviving moral sense that tends to stick in emotions of remorse; a yearning for the oblivion of drugs that is corrected by a seeking for strength in the work of the great artists and moralists; a disaffected attitude toward the war which lets him in for a feeling of guilt, and a sympathy with revolutionary forces which does not prevent him from dreading the advent of the coöperative state; a disgust with the contemporary world and a searching for the causes of its destructiveness. All this is attached, more or less, to the figure of Palinurus, the helmsman of the *Æneid*, who, succumbing to sleep and soft dreams, falls overboard holding the tiller, and who sustains himself for three days on a fragment of floating timber, but, reaching shore, is done to death by the natives. Mr. Connolly has his own version of the Palinurus story. The helmsman of the Trojans, he suggests, may have gone overboard on purpose, in disgust with the callousness of Æneas, for whom Dido has just killed herself, and discouragement with the expedition, which he has come to believe is doomed. It requires, he thinks, some explaining that Palinurus should have carried away, with the tiller, a part of the stern of the ship, which he was able to use as a raft. Virgil's helmsman, Mr. Connolly concludes, is "surely . . . a typical example of antisocial hysteroid resentment!" He signs his book "Palinurus."

This small volume—a scant hundred and fifty pages—is one of the books that has interested me most, as it is certainly one of the best written, that have come out of wartime England. They make no attempt, these pages, to impress by drama or message, and they are the better for being unpretentious. They keep free of all the wartime falsities, and, in rendering a candid account of the experience of one worried and dissatisfied man, they touch ailing layers of consciousness that are common to us all but which we have usually avoided discussing. In form, the little essays and epigrams by which the insights of the aphorist are conveyed are concentrated, exact and lucid (it is only when he is groping among general ideas that the thinking, not the style, becomes sometimes unclear). The passages that deal with memories of Paris and the Riviera are delicious and crisp, like good food to the taste, fresh and bright, like new sights to the eye; and there are descriptions of ferrets and lemurs, quinces and cantaloupes, that express in a novel way the affinities between human beings and the animal and vegetable kingdoms. The truth is, perhaps, that the unquiet grave has been but a kind of bomb-shelter which is giving up a still-living man.

One used to hear it said in London that Cyril Connolly was out of key with the wartime state of mind, but I think that we ought to be grateful that one editor has resisted all pressures and followed his own tastes, and that one good writer has persisted in producing, not what patriotism demanded, but a true natural history of his wartime morale.

October 27, 1945

Cyril Connolly's *The Condemned Playground* is a collection of essays, commentaries, burlesques and travel sketches. It is not so remarkable as *The Unquiet Grave*, but it makes extremely good reading. In matters of literature, Mr. Connolly is not quite a first-rate critic—his disparagement, for example, of A. E. Housman seems to me mistaken from beginning to end—but he is often more to the point than the heavier writers on literary subjects, who set out, with a vocabulary of jargon, to analyze them sociologically, aesthetically or philosophically. He has a genuine classical taste, he is not often influenced by fads, and he reads, and writes about what he reads, because he finds it an agreeable pastime. Literature is for him not a pretext for an impressive article but a strong appetite which he cannot help indulging and which he likes to discuss with others.

This one already knew if one had been reading Mr. Connolly in *Horizon*, but the burlesques in *The Condemned Playground* have come to me as a surprise. These imaginary memoirs and parodies are in a vein distinct from anyone else's, and some of them are really terrific. Mr. Connolly will invent a character—a Communist pansy, an arch young girl, the hero of an Aldous Huxley novel or a self-immolating member of a future totalitarian state—and allow it to possess him like a demon, carrying him away to lengths that are hilarious and a little hysterical. It reminds one of a passage in his early book of memoirs, *Enemies of Promise*, in which he tells of amusing his school-friends with feats of impersonation that would become more and more madly funny but end with his bursting into tears.

I was so much pleased by these burlesques, which seemed to show something like comic genius, that I looked up Mr. Connolly's one novel, *The Rock Pool*, which was published by Scribner's in 1936. Here one finds much the same sort of thing. A mediocre and snobbish young man from Oxford, with a comfortable regular income, spends a summer on the Riviera in an artists' and writers' colony. His first attitude is curious but patronizing: he tells himself that he has come as an observer and will study the community like a rock pool. But the denizens of the pool drag him down into it, demoralize him, plunder him and swindle him, until he finds himself, at last, with no money, left behind with the more abject derelicts who remain in the place through the winter, and in process of becoming one himself. This story, which owes something to *South Wind* and to Compton Mackenzie's novels of Capri, differs from them through its acceleration, which, as in the wildly speeded-up burlesques, has something demoniacal about it. *The Rock Pool* is not quite a success. It starts out as if it were meant for a straight novel and then sacrifices our sympathy for the hero by making his downfall so rapid and so complete that it can move us only to horrified laughter. Yet it convinces us that Cyril Connolly has a talent for the tragi-comic that ought to be given some fuller expression.

July 13, 1946

Both *Enemies of Promise* and *The Rock Pool* have been reprinted since this was written; but people still complain about Connolly. He is one of those writers who, though not aggressive, inspire moral indignation. Some feel that he has done too little and done that little too easily to deserve the prestige he enjoys—that one oughtn't to take seriously nowadays any writer so sybaritic as Connolly has confessed himself to be. It is no use being angry with Connolly. Whatever his faults may be —he has himself described them more brilliantly than anyone else is likely to do—he is one of those fortunate Irishmen, like Goldsmith and Sterne and Wilde, who are born with a gift of style, a natural grace and wit, so that their jobs have the freshness of *jeux d'esprit,* and sometimes their *jeux d'esprit* turn out to stick as classics.

TALES OF THE MARVELLOUS AND
THE RIDICULOUS

WHEN, a year and a half ago, I wrote a general article about horror stories, I was reproached by several correspondents for not having mentioned the work of H. P. Lovecraft. I had read some of Lovecraft's stories and had not cared much for them; but the books by and about him have been multiplying so and the enthusiasm of his admirers has been becoming so insistent that I have felt I ought to look into the subject more seriously. There have appeared, mostly in 1945, a collection of his *Best Supernatural Stories*; an unfinished novel, *The Lurker at the Threshold*, completed by August Derleth; a volume of his miscellaneous writings, with appreciations by various writers: *Marginalia*; an essay by him on *Supernatural Horror in Literature*; and *H. P. L. : A Memoir*, by August Derleth. Lovecraft, since his death in 1937, has rapidly been becoming a cult. He had already his circle of disciples who collaborated with him and imitated him, and the Arkham House (in Sauk Center, Wisconsin), which has published *Marginalia* and *The Lurker at the Threshold*, is named from the imaginary New England town that makes the scene of many of his stories. It seems to be exclusively devoted to the productions of Lovecraft and the Lovecraftians. A volume of his letters has been announced.

I regret that, after examining these books, I am no more enthusiastic than before. The principal feature of Lovecraft's work is an elaborate concocted myth which provides the supernatural element for his most admired stories. This myth assumes a race of outlandish gods and grotesque prehistoric peoples who are always playing tricks with time and space and breaking through into the contemporary world, usually somewhere in Massachusetts. One of these astonishing peoples, which flourished in the Triassic Age, a hundred and fifty million years ago, consisted of beings ten feet tall and shaped like giant cones. They were scaly and iridescent, and their blood was a deep green in color. The base of the cone was a viscous foot on which the creatures slid along like snails (they had no stairs in their cities and houses but only inclined planes), and at the apex grew four flexible members, one provided with a head that had three eyes and eight greenish antennae, one with four trumpetlike proboscises, through which they sucked up liquid nourishment, and two with enormous nippers. They were prodigiously inventive and learned, the most accomplished race that the earth has bred. They propagated, like mushrooms, by spores, which they developed in large shallow tanks. Their lifespan was four or five thousand years. Now, when the horror to the shuddering revelation of which a long and prolix story has been building up turns out to be something like this, you may laugh or you may be disgusted, but you are not likely to be terrified—though I confess, as a tribute to such power as H. P. Lovecraft possesses, that he at least, at this point in his series, in regard to the omniscient conical snails, induced me to suspend disbelief. It was the race from another planet which finally took their place, and which Lovecraft evidently relied on as creations of irresistible frightfulness, that I found myself unable to swallow: semi-invisible polypous monsters that uttered a shrill whistling sound and blasted their enemies with terrific winds. Such creatures would look very well on the covers of the pulp magazines, but they do not make good adult reading. And the truth is that these stories were hackwork contributed to such publications as *Weird Tales* and *Amazing Stories,* where, in my opinion, they ought to have been left.

The only real horror in most of these fictions is the horror of bad taste and bad art. Lovecraft was not a good writer. The fact that his verbose and undistinguished style has been compared to Poe's is only one of the many sad signs that almost nobody any more pays any real attention to writing. I have never yet found in Lovecraft a single sentence that Poe could have written, though there are some—not at all the same thing—that have evidently been influenced by Poe. (It is to me more terrifying than anything in Lovecraft that Professor T. O. Mabbott of Hunter College, who has been promising a definitive edition of Poe, should contribute to the Lovecraft *Marginalia* a tribute in which he asserts that "Lovecraft is one of the few authors of whom I can honestly say that I have enjoyed every word of his stories," and goes on to make a solemn comparison of Lovecraft's work with Poe's.) One of Lovecraft's worst faults is his incessant effort to work up the expectations of the reader by sprinkling his stories with such adjectives as "horrible," "terrible," "frightful," "awesome," "eerie," "weird," "forbidden," "unhallowed," "unholy," "blasphemous," "hellish" and "infernal." Surely one of the primary rules for writing an effective tale of horror is never to use any of these words—especially if you are going, at the end, to produce an invisible whistling octopus. I happened to read a horror story by Mérimée,

La Vénus d'Ille, just after I had been investigating Lovecraft, and was relieved to find it narrated—though it was almost as fantastic as Lovecraft—with the prosaic objectivity of an anecdote of travel.

Lovecraft himself, however, is a little more interesting than his stories. He was a Rhode Islander, who hardly left Providence and who led the life of a recluse. He knew a lot about the natural sciences, anthropology, the history of New England, American architecture, eighteenth-century literature and a number of other things. He was a literary man *manqué,* and the impression he made on his friends must partly have been due to abilities that hardly appear in his fiction. He wrote also a certain amount of poetry that echoes Edwin Arlington Robinson—like his fiction, quite second-rate; but his long essay on the literature of supernatural horror is a really able piece of work. He shows his lack of sound literary taste in his enthusiasm for Machen and Dunsany, whom he more or less acknowledged as models, but he had read comprehensively in this special field—he was strong on the Gothic novelists—and writes about it with much intelligence.

As a practitioner in this line of fiction, he regarded himself rightly as an amateur, and did not, therefore, collect his stories in book-form. This was done after his death by his friends. The "Cthulhu Mythos" and its fabricated authorities seem to have been for him a sort of boy's game which he diverted his solitary life by playing with other horror-story fanciers, who added details to the myth and figured in it under distorted names. It is all more amusing in his letters than it is in the stories themselves. His illustrator, Virgil Finlay, he would address as "Dear Monstro Ligriv," and he was in the habit of dating his letters not "66 College Street, Providence" but "Kadath in the Cold Waste: Hour of the Night-

Gaunts," "Brink of the Bottomless Gulf: Hour That the Stars Appear Below," "Burrow of the Dholes: Hour of the Charnal Feasting," "Bottomless Well of Yoguggon: Hour That the Snout Appears," etc. He cultivated a spectral pallor. "He never liked to tan," writes a friend, "and a trace of color in his cheeks seemed somehow to be a source of annoyance." The photograph which appears as a frontispiece in *H. P. L.: A Memoir* has been printed—with design, one supposes—in a pinkish transparent red that makes him look both insubstantial and sulphurous.

But Lovecraft's stories do show at times some traces of his more serious emotions and interests. He has a scientific imagination rather similar, though much inferior, to that of the early Wells. The story called *The Color Out of Space* more or less predicts the effects of the atomic bomb, and *The Shadow Out of Time* deals not altogether ineffectively with the perspectives of geological aeons and the idea of controlling the time-sequence. The notion of escaping from time seems the motif most valid in his fiction, stimulated as it was by an impulse toward evasion which had pressed upon him all his life: "Time, space, and natural law," he wrote, "hold for me suggestions of intolerable bondage, and I can form no picture of emotional satisfaction which does not involve their defeat—especially the defeat of time, so that one may merge oneself with the whole historic stream and be wholly emancipated from the transient and ephemeral."

But the Lovecraft cult, I fear, is on even a more infantile level than the Baker Street Irregulars and the cult of Sherlock Holmes.

November 24, 1945

THACKERAY'S LETTERS:
A VICTORIAN DOCUMENT

THERE IS no official biography of Thackeray, because
he left instructions that none should be written, and,
though groups of his letters have been printed, no comprehensive collection was published in the decades that
followed his death. A large collection had, however,
been made by one of the novelist's granddaughters, Mrs.
Richard Thackeray Fuller. In the summer of 1939, a
young man from the Harvard Graduate School, Mr.
Gordon N. Ray, who had just written a thesis on Thackeray, went to see Mrs. Fuller in England. She asked him
to edit these papers, and, since large-scale scholarly publishing seemed impossible in England in wartime, suggested his bringing them out in the United States. Mr.
Ray has added to Mrs. Fuller's collection whatever other
letters of Thackeray's it was possible to find in America and has published, through the Harvard University Press, the first two immense volumes of *The Letters and Private Papers of William Makepeace Thackeray*. Two more are to be brought out next year. The
collection includes "some sixteen hundred of Thackeray's letters, more than a hundred letters to and about
him (some of great biographical interest), and nineteen
of his diaries and account books." Three-fifths of these
letters of Thackeray's had never been published at all,

and less than a fourth had been published complete. The editor hopes to add later a fifth installment of letters from English collections, which the war made it impossible to assemble.

The appearance of these volumes is, of course, an event of the first importance. However tepidly one may admire Thackeray, it is impossible not to be fascinated by the extraordinary document they constitute on the London literary world, nineteenth-century society in both London and Paris (one had not realized before how much Thackeray and his family lived in France) and Victorian family life. Thackeray's stipulation that no biography of him should be written was prompted, no doubt, by reluctance to have the circumstances of his wife's insanity and of his attachment to Mrs. Brookfield made public; but we are profiting at last by the long delay, for never perhaps till our era would the descendants of a Victorian great man have consented to such a revelation of the celebrity's private life as these diaries and letters afford. I am not sure that a comparable record exists for any Victorian Englishman. Thackeray kept a diary at intervals, and, during the years that these volumes cover (1817-1851), he was always reporting himself at length to his mother or Mrs. Brookfield with a frankness we should hardly expect; and all the evidence thus provided has here been printed without excisions by the editor, though some had been made by Mrs. Brookfield in the letters written to her. (Certain letters, to Mrs. Brookfield and others, in the possession of Dr. Rosenbach have for some reason been withheld.)

These papers have been presented remarkably well. The edition is both a work of sound scholarship and a book for the ordinary reader. The editor has made it easy to identify Thackeray's friends and get the hang of his rather complicated family by compiling, in Volume I, a small encyclopedic guide to the principal personalities involved, and he has explained in indefatigable footnotes everything that can be explained, and included under the proper dates many anecdotes and descriptions of Thackeray from the memoirs of a variety of persons. The clarity and explicitness and fullness, as well as the good printing, of this Harvard job are unusual in such academic editing. These volumes, in spite of the scale of the material and the elaborateness of the apparatus, are remarkably agreeable to read and easy to find one's way in. (It is curious to note which literary and historical allusions Mr. Ray thinks it worth while to elucidate. When pre-revolutionary classics used to be reprinted in the Soviet Union, the editor always had to explain who such figures as Socrates and Napoleon were. The culture of the United States is not quite so meager as that, but its range of reference is different enough from that of the educated public of Thackeray's day so that we find Mr. Ray writing footnotes for allusions to the *Arabian Nights* and for once well-known names of Greek history. He must have had some nice problems in deciding what the reader would or would not be likely to know, for though he identifies Harmodius and Aristogeiton, he leaves Anaxagoras unexplained.)

The little drawings in Thackeray's letters, as well as a number of other sketches, have been carefully reproduced, and one finds that he had a delicacy as a draftsman that one would scarcely have suspected from the pictures with which he illustrated his books, since, as Mr. Ray points out and as Thackeray complains, the effect of his line was spoilt in transferring the drawings to steel or wood.

These documents offer an opportunity for a complete reconsideration of Thackeray (Mr. Ray promises an eventual biography), and they ought to be made the occasion of critical "reappraisals" of a writer to whom of late not much attention has been paid. I hope to return to the subject when the two remaining volumes come out. In the meantime, on the basis of these first two, one can only indicate disagreement with the opinion, expressed by Mr. Howard Mumford Jones in a leaflet describing the edition, that "the reason why Thackeray temporarily lacks readers is that we have not hitherto known him as a person. . . . There is no Thackeray legend as there is a Brontë legend and a Browning legend." If Thackeray today lacks readers, I believe that it is due to his defects as a novelist, and that, though *Vanity Fair* will remain, the rest of his work is not likely ever much to be read again. Nor can I imagine that this record of his life will create a "Thackeray legend." Interesting though the record is and good though some of his letters are (he is to be seen at his most entertaining in his correspondence with Mrs. Brookfield), we find in them the same weaknesses that prevented him from ever becoming a really top-flight novelist. His lack of intellectual interests appears strikingly in his youthful diary of his travels in Germany and France, where he visited the Weimar of Goethe (who received him for a half-hour's interview, of which Thackeray does not report a word) and the Paris of the early romantics and the early socialists without (though later he praised Victor Hugo and was on good terms with Louis Blanc) showing the faintest interest in either. Beside the great Englishmen of the Victorian era, Thackeray reveals himself here, even more clearly than in his published writings, rather a shallow commentator on life, and wherever we run into a letter by Dickens or by Edward FitzGerald, we get the impression of a soundness and dignity that contrasts with Thackeray's chatter. Snobbery, in the years of his success, became for him as much of a vice as gambling had been in his youth, and these letters show him alternately exulting in his connections with the titled world and trying to chasten or check this proclivity. In the earlier stages, he is as coy as a girl about his acquaintance with the Duke of Devonshire and boasts of having brought him to his (Thackeray's) door; in the later, he announces to someone that he has just destroyed a letter he has written because it is too full of offhand references to "the great," and, though he has sometimes to refuse invitations in order to be with his children or his relatives, he never fails, in writing about it, to mention just whom he has had to refuse.

Here, also, the falsity that one feels in his novels appears to much worse advantage, because here the human relations are real. Edmund Yates infuriated Thackeray in his later years by calling him a *"faux bonhomme,"* but the derogatory descriptions of Thackeray always tend to strike that note, and one is made rather uneasy, in these letters, by his professions of geniality and affection. He is always saying of people that "nothing . . . can be more kind, honest and good-natured," and of writers of his own kind, whom he calls "Satirical-Moralists," he writes to Mark Lemon, "Our profession seems to me as serious as the Parson's own. Please God we'll be honest and kind." Did Thackeray admire those qualities quite so much as he thought? One decides that, though a very demonstrative, he was rather a cold man. The result of his invariable habit of referring to his wife as "the dear little woman," even long after her mental condition has compelled him to put her away, is somehow to make us feel that he has never really cared much about her; and we are revolted, knowing the messy end of his relations with the Brookfield household, when on one occasion he writes to Brookfield invoking his own infant daughter in connection with Brookfield's wife:

"By my soul I think my love for the one is as pure as my love for the other—and believe I never had a bad thought for either. If I had, could I shake you by the hand, or have for you a sincere and generous regard? My dear old fellow, you and God Almighty may know all my thoughts about your wife; I'm not ashamed of one of them." I do not mean to imply that Thackeray was anything but attentive in his care of the insane Isabella or anything but formally correct in his attitude toward Mrs. Brookfield, but he is always protesting too much. The sentimentality that mars his novels was an element of his daily life. In the very act of recognizing it and castigating it, he is unable to shake it off: "It was pleasant walking about here in the fields on Thursday and thinking of Annie"—he is writing to his mother about his daughter—"my dear little girl, I hear her voice a dozen times a day, and when I write to her, it's a day's work—blubbering just as I used to do when I left you to go to school—not from any excess of affection filial or paternal as I very well know; but from sentiment as they call it—the situation is pathetic. Look what a sentimental man Sterne was, ditto Coleridge who would have sent his children to the poor house—by Jove, they are a contemptible, impracticable selfish race, Titmarsh [Thackeray] included and without any affectation: Depend upon it, a good honest kindly man not cursed by a genius, that doesn't prate about his affections, and cries very little, & loves his home—he is the real man to go through the world with." But his vision of the "good honest kindly man" is as sentimental as what went before. He is strongest when he is seeing through people and giving a shabby account of the world, but the bitter view he takes of human motives itself implies the sentimental vision, because what he is being bitter about is the fact that human behavior does not live up to this. He can never study motives coolly, as Stendhal or Tolstoy could, and, beside their journals and memoirs, these self-revelations of Thackeray's seem hopelessly second-rate.

December 22, 1945

SPLENDORS AND MISERIES OF
EVELYN WAUGH

THE NEW NOVEL by Evelyn Waugh—*Brideshead Revisited*—has been a bitter blow to this critic. I have admired and praised Mr. Waugh, and when I began reading *Brideshead Revisited*, I was excited at finding that he had broken away from the comic vein for which he is famous and expanded into a new dimension. The new story—with its subtitle, *The Sacred and Profane Memories of Captain Charles Ryder*—is a "serious" novel, in the conventional sense, and the opening is invested with a poetry and staged with a dramatic effectiveness which seem to promise much. An English officer, bored with the Army, finds himself stationed near a great country house which has been turned into soldiers' quarters. It is a place that he once used to visit—his life, indeed, has been deeply involved with the Catholic family who lived there. The story reverts to 1923, at the time when Charles Ryder was at Oxford and first met the younger son of the Marchmains, who became his most intimate friend. This early section is all quite brilliant, partly in the manner of the Waugh we know, partly with a new kind of glamor that is closer to Scott Fitzgerald and Compton Mackenzie. It is the period that these older writers celebrated, but seen now from the bleak shrivelled forties, so that everything—the freedom, the fun, the varied intoxications of youth—has taken on a remoteness and pathos. The introduction of the hero to the Catholic family and the gradual revelation of their queerness, their differences from Protestant England, is brought off with accomplished art, and through almost the whole of the first half of the book, the habitual reader of Waugh is likely to tell himself that his favorite has been fledged as a first-rank straight novelist.

But this enthusiasm is to be cruelly disappointed. What happens when Evelyn Waugh abandons his comic convention—as fundamental to his previous work as that of any Restoration dramatist—turns out to be more or less disastrous. The writer, in this more normal world, no longer knows his way: his deficiency in common sense here ceases to be an asset and gets him into some embarrassing situations, and his creative imagination, accustomed in his satirical fiction to work partly in two-dimensional caricature but now called upon for passions and motives, produces mere romantic fantasy. The hero is to have an affair with the married elder daughter of the house, and this is conducted on a plane of banality —the woman is quite unreal—reminiscent of the full-dress adulteries of the period in the early nineteen-hundreds when Galsworthy and other writers were making people throb and weep over such fiction as *The Dark Flower*. And as the author's taste thus fails him, his excellent style goes to seed. The writing—which, in the early chapters, is of Evelyn Waugh's best: felicitous, unobtrusive, exact—here runs to such dispiriting clichés as "Still the clouds gathered and did not break" and "So the year wore on and the secret of the engagement spread from Julia's confidantes and so, like ripples on the water, in ever widening circles." The stock characters —the worldly nobleman, the good old nurse—which have always been a feature of Waugh's fiction and

which are all right in a harlequinade, here simply become implausible and tiresome. The last scenes are extravagantly absurd, with an absurdity that would be
worthy of Waugh at his best if it were not—painful to
say—meant quite seriously. The worldly Lord Marchmain, when he left his wife, repudiated his Catholic
faith, and on his deathbed he sends the priest packing,
but when the old man has sunk lower, the priest is recalled. The family all kneel, and Charles, who is present, kneels, too. Stoutly though he has defended his Protestantism, his resistance breaks down today. He prays
that this time the dying man will not reject the final sacra-
ment, and lo, Lord Marchmain makes the sign of the
cross! The peer, as he has drifted toward death, has been
soliloquizing at eloquent length: "We were knights
then, barons since Agincourt, the larger honors came with
the Georges," etc., etc., and the reader has an uncomfortable feeling that what has caused Mr. Waugh's hero
to plump on his knees is not, perhaps, the sign of the
cross but the prestige, in the person of Lord Marchmain,
of one of the oldest families in England.

For Waugh's snobbery, hitherto held in check by his
satirical point of view, has here emerged shameless and
rampant. His admiration for the qualities of the older
British families, as contrasted with modern upstarts, had
its value in his earlier novels, where the standards of
morals and taste are kept in the background and merely
implied. But here the upstarts are rather crudely overdone and the aristocrats become terribly trashy, and his
cult of the high nobility is allowed to become so rapturous and solemn that it finally gives the impression of being the only real religion in the book.

Yet the novel is a Catholic tract. The Marchmain
family, in their various fashions, all yield, ultimately, to
the promptings of their faith and bear witness to its en-

during virtue; the skeptical hero, long hostile and mocking, eventually becomes converted; the old chapel is opened up and put at the disposition of the troops, and a "surprising lot use it, too." Now, this critic may perhaps be insensible to some value the book will have for other readers, since he is unsympathetic by conviction with the point of view of the Catholic convert, but he finds it impossible to feel that the author has conveyed in all this any actual religious experience. In the earlier novels of Waugh there was always a very important element of perverse, unregenerate self-will that, giving rise to confusion and impudence, was a great asset for a comic writer. In his new book, this theme is sounded explicitly, with an unaccustomed portentousness and rhetoric, at an early point in the story, when he speaks of "the hot spring of anarchy" that "rose from deep furnaces where was no solid earth, and burst into the sunlight— a rainbow in its cooling vapors with a power the rocks could not repress," and of course it is this hot spring of anarchy, this reckless, unredeemed humanity, that is supposed to be cooled and controlled by the discipline of the Catholic faith. But, once he has come to see this force as sin, Evelyn Waugh seems to be rather afraid of it: he does not allow it really to raise its head—boldly, outrageously, hilariously or horribly—as he has in his other books, and the result is that we feel something lacking. We have come to count on this Serpent; we are not used to seeing it handled so gingerly; and, at the same time, the religion that is invoked to subdue it seems more like an exorcistic rite than a force of regeneration.

There is, however, another subject in *Brideshead Revisited*—a subject which is incompletely developed but which has far more reality than the religious one: the situation of Charles Ryder between the Brideshead family on the one hand and his own family background on the other. This young man has no mother and his only home is with a scholarly and self-centered father, who reduces life to something so dry, so withdrawn, so devoid of affection or color that the boy is driven to look for a home in the family of his Oxford friend and to idealize their charm and grace. What are interesting to a non-Catholic reader are the origins and the evolution of the hero's beglamored snobbery, and the amusing and chilling picture of Charles's holidays at home with his father is one of the very good things in the book.

The comic parts of *Brideshead Revisited* are as funny as anything that the author has done, and the Catholic characters are sometimes good, when they are being observed as social types and get the same kind of relentless treatment as the characters in his satirical books. I do not mean to suggest, however, that Mr. Waugh should revert to his earlier vein. He has been steadily broadening his art, and when he next tries a serious novel, he may have learned how to avoid bathos.

In the meantime, I predict that *Brideshead Revisited* will prove to be the most successful, the only extremely successful, book that Evelyn Waugh has written, and that it will soon be up in the best-seller list somewhere between *The Black Rose* and *The Manatee*.

January 5, 1946

When Evelyn Waugh was converted to Catholicism by the Jesuit Father d'Arcy, he wrote, as a tribute to d'Arcy and in celebration of the rebuilding of Campion Hall, the Jesuit college at Oxford, a short biography of Edmund Campion, the Elizabethan Jesuit martyr. This book, which first appeared in 1935, has now been republished and given a new edition. The story is quite soberly and simply told—with no attempt to create historical atmosphere—and it is not uninteresting to read. Campion is very impressive in the utterances which Mr. Waugh quotes. A man of intellectual distinction, exalted religious vocation and great moral and physical courage, he was the victim, after the suppression of Catholicism in England, of one of those political frame-ups which, though not carried out on the same enormous scale or engineered with the same efficiency as those of our own day, were already a feature of the struggle between Catholicism and Protestantism.

Mr. Waugh's version of history, however, turns out, in its larger perspectives, to be more or less in the vein of 1066 and All That. Catholicism was a Good Thing and Protestantism was a Bad Thing, and that is all that needs to be said about it. The book is valuable mainly for providing a curious glimpse of the author's conception of modern England. The triumph of Protestantism under Elizabeth meant, he writes, that the country was "secure, independent, insular; the course of her history lay plain ahead: competitive nationalism, competitive industrialism, the looms and coal mines and counting houses, the joint stock companies and the cantonments; the power and the weakness of great possessions." For him, Protestantism is not merely one of the phases of the rise of the middle class; it is the cause of all the phenomena mentioned above. And, in recounting this incident of a period of general religious intolerance, he continually insists on the cruelties of the Protestant persecution of the Catholics but passes lightly over any instance—such as the St. Bartholomew Day's massacre—of the crimes committed by Catholics against Protestants. If we had no source but Mr. Waugh, we might assume that the Society of Jesus had always consisted solely of mild-spirited servants of God, who had never had anything to do with rigging racks or lighting fagots for their enemies.

July 13, 1946

Mr. Waugh has since published two books: *Scott-King's Modern Europe* and *The Loved One,* in which he returns to his earlier manner. Both are short stories rather than novels and both, in comparison with his other work, seem sketchy and incomplete. The first of these, rather like *Scoop,* deals with the misadventures of a teacher from an English public school in Communist-ridden post-war Europe; the second, much the better of the two, with a less ingenuous Englishman in Hollywood. *The Loved One* is extremely funny, but it suffers a little, for an American, from being full of familiar American jokes which Evelyn Waugh has just discovered. It recalls the Nathanael West of *Miss Lonelyhearts* as well as of *The Day of the Locust.* In connection with Mr. Waugh's Catholicism, it suggests one obvious criticism that nobody, I think, has made. *The Loved One* is a farcical satire on those de luxe California cemeteries that attempt to render death less unpleasant by exploiting all the resources of landscape-gardening and Hollywood mummery. To the non-religious reader, however, the patrons and proprietors of Whispering Glades seem more sensible and less absurd than the priest-guided Evelyn Waugh. What the former are trying to do is, after all, merely to gloss over physical death with smooth lawns and soothing rites; but, for the Catholic, the fact of death is not to be faced at all: he is solaced with the fantasy of another world in which everyone who has died in the flesh is somehow supposed to be still alive and in which it is supposed to be possible to help souls to advance themselves by buying candles to burn in churches. The trappings invented for this other world by imaginative believers in the Christian myth—since they need not meet the requirements of reality—beat anything concocted by Whispering Glades.

GEORGE SAINTSBURY'S CENTENARY

THE CENTENARY of George Saintsbury's birth has been celebrated in England by a memorial volume of his uncollected essays. In this country, Mr. Huntington Cairns has edited a volume of Saintsbury's articles on French literature from the *Encyclopaedia Britannica: French Literature and Its Masters*. These essays are not of Saintsbury's best. He needed more room to do himself justice. The article on *French Literature from the Beginning to 1900* has to account for too many names to have a chance to say anything very interesting about them, but the pieces on single figures—especially the Voltaire—are wonderful feats of condensation that manage, in summarizing a lifetime, to include a maximum of detail and, in their briefly expressed comments, to hit all the nails on the head.

It is a good thing to have these essays in book-form, but what are really most needed now are reprints of Saintsbury's important works, which are out of print and very hard to get. Saintsbury, since his death, has come more and more to stand out as the sole English literary critic of the late-nineteenth early-twentieth centuries, the sole full-length professional critic, who is really of first-rate stature. He is perhaps the only English critic, with the possible exception of Leslie Stephen, whose work is comparable, for comprehensiveness and brilliance, to the great French critics of the nineteenth century. Unlike them, he has no interest in ideas. In religion he was Church of England and in politics an extreme Tory, but his prejudices were rarely allowed to interfere with his appetite for good literature, wherever and by whomever written. He was probably the greatest connoisseur of literature—in the same sense that he was a connoisseur of wines, about which he also wrote—that we have ever had in English. In this, he stood quite outside the academic tradition. Though he contributed to the *Encyclopaedia* and to *The Cambridge History of English Literature,* he has always more or less the air of a man who is showing a friend the sights of some well-studied and loved locality.

In his *History of English Prose Rhythm,* Saintsbury apologizes for his own prose style; but the truth is that his prose is excellent: the rhythm of his own writing never falters. He had, in fact, invented a style of much charm and a certain significance: a modern, conversational prose that carries off asides, jokes and gossip as well as all the essential data by a very strong personal rhythm, that drops its voice to interpolate footnotes without seriously retarding the current, and that, however facetious or garrulous, never fails to cover the ground and make the points. The extreme development of this style is to be seen in the *History of the French Novel* written in Saintsbury's later years and one of the most entertaining of books on literature. It is all a gigantic after-dinner talk with an old gentleman who, to his immense entertainment, has read through the whole of French fiction. The only other writer I know who has created a style similar to Saintsbury's is the late Ford Madox Ford. Both these men are worth attention as writers because they found out how to manage a fine and flexible English prose on the rhythms of informal speech rather than on those of literary convention.

The *History of the French Novel* could never have been written by a Frenchman, because the books and the writers it deals with have not been organized and grouped as would have been done by a French professor. The literature of France itself has always been so much guided and rationalized by a criticism that was an integral part of it that it falls naturally into a well-ordered historical picture. Saintsbury's critical method had been evolved in connection with English literature, which, with its relative indifference to movements and schools and its miscellany of remarkable individuals, does not lend itself to this sort of treatment. In consequence, he stops a good deal longer over somebody like Pigault-Lebrun or Restif de La Bretonne than the ordinary French historian would. He does not need to make them fit into a scheme; he simply likes to tell you about them; and, since you will probably never read them, you do not mind getting them thus at second hand. Now, with English writing, this leisurely method of merely showing a guest the sights succeeds where other methods are inadequate. It is inevitable for academic surveys, English as well as French, to attempt to systematize, and since the material with which the English ones deal has been produced with a minimum of system, a great deal that is important and valuable is invariably left out or slighted. English surveys are likely to be dull, where French surveys may be stimulating, and are nearly always readable. But Saintsbury is never dull, because he misses no point of interest. He is to be seen at his very best in his studies of the minor nineteenth-century writers in his *Collected Essays and Papers*: such people as Peacock, Crabbe, George Borrow, Hogg, Praed and Barham of *The Ingoldsby Legends*. It is impossible to take

care of these writers by subsuming them under some
bigger name. Each is unlike anyone else, unique and
fully developed; each has to be explored for his own
sake. And Saintsbury explored and appraised them as
nobody else has done. Though more searching essays
than Saintsbury's have been written on some of the
greater nineteenth-century writers, it would be true in
a sense to say that the full history of English nineteenth-
century literature has never been written except by
Saintsbury.

Nor did his relish for such lesser figures confuse his
view of the greater. He made a few rather queer evalu-
ations, as every good critic does—his almost unqualified
enthusiasm for Thackeray and his contempt for *Liaisons
Dangereuses;* and it is true, as has sometimes been said of
him, that he does not plumb the deepest literature
deeply. But at least he has arrived by himself at his reasons for the greatness of the greatest. He never takes merits
for granted. If the relative amount of space assigned to
the various subjects may not always, in a given book of
Saintsbury's, seem proportionate to their importance, it
is likely to be due to the fact that he had, in his career as
a journalist, to treat some of the great figures so many
times. If you feel, say, that Shakespeare seems slighted in
his *History of Elizabethan Literature,* you will find that
he has done him magnificently in *The Cambridge History of English Literature;* if Bulwer-Lytton, in some
other work, seems to command as much attention as
Dickens, you will find Dickens studied on a larger scale
and in a more serious way somewhere else.

He had for a long time had some prejudice against
Dante and did not read him till rather late in life, when
the tastes of many critics would have already formed a
closed cosmos; but when he did sit down at last to *La
Commedia Divina,* he conceded its greatness at once.

It is curious to find this confession cropping up in the history of the French novel, and it is somehow characteristic of Saintsbury that he should be comparing Dante with some novelist of the nineteenth century, and mention incidentally that he puts him at the top of imaginative fiction. For, except in treating books chronologically, as he might arrange wines in his cellar, he has little real interest in history, and social changes tend merely to annoy him because they distract from the enjoyment of literature. The books are on his shelves like bottles, and it is the most natural thing in the world for him to take down a good medieval vintage made from astringent Italian grapes along with a good dry vintage of French nineteenth-century realism.

February 2, 1946

AMBUSHING A BEST-SELLER

THIS MAGAZINE has not always shown foresight in recognizing future successes, and it has sometimes ignored or dismissed in a note novels that were destined to sell hundreds of thousands and to go on selling for years. I have, therefore, lately been watching the publishers' lists in the hope of catching one of these books before it started on its triumphant progress; and, difficult though it seems to be to distinguish the coming best-seller from other specimens of inferior fiction, I have decided—from the amount and kind of advertising that the book is being given by the publisher and from the appearance of a picture of the heroine on the cover of *Publisher's Weekly* —that *The Turquoise,* by Anya Seton, has a good chance of landing in the upper brackets. I may be wrong, but I am going to report on it on the assumption that it will be widely read.

The heroine of *The Turquoise,* then, is, as I hardly need to say, a Cinderella. The child of the younger son of a Scottish baronet and of the daughter of a Spanish hidalgo resident in the American Southwest, she is early left a penniless orphan and grows up among the illiterate natives, part Indian, part Spanish, of New Mexico. "Her mouth, always wide, lost its childish innocence, and the lips revealed a passionate curve. Her skin grew moister and more glowing; beneath the dirt and tan shone the velvety whiteness of her Castilian heritage. She was still a thin, ugly child, her gray eyes were still too big for the small face and gave her a goblin look, but she now sometimes showed the first indications of the sex magnetism which was later to give her an illusion of beauty more seductive than actual symmetry." Her natural high breeding and dignity also asserted themselves in the sordid milieux of her early years, so that people instinctively deferred to her quality.

She had been named Santa Fe, after the place where she was born, but her father had been shy of the name for its association with her mother's death. " 'Santa Fe—' said Andrew bitterly, and at the sound of his voice the baby suddenly smiled. 'Aye, 'tis a daft name for ye, small wonder ye smile.' He repeated the name, and this time the last syllable echoed in his mind with a peculiar relevance. 'Fey! There's a true Scottish word will fit you, for ye're fated—doomed to die as we all are, poor bairnie.' " She was doomed, yet she was also chosen, for she had inherited from a Scottish grandmother a gift of mindreading and second sight, which enabled her not only, by a little concentration, accurately to predict the future but also to know what other people were thinking and to tell them what they had in their pockets. "You are born to great vision, little one," said an old Indian shaman in a "deep, singing tone." "For you they have made thin the curtain which hides the real. But there is danger. You must listen to the voice of the spirit, or your body and its passions will betray you." And he gave her a turquoise pendant, "the color of the Great Spirit's dwelling," in order that she should always remember that her power derives from the Spirit.

She ran away, at the age of seventeen, with a travelling Irish adventurer who had a one-man medicine show. She amazed him by divining at once the ingredients of the "Elixir" he was selling. "There came the sensation of light and a swift impression which she translated into words. 'In this bottle, there is river water—' She paused, then amplified, 'Water from the Rio Grande where you filled it.' Terry made an exclamation and uncrossed his legs. Fey continued calmly, 'There is also whiskey, a little sugar and—chile powder. No more.' She put the bottle on the floor beside her stool, and raised her eyes." He was impressed by her possible usefulness as a feature for his medicine show, a dependable mind-reading act which required no confederate or code; and she, on her side, was attracted to him strongly. "He was twenty-three and of that dashing Irish type which rouses many a woman's imagination. . . . The chin was pugnacious, the mouth, warmly sensual, also showed humor, while the greenish eyes, ill-tempered now, as they often were, seldom produced that impression on women because of their romantic setting of thick dark lashes. He was vivid and very male. Fey, unaccustomed to height and breadth of shoulder, gazed at the ripple of muscles beneath his white silk shirt, and thought him miraculous."

They took to the road together, got married. But her gift, when she debased it, failed her: she could no longer tell prostitutes their original names or inventory the contents of pocketbooks. Dashing Terry—who sincerely admires her but who has to be got out of the way —is rather implausibly made to desert her in a cheap lodging-house in New York. She had been pregnant, though he had not known it, but for a time she was able to earn a living at the Arcadia Concert Saloon. "While she sang, wandering from table to table strumming her guitar and smiling, she diffused sex magnetism, and she titivated the goggling out-of-towners who comprised three-quarters of the Arcadia's patronage." (The proper meaning of "titivate"—here, as often, used for titillate—seems hopelessly to have suffered the fate of "jejune" and "disinterested.") Then she goes to have her baby in a hospital, where a Quaker woman doctor befriends her and tries to persuade her to study medicine. Here she is nursing her baby: "The girl was beautiful; she [the woman doctor] had never realized it before. Or if not exactly beautiful, something far more disturbing. She was alluring, every line of her body, partly unclothed as it now was, pointed to seductive allure."

But the hospital is repellent to Fey: "I loathe sick people and poor people," she tells herself. "I want nothing now of life but luxury and refinement." She has conceived an audacious design on a certain Simeon Tower, the son of a Jewish peddler, who has become one of New York's richest men by dint of his native shrewdness and by "throwing plums to Big Bill Tweed as he rose to power by means of the most corrupt politics ever known in New York." She goes straight to his office in Wall Street and forces her way into his presence. "I think we would like each other," she says. " 'That is a trifle crude,' he said coldly. 'Will you kindly state your business?' His blunt, well-manicured hand made a slight gesture, the prelude to dismissal." But he looks "at the full high outline of her breasts under the leaf-brown silk, at the wide coral-tinted mouth," and succumbs to her seductive allure. He soon gets her a divorce and marries her, and there begins one of those period pageants which, with the recent patriotic exploitation of the American historical legend, have become a cheap and routine feature of so many of our books, plays and films. There is an "at home" at Phoebe and Alice Cary's, at which the visitor is "drawn over to a red settee where Susan B. Anthony and Elizabeth Cady Stanton are discussing . . . the advent of the bustle." (Fey has of course recognized early the greatness of Walt Whitman. Opening *Leaves of Grass* in a book store, " 'This is for me,' she said" at once, "her eyes shining. 'This man understands.' Mr. Tibbins had flushed a dull red. 'That's not a proper book for a young woman to read!' 'Oh, but it is!' said Fey, hardly conscious of him. 'It's true and good. It makes me strong.' And her rapt eyes reread a page.") Simeon is shocked and alarmed by the fact that "on January sixth, Jim Fisk had been shot and killed by Josie Mansfield's paramour, Edward Stokes," and he has a life-or-death struggle with Jay Gould, as "the Mephisto of Wall Street sits like a small black spider silently enmeshing enterprise after enterprise." Simeon Tower has hitherto been excluded from the social Four Hundred, the custodian of which is Ward McAllister; but Fey, with her usual directness—which Simeon "dimly recognized as the product of generations of breeding"—goes to McAllister and asks to be taken in. "It is," he tells her, "my privilege to help guard the—may I say—inner sanctum from pollution"; but "I'll see what I can do," he ends, bowing.

At the first great ball that the Towers give, with Mrs. Astor present, Fey's rascally ex-husband turns up, having impudently crashed the gate. Fey yields again to his Irish charm and spends a night in a raffish hotel with him. But Terry has conceived the idea of blackmailing Simeon Tower and, "sunk in an amorous drowsiness," he murmurs, " 'The old boy's an easy mark.' 'Why do you say that?' She pulled the light chain and the gas flared up, while she contemplated Terry with steady narrowed eyes." "Listen then, Terry," she announces, when she has grasped the situation. "It is finished at last, and I feel for myself a loathing. I was always a—an incident to you, as I have been now. I knew this. I even told myself this over and over, but I— Oh, what's the use! Perhaps it was necessary that by yielding to my body I might become free of it and you."

Unfortunately, Fey's second sight was still in abeyance at this time, so she could not prepare herself for what was about to happen. With the connivance of a villainous secretary, Terry launches his campaign of blackmail, and one day, when he has thrown it in Simeon's teeth that Fey has been unfaithful to him, Simeon takes out a revolver and shoots him. Simeon is sent to the Tombs, and we are led to believe that Fey is going to marry a Scottish relation who has been sent over by her grandfather to find her. But, on a visit to her husband in prison, her power of clairvoyance dramatically comes back (though it is now, it seems, moral insight rather than mind-reading or knowledge of the future). The words of the old Indian return; the past reveals itself to her in a series of blinding flashbacks. She knows she has been to blame. Her consciousness is penetrated "with annihilating truth": *"You are responsible, you!"* She tells her suitor that she can never be his and makes him return to Scotland; she trains herself in hospital work; she goes on the stand at her husband's trial and, by confessing her infidelity, obtains the acquittal of Simeon. Then she takes him away to New Mexico, where they live for the rest of their years in a four-room adobe house, while she ministers to the natives, who "regard her with semi-superstitious reverence." "She had much medical knowledge and she had an almost miraculous intuition as to what ailed the sick bodies or souls which came to her." After her death, she was known as "La Santa."

The Turquoise thus follows a familiar line. It is a typical American novel written by a woman for women. The great thing about this kind of fiction is that the heroine must combine, in one lifetime, as many enjoyable kinds of role as possible: she must be sexually desirable and successful, yet a competent professional woman; she must pass through picaresque adventures, yet attain the highest social position; she must be able to break men's hearts, yet be capable of prodigies of fidelity; she must have every kind of worldly success, yet rise at moments to the self-sacrifice of the saint. She must, in fact, have every possible kind of cake and manage to eat it, too. A bait is laid for masculine readers, also, by periodically disrobing the heroine and writing emphatically of her sexual appetite. And the whole book is written in that tone and prose of the women's magazines which is now so much a standard commodity that it is probably possible for the novelist to pick it up at the corner drugstore with her deodorant and her cold cream.

Yet *The Turquoise* sticks below the level of the more compelling specimens of this fiction by reason of the lack in it of any real feeling of even the feminine daydreaming kind that does sometimes enliven these books. There is not even a crude human motivation of either the woman or the men. The heroine, who is supposed to be intuitive, full of warm emotions and eager desires, is as incredible in her relations with her husbands as they are in their relations with her. She is made, for example, to lay siege to Simeon simply because she craves money and position, but the stigma of calculation is eliminated by showing her later as passionately in love with her husband—yet not so passionately, it appears still later, that she will not be tempted to slip with Terry. The whole thing is as synthetic, as arbitrary, as basically cold and dead, as a scenario for a film. And now the question presents itself: Will real men and women, in large numbers, as the publishers obviously hope, really buy and read this arid rubbish, which has not even the rankness of the juicier trash? Or have I been using up all this space merely to warn you against a dud? Watch the best-seller lists for the answer.

February 16, 1946

Several people who read this article imagined that it was a burlesque; they assumed, from the absurdity of the story, that I must have made the whole thing up. But *The Turquoise* was perfectly real, and it has justified my worst apprehensions by selling more than nine hundred thousand copies.

THE APOTHEOSIS OF
SOMERSET MAUGHAM

It HAS HAPPENED to me from time to time to run into some person of taste who tells me that I ought to take Somerset Maugham seriously, yet I have never been able to convince myself that he was anything but second-rate. His swelling reputation in America, which culminated the other day in his solemn presentation to the Library of Congress of the manuscript of *Of Human Bondage,* seems to me a conspicuous sign of the general decline of our standards. Thirty or thirty-five years ago the English novelists that were read in America were at least men like Wells and Bennett, who, though not quite of top rank, were at least by vocation real writers. Mr. Maugham, I cannot help feeling, is not, in the sense of "having the métier," really a writer at all. There are real writers, like Balzac and Dreiser, who may be said to write badly. Dreiser handles words abominably, but his prose has a compelling rhythm, which is his style and which induces the emotions that give his story its poetic meaning. But Mr. Maugham, whose language is always banal, has not even an interesting rhythm.

Now, unless I am looking for facts, I find it extremely difficult to get through books that are not "written." I can read Compton Mackenzie, for example, of the second rank though he is, because he has a gift of style of a not too common kind. But my experience has always been with Maugham that he disappoints my literary appetite and so discourages me from going on. His new novel, *Then and Now*—which I had sworn to explore to the end, if only in order to be able to say that I had read a book of Maugham's through—opposed to my progress, through all the first half, such thickets of unreadableness, that there were moments when I thought I should never succeed.

Then and Now is an historical novel: it deals with Niccolò Machiavelli and tells the story of his mission, as envoy from Florence, to the headquarters of Caesar Borgia, when the latter, in his campaign of domination, appeared at his most effective and most menacing. The way in which this promising subject is handled suggested, I was shocked to discover, one of the less brilliant contributions to a prep-school magazine. Here are Machiavelli and Borgia confronting one another: "Although he had but briefly seen him at Urbino, Machiavelli had been deeply impressed by him. He had heard there how the Duke Guidobaldo da Montefeltro, confiding in Caesar Borgia's friendship, had lost his state and barely escaped with his life; and though he recognized that Il Valentino had acted with shocking perfidy he could not but admire the energy and adroit planning with which he had conducted the enterprise. This was a man of parts, fearless, unscrupulous, ruthless and intelligent, not only a brilliant general but a capable organizer and an astute politician. A sarcastic smile played upon Machiavelli's thin lips and his eyes gleamed, for the prospect of matching his wits with such an antagonist excited him." This narrative from time to time is obstructed by the introduction of thick chunks of historical background that sound as if they had been copied out—so compressed and indigestible are they, so untouched by imagination—from some textbook in the history classroom: "In June of the year with which this narrative is concerned, Arezzo, a city subject to Florence, revolted and declared itself independent. Vitellozzo Vitelli, the ablest of Il Valentino's commanders and bitter enemy of the Florentines because they had executed his brother Paolo, and Baglioni, Lord of Perugia, went to the support of the rebellious citizens and defeated the forces of the Republic," etc., etc. As will be seen from the above sentence, in which, if we glide over the comma, we are at first misled into supposing that Baglioni was executed, before we find that he went with Vitelli, the writing is amateurish. The book is full of ill-composed sentences, bulging with disproportionate clauses that prevent them from coming out right, or confused by "he"s, "him"s and "his"s that apply to different antecedents: a kind of thing that an English master would have been sure to bluepencil in the young student's themes. The language is such a tissue of clichés that one's wonder is finally aroused at the writer's ability to assemble so many and at his unfailing inability to put anything in an individual way: "But Il Valentino appeared to be well pleased. It looked as though he were prepared to let bygones be bygones and restore the repentant rebels to his confidence. . . . But whatever sinister plans he turned round in that handsome head of his, the Duke was evidently not ready to resort to more than veiled threats to induce the Florentines to accede to his demands. . . . The Duke gazed at him thoughtfully. You might have imagined that he was asking himself what kind of a man this was, but with no ulterior motive, from idle curiosity rather. . . . The truth, the unpalatable truth, stared him in the face. . . . He had taken him on this trip from sheer good nature, he had introduced him to persons worth knowing, he had done his best to form him, to show him how to behave, to civilize him, in short; he had not spared his wit and wisdom to teach him the ways of the world, how to make friends and influence people. And this was his reward, to have his girl snatched away from under his very nose." This dullness is only relieved by an occasional dim sparkle of the Wildean wit that made comedies like *Our Betters* amusing without investing them with that distinction which, in Wilde, is the product of style: "If only she knew as much about life as he did she would know that it is not the temptations you have succumbed to that you regret, but those you resisted." But even this kind of thing would not be beyond the competence of a schoolboy.

About halfway through the book, however, we find that what the author has been doing, in his tiresome piling up of dead incident, is introducing the elements of a plot. This plot is pretty well contrived; it could hardly have been worked out by a schoolboy, for it shows a practiced hand, and it carries us through the rest of the book. We find here, furthermore, that the scheming of Caesar to accomplish his political ends is connected, not merely through ingenuities of plot but also by moral implication, with Machiavelli's scheming to make a conquest of the wife of a friend. Machiavelli as well as Borgia is cynical about human motives; Machiavelli (though politically a patriot working for republican Florence) is aiming in his personal relations at power for the sake of power, just as Borgia is. And the victims of both are equally cynics, equally double-dealers. The upshot of the whole affair is that Machiavelli, returning home with a certain admiration for Borgia but in a rage over the duplicity practiced on him by the young wife and her allies, meditates upon his experience and finds in it the material for *Il Principe,* his treatise on Realpolitik, and for his comedy, *La Mandragola*. This, too, shows more knowledge of the world than a schoolboy would have been likely to acquire, but that schoolboy, grown-up and much travelled, having somehow been diverted from his normal career of law, medicine, diplomacy or parliament, might have produced such a novel as *Then and Now;* did, in fact, produce it.

The defenders of Somerset Maugham will tell me that he is "old and tired" now, and that historical novels are not his forte—that it is quite unfair to judge him by *Then and Now,* which is one of the least of his books. I know that he has done better stories, but I am not sure that it *is* quite unfair to judge his quality by *Then and Now.* This quality is never, it seems to me, that either of a literary artist or of a first-rate critic of morals; and it may be worth while to say this at a moment when there seems to be a tendency to step up Mr. Maugham's standing to the higher ranks of English fiction, and when Mr. Maugham himself has been using his position of prestige for a nagging disparagement of his betters. Though Mr. Maugham's claims for himself are always carefully and correctly modest, he usually manages to sound invidious when he is speaking of his top-drawer contemporaries. In an anthology which he edited a few years ago, *Introduction to Modern English and American Literature*—a mixture of good writing and tripe that sets the teeth on edge—we find him patronizing, in what seems to me an insufferable way (and with his customary buzz of clichés), such writers as Henry James, James Joyce and W. B. Yeats. "His influence on fiction," he writes of James, "especially in England, has been great, and though I happen to think it has been a bad influence, its enduring power makes him an important figure. . . . He never succeeded in coming to grips with life. . . . This story (*The Beast in the Jungle*) reads to me like a lamentable admission of his own failure." Of

Ulysses: "I have read it twice, so I cannot say that I find it unreadable, but . . . like many of his countrymen, Joyce never discovered that enough is as good as a feast, and his prolixity is exhausting." Of Yeats: "Though he could at times be very good company, he was a pompous vain man; to hear him read his own verses was as excruciating a torture as anyone could be exposed to." Well, it is quite true of Henry James that his experience was incomplete and that he wrote about his own deficiencies, and that Joyce is sometimes too prolix, and it may be true that Yeats was sometimes pompous. It is also true that Mr. Maugham partly sweetens his detraction with praise. Yet, from reading this *Introduction,* you would never be able to discover that all these writers belong to a different plane from that of Michael Arlen and Katharine Brush, whose work is also included—to a plane on which Somerset Maugham does not exist at all. Mr. Maugham would apparently suggest to us that all novelists are entertainers who differ only in being more or less boring (though he grants, with a marked lack of enthusiasm, that Henry James supplied, "if not an incentive, at least an encouragement to those who came after him . . . to aim consciously at giving fiction the form and significance that may sometimes make it more than the pastime of an idle hour"). We get the impression of a malcontent eye cocked up from the brackish waters of the *Cosmopolitan* magazine, and a peevish and insistent grumbling. There is something going on, on the higher ground, that halfway compels his respect, but he does not quite understand what it is, and in any case he can never get up there.

There are cases in which Mr. Maugham is able to admire more cordially the work that is done on this higher plane, but even here his way of praising betrays his lack of real appreciation and almost always has a sound of impertinence. So, in his speech at the Library of Congress, we find the following remarks about Proust: "Proust, as we know, was enormously influenced by the now largely discredited philosophy of Henri Bergson and great stretches of his work turn upon it. I suppose we all read with a thrill of excitement Proust's volumes as they came out, but now when we reread them in a calmer mood I think what we find to admire in them is his wonderful humor and extraordinarily vivid and interesting characters that he created in profusion. We skip his philosophical disquisitions and we skip them without loss." Now, it is perfectly obvious here that Mr. Maugham does not know what he is talking about. Some aspects of Bergson's philosophy are still taken very seriously by first-rate philosophers of certain schools; and even if Bergson's whole system were regarded with universal disapproval, that might not affect the validity of the artistic use that Proust has made of one of its features. This feature—the difference between "time" and "duration": how long something takes by the clock and how long it seems while it is going on—is itself only one of the features of Proust's metaphysical picture, which in general has more in common with the implications of relativistic physics than with the Creative Evolution of Bergson. It is this play on the relativistic principle in the social and personal fields that gives Proust his philosophical interest and that makes his book, I suppose, the greatest philosophical novel ever written. In *A la Recherche du Temps Perdu*, the philosophy so pervades the narrative that it is difficult to see how you could skip it: if you jumped over the "disquisitions," you could still not escape from Proust, in a thousand intimations and asides, expounding his relativistic theory; and since the unexpected development of the characters, the astonishing reversals of relationships, all the contrasts and paradoxes that provide the main interest of the story, are dramatizations of this theory, it is difficult to understand how a reader can "admire" the former and yet disregard the latter. The inability of Mr. Maugham to grasp what there is in Proust helps to explain why he has not been able to make his own work more interesting.

June 8, 1946

Admirers of Somerset Maugham have protested that this article was unfair to him and have begged me to read his short stories. I have therefore procured *East Is West,* the collected volume of these, and made shift to dine on a dozen. They *are* readable—quite entertaining. The style is much tighter and neater than it is in *Then and Now*—Mr. Maugham writes best when his language is plainest. But when he wants to use a richer idiom, this is the kind of thing you get: "Be this as it may, Ashenden in the last twenty years had felt his heart go pit-a-pat because of one charming person after another. He had had a good deal of fun and had paid for it with a great deal of misery, but even when suffering most acutely from the pangs of unrequited love he had been able to say to himself, albeit with a wry face, after all, it's grist to the mill." These stories are magazine commodities—all but two of them came out in the *Cosmopolitan*—on about the same level as Sherlock Holmes; but Sherlock Holmes has more literary dignity precisely because it is less pretentious. Mr. Maugham makes play with more serious themes, but his work is full of bogus motivations that are needed to turn the monthly trick. He is for our day, I suppose, what Bulwer-Lytton was for Dickens's: a half-trashy novelist, who writes badly, but is patronized by half-serious readers, who do not care much about writing.

WILLIAM SAROYAN AND
HIS DARLING OLD PROVIDENCE

WILLIAM SAROYAN has written a novel evidently based
on his experience in the Army. *The Adventures of
Wesley Jackson* seems to be flavored with *Huckleberry Finn,* but, as a story of picaresque adventure, it has
the novelty of exploiting the idea that Army life may be
picaresque. The best things in it are such episodes as that
in which the Colonel brings a newspaperman to interview "the ordinary soldier" on how he likes being in the
Army, and the picture of the Hollywood directors and
writers mobilized to do training documentaries. Mr.
Saroyan is here at his strongest in showing the bewildered civilian inducted into his military role and drawing blank after blank as he submits to pointless indigni-
ties and finds himself shunted about from one post to another, at first disgruntled, then apathetic, learning how
to play tricks on the system and only at moments prod-
ded into spasms of mild rebellion, but uncontrollably
shrinking and skulking whenever the realization is thrust
on him that he is caught in a giant enterprise for the
slaughter of other human beings.

It is a relief, after *The Human Comedy,* Saroyan's
previous novel, to read the first part of *Wesley Jackson.*
In that earlier book (and film), which was written at a
time when the author had no first-hand knowledge of

the Army, nobody was ever cross or mean even when you might for a second have thought they were going to be; everybody was perfectly lovely; the whole thing was just a big chummy junket, and even when a good fellow got killed, he wasn't really and truly dead, because his spirit was still able to return (in the movie you could see him right there) and stay on with the people he loved. But there are spots in *Wesley Jackson* where a sharpness of tone and a satirical treatment indicate that Mr. Saroyan has run at last into a few human beings who have rubbed him the wrong way, and he is forced at least to admit that the destiny of man on this earth involves, among other things, deprivation, oppression and death. This new element of relative realism will help you through the sentimentality of the lovable old drunken father (so different from Huckleberry Finn's disreputable drunken father) who for a time follows his boy from post to post but finally goes home, like a dear old chap, to the family he has abandoned, and the erotic insipidity of the women who—ugly and awkward though Wesley is represented as being—are so wonderfully kind to the hero. But when you get to the part where the madam of a just-raided Ohio brothel fixes him up with a girl for nothing and is able, through pull, with no trouble at all, to have him and his friends sent back to New York, which, as a billet, they prefer to Ohio, your confidence begins to be shaken and your stomach gives an ominous quake. And the last part of *Wesley Jackson,* in which the hero finally gets to England and eventually takes part in the invasion of France, is the record of an appalling victory over Saroyan's realistic instincts of the impulse toward self-befuddling and self-protective fantasy. Wesley Jackson, who talks constantly of his trust in God, is specially exempted from misfortune by a darling old Providence who adores him. When

he picks up what appears to be a tart in Piccadilly Cir-
cus, she turns out to be a sweet little golden-haired seventeen-year-old girl who has run away from home and who,
never having slept with a man, is trying pathetically to
qualify as a prostitute. Wesley takes her home to his rooms
(God quickly got him out of barracks), gives her a bath
and makes her his wife, and they are soon going to have
a baby, to which Wesley looks forward with tears in his
eyes. At last he is sent to France. But don't be alarmed
for a minute. Two of his best friends are killed, to be
sure, but this becomes a very beautiful thing; and when
he is captured by the Germans, they prove charming and
presently run away, leaving their prisoners in the camp,
from which Wesley escapes back to England. He is pretty
well scared for a moment when he discovers that his
house has been bombed, but of course his little blue-eyed
bride had luckily gone away to the country the night
just before this happened, and he finds her safe and
sound with her people. Even when Wesley buys tips on
the races, both the horses he bets on wins, and the good
old tipster is *so* delighted!

It is curious that this part of the novel should sound
like an anachronistic regression to the literature of sensibility of the late eighteenth and early nineteenth centuries.
There are some passages which seem to indicate that Saroyan has just been reading Dickens—and make us long
for one of Dickens' hooting hobgoblins to offset such stuff
as this: "I winked back at the flowers and thanked them as
if they were God for having me around that way—out in
England, out where the Kings and Queens had strolled,
out by the lazy old Thames, out with my lovely English
girl. After we had slept in the green of Windsor and
wakened and kissed and played games involving clouds
and their shapes and what they'd changed to, we ate our
lunch. Then Jill took off her shoes and stockings to run

bare-footed in the grass and dance for me, and oh Jill, I love thy blessed little feet. I chased her and caught her and lifted her off her feet and set her down in the green grass of England and kissed her feet because they were so twinkling and funny and serious. I kissed every toe of each foot, each sole, each arch and each ankle, so Jill kissed my Army shoes to make me laugh, and I laughed, and the flowers winked and laughed and didn't care about the lousy War." But the ready and fluent weeping that Wesley Jackson turns on whenever his finer feelings are touched, as they more and more often are, suggests, though it would probably embarrass, Henry Mackenzie's Man of Feeling or the Sterne of the *Sentimental Journey*. I forbear to quote further. There is a chapter in which Wesley recapitulates practically every thing that has happened in the book and cries over every item, including every individual who has at any time affected him unpleasantly. This is surely some of the silliest nonsense ever published by a talented writer.

June 15, 1946

OSCAR WILDE: "ONE MUST ALWAYS SEEK WHAT IS MOST TRAGIC"

THE VIKING PRESS has brought out in its Portable Library series a selection from the writings of Oscar Wilde, with a dozen unpublished letters and an introduction by Richard Aldington, and Harper is about to publish a new biography of Wilde by Hesketh Pearson: *Oscar Wilde: His Life and Wit.* This last book is a journalistic job. Mr. Pearson is an actor turned writer, who has also done biographies of Erasmus Darwin, Sydney Smith, Hazlitt, Gilbert and Sullivan, Labouchère, Anna Seward, Tom Paine, Shakespeare, Bernard Shaw and Conan Doyle. His book makes interesting reading, for he has assembled from various sources an immense number of anecdotes and sayings, and he has managed to tell a straighter story than we usually get where Wilde is concerned. Oscar Wilde has hitherto been written about mostly by his personal friends, among whom the vituperative controversies seem with time to become more embittered. Mr. Pearson stands quite clear of all these disputes, and he writes with good sense and good temper. But his book is only another example of the current kind of popular biography that adds little to our knowledge of its subject: non-critical, non-analytic and, though dealing with literary matters, essentially non-literary.

Mr. Pearson does, however, tell Wilde's story with a

new emphasis which is all to the good. The public disgrace of Wilde's trial has been allowed so much to blur the outline of the whole of his preceding career and to tarnish the brilliance of his abilities that it is a good thing to have him presented by someone, not afraid to admire him, who restores to him the pride and prestige of the days before his disaster. From Frank Harris's biography, for example, you get an almost completely grotesque picture of Oscar's parents, Sir William and Lady Wilde. Frank Harris, with gusto, makes the most of Sir William's bad reputation as an insatiable seducer of women, and there is little in his chapter on the Wilde family save an account of the scandalous lawsuit in which the elder Wilde became involved, when a more or less deranged young lady, who had come to him as a patient, accused him of having raped her while she was under an anesthetic. Nor does he tell us much more about Lady Wilde than that R. Y. Tyrrell considers her "a hifalutin, pretentious creature" with a "reputation founded on second-rate verse-making." Lord Alfred Douglas, in his ghost-written book *Oscar Wilde and Myself*, permitted his name to be signed to sneers that were quite unwarranted about the origins and standing of the Wildes. Mr. Pearson is, so far as I know, the first of Oscar Wilde's biographers to do his remarkable parents justice, and a new biography of the elder Wilde—*Victorian Doctor*, by T. G. Wilson— gives an even more complete account of the family background of Oscar. This latter book, the work of a Dublin doctor, is a variedly interesting chronicle of political and medical events and of antiquarian research in Ireland, and it confirms Mr. Pearson in establishing the importance of Lady Wilde in the first of these fields and the distinction of her husband in the others. William Wilde, who was knighted for his achievements, was, it seems, one of the greatest aurists and oculists of the English-speaking world of his time; Jane Francesca Elgee (the Elgees were Algiati of Florence, and Oscar's Italian blood should be taken into account in considering his theatrical instincts and his appetite for the ornate), though a somewhat worse than mediocre poet, had played in youth a conspicuous role as a champion of Irish nationalism and later translated from German and French and wrote books on social problems. Both were persons of wide cultivation and remarkable intellectual ability, and they shared also an independence of character and a personal eccentricity that sometimes got them disliked in Dublin.

Oscar was brought up in this tradition, and he followed it from his earliest years. Though he liked to appear offhand and lazy, his assimilative powers were prodigious, and he seems to have been at Oxford the best Greek scholar of his day. Nor was he lacking in strength or courage. The notion of him as soft and wilting has been partly the result of his "aesthetic pose," parodied by Gilbert in *Patience*, partly an unjustified inference from his homosexual habits. On a trip through one of the wilder parts of Greece in his undergraduate days, he carried a gun, Mr. Pearson tells us, and seems to have stood up to the natives as boldly as Byron did, just as later, on his visit to the United States, he won the respect of the cowboys, the Colorado miners and the San Francisco Bohemian Club by the intrepid good humor with which he accepted the crudeness and the outlandishness of pioneer life and by his indomitable head for liquor (a virtue which Lord Alfred Douglas, even at his most vindictive, admits that Wilde retained till a short time before his death). Mr. Pearson, on the testimony of an Oxford Blue of Oscar Wilde's time at Magdalen, is able to explode the story of his having been held under the pump by a group of jeering students, who had also smashed his china. "So far from being a flabby aesthete," says this contemporary, Sir Frank Benson, "there was only one man in the college, and he rowed seven in the Varsity Eight, who had the ghost of a chance in a tussle with Wilde." When a mob that had set out to maul him sent four boys in their cups to his rooms, Wilde succeeded in throwing them out and, picking the last of them up like a baby, "carried him to his rooms, and, having ceremoniously buried him beneath a pile of his own luxurious furniture, invited the spectators, now pro-Oscar to a man, to sample the fellow's wines and spirits, an invitation that was accepted with peculiar pleasure on account of the owner's present plight and past stinginess." It was precisely this self-confidence and audacity that misled him into bringing his libel suit against the Marquess of Queensberry and that sustained him to face trial when the Crown brought its action against him. Mr. Pearson gives an exhilarating version—for which, of course, we can have only Wilde's word—of his reception of the Marquess and a pugilist bodyguard when Queensberry came to his house to insult him: "This is the Marquess of Queensberry," he told his seventeen-year-old footman, "the most infamous brute in London. You are never to allow him to enter my house again." There is thus much in Mr. Pearson's book to confirm W. B. Yeats's view, expressed in his autobiography, that Wilde was "essentially a man of action, that he was a writer by perversity and accident, and would have been more important as soldier or politician."

After the decades of bickering among Wilde's friends as to who was the cause of his downfall and as to who, in his years of exile, did or did not give him money, it is a relief to read an account that brings out the stronger side of Wilde's personality, as well as his natural generosity and kindness, of which Mr. Pearson gives many instances. But it is a weakness of Mr. Pearson as a biographer of Wilde that he tends to ignore, though he cannot exclude, his subject's fundamental perversity. Mr. Pearson's sole attempt to throw light on the complexities and conflicts of Wilde's nature is a theory that his intellect had developed while his emotions remained immature. But the perversity of Oscar Wilde—by which I do not mean merely his sexual inversion—was as much a part of his thought as it was of his emotional life. The whole force of his wit is derived from it. He regarded himself, as he wrote in *De Profundis,* as "one of those who are made for exceptions, not for laws." It was Wilde's special gift, in his writings, to find expression for this impulse in a form that charms at the same time that it startles, but this perversity was also the mainspring of the tragedy of Wilde's career which is somehow so much more impressive than anything he ever wrote, or, rather, which gives to his writings an impressiveness they might not otherwise have.

This drama has never as yet really been dealt with by any of his biographers. The homosexuality that grew on Wilde was merely among its elements. There was nothing inevitable, from the moral point of view, in his having been punished for this. It is absurd for Bernard Shaw to say, as he does in his preface to the new edition of Frank Harris's book on Wilde, that "Oscar's ruin was caused by his breach of the Criminal Law Amendment Act and by nothing else." His suit against the Marquess of Queensberry was a disinterested though an ill-advised action, prompted by his infatuation with Lord Alfred Douglas, who, childish and hysterical himself, wanted revenge against his rabid father, and who never for a second hesitated, in gratifying his selfish spite, to let Oscar run terrible risks. Lord Alfred, as he appears in the descriptions of him written by other people and in his own self-justificatory polemics, makes such an unpleasant impression that it is only by reading *Dorian Gray* and *The Portrait of Mr. W. H.*, in which Wilde, writing before he met Douglas, describes his romantic ideal, that we can see how Lord Alfred represented it, and it is only by reading Douglas' sonnet on Wilde, written after the latter's death, that we can see that Wilde's admiration was not entirely misplaced. But it was certainly, on Wilde's side, this idealization of Douglas, and, on Douglas' side, his adoption of Wilde as a kind of substitute father, who, as he thought, could stand up to his real father, that set the machinery of disaster in motion.

The next question, however, is why Oscar, after losing his suit against Queensberry, insisted on remaining in England to face the second of the criminal trials—the jury having disagreed in the first—in which he was prosecuted by the public authorities on charges arising from the evidence presented by Queensberry in the original suit, when he could perfectly well have escaped to the Continent. The explanations usually given are Wilde's pugnacious Irish pride, stimulated by that of his mother, who had told him that if he ran away she would never speak to him again, and his desire to vindicate his character in the interests of his wife and children. But by that time he already knew what the evidence against him was and he should have foreseen his defeat, as, in fact, he should have had the foresight not to take the legal offensive against Queensberry (Bernard Shaw says he was drunk when he did this). I want to point out that a sense of damnation, a foreboding of tragic failure, is to be found in the writing of Wilde from a time long before he was caught in the particular noose that landed him in Reading Jail. It is the theme of the sonnet *Hélas!* as it is of *Dorian Gray*: it is sounded, as Mr. Pearson notes, even in *An Ideal Husband*. And the conflict that is to end in collapse is reflected by his continual antithesis of what he regarded as his "pagan" side to what he regarded as his "Christian" instincts, by which literary phrases he really referred to his appetites and his moral sense. For an "aesthete" like Wilde's master, Pater, it was possible to savor both points of view in a state of serene contemplation; but, though Wilde could see "beauty" alike in the sensuous pleasures of the one and in the suffering implied by the other, he could not help, behind his smiling boldness, being troubled and torn between them. The impulse of perversity in him was constantly working both ways: it impelled him not only to disconcert the expectations of the conventional world by shocking paradoxes and scandalous behavior, it caused him also to betray his pagan creed by indulgence in Christian compunction. There are moments when we get the impression not merely that he apprehended catastrophe but that he even in some sense invited it; when we feel that, having flouted the respectable world by making an immense amount of money and a conspicuous social success through mockery of its codes and standards, he turned against his own arrogance and kicked wealth and success downstairs.

It throws some light on this psychological procedure of Wilde's to refer to Yeats's portrait of him in *The Trembling of the Veil*. Yeats describes the Wilde family in Ireland as "very imaginative and learned," "dirty, untidy" and "daring," and speaks of Wilde's "half-civilized blood," which did not allow him to "endure the sedentary toil of creative art." It is certainly true of Wilde that, with much sensitivity and nobility, he had also a certain coarseness, and his pursuit of the "pagan" ideal always had a tendency to lead him into vulgar ostentation and self-indulgence. The trouble is that, when, fed up with luxury, he turns away in disgust, it is usually not in the direction of the "sedentary toil of creative art" but in the direction of a version of the Christian ideal of humility and abnegation—some of his fairy-stories illustrate this appallingly—that is itself ostentatious and vulgar. Yet one finds in him, also, at moments, a sense of guilt and a bitter chagrin at having fallen very far short of the best that he could imagine. There is, of course, in *De Profundis,* a certain amount of maudlin Christian emotion, but there is also the other thing. "While I see," he says soberly enough, "that there is nothing wrong in what one does, I see that there is something wrong in what one becomes." One of his principal reproaches against Lord Alfred Douglas, whether the latter deserved it or not, is that Douglas interfered with his work, and it is his consciousness of sin for the neglect of this work rather than grief at having injured his family which seems to make him feel, in prison, that it is just for him to expiate his debaucheries. Even here, to be sure, he is acting, and there is testimony, as Mr. Pearson indicates (he might have added that of Ford Madox Ford), that Oscar sometimes overacted the poverty and misery of his final years. But the fact that he is always acting does not deprive his performance of value. This performance is not merely literary. In his writing, his imagination often dresses itself floridly and trashily; it is only at his most intellectual— that is, when we get his wit at its purest and its least arty —that he arrives at an excellent style. One has to combine his writing, the records of his conversation and the sequence of events in his life in order to appreciate Wilde and to see that, though one cannot describe him as precisely a first-rate writer, he did somehow put on a first-rate show.

There is as yet no biography of Wilde which goes at all behind the scenes of this drama, and the only descriptions of him which show any real psychological insight are those of Yeats and Gide. It seems to have been to Gide, always conscious of moral problems, that Wilde, always sensitive to his audience, made the most vivid revelation of his own conception of his role in the successive scenes of the play. "My duty to myself," he told Gide when he saw him in Algeria in January, 1895, at the time when the Marquess of Queensberry had already begun to bait him, "is to amuse myself terrifically . . . . no happiness—only pleasure. One must always seek what is most tragic.*. . . My friends are extraordinary; they advise me to be prudent. But prudence!— is that possible for me? It would be to return on my tracks. I must push things as far as possible. I cannot go any further, and something will have to happen—something different." And later, when he had come out of prison and Gide had gone to see him in France: "One must never take up again the same existence one has had before. My life is like a work of art: an artist never repeats the same work—or if he does, it is only for the reason that he did not succeed the first time. My life before I went to prison was the greatest success possible. Now it is a completed thing."

As for the clinical aspect of Oscar Wilde's case, there has been no careful study of it—though he deserves the same kind of attention that has been given to Maupassant and Swift. Mr. Pearson, Dr. Wilson and Frank Har-

---

* "Pas le bonheur! Surtout pas le bonheur. Le plaisir! Il faut vouloir toujours le plus tragique." These quotations are from Gide's little book on Wilde. He adds: "Je n'ai rien inventé, rien arrangé, dans les derniers propos que je cite. Les paroles de Wilde sont présentes à mon esprit, et j'allais dire à mon oreille."

ris have pointed out the striking parallel between the last years of Oscar's life and the last years of Sir William Wilde's. Both were dragged down, at the height of their fame, by sexual scandals that brought them into court, and the father withdrew afterward from Dublin and almost completely abandoned his profession, just as the son fled to France and ceased to write. Did the father's example here exert a compulsive influence or was some pathological principle operating in both cases? Bernard Shaw suggested, in his memoir in the first edition of Harris's life, that both Oscar and his mother had the physical signs of a derangement of the pituitary gland, and Dr. Wilson has discussed this idea on the basis of more recent researches into the various glandular types. But there is apparently another factor in the pathology of Oscar Wilde—a factor which, so far as I know, has never been emphasized save in the writings of Wilde's quixotic and non-homosexual friend, Robert Harborough Sherard. We are usually told in the books about Wilde, as if it were something of merely casual interest, that he probably died of syphilis. But if he was really a victim of syphilis, it is surely important to know how this malady had been acquired and how long and how severely he had been suffering from it. We learn now from Dr. Wilson's book that he is supposed to have contracted it at Oxford, but he does not pursue the subject. It would help to explain Wilde if it were proved that he was haunted through his adult life by an uncured syphilitic infection, and his illness—made rapidly worse, it is said, by the drinking of his last years—should certainly be taken into account in considering the demoralization into which he finally sank. In the cases of Baudelaire and Maupassant, it seems obvious that the morose disaffection of the one and the desperate pessimism of the other were the shadows of the syphilitic's doom in the days when the disease was incurable. In Wilde's case, the man is so bland, the work so bright-hued and amusing, that his biographers—having already to deal with the problem of his homosexuality—seem reluctant to come to grips with another distasteful factor; but, in shirking it, I believe, they slight also both the interest of Oscar Wilde's work and the tragedy of his life. Read *The Picture of Dorian Gray,* or even the best of his fairy tales, *The Birthday of the Infanta,* with the *Spirochaeta pallida* in mind. In such stories, the tragic heroes are shown in the peculiar position of suffering from organic maladies—in the one case, a moral corruption which grows; in the other, a permanent repulsiveness—without, up to a point, being forced to experience the evils entailed by them. Dorian Gray conceals his vices and is able to evade their consequences; the Dwarf in *The Birthday of the Infanta* is not saddened or embittered by his ugliness because he does not know how he looks. But in the end, in both cases, the horror breaks out: the afflicted one must recognize himself and be recognized by other people as the odious creature he is, and his disease or disability will kill him. This theme of impending collapse is a recurrent one with Oscar Wilde, and it must have some very close connection with his conception of his own nature and its destiny. One can account for it purely in terms of Wilde's sexual and moral life, without supposing him to have been doomed by syphilis; yet it is hard to believe that a nature so elastic and so insouciant could have been broken so completely and so quickly without some shattering physical cause.

June 29, 1946

Since the above was written, a volume called *The Trials of Oscar Wilde* in the *Notable British Trials* series has supplied the clinical facts that the biographies of Wilde lack. I quote from Appendix E by the editor, H. Montgomery Hyde: "Certain it is that Wilde betrayed no signs of abnormality in adolescence and early manhood. On the contrary, his inclinations seem to have been decidedly heterosexual. While an undergraduate at Oxford, he contracted syphilis as the result of a casual connexion, probably with a prostitute. In those days the recognized treatment for this disease was with mercury. In Wilde's case this treatment undoubtedly produced the discolouration and decay of his teeth, which remained a permanent feature of his appearance for the remainder of his life and added to the general impression of physical overgrowth and ugliness which his person presented on acquaintance. Nor, it may be added, was there the slightest suggestion of effeminacy about him, either at Oxford or at any subsequent period. . . . We know, too, that he was deeply in love with his wife at the time of their marriage, and that they experienced normal sexual intercourse. Indeed, two sons were born of the union before the rift between them took place. . . . Before proposing to his wife, Wilde had been to consult a doctor in London, who had assured him that he was completely cured of his youthful malady. On the strength of his assurance he got married. About two years later he discovered to his dismay that all traces of syphilis had not been eradicated from his system, and it was this unpleasant discovery which obliged him to discontinue physical relations with his wife. In the result, *inter alia,* he turned toward homosexuality." The doctor who attended him in prison reported that Wilde's disease was then in an advanced stage. No wonder he soon ceased to function when he finally got away to the Continent.

GEORGE GROSZ IN THE UNITED STATES

THE AUTOBIOGRAPHY OF GEORGE GROSZ—*A Little Yes and a Big No*—is a most entertaining book and an important document on Germany. Here is the record of a German artist who was disgusted by German war-making and who attacked the makers of war; who spent his youth as a Dadaist rebel in the years of bad food and inflation between the two wars in Germany; who felt the pressure of impending tyranny and, warned, he says, by a Kafka-esque nightmare of blind alleys, covert persecution and a plague of stinking fish, decided to de-camp to America at the beginning of 1933. "Yes, it was indeed strange," he writes, "that the deeper significance of my dream remained hidden from me at that time. I know today that a definite Power wanted to save me from annihilation. Why I was to be spared, I do not know. Perhaps it was to serve as a witness." I have not read anything else which has made me feel to what degree life in Germany became intolerable during the years after the Treaty of Versailles. From George Grosz you get the impression that there were only two real courses possible: Hitlerism or flight. Though for a time, after the first of the wars, he allied himself with the political Left, he has a Nietzschean scorn of the masses, and seems never to have believed very strongly in the ability of the working class to recreate

343

contemporary society. He says that he shocked Thomas
Mann, when he met him in America in 1933, by pre-
dicting that Hitler would last.

Mr. Grosz is also a valuable witness, in his account of
his experience in this country, on the subject of the foreign artist who comes to live in the United States. It
more or less happened in Grosz's case, as it did with
Stravinsky and Auden, that, in obedience to some curious law, his prestige for Americans dwindled from the
moment that we had him among us. George Grosz, unlike these other two artists, wanted very much at first to
make money in the American way; he admired the
American illustrators who drew for our magazines and
thought, apparently, that he would like nothing better
than to do this sort of work himself, but somehow he was
not acceptable. He had hoped to drop the vein of satire
which had made him so famous abroad, along with the
society it caricatured; but, in spite of his determined efforts to deal with American life in a forward-looking
and clean-cut way, the colors that he applied to his street
scenes were always overflowing their outlines and the
Americans he would have liked to idealize turned out to
be "mostly middle-aged and uglier than I had intended."
He could only remain himself: an artist with a vision of
the world which he could no more prevent his faculties
from concentrating their forces to realize than a wild
pig in labor with a litter of boars can give birth to
china-pig savings-banks.

Eventually, left free in America by the lapse of his
reputation and obliged to dig himself in, as is necessary
for artistic survival in a country that has no artists' cafés,
he worked on into a new phase of development which
was for a long time completely "straight"—doing landscapes, lay figures, portraits and nudes that sometimes
seemed strangely inexpressive after the extraordinary va-

riety and humanity of his earlier satirical period. (The satirical side of his art is admirably represented by the dozens of drawings included in *A Little Yes and a Big No*). And at last we found him turning out studies of the grass-fringed contours of sand-dunes, the broken stumps of Adirondack lakes and the filigree of Cape Cod scrub-pine that—quite different in everything save mastery of line from the deliberately ragged caricatures of the pre-Hitler bourgeoisie—had a firmness, a steel-shaving delicacy, only a little softened in its descent from the leaf-drawings of Dürer. The album of George Grosz's work published by Bittner in 1944 gave a retrospective view of this work; and the exhibition of last autumn, at the Associated American Artists, added to it the remarkable water colors of the atrocities of the Nazi movement which represent a further development, more bitter and more brilliant, of his original satirical vein, and a series of apocalyptic paintings, not always perhaps successful but at their best of a frightening tragic force, in which the remnants of a decrepit civilization are seen wallowing on their bellies or frying in an inferno of fire and mud. In the field of the arts, it seems to me that these pictures, with André Malraux's last novel, *La Lutte avec l'Ange*, and Benjamin Britten's opera *Peter Grimes*, are the only productions I know that have expressed the despair and anguish of the years we have been living through and that yet do not discourage but fortify, since they make us feel the vigor of the craftsman who, in grappling with a terrible subject, scores a victory over its terrors. And just as Stravinsky has emerged as a popular national figure whose new music, that was at first ignored, is now played to crowded houses and whose albums of phonograph records are sold out as soon as issued; as the collected poems of Auden have recently caused him to shine far beyond the academic penumbra of the colleges in which he has been teaching, and won him almost the circulation of an American family poet—so the reception of this recent exhibition seemed to indicate that at last George Grosz was coming to play a role in America which, if not quite the one he imagined—since it does not bring him the biggest income—does confer upon him the highest rank.

This exceptionally honest and amusing and revelatory autobiography should effect his complete emergence. What is most striking, as in the artist's pictures, is his freedom from the inveterate myth-mindedness which leads the Germans, so often disastrously, to substitute heroic abstractions for realistic observation and ordinary common sense. There are striking examples of this habit of mind in Stephen Spender's recent book, *European Witness*—not only the excerpts he gives us from a youthful novel of Goebbels', but the blood-chilling battle scene that he translates from a novel by Ernest Jünger, in which the excitement of war is raised to a pitch of barbaric ecstasy that disconcertingly recalls the old sagas. It can be seen also in a most curious form, in the last issue of *Partisan Review*, in the memoirs of a German soldier who was assigned to guard a prison-camp in Poland. This man, whose duty it was to beat, torture and kill other men, writes of the happenings of the life of this prison-camp in terms of a mythology of stalking Deaths, white watching Ghosts, Hills of Calvary and Angels of Vengeance. But this element of grandiose allegory is quite absent from George Grosz's story: he is homely, concrete and human. There is no touch of the mystical imagination, unless his prophetic dream be one—but that is concrete and homely, too. One remembers that the German tradition is not necessarily Hegelian, not necessarily Wagnerian: there are Dürer, Beethoven and Hauptmann. And one realizes today that George Grosz, in these dark days for the German intellect, has represented what is stoutest and noblest in this other German tradition. The hand that sketched the moral tatters, the deliquescence, of the bourgeoisie could trace the distinct stems and twigs, and fill in the big sweep, of the dunes; and the man who directed the hand may be met in this autobiography: a great German artist, we recognize, who, in becoming an American citizen, has acquired an international passport.

January 4, 1947

AN OLD FRIEND OF THE FAMILY:
THACKERAY

THE TWO NEW VOLUMES of the Thackeray papers edited by Gordon N. Ray—*The Letters and Private Papers
of William Makepeace Thackeray*—cover the years
from the beginning of 1852 to Thackeray's death at
the end of 1863, and they include his two trips to America, where he lectured and made a great deal of money;
his row with Dickens and Edmund Yates over the publication of the latter's description of him and the expulsion
of Yates from the Garrick Club; Thackeray's campaign and
defeat as a parliamentary candidate for Oxford; his editorship of the *Cornhill Magazine*, which gave rise to
some curious correspondence between him and his
fellow-writers; and his attempts to bring up his two
daughters, who had been motherless since his wife went
insane and whom he had sometimes, when away on
tours, to leave with his own mother—thus precipitating
long arguments by letter about the little girls' religious
education, in which the strongly anti-fundamentalist
Thackeray had to stand up to the formidably pious lady
who had sat for Helen Pendennis. There are also some
hitherto unpublished comments on the personality and
work of Charlotte Brontë, whom Thackeray publicly
praised but who seems rather to have nagged him and
got under his skin by the challenging and birdlike at-

tacks which she made on him whenever they met; and a long letter to George Henry Lewes, giving an account, at the latter's request, of Thackeray's visit to Weimar in his youth and a conversation he had with Goethe, incidents which he had then recorded on a casual and captious tone but now suffuses with a mellow light of memory. An appendix contains passages from the letters, written by Thackeray to Mrs. Brookfield or to common friends of theirs, which Mr. Ray has been unable to obtain and for which he has been obliged to rely on the fragmentary extracts in auction catalogues. These sometimes give more intimate glimpses into the passions and unpleasantness of the period when Thackeray was in love with Mrs. Brookfield than do the more complete texts in Volume II.

The Thackeray of this final decade makes, in general, a more amiable impression than the Thackeray of the first forty years. A Victorian paterfamilias tied to an insane wife, his flirtations are always painful, but his relations with Sally Baxter, the young American girl he met in New York, are very much lighter and straighter than the depressing affair of Mrs. Brookfield. And, though he seems to have been made rather intolerable by his first social success in London, he cools off later and becomes more civil. At the beginning of Volume III, we still find him boasting rather embarrassingly to a humble woman friend in the country who is coming to teach his daughters music: "Thursday will be the best day to come, that's the soonest. I dine out with the Dean of St. Paul's (you have heard of a large meeting house we have between Ludgate Hill & Cheapside with a round roof?) but by the time I come home, you will have made friends of Miss Trulock & Miss Anny & Miss Harriet." And he still likes to let people know it even when he has to decline an invitation: "Some of the immensest bigwigs have asked me to dinner: but I refuse all to go to the children. My dears. . . . I would rather sit in the brown house [of the American friends to whom he is writing] than at the bigwiggest table." He had evidently had a chip on his shoulder in regard to the aristocracy, for he now bubbles over to his mother: "How much kindness haven't I had from people eager to serve me? It's we who make the haughtiness of the grandees—not they. They're never thinking of it . . . and coming to know people whom I have thought insolent & air-giving, such as Lord & Lady John for instance, I find 2 as simple folks as you & G P—and no more *gêne* at their tea-table than yours"; and, "Did they [his daughters] write to you about Blanche Stanley, who is Lady Airlie now, asking me for a dinner, and walking away to the front drawing room from the other ladies, and only talking to the children till the gentlemen came in? I called her Lady Give-yourself Airlie and that's the only Air giving I've seen amongst the great ladies. The small ones are just as vulgar sometimes: and quite as overbearing."

But he got over this intoxication. His earnings made him independent; and his visit to the United States in 1852–53 gave him for the first time the vision of a completely non-feudal world where one's social position did not depend on the good nature and the good taste of the titled. "There's nothing to sneer at," he writes friends in England, "—some usages different to ours, but a manliness and fairness that puts our society to shame often. I like to see the equality, I wince a little at first when a shopman doesn't say 'Sir' or a coachman says 'Help that man with his luggage'—but y not? I'm sure that Society sh^d be as it here is, that no harm should attach to a man for any honest way of working for his bread, and that a man should be allowed to be poor. We allow *certain*

men to be poor at home, but not every one." America
even goes to his head, as his first taste of the nobility
had: "In travelling in Europe our confounded English pride only fortifies itself, and we feel that we are
better than 'those foreigners,' but it's worth while coming here that we may think small beer of ourselves afterwards. Greater nations than ours ever have been are
born in America and Australia—and Truth will be
spoken and Freedom will be practiced, and God will be
worshipped among them, as they never have been with
the antiquarian trammels that bind us in the Old World.
I look at this, and speculate on this bright Future, as an
Astronomer of a Star; and admire and worship the beautiful goodness of God." In the South, though he disapproved of slavery, he thought that the Negroes were
an inferior race and that they were very well off as they
were: "The negroes are happy whatever is said of them,
at least all we see, and the country Planters beg and im-
plore any Englishman to go to their estates and see for
themselves."

But later, again, he somewhat cools off. Returning
to Europe, he is disgusted, in Switzerland, to find Americans eating with their knives and talking bad French
or no French, and he makes a point of writing repeatedly
to his friends in the States about it. And, visiting America a second time, in 1855–56, when he is older and
suffering from two complaints, malaria and urethral
stricture, he finds he does not like it so well. Sally Baxter
is getting married; an antagonism toward England is
mounting; and he sees more of barbarity and squalor
when he explores, with his new series of lectures, the
Deep South and the Mississippi—having, on one occasion, as competitors and fellow-travellers, a freak show
with Wild Men and a Giantess. "It seems to me," he
writes to his daughters, "I am not near so much in love

with the country this time as before—doesn't it seem so
to you?" He still finds "slavery nowhere repulsive—the
black faces invariably happy and plump, the white ones
eager and hard . . . but you read that the other day a
woman killed one child, and tried to kill another and
herself rather than go back to slavery—that a party of
fugitives were discovered in a leaky river boat rather
than return."

Yet—his celibate life and his worsening ailments have
evidently affected his views of the New and the Old
World both—he does not like England any the better.
He becomes, on the contrary, in his final years, even
more bitter against the life of society and more critical
of the aristocracy. "B—— is spoiled by the heartlessness of
London," he had written already in 1853, "which is
awful to think of—the most godless respectable thing—
thing's not the word but I can't get it—I mean that world
is base and prosperous and content, not unkind—very
well bred—very unaffected in manner, not dissolute—
clean in person and raiment and going to church every
Sunday—but in the eyes of the Great Judge of right &
wrong what rank will those people have with all their
fine characters and linen? They never feel love, but
directly it's born, they throttle it and fling it under the
sewer as poor girls do their unlawful children—they
make up money-marriages and are content—then the
father goes to the House of Commons or the Counting
House, the mother to her balls and visits—the children
lurk upstairs with their governess, and when their turn
comes are bought and sold, and respectable and heartless
as their parents before them." And when, in 1857, he ran
for Parliament as an independent candidate, he declared
that he had incurred "a good deal of ill-will in certain
very genteel quarters in London" for having said "that
those gentlemen with handles to their names, that the

members of great aristocratic families had a very great share of public patronage and government, and that for my part I heartily desired that men of the people—the working men and educated men of the people—should have a share in the government." "We hope to meet in April or May," he writes, in connection with Bayard Taylor, to an American correspondent, "when I bragged about taking him into the fashionable world. But I hear that I am in disgrace with the fashionable world for speaking disrespectfully of the Georgy-porgies —and am not to be invited myself, much more to be allowed to take others into polight Society. I writhe at the exclusion. . . . I MUST come back & see you all. I praise Mr. Washington five times more here than I did in the States— Our people cheer—the fine folks look a little glum but the celebrated Thacker does not care for their natural ill-temper." And elsewhere, to his mother: "The bigwigs and great folks are furious. The halls of splendor are to be shut to me—and having had pretty nearly enough of the halls of splendor I shall be quite resigned to a quiet life outside them." That phrase "our people" above is significant of the later Thackeray. He had always been, even for an Englishman, excessively and uncomfortably class-conscious; but he had never identified himself so frankly, taking this tone of outspoken defiance, with an educated upper middle class which has interests in conflict with the nobility.

It is particularly, thus, in these later years that what Chesterton called somewhere, I think, Thackeray's "strong but sleepy virility" most resoundingly comes to life. And, as he grows older, the inextinguishable boyishness, which somehow continued to exist in the face of disillusion and illness, becomes more of a saving grace as his age throws it into relief. Thackeray, even for an Englishman, talks a great deal too much about money and, even for a respectable Victorian, too much about his duty to his family and the sacrifices and efforts he is making for them. But he did so love having the dollars and the pounds roll in that he communicates his exhilaration. He never seems to perform a benefaction without publishing it to some correspondent, and he was too eager on one occasion to make himself disagreeable at the expense of a member of his club who had failed to chip in for a fund to help a friend out of serious straits—passing around a malicious cartoon of the Pharisee and the Good Samaritan—till he discovered that the supposed Pharisee had already done his best for the man in a less conspicuous fashion. But he was spontaneously and lavishly generous, and such an incident is counterbalanced by the story told by Mr. Lionel Stevenson, in his recent biography of Thackeray, of his climbing to the garret of another old friend, scolding him for his evil courses, and hiding a hundred-pound note to be discovered after he left. His humor, which in earlier days he had often used to solace his envy or to revenge himself for slights, now becomes more like Edward Lear's, in Lear's familiar letters: an impulsive spilling-over of fun, that has the merit of making hay of formalities. And, though he ate and drank himself to death at the age of fifty-two, just at the moment when he was on the threshold of what he had planned as his most important work, a history of the reign of Queen Anne, he did love a party so, he enjoyed it so much more than research, that we can't be entirely sorry to miss seeing him bore himself. Yet the amiable qualities of Thackeray have at last been so liberally released in proportion as he has found himself freed from the anxieties and constraints of his earlier years that, fatigued with him though we may have come to be in going through these four long volumes, we regret it when we get to the letters in which his daughter writes to the Baxters to tell them about his death—from apoplexy, after dining out, just a day or two before Christmas.

One of the things that have made us impatient with Thackeray is his reluctance to take literature seriously and that carelessness about his novels of which Trollope and Henry James complained. These letters are full of the evidences of his boredom with his later books. On one occasion, when travelling on the Continent, he had to write back to England to find out the Christian names of some of the characters in *The Newcomes*, which he was then still engaged in writing. He *did* take a lot of trouble over *Henry Esmond*, but when it failed to have the success he had hoped for—the result, as he thought, of a bad review—he seems quite to have dropped any idea of classical form or artistic intensity. When Trollope told him that *Esmond* was "not only his best work, but so much the best that there was none second to it," Thackeray answered, "That was what I intended, but I have failed. Nobody reads it. After all, what does it matter?"

Nor, so negligent about literary form, was he remarkably courageous about subject. In spite of his prayers, after *Vanity Fair*, to be given the strength to tell "the Truth," he was easily discouraged by the conventions of the day. He violated the probabilities in *The Newcomes* by allowing Clive to marry Ethel, and, when James Russell Lowell remonstrated with him, begged, "What could a fellow do? So many people wanted 'em married. [The novel had been appearing in monthly parts.] To be sure, I had to kill off poor little Rosey rather suddenly, but shall not a man do what he will with his own?" There was a moment, after the Brookfield affair, when he wanted to write a novel about a man who fell in love with a married woman—she and her husband to be reunited by their affection for their children—but he seems to have been dissuaded by a horrified friend; at any rate, he gave up the idea. When *Madame Bovary* came out, he loathed it. "The book is bad," he declared. "It is a heartless cold-blooded study of the downfall and degradation of a woman." As editor of the *Cornhill Magazine*, he sent back a story of Trollope's on the ground, Trollope says, that it "alluded to a man with illegitimate children, and to the existence of a woman not as pure as she should be"; and a poem of Mrs. Browning's on the ground that it was "an account," as Thackeray wrote her, "of unlawful passion felt by a man for a woman." Trollope retorted: How about *Adam Bede*, *Jane Eyre* and *The Heart of Midlothian*, and, for that matter, how about *The Four Georges*? And Mrs. Browning replied with some spirit: "I am not a 'fast woman'— I don't like coarse subjects, or the coarse treatment of any subject— But I am deeply convinced that the corruption of our society requires, not shut doors and windows, but light and air." He started running the essays of Ruskin later published as *Unto This Last*, but was so frightened by the protests aroused when their socialistic tendencies became apparent that he wrote Ruskin with "many apologies" and "great discomfort to himself," explaining that he must stop them short. (It should be said, in justice to Thackeray, that he liked his job of editor so little that he resigned before the end of the three years that he had originally engaged to serve.)

My own experience in rereading Thackeray has been rather disappointing. In going back to Jane Austen and Dickens, I have found more than I had known was there, and have been even more impressed by them than I had been before. But to go back to Thackeray, in one's later years, when one no longer takes great writers on faith, is to be made more aware of his weaknesses without discovering much that is new. Of course, his vein at its best was excellent; but it is so much merely a vein that is always running thin or insipid. One cannot count on him to do anything solid, and even *Henry Esmond*, though carefully built, has always seemed to me rather flimsy. One falls back on the conclusion, borne out by these letters, that Thackeray had in his day and for a certain length of time thereafter a kind of social value that made him seem a greater writer than he was. He was the chronicler of a middle-class world which, though sometimes humiliated by poverty, always pretended to education and gentility. Dissociating itself from its background of trade, which it had now begun to ridicule, or assimilating itself to the nobility, whose standards it partly adopted, it sought exclusively to identify itself with the professions, with literature and painting, and with the Army and Navy and the Civil Service. The ups and downs of this world and the assertion of its fundamental dignity, as well as a certain dissatisfaction with its methods, aims and rewards, really constitutes Thackeray's whole subject, and he never gets outside that subject. He cannot see society as a whole as Dickens was able to do, with all the paradoxes involved in its structure and the dislocations caused by its growth. He is unable to interest himself in personalities or relations for their own sake, as Henry James or Jane Austen did—in such a way as to use them for materials in composing a work of art. His situations and characters are sketches on a somewhat higher plane, to be sure, than the drawings he dashed off in his letters, but more or less the same sort of thing.

To readers of the group that he wrote for, the monthly installments of his novels were all like a series of

letters—full of personal appeals and confidings and whatever reflections on life the event or the mood might
suggest—in which Thackeray talked about people that
he and they both knew. This explains his popularity
in the United States, where he felt so much more at
home than Dickens did. Realizing how pleasant and
how profitable it would be to enlarge his circle of correspondents, he more or less directly addressed to the
American upper classes, with their republican point of
view, *The Four Georges* and *The Virginians*, and he
cemented this *entente cordiale* by embodying Miss Sally
Baxter in the English Ethel Newcome. To such "nice
people" on both sides of the water, he became a kind of
friend of the family: a gossip who was mostly entertaining, a moralist who was not too severe, a man of the
world who had met everyone worth meeting yet did not
make his hosts feel provincial, a man of breeding who
was always avuncular in correcting the bad manners
of the children and a dinner guest who always did
justice to the company, the wine and the food. And this
role that Thackeray played for his own and the next
generation accounts partly, I think, for the high esteem
in which his books have been held by such Old World
"bourgeois" critics as George Saintsbury and H. L.
Mencken. The extravagant praise which has been given
by the latter of these to *The Newcomes* and by the
former to Thackeray's work as a whole may be due to
very early impressions, to their identifying themselves
in boyhood with Pendennis and Clive Newcome and
Esmond. Up through 1910, I suppose, boys and girls
still continued to read Thackeray; but by that time
he was no longer so close to the life that they actually
knew. I do not believe that his novels will ever mean so
much again to either younger or older readers.

February 8, 1947

GILBERT WITHOUT SULLIVAN

Random House has reprinted its collected volume of the *Plays and Poems of W. S. Gilbert*, first published in 1932. It is, in the main, a satisfactory job: it contains all the librettos of the Gilbert and Sullivan operas, two operas written with other composers, and the whole of the *Bab Ballads*. Operas and ballads are illustrated with Gilbert's droll little drawings; and there is a fifty-page preface by Deems Taylor which admirably covers Gilbert's career and the history of the operas. The book is well printed and not too heavy.

One's only complaint would be that the editor has taken space to include an inferior set of *Bab Ballads*, which Gilbert rightly discarded, and a blank-verse play, *The Palace of Truth*, which is certainly not one of his most brilliant things, while he has left out *Haste to the Wedding*, Gilbert's very amusing version of *Le Chapeau de Paille d'Italie*, and has failed to give any examples of his non-operatic farces. Surely it would have been worth while to preserve the burlesque *Hamlet*, called *Rosenkrantz and Guildenstern*, and the once popular comedy *Engaged*, which was revived in New York so recently as the twenties. Even aside from the operas, Gilbert had some importance as a dramatist. His serious plays were dreadful. When he tried to drop his characteristic mixture of satire and pure nonsense, he lapsed immediately into sentimental melodrama of the kind that, as Mr. Taylor remarks, he frequently parodied in his comic writings. But he had also another vein, which was anti-sentimental and somewhat tougher than anything in the operas. Such comedies as *Tom Cobb* and *Sweethearts*, which had considerable success in the seventies, must have struck a new note in the theater. What Gilbert seems to have invented was a curious comic convention, derived from a mercantile society, according to which the characters, full of tender and noble sentiments, were shown never to act from any other motives than those of the grimmest self-interest. Their amorous affairs are conducted on a basis of hard cash and advantage, without an atom of human feeling; and they are thus not merely fairy-tale creatures, like the characters in the operas, who make British officials delightful at the same time that they make them absurd and have fun with the British caste system by turning it upside down, but caricatures of a harsher kind. And this abstraction of the motive of cupidity from all the other impulses and passions had its influence on the dramatists who came after Gilbert. If the earlier comedies of Wilde went back to the tradition of Congreve, *The Importance of Being Earnest* unquestionably derived from Gilbert; and though Shaw, in his youthful days as a reviewer of theater and opera, was in general rather snooty about Gilbert, the latter evidently counted for something in the readiness with which it was possible for Shaw to substitute, in such of his early plays as *Arms and the Man* and *You Never Can Tell*, the common-sense motivations, in situations of love and war, for the expected romantic ones.

With Barrie, too, the reversal of social roles that makes the interest of *The Admirable Crichton* probably dates back to *Pinafore*; and the pirates of *Peter Pan* must owe something to those of Penzance. As a figure in this whole development of the modern school of British comedy, Gilbert has, I think, been rather slighted. He has become, in the popular mind, so closely and exclusively associated with Sullivan that he is rarely given serious attention as a dramatist with an independent existence. Yet, as one reads these librettos, one realizes how sharp and how permanent the differences were between the two collaborators, and to what degree these must have been responsible for their finally falling out. They were differences of a kind which made it almost impossible for Gilbert to adapt himself to Sullivan, so that Sullivan was always in the position of trying to assimilate Gilbert. For the latter, though metrically adroit, a marvellous wit in verse, was quite devoid of real lyric talent. Gilbert had no ear for music, and of the magical music of words that distinguishes the meanest lyric of the Elizabethan song-writer Campion, the most ambitious aria of Gilbert is not able to muster a trace; nor could he manage the more commonplace sweetness which, in so many of the poems of Moore, married itself to Irish melodies. Bernard Shaw put his finger on the deficiencies of Gilbert when he called his lyrics "aridly fanciful," and, contrasting his librettos with those that Meilhac and Halévy had written for Offenbach, described them as "a curiously brutalized, embittered, stolidified, middle-classical, mechanical equivalent" for these.

One cannot help sympathizing with Sullivan when he complained that he had to fit his music into a rigid and inhuman mold (one sympathizes particularly with his protest against "the middle-aged woman with fading charms," the inevitable appearance of whom became such a tiresome betrayal of all that was worst in Gilbert: a streak of vulgar cruelty and a tendency to rely on formula). Sullivan's own talent was

Irish and Italian: he loved to write pretty music. And Gilbert could never really write prettily—that is, he could never write without a certain hard facetious touch that was then and has remained characteristic of the kind of humorous verse that one finds in English comic weeklies. Sullivan was graceful and romantic; Gilbert, though fantastic, flat-footed. They soon learned how to work together in a well-oiled coördination, but their talents never really blended. Sullivan first expressed his dissatisfaction after the run of *Princess Ida*, requesting from Gilbert "a story of human interest and probability, where the humorous words would come in a humorous (not serious) situation." Gilbert was angry at first, but presently told Sullivan that he had for him just the kind of thing he wanted, and presented him with the libretto of *The Mikado*, which, if it did not precisely meet the requirements, proved such a stupendous success that Sullivan, for the moment, evidently ceased to worry. They went on to *Ruddigore*, and then Gilbert made a real effort to give Sullivan what he wanted by turning out *The Yeomen of the Guard*, for which Sullivan wrote an excellent score, but in which Gilbert, making desperate efforts to arrive at the poignant and the somber, is workmanlike but not at his best.

Gilbert himself, it seems to me, is successful in achieving an aesthetic effect only in those operas where outlandish combinations produce piquant and surprising contrasts that eventually become resolved: the descent of the Heavy Dragoons upon the aesthetes and love-sick maidens of *Patience*, the intrusion into fairyland, in *Iolanthe*, of the Lord Chancellor and the House of Lords. And in these cases it is hard to tell how much the happy result was a matter of calculation. Gilbert *did* have some instinct for dramatic color; and his charming little drawings show that his characters were not quite

all conceived as disputatious two-dimensional monsters;
but, if you read the librettos of the operas, without
reference to Sullivan's scores, you would hardly be able
to imagine, any more than in reading the *Bab Ballads*,
that vivifying them by stage production would bring
out in them a poetic beauty. There is no color in Gilbert's *writing*: it all comes with the costumes and the
settings, and with the brightness of Sullivan's music.
The worst operas as aesthetic creations are, in my opinion, *The Mikado* and *The Gondoliers* (admirably solid
though the former is as a job of theatrical carpentry), in
which a definite national background has no real relevance to either text or music (though Sullivan put into
the latter some delightful parodies of Italian opera), the
text and the music, as usual, pulling a little against one
another. It may be that *Pinafore* is the only point in
the series at which the two men are really at one. Here
Gilbert approaches Sullivan's prettiness and Sullivan
Gilbert's frivolity, and the piece is not complex enough
for their divergences to set up a strain.

For years during the period of their first collaboration—
as we learn from the biography of Sullivan by his
nephew, Herbert Sullivan—Gilbert had been trying to
foist upon his partner what he considered a magnificent
theme: a magic charm which would convert human
beings into the realities of what they pretended to be,
one of its effects, by a farfetched and tasteless touch,
being the transformation of certain of the characters
into a pair of clockwork figures. The composer had
fought this off, had had to turn it down again and
again. The recurrence, in Sullivan's diary and letters,
of his phrase for it, "the lozenge story," comes to suggest
an insane obsession on the part of his collaborator to
which Sullivan has had to resign himself, a peril which
he has learned to evade; and that Gilbert should have

thought this idea attractive does show a queer stupidity in him. But when he at last made the break with Sullivan, the librettist's very first act was to exploit this frustrated plot in the incredibly unamusing opera written with Alfred Cellier under the title of *The Mountebanks*. One has only to read its text to appreciate the kind of thing that Sullivan had saved himself and Gilbert from.

After their quarrel and reconciliation, Gilbert and Sullivan did two more operas together: *Utopia, Limited; or The Flowers of Progress* (1893) and *The Grand Duke; or The Statutory Duel* (1896). *The Grand Duke*, written when Gilbert was nearing sixty, is one of his most labored librettos, alternating weary Gilbertianisms with Christmas-pantomime gags of a crudeness that hardly occurs in any of his other librettos. But *Utopia, Limited* is a different matter. The reunion with Sullivan seems to have stimulated him, after the two desolating librettos that he had written for other composers. One wonders why *Utopia* has never been revived by the D'Oyly Carte Company. (The public, when it was first produced, is said to have followed the lead of the Court, who disapproved of the royal drawing-room put on the stage in the Second Act.) Shaw said that he enjoyed the score more than that of any of the other operas, and the libretto, perhaps Gilbert's most ambitious, is, it seems to me, a great deal more amusing than that of either *Princess Ida* or *The Gondoliers*. In this fantasy, a Utopian king, impressed by the glories of England, decides that his country is behind the times and in need of fundamental renovation. He gives his daughters an English education, and he imports six "Flowers of Progress" in the shape of selected representatives of key English institutions: a barrister M.P., a Lord Chamberlain who censors plays, a county councillor who makes municipal improvements, a captain of the First Life Guards, Captain Corcoran of H.M.S. *Pinafore* and Mr. Goldbury, a company promoter—the last of whom re-organizes Utopia as a limited-liability company. Here the satire on contemporary England becomes less elfin and somewhat bolder than in any of the previous pieces. In fact, it leads the way quite plainly for the social-economic comedy of the early nineteen-hundreds. *Utopia* ought, I should think, to be brought into currency again (as *Ruddigore* was so successfully after its relative fail-ure when it was first performed), both as a creditable culmination of the last phase of the partnership and as a link that has been unfairly dropped out of the history of British drama. The other operas have grown so fa-miliar that they are getting to be a bore, and it would be pleasant to hear a fresh one.

April 12, 1947

GEORGE SAINTSBURY:
GOURMET AND GLUTTON

IT IS SOMETIMES SAID of entertaining writers that reading them is like eating peanuts. The literary criticism of George Saintsbury has for a long time had this effect on me. I cannot start one of his books, or even dip into one, without reading more than I meant to, and my appetite still carries me on even after the pleasure has cloyed. I have recently had this experience with the new reprint of *The Peace of the Augustans* in the *World's Classics* series, published by the Oxford Press. This *Survey of Eighteenth Century Literature as a Place of Rest and Refreshment* is in Saintsbury's later and more personal manner, but not so garrulous as the *History of the French Novel*, which came after it, and it would be, I should think, an ideal book with which to begin reading this author. Here you have at their best his easy handling of biography and history, his expert analysis of the technique of writing, his unexpected and witty allusions, his warm and luminous glow and his inexhaustible curiosity.

Reading *The Peace of the Augustans*, I came at last to realize that Saintsbury, besides being a great critic and scholar, was one of the best English *writers* of his time. The spell that he can cast in his more mature work is of a kind that is not common in literary criticism;

it is more like the spell of fiction or memoirs—though the critical histories of Saintsbury are not in the least like the work of the great French historian-critics, for Saintsbury had neither Taine's interest in the development of human society nor Renan's in the growth of ideas. What he has done is create an imaginative world composed almost exclusively of books and their makers, with an admixture of foods and wines. In this world, his ostensible occupation is tasting and digesting the authors (as well as the vintages and dinners) and appraising them with scrupulous fairness from the point of view of the enjoyment they afford; but this record becomes an adventure story and a commentary on human experience; and there is even a dramatic element provided by the recurring conflict between Saintsbury's Tory principles and the productions of those of his subjects who hold contrary opinions. The thrill for the reader results from Saintsbury's displays of gallantry in recognizing and applauding the literary merit of writers whose views he abhors; and there are moments when one nearly suspects him of having invented the Tory background—in the same way that a dramatist or novelist arranges contrasting elements—on purpose so that his passion for literature might find itself pitted against this and score unexpected victories over it.

I had been wondering what Saintsbury was like as a man and how he had spent his life, when I came upon the new memorial volume, *A Saintsbury Miscellany*. This selection from his essays and scrapbooks is introduced by "personal portraits" by Oliver Elton, Sir Herbert Grierson and others of Saintsbury's friends, and I expected that it would contain some biographical information that would satisfy my curiosity. One does not, however, find much. There are memoirs of his lectures, his dinners and his conversation, which present him in a sympathetic light, but no real revelation of his character or description of his intimate life. We learn that George Saintsbury, like Thackeray, asked that no life of him or biography of him should be written (rather unfairly, one feels, when he read other people's biographies so avidly and so much enjoyed discussing their personal affairs); and we conclude from certain intimations that the reason was the same as in Thackeray's case: some sort of domestic tragedy that had dislocated and that shadowed his life. This would explain the peculiar voracity with which he fed himself on books. Emotional deprivation sometimes drives people to eating and drinking as a substitute for what has been lost, and this may have been the case with Saintsbury, who certainly loved the pleasures of the table—he liked to write about cookery and wines—and seems to have taken to letters as both a gourmet and something of a glutton. Beginning as a reviewer of current books and a writer of short literary histories of the kind that may be used as textbooks, he gave himself up to literature in a way that was very different from the way of the ordinary scholar, with his tendency toward specialization and his ambition for academic prestige. It was as if he had transferred to literature his whole emotional and moral life, so that presently he appeared as an artist whose contacts were all with books instead of with places and people. One may even say "athletic life," for he has travelled in literature, too, and climbed mountains and done long-distance swimming. Saintsbury must have come as close to reading the whole of English literature as anyone who has ever lived, and he knew French literature almost as well. Academic fashions and categories, conventional assumptions and beaten trails, meant very little to him: he had to explore every inch for himself, see everything with his own eyes and formulate his own opinions.

His thus having the consumption of books for his only serious interest did, however, lead in some ways to a slightly distorted point of view. We find him, for example, in *The Peace of the Augustans* talking as if the enjoyment of literature were somehow a moral matter. He might be justified in this if it were merely a question of acquainting ourselves with the great books of the great writers. But for Saintsbury this is not enough. He seems to want to make us feel that we are under some obligation to gratify the literary palate with everything that can possibly be relished—implying that it is no more than our duty to go all through Dodsley's *Miscellany*, "especially as supplemented later by Pearch," in order to glean some minor poetry, and declaring, after a lengthy review of eighteenth-century periodical literature, that "as one looks over the two score and more little volumes of Chalmer's set, a sacred shame invades [him] at the thought of leaving such a various collection of pastime with the scanty inventory above selected." If an author that he particularly likes has been recently disparaged or attacked, he usually becomes pugnacious, and is quick to suggest that the critic is either a fool or a scoundrel. And he certainly praises too much and praises too many people. While I was reading *The Peace of the Augustans*, I was stimulated by Saintsbury's enthusiasm to look up certain things which I did not know. I had never had much luck with Cowper, and Saintsbury induced me to read two poems, *Yardley Oak* and *The Castaway*, which he extols in the strongest terms; but these seemed to me on just the same level, only a little above mediocrity, as every other serious piece of Cowper's that I had ever tried to read. Then the eye-twinkling and chuckling of this connoisseur over the humor of the satirical verse of Canning, Ellis and Frere in the *Anti-Jacobin Review*, which I had seen only scattered in anthologies, led me to look into the collected volume—only to find it rather disappointing. The merits of the Anti-Jacobins are hardly of such proportions as to warrant this gourmet's delight in them. Here his political prejudice and his snobbery have really for the moment betrayed him—for he becomes a little sickening on the subject of the good family and good breeding of these writers, who, as a matter of fact, in the work that he admires, are not merely reactionary but sometimes stupid and crude. A burlesque of Schiller, *The Rovers*, besides being aggressively Philistine, is slapstick and uninventive.

George Saintsbury's powers of appreciation were limited in one direction in a way that it is hard to account for. In his attitude toward contemporary writing, he practiced a consistent old-fogyism that seems to have no connection with his attitude toward works of the past, in judging which, as I have said, he never depends on conventional views. He does not hesitate either to tell us that a classic like Richardson bores him or, as in the case of George Borrow, to push into prominence a writer who had been rather underrated and neglected. But in regard to anything of importance that had happened since about 1880, he seems to have been not merely cool but hostile, and when he did have a good word for a contemporary, it was usually for someone of the second order: an R. L. Stevenson or a Norman Douglas. He lashed himself into a strange indignation over the movement at the end of the century to introduce form into the English novel. We find in *The Peace of the Augustans* a veritable diatribe on this subject, evidently directed at Henry James. This animus was as much out of harmony with his sensitive feeling for form in verse as it was with his respect for French fiction.

But neither this limitation nor his sometimes exaggerated enthusiasm seriously mars his work; and, in bringing them to notice here, I have merely been making an effort to arrive at an objective view, to correct the bemused condition to which Saintsbury has the power to reduce me. Once you fall under his spell, it will be long before you are troubled by these aspects of him or begin to feel the incompleteness of an entire artistic world of wide scope and huge dimensions that is populated entirely by books.

May 17, 1947

BOOKS OF ETIQUETTE AND EMILY POST

PROFESSOR ARTHUR M. SCHLESINGER, the Harvard historian, has written an entertaining little treatise called *Learning How to Behave: A Historical Study of American Etiquette Books*. It is curious and rather instructive to look at the development of the United States from the point of view of the literature of etiquette. The first manuals derived from Europe and emphasized deference to rank to the point of, in one case, admonishing the young: "If thy superior be relating a story, say not, 'I have heard it before.' . . . If he tell it not right, snigger not"; but after the Revolution, and especially after the advent of Jackson, the object became not to define class differences but to provide a set of prescriptions which would show anyone how to become a gentleman. The Southerners had, however, based their practice on seventeenth-century guides which helped the planter "to model his life on that of the English landed gentry" and "provided a fairly consistent chart of behavior . . . in emulation of the ancient ideals of Christian chivalry"; and they continued to follow this code. In the period after the Civil War, when the big fortunes were being made, a fresh crop of volumes appeared which had the purpose of orienting the newly rich among the refinements and complications of calling cards and formal dinners. There was an average of five such a year, and this continued through to 1945.

The two greatest publishing successes in the department of etiquette date from the beginning of the nineteen-twenties. At this time, a Miss Lillian Eichler, an advertising copywriter, then eighteen and just out of high school, sold thousands of copies of an *Encyclopedia of Etiquette* by means of a series of advertisements with the caption "What's Wrong with This Picture?" But the book—which had been written in 1901—was by that time, it seems, obsolete (Mr. Schlesinger does not tell us in what respect), for it was returned by "droves of dissatisfied customers." The publisher then proposed to Miss Eichler that she should herself do an up-to-date book, and the result was *The Book of Etiquette,* which between 1921 and 1945 sold over a million copies. In 1922, Emily Post brought out her *Etiquette,* which by 1945 had sold more than two-thirds of a million.

An examination of these two manuals reveals fundamental differences between them and suggests that they have been appealing to two rather different publics. Miss Eichler is practical and comfortable (her book is now frankly called *Today's Etiquette*). She tells you how to teach the children table manners and how to give a dinner without servants. She makes rough tabulations of vintage wines and supplies reliable recipes for half-a-dozen well-known cocktails; she recommends, in a chapter on *The Nature and Meaning of Culture,* that one "read more than one kind of literature: not mystery stories alone, nor light fiction alone," and she lists "nine painters of undisputed glory, with whose work every person of culture should be at least familiar." The precepts are mostly appropriate for anyone of moderate income, and the whole tone is non-invidious. She makes social life sound easy and jolly. But Mrs. Post is another affair. I had had no conception of her extraordinary book till I looked into it recently, fell under its spell and read it almost through. Mrs. Post is not merely the author of a comprehensive textbook on manners: she is a considerable imaginative writer, and her book has some of the excitement of a novel. It has also the snob-appeal which is evidently an important factor in the success of a Marquand or a Galsworthy. (I should explain that the edition I read was the third printing, of 1922.)

Mrs. Post has produced a world which has its characters, its atmosphere, its drama. I was reminded, after reading *Etiquette,* of the late Scott Fitzgerald's once telling me that he had looked into Emily Post and been inspired with the idea of a play in which all the motivations should consist of trying to do the right thing. The element of dramatic conflict would be produced by setting people at cross-purposes through stalemates of good form, from which the only possible rescue would be though the intervention of some bounder as *deus ex machina* to put an end to the sufferings of the gentlefolk who had been paralyzed by Mrs. Post's principles. (There are actually novels by Howells, and even by Henry James, which very nearly fulfill this formula.) For it is true that Mrs. Post has supplied all the materials for such a drama. Her ideal gentleman-clubman and her ideal feminine house guest—described in little essays like the "characters" of La Bruyère or the *Spectator*—are models which can never deviate, and thoroughly priggish figures which would lend themselves to satirical comedy. The "considerate guest," in particular, who is always perfectly sweet to everyone and always wants to do what the others are doing, who pretends to like children and dogs and lets them "climb over her" though she loathes them, could easily be shown as a menace from whom the party would have to be saved by Mrs.

Post's hideous villain: "The Guest No One Invites Again."

But Mrs. Post, in providing illustrations, has also invented types that have names, personalities and histories, and that are threaded, like the characters of Proust, in and out all through her book. These figures were originally intended merely as convenient dummies to stand in the places of hosts and guests when she was showing how the right kind of entertaining might be done on various scales by people on different income levels; but they have taken such a hold on the author that they have gratuitously been developed to exemplify, like the groups in Proust, a variety of social milieux. They do, however, all belong to Society, and the author, unlike Miss Eichler, always assumes that the reader wants to belong to Society, too.

At the top of Mrs. Post's structure, from the point of view of a wealth which is combined with "social credentials," stand the Worldlys of Great Estates (run by their butler Hastings) and the Gildings of Golden Hall. The Worldlys are a little difficult, they are constrained by the expensive habits and the inflated self-importance of the rich; but the Gildings are more human and always fun. Of Golden Hall, Mrs. Post writes: "The house is a palace, the grounds are a park. There is not only a long wing of magnificent guest rooms in the house, occupied by young girls or important older people, but there is also a guest annex, a separate building designed and run like the most luxurious country club. . . . Perfectly equipped Turkish and Russian baths in charge of the best Swedish masseur and masseuse procurable . . . a glass-roofed and enclosed riding ring—not big enough for games of polo, but big enough to practise in winter," etc. It was after a party at Golden Hall that

Mrs. Toplofty, Bobo Gilding's great-aunt, exclaimed, "How are any of us ever going to amuse any one after *this?* I feel like doing my guest rooms up in moth balls." Bobo Gilding (whose nickname is incidentally explained in a section intended to discourage what Mrs. Post calls conversational "door-slammers": "As for the name 'Bobo,' it's asinine." "Oh, it's just one of those children's names that stick sometimes for life." "Perfect rot. Ought to be called by his name.")—Bobo Gilding, on his side, does not care for his aunt's rather pompous parties, since "entering a drawing-room [for Bobo] was more suggestive of the daily afternoon tea ordeal of his early nursery days than a voluntary act of pleasure." And Mrs. Gilding (who was Lucy Wellborn) "did not care much to go either if none of her particular men friends were to be there. Little she cared to dance the cotillion with old Colonel Bluffington or to go to supper with that odious Hector Newman." Yet old Mrs. Toplofty is by no means dull, for, finding herself once at dinner "next to a man she quite openly despised, [she] said to him with apparent placidity, 'I shall not talk to you—because I don't care to. But for the sake of the hostess I shall say my multiplication tables. Twice one are two, twice two are four—' and she continued on through the tables, making him alternate them with her. As soon as she politely could, she turned to her other companion."

Lucy Gilding "smokes like a furnace and is miserable unless she can play bridge for high stakes." At her wedding, the bridesmaids were dressed "in deep shades of burnt orange and yellow, wood-colored slippers and stockings, skirts that shaded from brown through orange to yellow; yellow leghorn hats trimmed with jonquils, and jonquil bouquets"; and the affair was a great success for everybody except a "distinguished uncle," with whom Mrs. Post frankly sympathizes, who declared: "I did not think it was lovely at all. Every one of the bridesmaids was so powdered and painted that there was not a sweet or fresh face among them."

The Gildings' especial friends are rich young people like the Lovejoys and the Gailys, rich bachelors like Jim Smartlington and Clubwin Doe (the former of whom was elected "with little difficulty" to Clubwin Doe's club, at the same time that young Breezy was kept out by two men who "disliked his 'manner'"). But there are also, in the higher brackets, Mr. and Mrs. Kindhart. Mrs. Kindhart, unlike Mrs. Worldly, "talks to everyone, everywhere and always." Her "position is as good as Mrs. Worldly's every bit, but perhaps she can be more relaxed." It is the Kindharts who try to be helpful at the catastrophic "bungled dinner" which is given by "you," the reader—the evening when the fire smokes and Mrs. Toplofty issues orders that the logs are to be thrown out into the yard; when the Swedish maid says "Dinner's all ready!" instead of "Dinner is served" and deals the plates out like cards and then stacks them; when the clear soup turns out a "greasy-looking brown" and the hollandaise sauce "a curdled yellow mess"—the evening after which Mrs. Toplofty, Clubwin Doe and the Worldlys and the Gildings, all of whom you invited together, will, as you well know, be telling their friends: "Whatever you do, don't dine with the Newweds unless you eat your dinner before you go, and wear black glasses so no sight can offend you." On that occasion, Mr. Kindhart is the only guest who tries to eat the soup, and Mrs. Kindhart says to you gently: "Cheer up, little girl, it doesn't really matter"—making you know for the first time "to the full how terrible the situation is." (The other guests, on this unfortunate occasion, seem to have fallen a little short of the qualities of

delicacy and grace which the author has elsewhere as-
cribed to the truly well bred.) It was the Kindharts
who gave the houseparty at informal Mountain Sum-
mit Camp which inspires Mrs. Post to one of her most
memorable chapters—that party at which Mr. Kindhart
points out after lunch to the guests "a dozen guides who
are waiting at the boat-house" and "a small swimming
pool which can be warmed artificially" for those who
find the lake too cold, but at which the Worldlys strike
a false note, for Mr. Worldly insists on bringing his valet,
though he well knows that this was not expected, and
Mrs. Worldly, at the long pine lunch-table, "looks at her
napkin ring as though it were an insect"—till Mrs. Kindhart smiles and says: "I'm sorry, but I told you 'it was
roughing it.'"

And then there are the Littlehouses (Mrs. Littlehouse
was Sally Titherington), who, when you visit them,
may "press you into service as auxiliary nurse, gardener
or chauffeur," but whose "personality" is "such that there
is scarcely a day in the week when the motors of the
most popular of the younger set are not parked at the
Littlehouse door." And, on the fringes, such occasional
guests as Grace Smalltalk, who *did* write to Mrs. Norman an admirable bread-and-butter letter, and the boring Professor Bugge, who was rather a social problem
till he was seated by a clever hostess next to Mrs. En-
tomoid. In a somewhat different category, not frowned
on but not included in the Eastern set, are Mr. and
Mrs. Spendeasy Western and Mr. and Mrs. Jameson
Greatlake, of 24 Michigan Avenue, Chicago.

But Mrs. Post's real hero and heroine are Mr. and
Mrs. Oldname. Mrs. Oldname is *"une dame élégante"*—
because, as Mrs. Post tells us, there is no English word to
"express the individuality of beautiful taste combined with
personal dignity and grace which gives to a perfect cos-

tume an inimitable air of distinction." Her tact is unfailing
and consummate: to a lady going in to dinner, she will
say quietly: "Mr. Traveler, who is sitting next to you at
the table, has just come back from two years alone
with the cannibals." And "how does Mrs. Oldname
walk? One might answer by describing how Pavlowa
dances. Her body is perfectly balanced, she holds herself
straight, and yet nothing suggests a ramrod. She takes
steps of medium length, and, like all people who move
and dance well, walks from the hip, not the knee. On
no account does she swing her arms, nor does she rest a
hand on her hip! Nor, when walking, does she wave
her hands about in gesticulation." One of the most telling of the little episodes with which Mrs. Post's commentary is interspersed is her account of a visit to the
Oldnames, which has the title *The Small House of Perfection.* "A great friend of the Oldnames, but not a man
who went at all into society, or considered whether people had position or not, was invited with his new
wife—a woman from another State and of much wealth
and discernment—to stay over a weekend at Brook
Meadows." She asks her husband what sort of clothes to
take, and he tells her that he has never seen Mrs. Oldname "dressed up a bit." The wife wonders whether to
pack her cerise satin. The husband thinks it "much too
handsome," but the wife decides to put it in. They drive
up to a low, white shingled house, and the visitor notices that the flowers bordering the old-fashioned brick
walk are "all of one color, all in perfect bloom." "She
knew no inexperienced gardener produced that apparently simple approach to a door that has been chosen as
frontispiece in more than one book on Colonial architecture. The door was opened by a maid in a silver gray
taffeta dress, with organdie collar, cuffs and apron, white
stockings and silver buckles on black slippers, and the

guest saw a quaint hall and vista of rooms that at first sight might easily be thought 'simple' by an inexpert appraiser." Mrs. Oldname herself was electrifying to the visitor of wealth from another State. To describe her as "simple," exclaims Mrs. Post, "is about as apt as to call a pearl 'simple' because it doesn't dazzle; nor was there an article in the apparently simple living-room that would be refused if it were offered to a museum." The furniture, the appointments, the other guests are filled in with glowing rapture. "That night the bride wore her cerise dress to one of the smartest dinners she ever went down to"; and when later she is alone with her husband she bursts out: "Why in the name of goodness didn't you tell me the truth about these people?" The husband misunderstands: "I told you it was a little house —it was you who insisted on bringing that red dress. I told you it was much too handsome!" "Handsome!" she cries in tears. "I don't own anything half good enough to compare with the least article in this house. That 'simple' little woman, as you call her, would, I think, almost make a queen seem provincial! And as for her clothes, they are priceless—just as everything is in this little gem of a house. Why, the window curtains are as fine as the best things in my trousseau."

There is only one instance on record of anybody's scoring off the Oldnames. Mrs. Oldname had hanging in her dining-room a portrait of a Colonial officer, to which she was rather attached. One day, however, "an art critic, whose knowledge was better than his manners, blurted out, 'Will you please tell me why you have that dreadful thing in this otherwise perfect room?' Mrs. Oldname, somewhat taken aback, answered rather wonderingly: 'Is it dreadful?—Really? I have a feeling of affection for him and his dog!' The critic was merciless. 'If you call a cotton-flannel effigy a dog! And as for the figure, it is equally false and lifeless! It is amazing how anyone with your taste can bear looking at it!' In spite of his rudeness, Mrs. Oldname saw that what he said was quite true, but not until the fact had been pointed out to her. Gradually she grew to dislike the poor officer so much that he was finally relegated to the attic." It will be noted that, though the art critic carried his point, he was still guilty of a grave breach of manners.

The latest edition of Emily Post omits, as she says on the jacket, "certain non-essential customs and old-fashioned ideas," and aims to accommodate itself to the habits of later decades—including even those of the war and post-war young people—when formalities have been going by the board. The chapter, for example, which in the 1922 edition is called *The Chaperon and Other Conventions* is now headed *The Vanished Chaperon and Other Lost Conventions*. But the book is still dominated by the prestige of the Oldnames and the Gildings. Their prestige for Mrs. Post may finally have the effect of making some of her readers sympathetic toward the characters who are awful examples: the Upstarts, Mr. and Mrs. Unsuitable and that touching Mr. Richan Vulgar, who crossed the Atlantic four times a year in order to meet the smart people on shipboard and who, by capturing an innocent celebrity, attracted for a time to his table the Smartlys, the Wellborns and the Lovejoys, only to lose them every one when they found out what he was really like and took to eating their meals on deck. (The story of Mr. Richan Vulgar has been dropped from the new edition, as have also, the Unsuitables and the Upstarts, but a pathetic Miss Nobackground has appeared.) One feels, in fact, something like sadism in the whole approach of Mrs. Post. She likes to humiliate. She cannot tell us how charming Miss Wellborn is or how perfect is

Mrs. Oldname's taste without putting in a little incident to show us this polish or grace making somebody else uncomfortable. Mrs. Post's popularity, I think, is partly due to precisely this.

It is obvious that the Gildings and the Oldnames do not themselves need Mrs. Post's book of etiquette; and that the ordinary amiable American, to whom Miss Eichler addresses herself, does not necessarily need to hear about either Great Estates or the Small House of Perfection. But there are people who want to believe in the existence of a social Olympus and who find here the satisfaction that is somehow derived at once from imagining the enjoyment of glamor and power and from immolating oneself before them—since the reader is let in on the lives of the dwellers in these privileged places but is constantly being reminded how desperately he should have to watch his step if he were ever admitted among them.

What you get in Emily Post, for all her concessions to the age's vulgarization, is a crude version of the social ideal to which the mass of Americans aspired after the Civil War: an ideal that was costly and glossy, smart, self-conscious and a little disgusting in a period when even Mrs. Oldname reflected the lavish Gildings in stimulating her visitors to realize that the clothes she wore were "priceless" and her tableware and furniture museum pieces. Today this ideal must be fading with the money that kept it up, but, such as it is, a great many people must still enjoy reading about it. The publishers of Mrs. Post's *Etiquette* have announced that it has sold fifty thousand copies since the beginning of this year: its biggest sale in a decade.

July 19, 1947

A DISSENTING OPINION ON KAFKA

FRANZ KAFKA has been looming on the literary world like the meteorological phenomenon called the Brocken specter: a human shadow thrown on the mist in such a way that it seems monstrous and remote when it may really be quite close at hand, and with a rainbow halo around it. Since the publication in English of *The Trial* in 1937 (*The Castle* came out in 1930 but did not attract much attention), Kafka's reputation and influence have been growing till his figure has been projected on the consciousness of our literary reviews on a scale which gives the illusion that he is a writer of towering stature. New translations of him are constantly appearing, an endless discussion of his writing goes on, and a new collected edition in German is being brought out in New York. This edition, under the imprint of Schocken Books, is in part a reprinting of the old German edition which the war made unavailable, but, when complete, it will include ten or eleven volumes instead of the original six, with two volumes of Kafka's diaries, two of his letters and one or two of his miscellaneous fragments, of all of which only selections were given in a single volume before. We may be proud that this admirably produced and authoritatively edited version of a modern German classic, which was begun in Berlin under Hitler and only finished in Prague on the eve of the German occupation of Czechoslovakia, should thus have been salvaged from the ruins of Central European culture and brought out in the United States. Schocken has also published, both in German and English, *Franz Kafka: A Biography,* by Max Brod, and a selection, in English translation, from Kafka's "stories and reflections" under the title *The Great Wall of China;* and it has announced some further translations. In the meantime, a translation of *Metamorphosis,* one of the most important of Kafka's short stories, has recently been brought out by the Vanguard Press; and *A Franz Kafka Miscellany,* which contains translated scraps of Kafka as well as essays on his work, has been published by the Twice A Year Press. A compilation of essays and memoirs called *The Kafka Problem* has been published by New Directions; and *Kafka's Prayer,* an interpretation by Paul Goodman, has just been brought out by Vanguard.

These last two volumes, in the first of which the editor, Mr. Angel Flores, has assembled no less than forty-one pieces by writers of all nationalities, oversaturate and stupefy the reader and finally give rise to the suspicion that Kafka is being wildly overdone. One realizes that it is not merely a question of appreciating Kafka as a poet who gives expression for the intellectuals to their emotions of helplessness and self-contempt but of building him up as a theologian and saint who can somehow also justify for them—or help them to accept without justification—the ways of a banal, bureaucratic and incomprehensible God to sensitive and anxious men. Now, it may make a good deal of difference whether one was born, like the present writer, before the end of the nineteenth century, when stability and progress were taken for granted, instead of in a period when upheaval and backsliding seemed the normal conditions of life; but, with much admiration for Kafka, I find it impossible to take him seriously as a major writer and have never ceased to be amazed at the number of people who can. Some of his short stories are absolutely first-rate, comparable to Gogol's and Poe's. Like them, they are realistic nightmares that embody in concrete imagery the manias of neurotic states. And Kafka's novels have exploited a vein of the comedy and pathos of futile effort which is likely to make "Kafka-esque" a permanent word. But the two of these novels, *The Trial* and *The Castle*, which have become for the cultists of Kafka something like sacred writings, are after all rather ragged performances—never finished and never really worked out. Their themes, as far as Kafka had got, had been developed with so little rigor that Max Brod, when he came to edit them, found mere loose collections of episodes, which he had to piece together as best he could so as to give them a consistent progression, though he was not always able to tell in precisely what order they should come. To compare Kafka, as some of the writers in *The Kafka Problem* do, with Joyce and Proust and even with Dante, great naturalists of personality, great organizers of human experience, is obviously quite absurd. As for the religious implications of these books, they seem to me to be practically nil. I agree with Mr. D. S. Savage, who contributes to *The Kafka Problem* one of its most sensible essays, that the trouble with Kafka was that he could never let go of the world—of his family, of his job, of his yearning for bourgeois happiness—in the interest of divine revelation, and that you cannot have a first-rate saint or prophet without a faith of a very much higher potential than is ever to be felt in Kafka.

All that insulated and eventually nullified the spiritual charge that he carried is indicated in Max Brod's biography. Franz Kafka was the delicate son of a self-made Jewish merchant in the wholesale-women's-wear business in Prague, a vigorous and practical man, who inspired him with fear and respect, and gave him a life-long inferiority complex. The son was a pure intellectual, who derived from the rabbinical tradition of the mother's side of the family; but he yielded to the insistence of the father and, though at times reduced to thoughts of suicide, he took his place in the drygoods warehouse. His real interest had always been writing, which represented for him not merely an art but also somehow a pursuit of righteousness—he said he regarded it as a form of prayer—and he finally got himself a job in a workers' accident-insurance office, which left him his afternoons free. He wanted, or thought he ought to want, to get married, but his relationship with his father seems to have deprived him of sexual self-confidence. He became engaged to a girl whom he described as "wholesome, merry, natural, robust"; and, after five years of gruelling hesitation, developed tuberculosis, on purpose, in his own opinion, to make it impossible for him to marry. He was by this time, one supposes, too much at home in his isolation to be able to bring himself to the point of taking the risk of trying to get out of it; and he now, at the age of thirty-six, addressed to his father an enormous letter (never yet printed in full), an apologia for his own life, in which he seems to have blamed his failure on him. Later he did get away to Berlin. He had found an intellectual girl who studied Hebrew with him and whom he seems really to have wanted to marry. Her orthodox Chassidic father was forbidden by the rabbi to allow it when Franz confessed that he was not a practicing Jew; but the girl, in revolt against her family tradition, set up housekeeping with him and took care of him. Though he was eager now to work and to live, his disease had left him little time, and, after less than a year of this life, he was dead at forty-one.

The connection of all this with what Kafka wrote is made plain by his friend Max Brod in a book full of understanding. Herr Brod—whom the more metaphysical Kafkians tend to accuse of Philistinism—has, it seems to me, precisely the merit of looking in Kafka's work less for divine than for human meanings. That Kafka was weak-willed, that he was psychologically crippled, Max Brod is quite ready to admit, since he had made it his task during Kafka's life to keep his friend's morale up and make him work. He did stimulate Kafka to write and to have a few of his stories published, but he was very much less successful in his efforts to get him to break with his family. Other people escape from their parents, protests Herr Brod in astonishment and sorrow, so why on earth couldn't Kafka? Why *should* he have allowed his father so to crush and maim his abilities? Why, the reader may second Max Brod, remembering one of Kafka's most effective stories, should this artist have gone on past boyhood accepting the role of cockroach for which, like the hero of *Metamorphosis,* he had been cast by the bourgeois businessman? Well, the cards were stacked against poor Kafka in an overpowering way. His impotence was that of a man constitutionally lacking in vitality and walled in by a whole series of prisons that fitted one into the other like Chinese eggs. There was, first, the strangling father relationship; then the pressure of the tight little group of the Jewish orthodox family; then the constraints of the Jewish community incompletely emerged from the ghetto (Brod points out that the problems of Kafka's heroes are often those of the Jew among semi-alien neighbors—that the wanderer of *The Castle,* for example, is always trying to get himself accepted; he might have added that Joseph K., in *The Trial,* is constantly pursued for some crime which he is not aware of having committed); then the boredom and the spiritual starvation of the writer tied down to business hours—with the impression of hopelessness made on him by the workers who came to his office in the attempt to collect their insurance and who were met by all sorts of evasions and subjected to endless delays ("How modest these men are," he once said to Max Brod. "They come to us and beg, instead of storming the institute and smashing it to little bits."); then the deep-seated inhibitions which seem to have made his love affairs difficult; then the position of the Czechs in the Austrian Empire as an oppressed and somewhat scorned minority; then the privations of a defeated Central Europe, blighted, among other plagues, by the tuberculosis that undermined Kafka. This bewildered and darkened captivity, which may have seemed at the time rather special, was later to become, in Europe, more or less the common lot, and Kafka's fantasies were to gain a validity which could hardly have been foreseen—when, under the rule of the Nazis and the Soviets, men were to find themselves arrested and condemned on charges that had no relation to any accepted code of morals or law, or were driven from place to place to labor or to fight by first one then another inhuman unpetitionable government, which they hadn't the force to defy or the intellect to grasp and disintegrate.

But must we really, as his admirers pretend, accept the plights of Kafka's abject heroes as parables of the human condition? We can hardly feel toward Kafka's father, whose aspect Kafka's God always wears, the same childish awe that Kafka did—especially when the truth is that Kafka himself cannot help satirizing this Father-God as well as his own pusillanimity in remaining in bondage to him. A good deal has been made of the influence on Kafka of the Danish theologian Kierkegaard; but we learn from Max Brod that Kafka was at least equally influenced by Flaubert, and his work is full of a Flaubertian irony which the critics have tended to disregard. There is a story of Kafka's, for example, called *Investigations of a Dog* (included in *The Great Wall of China*), in which a dog is supposed to be inquiring into certain rather puzzling phenomena that are basic to the dog world. Where, he asks, does the food for dogs come from? The conventional explanation—which all right-minded dogs have been taught—is that this food comes out of the earth and is elicited by watering the earth and by singing incantatory hymns and performing ritual dances. Yet, as the scientist-dog has observed, the dogs, when they are invoking food, look not down toward the ground but up. Why *do* they look up, and is this essential? Then there are other unsolved problems: the dogs that roll over in unison and walk on their hind legs to the sound of mysterious music, and the small dandified dogs that seem to float through the air. The point is, of course, that the dogs have had their own reasons for pretending that human beings do not exist. Now, if you read the interpretations of this story which have recently been appearing, you will gather that it is simply an allegory of the relation of man to God—though the analogy does not hold, in view of the fact that the dogs *can* perfectly well see their masters, as man cannot do God, and are dependent on them in a practical way. Kafka remarked of this story, started—and never finished—not long before he died, that it was his *Bouvard et Pécuchet,* by which he must certainly have meant, not merely, as he said, that he thought it was a late work rather lacking in vitality, but also that it had something in common with Flaubert's most contemptuous indictment of the pettiness and ineptitude of the modern world. The sting of Kafka's story resides in the reluctance of the dogs to admit that they are in servitude to men—so that they have all entered into a conspiracy to conceal this fact from themselves, and even their boldest thinker cannot allow himself to find out the secret because it would rob him of his own self-respect. This is much less like an edifying allegory of the relations between God and man than like a Marxist-Flaubertian satire on the parasites of the bourgeoisie.

I do not deny that the enslaver, the master, is often given, in Kafka's stories, a serious theological meaning; but this side is never developed in anything like equal proportion to the ironical self-mocking side. Is the man condemned to death in *The Trial,* and finally convinced of his guilt for some crime which is never named, really either adapted or intended to illustrate Original Sin?— or is Kafka not rather satirizing the absurdities of his own bad conscience? In *The Castle,* there is also self-irony, but, besides this, a genuine wistfulness in K.'s longing to settle down and find a modest place in life for himself. But neither—unless one takes them as parodies of the Calvinist doctrine of Grace—seems to me to possess much interest as the expression of a religious point of view. The Christian of *Pilgrim's Progress* had obstacles to overcome and required moral fortitude to meet them; but all the struggling, such as it is, that is done by Kafka's K. is against an omnipotent and omniscient authority whose power and lights he can never share but to whose will he is doomed to succumb. And Dante, whose religious vision is all an exercise in control and direction, makes even his pagan Ulysses urge his men not to sleep before evening and tells them they were not made "to live like brutes but to follow virile courage and knowledge"; whereas Kafka is at his most characteristic when he is assimilating men to beasts—dogs, insects, mice and apes—which can neither dare nor know. On the other hand, for me, these stories too often forfeit their effectiveness as satires through Kafka's rather meaching compliance, his little-boylike respect and fear in the presence of the things he would satirize: the boring diligence of commercial activity, the stuffiness of middle-class family life, the arid reasonings and tyrannous rigidities of Orthodox Judaism (which have a good deal in common with those of our old-fashioned Puritan Protestantism).

If, however, one puts Kafka beside writers with whom he may properly be compared, he still seems rather unsatisfactory. Gogol and Poe were equally neurotic, in their destinies they were equally unhappy; and if it is true, as Mr. Savage says, that there is present in Kafka's world neither personality nor love, there is no love in either Gogol or Poe, and though there are plenty of personalities in Gogol, the actors of Poe, as a rule, are even less characterized than Kafka's. But, though the symbols that these writers generate are just as unpleasant as Kafka's, though, like his, they represent mostly the intense and painful realization of emotional culs-de-sac, yet they have both certain advantages over Kafka—for Gogol was nourished and fortified by his heroic conception of Russia, and Poe, for all his Tory views, is post-Revolutionary American in his challenging, defiant temper, his alert and curious mind. In their ways, they are both tonic. But the denationalized, discouraged, disaffected, disabled Kafka, though for the moment he may frighten or amuse us, can in the end only let us down. He is quite true to his time and place, but it is surely a time and place in which few of us will want to linger—whether as stunned and hypnotized helots of totalitarian states or as citizens of freer societies, who have re-lapsed into taking Kafka's stories as evidence that God's law and man's purpose are conceived in terms so differ-ent that we may as well give up hope of ever identifying the one with the other.

"One must not cheat anybody," says Kafka, in an aphorism which has been much applauded, "not even the world of its triumph." But what are we writers here for if it is not to cheat the world of its triumph? In Kafka's case, it was he who was cheated and never lived to get his own back. What he has left us is the half-expressed gasp of a self-doubting soul trampled under. I do not see how one can possibly take him for either a great artist or a moral guide.

July 26, 1947

JEAN-PAUL SARTRE: THE NOVELIST
AND THE EXISTENTIALIST

The Age of Reason is the first novel of Jean-Paul Sartre's to be translated into English. It is the first installment of a trilogy under the general title *The Roads to Freedom,* of which the second installment in translation has been announced for the fall. *The Age of Reason* deals with a group of young people in Paris—*lycée* teachers and students, Bohemians and night-club entertainers—in the summer of 1938. The second novel, *The Reprieve,* which has already appeared in French, carries the same characters along but works them into a more populous picture of what was going on in France during the days of the Munich Conference. The third volume, *The Last Chance,** has not yet been published in French, so it is impossible at the present time to judge the work as a whole or even to know precisely what the author is aiming at.

The Age of Reason, however, stands by itself as a story. Sartre displays here the same skill at creating suspense and at manipulating the interactions of characters that we have already seen in his plays. His main theme is simply the odyssey of an ill-paid *lycée* teacher

---

* There are now to be four volumes instead of three. The third, *La Mort dans L'Âme,* has appeared in French. 1950.

who does not want to marry his pregnant mistress and who is trying to raise the relatively large fee required for a competent abortion; but though the author makes this provide a long narrative, in which we follow the hero's every move and in which every conversation is reported in its banal entirety, he stimulates considerable excitement, holds our attention from beginning to end and engineers an unexpected dénouement which has both moral point and dramatic effectiveness. The incidents are mostly sordid, but, if you don't mind this, entertaining. The characters are well observed and conscientiously and intelligently studied, so that the book makes an interesting document on the quality and morale of the French just before their great capitulation. An American reader is struck by the close similarity of these young people, with their irresponsible love affairs, their half-hearted intellectual allegiances and their long drinking conversations, to the same kind of men and girls at the same period in the United States—just as the novel has itself much in common with certain novels that these young people produced. I do not believe, however, that this is the result of imitation by Sartre of the contemporary American novelists whom he is known to admire so much. It is rather that such young people everywhere have come to be more alike, so that the originals for Sartre's Parisians must have been far less specifically Parisian than the Parisians of Balzac or Flaubert or Anatole France or Proust.

It is true, besides, that the writing of the book shows few of the traditional traits that we have been used to in French fiction. It tells the story with a "functional" efficiency, but it is colorless, relaxed, rather flat. It loses little in the English translation, not merely because the translator knows his business, but also because Sartre's style does not put upon him any very severe strain. The conversation is mainly conducted in a monotonous colloquialism of catch-words, where some expression like "*C'est marrant*" does duty for as many emotions as our own ever-recurring "terrific"; and for this Mr. Eric Sutton has been able to find a ready equivalent in a jargon basically British with a liberal admixture of Americanisms.

Of Sartre's imaginative work, I have read, besides this novel, only his plays and a few of his short stories. On this showing, I get the impression of a talent rather like that of John Steinbeck. Like Steinbeck, Sartre is a writer of undeniably exceptional gifts: on the one hand, a fluent inventor, who can always make something interesting happen, and, on the other, a serious student of life, with a good deal of public spirit. Yet he somehow does not seem quite first-rate. A play of Sartre's, for example, such as his recent *Morts sans Sépulture*—which is, I suppose, his best drama so far—affects me rather like *Grapes of Wrath*. Here he has exploited with both cleverness and conviction the ordeal of the French Resistance, as Steinbeck has done that of the sharecroppers; but what you get are a virtuosity of realism and a rhetoric of moral passion which make you feel not merely that the fiction is a dramatic heightening of life but that the literary fantasy takes place on a plane that does not have any real connection with the actual human experience which it is pretending to represent.

I have approached *The Age of Reason* purposely from the point of view of its merits as a novel without reference to the Existentialist philosophy of which Sartre is one of the principal exponents and which the story is supposed to embody. But, with the publication, also, of a translation of a lecture of Sartre's called *Existentialism* and a pamphlet called *What Is Existentialism?* by William Barrett, this demands consideration, too. It should, however, be said that neither of these discussions of the subject provides for the ordinary person the best possible key to Sartre's ideas. The Barrett essay, though very able, is mainly an exposition of the ideas of Martin Heidegger, a contemporary German philosopher, from whom Sartre took some of his prime assumptions, and it presupposes on the part of the reader a certain familiarity with the technical language of philosophy. The lecture by Sartre himself has the special object of defending Existentialism against charges which have been brought against it by the Communists, so that it emphasizes certain aspects of the theory without attempting to state its fundamental principles. It would have been well if the publisher had included a translation of the article called *Présentation*, in which Sartre explained his position in the first number of his magazine, *Les Temps Modernes* (October 1, 1945), and which gives the best popular account I have seen of what this literary school is up to. I can also recommend especially a short summary of the history of Existentialist thought and of its political and social implications—*Existentialism: A New Trend in Philosophy*—contributed by Paul Kecskemeti, a former U.P. foreign correspondent who is also a trained philosopher, to the March, 1947, issue of a magazine called *Modern Review* (published in New York by the American Labor Conference on International Affairs). This study has the unusual merit of not getting so deeply enmeshed in the metaphysical background of Existentialism that it fails to focus clearly on the picture of mankind on the earth which is the most important thing to grasp in a doctrine that is nothing if not realistic.

What is this picture, then? In Sartre's version—to skip altogether the structure of philosophical reasoning on which it is made to rest and which Sartre has set forth at length in a book called *L'Etre et le Néant*—it places man in a world without God (though not all Existentialists are atheists), in which all the moral values are developed by man himself. Human nature is not permanent and invariable: it is whatever man himself makes it, and it changes from age to age. Man is free, beyond certain limits, to choose what he is to be and do. His life has significance solely in its relation to the lives of others —in his actions or refrainings from action: to use a favorite phrase of Sartre's, the individual must "engage himself."

Now, this conception of man's situation may appear to the non-religious reader, if he has also the "historical" point of view, precisely what he has always assumed, and may cause him to conclude with surprise that he was already an Existentialist without knowing it. To a Marxist, when he has further discovered that Sartre assigns human beings to the categories of the social classes almost as relentlessly as Marx, it will be evident that Sartre has borrowed from Marxism, and he may ask in what way Existentialism is an improvement over Marxism. In a debate between Sartre and a Marxist, a record of which follows the printed lecture, the Marxist actually scores rather heavily. The one advantage, it seems to me, that the doctrine of Sartre has is that it does away with Dialetical Materialism and its disguised theological content. There is for Sartre no dialectical process which will carry you straight to salvation if you get on the proletarian train. He sides with the proletariat, but intellectual or proletarian has to put up his own battle, with the odds looking rather against him. Yet Sartre does insist like a Marxist that every member of modern society belongs to a social class, and that "every one of his feelings, as well as every other form of his psychological life, is revelatory of his social situation." This molding of the individual by class—and Sartre allows also for the effects of "origin," "milieu," nationality and sexual constitution—produces the limitation on freedom which I mentioned in passing above. One finds oneself in a situation which one did not make for oneself, but, given that situation, one can choose various ways of behaving in it. The bourgeois—with whom Sartre is particularly concerned—can either go along with his class or rebel against it and try to get away from it. The Marxist may inquire how this differs from the classical Marxist formulation that "men make their own history, but . . . do not choose the circumstances for themselves," and how Sartre's practical doctrine of man realizing himself through action differs from Marx's conception of testing our ideas through action. To the writer, the conception of a wholly free will seems as naïve as the contrary conception of a wholly mechanistic determinism, and it is surely hardly less naïve to declare, as Sartre appears to do, that we are determined up to a certain point, but that beyond that we can exercise choice. If Marx and Engels, in exploring these problems, are somewhat less schoolmasterishly clear than Sartre, they seem to me, in their tentative way, to give a more recognizable picture than he does of what happens when what we take for the will tries to act on what we take for the world, and of the relation between man and his environment.

But the Existentialist philosophy of Sartre is the reflection of a different age from that which stimulated the activist materialism of Marx, and it has the immense advantages of sincerity and human sympathy over the very peculiar version of Marxism, totalitarian and imperialistic, now exported by the Soviet Union. Let us see it in its historical setting. Mr. Kecskemeti has shown in his essay how the neo-Kantian idealism of the pre-1914 period in Germany, which "admirably expressed the average German's awe in the presence of every kind of expert and official," had to give way, after the first German defeat, which shook this faith in specialized authority, to an effort to find principles of morality in the study of human conduct itself. So, eventually, the Germans got Heidegger. In the same way, Kecskemeti says, the defeat of the French in 1940 deprived them of all they had leaned on: they had at one stroke lost both their great traditions—the tradition of the French Revolution, which collapsed with the Third Republic, and the monarchist-Catholic tradition, which, through Pétain, had sold them out to the invaders. It is characteristic of the French that the destruction of French institutions should have seemed to them a catastrophe as complete as the Flood and caused them to evolve a philosophy which assumes that the predicament of the patriotic Frenchmen oppressed by the German occupation represented the condition of all mankind. They felt imperatively the duty to resist, with no certainty of proving effective, and they had, as Albert Camus has said, to formulate for themselves a doctrine which would "reconcile negative thought and the possibility of affirmative action." Hence the emphasis on the individual—since the Resistance was always an effort of scattered men and women—so different from the emphasis of Marx on the importance of collective action at a time when a great working-class movement was looming and gathering strength. Hence, also, the suffocating atmosphere of corruption, degradation and depression which is a feature of Sartre's work and for which the French Communists, hopped up by the Kremlin to the cocksureness of propaganda, are in the habit of showering him with scorn. But such reproaches have no real validity, either artistic or moral: this atmosphere is Sartre's subject, and he has not allowed it to drug his intelligence or his conscience. It is the climate of the Oc-

cupation, and the chief literary achievement of Sartre
is to have dramatized the moral poisoning of a France
humiliated and helpless, in which people, brooding
guiltily or blaming someone else, squabbled horribly, betrayed one another or performed acts of desperate heroism. For, says Sartre, though you cannot appeal to God,
you have always a margin of freedom: you can submit,
you can kill yourself or you can sell your life dear by
resisting. Where this freedom is now to lead Frenchmen
since the Germans have been driven out, I do not think
that Sartre has yet made clear. Though anti-bourgeois
and pro-working-class, he is evidently not an orthodox
Communist of the kind who takes his directives from
Moscow. One has a little the feeling about him that his
basic point of view has been forged, as his material
has been supplied, so completely under pressure of the
pain and constraint of the collapse and the Occupation
that he may never readapt himself to the temper of any
new period.

And now how does *The Age of Reason* point the
morals of Existentialist principles? Well, if you already
know something of the subject, you will recognize
some of its concepts turning up in the reflections of the
hero as he drearily walks through the Paris streets. And
the conflict of classes is there: a seceder from the bourgeoisie, we see this hero, Mathieu, revolving in a lonely
orbit but experiencing gravitational pulls from a successful lawyer brother who represents the bourgeoisie,
an old friend who has become a Communist and represents the proletariat, and a young girl of Russian émigré
parents who represents the old nobility. It is not, however, this central character, so far as this volume takes
him, who "engages himself" by a choice: his choices
are all of the negative kind. It is the sexual invert Daniel,

a neurotic and disconcerting personality, who, exercising free will, resists his suicidal impulses and performs, unexpectedly and for devious reasons, a responsible and morally positive act. Here the difficult "situation" is a matter not of social class but of biological dislocation; and the triumph of Daniel's decision is to be measured by the gravity of his handicap.

Yet it is difficult to see how *The Age of Reason* can have been very profoundly affected by Sartre's Existentialist theory. In such a production of his as his play *Les Mouches,* the dramatist turns academic and rather destroys the illusion by making the characters argue his doctrine; but this novel might perfectly have been written if Sartre had never worked up Existentialism. It does differ from the picture of life presented by the embittered French naturalists after the French defeat of 1871, whose characters were invariably seen as caught in traps of heredity and circumstance and rarely allowed to escape—though Sartre's mood, as in his play *A Huis Clos (No Exit),* is sometimes quite close to theirs. But this book does not essentially differ from the novels of other post-naturalistic writers, such as Malraux, Dos Passos and Hemingway, for whom the international socialist movement has opened a door to hope and provided a stimulus to action that were unknown to such a Frenchman as Maupassant or to the Americans who paralleled his pessimism. In Sartre, as in these other writers, you have a study of the mixture in man's nature of moral strength and weakness, and a conviction that, although the individual may not win the stakes he is playing for, his effort will not be lost.

Since *Partisan Review* has published, in the same series as Mr. Barrett's pamphlet, a translation of one of Sartre's long articles, *Portrait of the Anti-Semite,* one should say something about his activity as a journalist. These essays that he contributes to his *Temps Modernes* seem to me among the most interesting work of their kind that has appeared during the current slump in serious periodical writing. In this field, Sartre can be compared only with George Orwell in England; we have nobody so good over here. Mr. Barrett, in an article on Sartre, has complained that he ignores, in his *Portrait,* the Freudian springs of anti-Semitism. It is true that Sartre makes no attempt to explain this phenomenon historically in its political and social connections; but he does pursue with merciless insight at least one of the psychological factors involved: the need of small frustrated people to fake up some inalienable warrant for considering themselves superior to somebody. Sartre's whole essay, in fact, pretends to be nothing else than an elaborate development of this theme. It is no scientific inquiry but an exercise in classical irony, which might almost have been written, we reflect, by one of the more mordant eighteenth-century Encyclopedists. *The Age of Reason* of Sartre's novel is the intellectual maturity of the hero, but the phrase recalls also a period with which Sartre has a good deal in common. In penetrating these enormous editorials that mix comment on current affairs with a philosophy which, whatever its deficiencies, is always clearly and firmly expressed, we are surprised and reassured to find ourselves chewing on something which we might have feared the French had lost. For it is Sartre's great strength in his time that he has managed to remain quite uninfected by the Cocteau-esque Parisian chichi of the interval between the wars. If Existentialism has become, like surrealism, something of a *mouvement à exporter,* no one has probed so shrewdly as Sartre, in one of his articles in *Les Temps Modernes,* the recent attempts of the French to distract the attention of the world from their political and military discredit by exploiting the glory of their writers, or pointed out so boldly the abuses to which this practice may lead. If he sometimes has the air of pontificating, it is probably almost impossible for a French literary man whose influence is being felt to refrain from playing the role of *chef d'école*. And Sartre, bourgeois and provincial, has succeeded in preserving for the French qualities which they very much need and which it is cheering to see still flourish: an industry, an outspokenness and a common sense which are the virtues of a prosaic intelligence and a canny and practical character. This does not, perhaps, necessarily make Sartre a top-flight writer, but, in these articles of *Les Temps Modernes,* it does provide some very good reading.

August 2, 1947

THE MUSICAL GLASSES OF PEACOCK

An omnibus of Thomas Love Peacock, under the title *The Pleasures of Peacock,* has been brought out by a New York publisher. It is a good thing to have these novels reprinted, and Mr. Ben Ray Redman, who has edited the volume, contributes a well-informed introduction that touches briefly on almost every side of Peacock. But this book has what seems to me the serious defect of being mainly a collection of excerpts. Only two novels are given complete: *Nightmare Abbey* and *Crotchet Castle.* The other five appear merely in selections. Now, it is true that from one point of view Peacock lends himself easily to anthologizing: his plots are not usually important, and his narrative is a loose series of episodes. Yet each of his books as a whole shows the same delicate sense of form as each of the episodes and each of the sentences, and it is a pity to take them to pieces—especially since they are all so short that it was possible, in a thin-paper edition published some years ago, to include the complete novels in one pocket-size volume. It is also rather unfair, it seems to me, to shear off, as Mr. Redman has done, all the quotations that head Peacock's chapters, and to trim away a part of his learned notes. The main text can stand without them, but they do represent the soil out of which that text has grown and help to situate Peacock's mood in an early-nineteenth-century library, where the Greek and Latin classics are mingled with Italian light comedies and the wild folk ballads of Wales. Surely anyone who can care for Peacock would prefer to have him intact.

The Pleasures of Peacock, however, serve to remind us, in any case, of a very fine writer and to offer a pretext for talking about him. We have already seen one revival of Peacock—during the twenties, when J. B. Priestley did a book about him and when Aldous Huxley gave him some vogue by deliberately imitating him. The element that Huxley exploited was the characteristic Peacock symposium: the conversation in a country house, with much passing of port and claret, among highly intellectual guests, each of whom appears as the exponent of some current tendency or doctrine reduced to its simplest terms and carried to its most absurd lengths. This is the critical side of Peacock, for which he is now perhaps most famous because Huxley has seized upon it, injected into it moral earnestness and transposed it into a peevish key. But it is by no means the whole of Peacock, as one can see by comparing him and Huxley. With the later as with the earlier writer, the opinions of the various philosophers more or less cancel one another out; but for Huxley this leads to bitterness and a demand for religious certainties, whereas in Peacock it leads to a final drink and a song in which everyone joins. And this fencing by Peacock's cranks with rigid contradictory ideas— excellent sometimes, of course, but not always remarkably clever—is hardly enough to have preserved him so long. What is it, then, that makes Peacock live? Why is it that Mr. Redman believes that we can still enjoy reading his novels?

Another critic, Mr. Ronald Mason, asked this question three years ago in the English review *Horizon,* and, after discounting almost every source of interest that one may expect to find in a novel, came to the conclusion that Peacock's strength lay mainly in his firmness as a nipper of extremes and in his admirable prose style. Both these merits Peacock certainly had. It was a godsend that in the early nineteenth century, with its seraphic utopianisms, its attitudinizing anti-social romanticisms and its cannibalistic materialisms, one man who had the intelligence to understand and the aesthetic sensibility to appreciate the new movements and the new techniques that were going to people's heads, should have been able to apply to their extravagances a kind of classical common sense; and Peacock's value, as Mr. Mason suggests, should by no means be less today, at a time when extreme ideas are being violently put into practice. As for his style: to the mature reader, whom mere sonority and movement and color do not intoxicate as they did in youth, it seems one of the best in English. Light, lucid, neat and dry, it is as far from the prose of his own period, mossily clogged or grassily luxuriating, as from the showy upholstery of the later age. It redeems him from insipidity at the moments when he is running thinnest; it gives charm to his most telling jokes by slipping them in with a minimum of emphasis. "Nothing superfluous and nothing wanting" was the comment of India House on the papers that won Peacock his job there. If one compares him, particularly, with Thackeray, who liked his work and who is sometimes praised for qualities similar to his, one is struck by the relative coarseness of the texture of the Victorian's writing, with its dilutions and its repetitions, and by the relative commonplaceness of his mind, with its worldly preoccupations and its embarrassing exhibitions of benevolence. When we come to Peacock from this, we are aware of his restraint and distinction, of the spareness and sureness of the pencil which he uses for his prose line-drawings.

This brings us to an aspect of Peacock which Mr. Mason leaves out of account. The fact that Peacock's *imagination* is not vigorous, varied or rich has, I believe, rather kept people from realizing how exquisite his effects sometimes are. It is usual to treat him as a satirist whose power is more or less weakened by his scoring off both sides of every question; but the truth is that Peacock is an artist the aim of whose art is to achieve not merely a weaving of ideas but also an atmosphere—an aroma, a flavor, a harmony. You get closer to what Peacock is trying to do by approaching him through his admiration for Mozart—"There is," he wrote, "nothing perfect in this world except Mozart's music"—than by assimilating him to Lucian or Voltaire. His books are more like light operas than novels (it was quite natural that *Maid Marian* should have been made into one) and the elements of fantasy with which they play—the civilized orangutan of *Melincourt*, who is chivalrous with the ladies, the seven lovely maidens of *Gryll Grange* who keep house for the young man in the tower—as well as the landscapes of mountain streams, the drives and rides in the New Forest, the boating and skating parties, are as important as the conversations. It all makes a delicious music, at the same time sober and gay, in which the words fall like notes from a flute, like progressions on an old-fashioned pianoforte, lighted by slim white candles. In *Gryll Grange,* when we come to the snowstorm, we almost have the illusion that these pale and sifted words of Peacock's are dropping on the page like snowflakes and that they melt away as we read. Even the openings of Peacock's unfinished novels—so sure is his touch on the keyboard to convey us at once to his realm—may be enjoyed as little works in themselves, like the "preludes" of Debussy or Chopin.

It seems to me, too, that the nonchalance of Peacock in dealing with political and moral systems has been given a wrong meaning by his critics—for he is always, in some way, on the *human* side, and he shared the generous ideas of the romantic and utopian generation to an extent that his conservative encomiasts are sometimes reluctant to recognize. I have a suspicion that the relative indifference of the typical Peacockian to *Melincourt* may be partly due to the fact that the hero of this early novel gives expression to such ideas with an eloquence which can almost be called glowing and which suggests real conviction on Peacock's part. The book does go on a little too long, for Peacock has not yet quite found his form; but it is certainly one of his best—with its gentleman anthropoid, its beautiful blue-stocking oread, its forthright and very funny satire on rotten-borough politics and the publishing business, and its admirable discussion, at the end, under the title *The Hopes of the World,* of the future of civilization. Mr. Redman could not have remembered *Melincourt* when he wrote in his introduction in such a way as to give the impression that Peacock's friendship with Shelley is only to be explained on the ground of the attraction of opposites. The creator of the Rousseauist Mr. Forester had no difficulty in sympathizing with the poet's utopian yearnings toward a happier and freer society. It was only that he could not help kidding his friend in the skit of *Nightmare Abbey*—the dry diagnosis of which is a corrective to more impassioned portraits—for the self-delusions of Shelley in his childish relations with women; and that the cool human sympathy I have spoken of compelled him to defend Harriet—in his *Memoirs of Percy Bysshe Shelley*—against the slanders of the Shelley-worshippers.

The mountain-loving Anthelia of *Melincourt* is one of Peacock's most attractive versions of his ideal young Englishwoman—always a strongly positive element in his stories. These girls of his—frank, independent, brave, intelligent and rather intellectual—stand somewhere between the heroines of Shelley and the heroines of Jane Austen. I find them a great deal more attractive, as well as a great deal more convincing, than the women of Victorian fiction. That these latter could not have been found particularly sympathetic by Peacock may be concluded from the unfinished *Cotswold Chace,* in which he is careful to explain that his heroine "wears no crinoline, and, if I might venture to divine, no stays." It is obvious that Peacock's young girls—witty, athletic and fresh—are the mothers of the anti-Victorian goddesses of his son-in-law George Meredith's novels.

The later Peacock was less interested in reformers, less "progressive" and less optimistic. But it is true, as Mr. Redman reminds us, that he had already in the sixties lived long enough to see a great many reforms accomplished but life rendered rather less agreeable than it had been in the early years of the century, and to foresee the mechanical developments—prophesied in *Gryll Grange*—which were to increase men's productive powers and at the same time to reduce them to bondage. When he had retired from his job at India House, he took his family to live in the country, where he spent most of his time with books—though he liked to go to visit Lord Broughton, who, as John Hobhouse, had been Byron's friend and who could give Peacock the good entertainment and the free-ranging conversation with which he had filled his novels. Thackeray met Peacock once in 1850 and called him "a white-headed jolly old worldling"; but he was never really a Thackeray character. He was not worldly in Thackeray's sense. The world he loved was the world of his library—to which he fled when, at the age of eighty, he was warned that the house was on fire, declaring, when they tried to get him out: "By the immortal gods, I will not move!" He was upset when his favorite daughter, who had been educated, on the model of his heroines, both in literature and in outdoor sports and who is said to have been both brilliant and beautiful, married the young George Meredith. Meredith wore a beard, which Peacock could not abide; and, though the young man respected his father-in-law and was influenced in his own work by Peacock's, his ardors, energetic and uneasy, annoyed the old man and made him nervous. It was quite a different thing from Shelley.

Nor did Meredith and his bride get along together. They were both sharp-tongued and self-willed, and they had very little money to live on. They tormented one another unbearably. Mary Meredith, at the end of nine years, ran away to Capri with another man, but soon came back to die in England. Peacock, then seventy-nine, did not go to her funeral, but he composed for her an epitaph in Latin and Greek, which was never inscribed on her grave. Meredith published soon after, as a commentary on his tragic marriage, the great sequence of sonnets called *Modern Love,* full of self-probings and passionate frustrations of a kind that must have been inconceivable to Peacock; and when one glances back on this mid-century Peacock from the point of view of *Modern Love,* one seems to see an old man in a bottle, whose unshakable poise and calm depend on his not coming out.

For when we look back on Peacock from Meredith's time instead of seeing him in the dawn of the century, he seems to us less mobile and cooler. Peacock's father was a dealer in glassware, and there is sometimes a glint of glassware in the clear, sound and smooth work of Peacock. The editors of the Halliford Edition of Peacock have included in his last novel, *Gryll Grange*, a peculiarly appropriate frontispiece which shows a spun-glass bust of Homer that Peacock had hung in his library. It makes us reflect that the classics in Peacock's hands do a little take on the aspect of having been deftly spun into glass; and his own work may look to us at moments like a fine antique sideboard display, with rows of graceful flower-calyxed goblets all ready for the very best wine—which you will have to buy from somebody else: somebody like Meredith or Shelley. In the meantime, however, Peacock can elicit from them a very pretty music by delicately moistening the rims and rubbing them with the tips of his fingers.

August 23, 1947

EDITH WHARTON: A MEMOIR BY
AN ENGLISH FRIEND

Portrait of Edith Wharton, by Percy Lubbock, will be read with fascination by anyone interested in its subject. It is the first important memoir of the novelist that has been published since her death; and it is a literary performance of some distinction—not the usual sketch by a friend, but a real portrait, carefully composed with every brush-stroke studied. The book is, in fact, so very much "written" that the writing sometimes has the effect of obscuring the actualities which the author is trying to describe. Mr. Lubbock, who edited Henry James's letters, is one of James's most faithful disciples, and he here follows the Jamesian procedure of writing around his subject instead of showing it to us directly. He prefers to adumbrate Mrs. Wharton with metaphors or to generalize about her with abstractions rather than tell you what she said and did, how she looked and what she wore; and the result is that we seem to be gazing at her through a kind of sea-mist that never clears and through which we can make out her movements and shape but are unable to scrutinize her features. It is a pleasure to read prose so well worked, in the sense that a tapestry is worked, but, like a tapestry, the book presents a series of somewhat conventionally posed tableaux—Edith Wharton just arrived in England, Edith

Wharton in her household in the Faubourg St. Germain,
Edith Wharton in Morocco, etc.—which rather lack
depth and detail.

The concrete questions that one would have to have
answered in order to understand Edith Wharton's career
are mostly either ignored or evaded by Mr. Lubbock.
Mrs. Wharton was always quite rich. Where did her
money come from? Was it her own or was it her husband's? And why did she marry Edward Wharton, with
whom she obviously had little in common and was not
very much in love? What, precisely, was the matter with
him when he became deranged and Mrs. Wharton finally
divorced him? Mr. Lubbock tries to put their relationship in as attractive a light as possible, but then he
later speaks of Walter Berry, the American lawyer in
Paris with whom Edith Wharton's name has always been
associated, as "the man she had loved for a lifetime, in
youth and age." To what kind of situation had this
given rise? There is a legend that Edith Jones's first love
was broken up by her mother, who disapproved of it and
sent her abroad; and that her first book of poems, which
she had secretly had printed, was discovered and destroyed by her family. Is it true? And is it true that she
began writing fiction, some years after her marriage, as
the result of a nervous breakdown at the suggestion
of S. Weir Mitchell, the novelist and neurologist? It has
been asserted by persons who should be in a position to
know that Edith Wharton had some reason for believing
herself to have been an illegitimate child and that
her family rather let her down from the point of view of
social backing—which would account for the curiously
perfunctory, idyllic and unreal way in which she writes
of her parents in *A Backward Glance,* as contrasted with
her bitter picture, in her novels of old New York, of the
cruelty of social convention and the tyranny of the fam-

ily group, as well as for her preoccupation with the miseries of extramarital love affairs and the problems of young women who have to think about marrying for money and position. The last of these themes, especially —exploited so successfully in *The House of Mirth*—is difficult to account for on the basis of Edith Wharton's being simply the well-born Miss Jones, as is, perhaps, that insistence on her social prerogatives which many who knew her, including Mr. Lubbock, found unnecessary and exaggerated. Of all the conflicts of purpose and the stifled emotions that are expressed in Mrs. Wharton's books, you will find little trace in the figure presented by Mr. Lubbock. Here she is always seen as the hostess or the traveller *de grand luxe*. He intimates that her love for Berry was the source of a good deal of unhappiness, that her perfectly appointed houses and her retinue of clever guests still left her unsatisfied, that her going to live in Europe and breaking her ties with America were a misfortune for her art and her life, and uneasily felt by her as such. But he fails to explain a career which has always appeared rather freakish. The vexed and aggrieved spirit that wrote Edith Wharton's best novels has no part in Mr. Lubbock's portrait, and the novels themselves—for reasons which Mr. Lubbock does not quite make clear—are mentioned only incidentally.

Mr. Lubbock, however, is not to be blamed. Since he was an old and intimate friend, it was probably impossible for him to go behind his subject's façade less discreetly than he has done; and the fact that he is an Englishman—he has apparently never been in the United States—makes it difficult for him to understand the background and the significance of Edith Wharton's work. What we get from him is a pretty full account of how she behaved in Europe and how she seemed to Europeans. He has added to those we already have a new picture of the literary group—which comes to seem more important as time goes on—that centered around Mrs. Wharton, Henry James and Howard Sturgis, the Anglicized American who wrote *Belchamber*. And he has supplemented his own impressions with those of various other friends, American, English and French, which Mr. Gaillard Lapsley, Edith Wharton's literary executor, has persuaded them to write down at length.

But the American end of the story is largely left a blank. You cannot even see the "port of New York"—it lies beyond the Atlantic and Mr. Lubbock's vision—where Edith Wharton was born, which did as much to mold her mind as Europe (it is precisely one of the functions of Manhattan to blend and to concentrate the influences of the rest of the world), and which—in her sharpness and smartness, her efficiency, her glitter and her cruelty—she so brilliantly reflected in her work. Mr. Lubbock, in his ignorance of America, has made several glaring blunders. When he comes to do a kindly little sketch of the history of American fiction up to what he calls "the uproarious Boston tea party" of the movement that came of age in the twenties, he describes it as if it mainly consisted of or were adequately represented by Hawthorne, Howells and James—a "procession . . . united in their order for all their disparity, marching in honor and sobriety," of which Edith Wharton brings up the rear. Not to attempt to supply the deficiencies of Mr. Lubbock's picture, I will point out that Mrs. Wharton was as much a contributor to the realism of the age that followed hers as she was an inheritor from James, and that a book like *The Custom of the Country* opened the way for novels like *Babbitt* and *Manhattan Transfer*. What she did that these older American writers mentioned by Mr. Lubbock had hardly attempted at all, but that the later writers made their chief business, was draw up a terrific indictment against the new America of money values that, swelling to monstrous proportions during the years after the Civil War, confronted the world at the end of the century. Nor is it true, as Mr. Lubbock asserts, that this later group of writers "cast overboard the wares of the old world," whereas all the earlier ones had been "still of Europe in their art, and in much more than their art, in the climate of their culture, in the style and habit of their thought." Lewis, Dos Passos, Faulkner and Hemingway have obviously owed as much to European writers and European travel as Hawthorne and Howells had done, and if the stories of Sherwood Anderson grew up, like the native grass, without any foreign fertilizer, so had those of Mark Twain, who belonged to the Howells era.

Another error of Mr. Lubbock's appears in connection with his attitude toward Edith Wharton's heroes. We can agree with him that many of these heroes must have been inspired by Walter Berry, and we lack evidence to dispute his contention that Edith Wharton's closest male friend was dry, empty-hearted and worldly, a pretentious and unlikable snob. We certainly get the impression that Mr. Lubbock has a grudge against Berry for encouraging Edith Wharton in her skepticism about religion, and that he would like to believe that, without him, she might at last have accepted the Catholic faith. In any case, Mr. Lubbock believes that Walter Berry, to whom Edith Wharton showed all her work and who sat in judgment on it, was responsible for some of its faults. But he is certainly mistaken in supposing that Mrs. Wharton idealized uncritically those of her characters who were based on Berry. On the contrary, the male type which most conspicuously recurs in her novels is the cultivated intelligent man who cannot bear to offend social convention, the reformer who gets bribed without knowing it in marrying a rich wife, the family man who falls in love with someone more exciting than his wife but doesn't have the courage of his passion; and the treatment of these characters by the author, though outwardly sympathetic, is always well chilled with an irony that has an undercurrent of scorn. It is a phenomenon unfamiliar to Europe, this connoisseur whose culture is sterile, this idealist whose impulses are thwarted, this romantic who cannot act his romance, because, in every one of these roles, he is made helpless by a commercial civilization. But Edith Wharton knew him well, and she never ceased to resent him because he had failed to stand up to the temptations and threats of that civilization and because he had not been strong enough to save from that moneyed world, in which it was even easier for a woman than for a man to be caught, a woman, courageous herself, whom he might have, whom he should have, loved.

Certainly the question of money had been and always remained extremely important for Edith Wharton. Her work is the record of a struggle between wealth and its advantages, on the one hand, and aesthetic and moral values, on the other. (The fortunes of her family, Mr. Lubbock implies, was derived from New York real estate, and insofar as she was dependent on this, she must have found herself in the situation of owing her standard of living to the very extravagances of the speculative and vulgar society which she was constantly castigating.) And for this reason, if her life is to be understood, the facts about it should be brought to light. Her work, I believe, has never been—and was not, even at the time of her greatest success—appreciated or interpreted as it should be; and it is possible that her personal history, which now appears merely puzzling, would provide a dramatic illustration of the tragedy often incurred and the heroism sometimes engendered by a period of American life which imposed upon human beings peculiar and extreme conditions. The papers of Edith Wharton now deposited in the Yale University Library are not, I understand, to be published before 1967, but we may hope to have eventually a biography that will tell the whole of her story and show her in her full dimensions.

October 4, 1947

THE SANCTITY OF BAUDELAIRE

A TRANSLATION by Christopher Isherwood of Baudelaire's *Intimate Journals* was published in England in
1930, with an introduction by T. S. Eliot. It has now been
brought out here for the first time, in a somewhat revised text and with an introduction by W. H. Auden
instead of the one by Eliot, which in the meantime had
been included in the volume of the latter's *Selected
Essays* and become one of the principal stimuli for the
recent vogue of Baudelaire.

When I speak of Baudelaire's "recent vogue," I do not,
of course, mean to imply that his reputation has at any
time seriously declined. Baudelaire was one of the greatest of French poets, and has been recognized as such by
writers of all periods and many schools. But during the
last fifteen years or so, he has been pressed into service
by certain elements in the literary world who want to
claim him for their own cause, and his career has been
shown in a light which falsifies the meaning of his work.
Messrs. Eliot, Auden and Isherwood are all, in their several ways, active champions of Christian doctrine. In
times of disillusion with politics, it is usual to find a retreat in the direction of traditional religion, and that is
what we have been getting lately. Now, Baudelaire, after
his exploit of 1848, when he leapt on the barricades and
shouted "Down with General Aupick!" (his stepfather),

became cynical enough about politics. But this is not enough for Eliot and Auden and Isherwood: they want to have him a good Catholic, too. Eliot and Auden both have attached tremendous importance to the last disjointed entries in his journals, written four or five years before Baudelaire died, in which he alternates programs of diet with desperate expressions of piety. These were dictated, Auden believes, by a "real change of heart." Baudelaire was suffering at the time from the penultimate stage of syphilis. "I have," he wrote at this time, "cultivated my hysteria with delight and terror . . . and today I have received a singular warning. I have felt the wind of the wing of madness pass over me." "To the eye of nature," says Auden, his repentance "was too late. As he spoke, the bird swooped and struck. But, to the eye of the spirit, we are entitled to believe he was in time—for, though the spirit needs time, an instant of it is enough."

But Baudelaire's great book *Les Fleurs du Mal*, the work by which he is known, had been published years before, and, though its poems in praise of Satan and of Peter's denial of Christ are occasionally set off by the brusque descent of disciplinary angels and by favorable references to Jesus, it is hardly a work of piety. I agree with Anatole France (whose critical point of view has become so unfashionable in the present day, with the dogmatisms of unsure people) that "Baudelaire is a very bad Christian. He loves sin and deliciously savors the feeling that he is lost to God. He knows that he is being damned, and thereby he renders to the divine wisdom a tribute which will be counted to him for righteousness, but he is intoxicated by the idea of damnation and his appetite for women goes no further than what is necessary to guarantee that he has definitely forfeited his soul." (So Baudelaire writes in these journals: "For my part, I say: the sole and supreme pleasure in Love lies in the absolute knowledge of doing *evil*. And men and women know, from birth, that in Evil is to be found all voluptuousness.") His references to God, says France, were stimulated by egoism. "In his arrogance he wished to believe that everything he did was important, even his little impurities; so that he wanted them all to be sins that would interest heaven and hell. But at bottom he had only a half-faith. His spirit alone was Christian. His heart and his mind remained empty."

The puritanical side of the Catholic Church had evidently combined with an Oedipus complex to produce in Baudelaire his curious view of love. Is it possible to show that religion contributed much else to his work? He had some sympathy of fellow-feeling for the poor and the ignored and the ill. Yet it is characteristic of him that when he writes his memorable poem about the "bighearted servant" of whom he had been jealous in childhood, he imagines her returning from the grave to weep over his fallen state. This is moving; but so is his satanic pride, and there is a good deal more pride in him than pity. Baudelaire is one of the great modern poets, as Eliot and Auden themselves are poets of at least the first rank. Eliot, in *Ash Wednesday*, can move us when his weakness and chagrin tremble into the accents of prayer; Auden, in his *Christmas Oratorio*, can move us with the spectacle of Joseph and Mary staggered by an Annunciation which seems to be breaking the news of the arrival of a difficult and topflight poet. But are such things as these religion? Are Baudelaire's angels religion? Aren't they rather the literary devices of uncomfortable rationalists who, disgusted by the dullness of democracy, the vulgarity of revolution, have resorted for protection against them to the mythology and animism of childhood? When Baudelaire prayed to Poe (not remarkable for his Christian feeling and rather perfunctory about his faith), as he did in the last entry of his journal; when Eliot and Auden and Isherwood invoke the example of Baudelaire, they are appealing to a passion for literature which has managed to burn pure and intense through suffering and degradation. But what has this to do with the Christian cults for whose rites the churches are built and the parsons and priests ordained?

November 1, 1947

VAN WYCK BROOKS ON THE
CIVIL WAR PERIOD

The Times of Melville and Whitman is the fourth volume in order of appearance in Van Wyck Brooks's history of American literature, but in the chronology of the series it takes its place between the two New England volumes, *The Flowering of New England* and *New England: Indian Summer*. It is not quite so exciting, perhaps, as the volume published just before (chronologically, the first of the series), *The World of Washington Irving*, which revived the intellectual ferment of the period just after the Revolution, but it is distinguished by the same kind of qualities. These two volumes which do not deal with New England seem to me to have a freedom of movement and an exhilaration of spirit, as well as a brilliance of writing, that the New England volumes, remarkable though they are, do not display to the same degree. This is partly because Mr. Brooks has been growing more and more adept and partly because his story in these later-written installments ranges more widely and becomes more varied; but it is also, I believe, partly because the author, being himself a New Yorker, does better when he gets away from New England.

There has always been in American literature a New York tradition as well as a New England one, but it has never been so much talked about precisely because it is less provincial. The New Yorkers, all facing, as it were, in the direction of the mouth of the Hudson, have more easily passed out into the larger world, and the great city in which they have all sojourned has been cosmopolitan and always changing. The New Englanders of the classical generation did derive a certain strength from their relation to small strongly-rooted communities—Cambridge, Concord, Beacon Hill, etc.—but they suffered from the crampedness of these places. The New Yorkers—Irving, Cooper, Melville, Whitman, the Jameses, Edith Wharton, Stephen Crane, John Jay Chapman, Van Wyck Brooks himself—are all men or women of the world in a way that no New Englander is, and they have, most of them, a sense of the country as a whole such as few New Englanders have had. (If one is going in for regional competition, the New Yorkers stand up very well beside Emerson, Hawthorne and Thoreau, the only first-rate New Englanders of the classical age; and they outshine the later New Englanders, from Henry Adams to E. A. Robinson, who mostly did not live in New England.)

This volume of Brooks's history, at any rate, unrolls a lively panorama of the filling-out of the continent between the middle of the century and the eighties. It extends a whole network of literary lines through the South, the Middle West and the Far West, each pegged here and there with the colored pin of some writer of particular note—though a map does not give quite the right metaphor, since the trail is always represented with the scenery, the people, the kinds of life, that the traveller himself saw: Miss Murfree's Tennessee mountaineers, the Illinois and Indiana towns of Joseph Kirkland and Edward Eggleston, the frozen Sierras of John Muir, the stagecoaches, miners and gamblers of Bret

Harte and Mark Twain. And you have, also, the long voyages of Melville and the extraordinary wanderings as a folklorist among the American Indians, the European gypsies and the Etruscan Romagnoli of the forgotten Charles Godfrey Leland, one of Mr. Brooks's *trouvailles*. The fluent presentation of all this—which accommodates so much information and keeps straight so many intertwined destinies—is a triumph of the flexibility that Mr. Brooks has developed in applying his method; and these summaries of individual careers are accompanied by the usual formulations, perhaps the most valuable part of the history, of insights into cultural phenomena: the swift fading-out in the South, with the ascendancy of the "cotton snobs," of the Jeffersonian taste and enlightenment, leaving literature in complete discredit and publishing subjected to a censorship imposed by the slave-holding interests in a society without even the town records, without even the private diaries that might allow the nostalgic novelists of the period after the Southern defeat to reconstruct the good old days; the influence of periodical journalism on American writing in general at the time when Stedman wrote that "the worlds before and after the Deluge were not more different than our republics of letters before and after the late war" and that "for ten years the younger generation" had "read nothing but newspapers"; the going-underground, at this time, of our more serious writers for the purpose of escaping the oppression of the twin tyrants of vulgarity and gentility that were established during the reign of commercialism (a tendency which was carried to extreme lengths in Emily Dickinson's secret poems and Henry Adams' unsigned or unpublished writings but which had already manifested itself in the later careers of Whitman and Melville, when the former, retired to Camden, was a prophet without honor and a scandal, and the latter, after the first success of his South Sea island books, had passed into an eclipse so complete that, though he was still alive and writing at the time when Robert Buchanan visited New York in 1885, this English admirer of Melville was unable to find out where he lived); the cult of the common man, to which both Whitman and Melville were dedicated, and the rift between rich and poor, which, widening as the century wore on, was felt to be un-American by the writers of the older generation—with the beginnings in 1861, in the work of Rebecca Harding Davis, of a new kind of realism in fiction dealing with industrial life— the conditions of which, as she said, had an "awful significance we do not see."

What is treated here least satisfactorily—though its effects are thus to some extent allowed for—is the Civil War itself, which, in breaking and embittering the South, in inflating and corrupting the North, left the American republican idealism in a wrecked and demoralized state, dislocating the points of view of writers, Northern and Southern alike, whose training had prepared them for a different kind of world from that with which they were later confronted. Mr. Brooks has shown admirably in Whitman's case his growing dismay and doubt as he lived on after those years of the war that had "trembled and reeled" beneath him; but he is diverted by the scheme of his work from featuring the war as the crisis it was in the development of American society. One feels guilty in complaining at one's ease of a scheme which has enabled the historian to organize so large a body of various and tangled material, but one comes to regret more and more some of the results of his having decided to make two volumes center about New England. For one thing, this has led him to attach to New England, and thus remove from their true frame

of reference, writers like Henry James and W. D. Howells whose connection with New England was incidental
or who, like Henry Adams, though born in New England of New England stock, had their real careers somewhere else; and it has also involved him in the awkward-
ness of covering the war in two different volumes, so that
the lives of a Northerner like John De Forest, a Westerner like Ambrose Bierce and a Southerner like Sidney
Lanier cannot be considered together in relation to their
experience as soldiers; nor can the simultaneous disillu-
sionments with democratic civilization of Henry Adams,
of Henry James and of Mark Twain be easily seen as
cases of a general shrinking and chill on the part of
American idealism.

Another unsatisfactory feature of *The Times of Melville and Whitman* is the discussion of Melville himself.
One feels here, too, a certain diffidence about criticizing
so large a work, which, in accepting deliberate limitations, has so splendidly justified itself. It has, of course,
been one of the conditions of carrying out the program
at all that the historian should not treat too elaborately
or explore with too much curiosity even the most important or interesting of his individual subjects. Mr.
Brooks has handled some difficult cases—Poe in the preceding volume, Whitman and Mark Twain in this—
with an intelligence and an expert tact that have managed to summarize these writers without oversimplification, touching on every aspect of their work (he is
particularly good with Whitman, who has always been
one of his admirations). But in the case of Herman
Melville, he seems never to have got into his subject.
The situation here is worse even than it was in his treatment of Henry James, for there were certain sides of
James that he understood, whereas it can almost be said
that he simply passes Melville by—or at least that he

sees him only in relation to the national idealism. At the end of the previous volume, the historian told us quite truly that "with Poe another age had opened—intenser, profounder than this" (that is, than Irving's age); but the depths and intensity of Melville, which are surely the most obvious examples of this, he skims over with less insight than he had for Poe's, and when we discover that he has here devoted about the same amount of space to Melville that he had, in the New England volumes, to Oliver Wendell Holmes, we feel that he has let us down. It is possible to agree with Mr. Brooks that Melville did somehow fail to live out his career as a writer, that he always remained something of an amateur; but one cannot admit the implications of Mr. Brooks's theoretical questions as to whether Melville's short stories, "after all . . . would have been recalled at all" if he had not written *Moby Dick* and the three or four books of travel that appeared before it," and as to whether his "metaphysical cogitations . . . were in reality of greater moment than the thoughts of a hundred other men who were obsessed at the time with the conflict of religion and science." Mr. Brooks speaks respectfully of *Moby Dick,* but he sidesteps a real discussion of it in a sentence beginning as follows: "Aside from the innermost meaning of the book—and this seemed clear enough—with what an astonishing skill he sustained the mood"; yet one cannot find out from his chapters on Melville what he supposes this clear meaning to be. The systole and diastole of Melville, the alternations of attraction and repulsion, of ecstatic rapture and horror, that supply the dark fable of *Benito Cereno* as well as that of *Moby Dick,* do not pulse in Mr. Brooks's pages.

Mr. Brooks's *The Ordeal of Mark Twain,* published now twenty-seven years ago, was one of the best of his books. Here he studied Mark Twain in his origins, in his family relations and in his relations with his public, and produced in its tragic closing pages one of the great passages of the American prose-writing of our period—a passionate peroration, which must have set up responsive vibrations in many young American writers who read it. Now, if any American of genius ever went through an ordeal, it was Melville. Precisely what this ordeal consisted of has never, so far as I know, been investigated, and one would have thought that Van Wyck Brooks would have been just the man to do it. But nothing could be further from his procedure with Mark Twain than his way of approaching Melville. He barely mentions Melville's family and marriage, which would make, one imagines, in connection with his wanderings, a gloomy but significant story; and, although Mr. Brooks sticks here to his original version of Mark Twain's career, it is curious to see him resorting to a superficial explanation for Melville's feeling, after writing *Pierre*, that the "thews of a Titan" had been cut in him: simply eye-strain and overwork and a fire at Harper's that destroyed the plates and most of the stock of his books—an explanation that has a disconcerting resemblance to that put forward by Bernard De Voto, Mr. Brooks's implacable antagonist, as an alternative explanation to Brooks's for the pessimism of Mark Twain's later years: simply the failure of Mark Twain's speculations following his early success.

It is the stress of the period one misses. This was the moment of bankruptcies and wounds, of miscarriages, distortions, frustrations. Even the life of a second-rank writer like Cable, homeless between South and North, has an element of strain and waste that does not come through in Mr. Brooks's account of him. If one thinks of it from this point of view, *The Times of Melville and*

Whitman seems a little too even and cheerful. But if one thinks of it from the point of view of the distance that Mr. Brooks has already come and the energy he must already have expended, one is amazed that he has still so much to give, that he can still deal so freshly and vividly with so many kinds of subjects, that, at the end of two thousand pages, he is still exerting his spell.

November 29, 1947

AN ANALYSIS OF MAX BEERBOHM

THIS REVIEWER is a little late in getting around to Max Beerbohm's *Mainly on the Air,* which was brought out as long ago as last year; but it may be pleaded that the book itself is not strictly up to date, containing as it does three pieces that first appeared in the early twenties and two that have been published before in earlier volumes of Max's essays. The other pieces, with one or two exceptions, are not—agreeable reading though they make—quite of the author's best. About half of the thin book is made up of B.B.C. broadcasts—three from the thirties, three from the forties—which deal mainly with the London of Max Beerbohm's youth (music halls, glimpses of Gladstone, the old quiet London squares), and most of the non-broadcast pieces are in a similar mild reminiscent vein (top hats and Charterhouse school-days). So the occasion, not important in itself, may conveniently serve as a pretext for a general discussion of the author.

The book has been already so used by Mr. Louis Kronenberger in an admirable little essay called *The Perfect Trifler,* in the *Saturday Review of Literature.* Mr. Kronenberger begins by assuming that Max is already a classic, and he tries to discriminate the qualities that are likely to ensure his permanence. I agree with Mr. Kronenberger that Max Beerbohm is likely to be read much longer than certain of his British contemporaries who at one time attracted as much attention. Chesterton and Belloc, for example, seem today merely literary journalists advertising their barbarous prejudices with the rattle of a coarse verbal cleverness. Their prose is unreadable now, when Max Beerbohm's seems even better than it did when it first appeared. Though I am not much given to rereading books, I have often reread Max Beerbohm, and my respect for his writing has immensely increased since the early nineteen-hundreds, when it was natural to see him as a mere minor sparkler suspended in rather an anomalous position between the constellation of Wilde, Beardsley, Whistler, the *Yellow Book* and the Rhymers' Club, and that of Shaw, Bennett, Wells, Chesterton, Galsworthy and Barrie. But for an expert appreciation of his writing, I refer you to Mr. Kronenberger. What I want to try to do here is go a little behind Max's engaging mask and analyze the point of view which gets expression in his writings and his caricatures, and which it seems to me that Mr. Kronenberger has made to look somewhat simpler than it is.

The truth is that Max is quite complex, and that complexity and the intelligence it generates are what— given his double talent, a complexity in itself—have made him interesting beyond what one might expect from work that seems at first sight so playful. We learn from the memorial volume edited by Max for his half-brother, the actor Sir Herbert Beerbohm Tree, that their father, who was born in Memel, was "of German and Dutch and Lithuanian extraction," and that he "settled in England when he was twenty-three," where he became a successful grain merchant in London and married a lady with an English name. His three sons by this first marriage were sent to be educated in Germany, at the same college where the father had studied. Thereafter one of them went to Cape Colony and decided to

spend the rest of his life there, another explored Pata-
gonia and wrote a book on the subject, and the third
took to the stage (adopting the name of Tree, derived
from the original *baum* of Beerbohm), where he enjoyed, if any actor ever did, a life of fantasy that blithely
soared above his actual milieu and era. When, later,
their mother died, their father married her sister, and
Max was born when his father was sixty-one. (There
has always perhaps been about Max something of the
enfant de vieux, with his frailness, his elfin aspect and
that poise and air of experience that caused Wilde to
say about him, in his twenties, that he had mastered the
secret of perpetual old age.) These are the only data
available in regard to Max Beerbohm's antecedents, but
they suggest a mixture of foreign with English blood,
and an element unassimilated by England that inevitably gravitated away from her. Max himself did not study
abroad; he was sent to Charterhouse and Oxford, and
seems to have grown up entirely in England; yet, though
odd, it did not seem unnatural that, when he married in
1910, this master of English style, who had absorbed so
much of Oxford and London, this popular English caricaturist, who had depended on first-hand observation
of Parliament, the Court and the theater, should, at
the age of thirty-eight, have taken his wife to live in
Italy, and should only have returned, under pressure of
events, just before the second World War. There had
always been perceptible in his work an alien point of view
not amenable to English standards.

This alien side of Max Beerbohm declares itself most
fully and frankly in the album of drawings called *Rossetti and His Circle,* published in 1922, when Max
had lived more than a decade in the country of Rossetti's
origins. "Byron, Disraeli, and Rossetti," he explains to us
in his preface, "these seem to me the most interesting

men that England had in the nineteenth century. . . .
To be interesting, a man must be complex and elusive.
And I rather fancy it must be a great advantage for him
to be born outside his proper time and place." As for the
drawings themselves, they are mainly a set of variations
on the theme of Rossetti's relation, not to his romantic
art, but to the influences of Victorian England that try
to distract him from it. You see him—preoccupied, obstinate, brooding, unkempt, ill-dressed—resisting impor-
tunity and pressure: the blighting smugness of the academic Jowett, the slick eloquence of the fashionable
Leighton, Meredith's self-conscious nature cult, Mill's
shy, pale and gentle rationalism, the bohemianism of
Sala and Browning's society ladies.

For the alien element in Max is at least as exotic as
Rossetti. He says somewhere in his theatrical criticism
that the rococo is his favorite style; but this element,
when he gives it its head, does not stop with being
rococo. In its gemminess, its artificiality, its excrescences
of grotesque fancy, it sometimes becomes positively Byzantine. The Englishman in Max, on the other hand, is
moderate and unassertive, dominated by common sense—
and not merely correct and prosaic, but even occasionally a bit of a Philistine. It was the Byzantine that made
him love the nineties and led him to find Beardsley
enchanting; it was the Englishman that kept him steady,
so that, almost alone of his group, he survived the *fin de
siècle* without tragedy, breakdown or scandal—and he
walked out of the pages of the *Yellow Book* and into
those of the *Saturday Review* as politely and unperturbedly as he might have gone to dine at Simpson's after
absinthe at the Café Royal. It was the Byzantine that
pricked him to cultivate his early preciosity of style; the
Englishman that taught him the trick, which it has
amused him to practise so often, of letting this preciosity

down, with deprecating and comic effect, by a descent into the flatly colloquial.

This mixture of contrasting tendencies appears in all Max Beerbohm's work, sometimes with confusing results. In the title of *Zuleika Dobson* there is a simple juxtaposition of the exotic and the British; but in the novel itself the two are entangled in a curious way. I agree with Mr. Kronenberger—though I know we are in a minority—that there is something unsatisfactory and, as he says, "unpalatable" about this book. The trouble, I believe, is due to the fact that in this case the two sets of colors, instead of being blended in a fabric, have got into a kind of snarl. What is the pattern or the point of *Zuleika?* Is it satire or parody or nonsense or what? It is full of amusing things and patches of clever writing, but it has also tiresome stretches of the thought and conversations of characters who do not even have the two-dimensional kind of life—like that of the people of Congreve or Firbank—that is possible within a comic convention. Max Beerbohm may be trying to satirize the admiration of Oxford for a duke, but, just as he frankly himself adores Oxford, so he seems fascinated, less frankly, by his duke, who sets the fashion for all the other undergraduates. (One remembers Max's eulogy of Ouida; and his attitude toward the Duke is closely related to his attitude toward royalty, a subject with which he was preoccupied in his first two collections of essays and to which, in both his writings and his drawings, he has constantly returned. Though he has made a good deal of fun of English monarchs and their households, one feels that he has been somewhat beglamored by them. The waspishness he sometimes displayed at the expense of George V and his family—whom he saluted with satirical verses at the time of the coronation and later caricatured so sharply that a protest from an official

source compelled Max to remove certain drawings from
one of his exhibitions—seems largely to have been
prompted by resentment at their failure to be glamorous
enough.) But though it is English to love a duke, the
Duke of Dorset projected by Beerbohm is Byzantine
and apocalyptic. The hyperbole of magnificence here
has its effectiveness, poetic and comic, but it is surely
not of Oxford. The wholesale suicide at the end of the
book is also apocalyptic, but it seems to me completely
unreal, completely unamusing. An exotic imagination
has lost touch with an English subject.

And Max Beerbohm's imagination has in itself never
been very strong. It is, in general—to my taste, at any
rate—in this department of fairy-tale fantasy that he is
usually least successful. Neither *Zuleika* nor *The Happy
Hypocrite* is a favorite of mine among his works; and
The Dreadful Dragon of Hay Hill is perhaps the only
really bad thing that he has allowed to get into a book.
These stories force unworkable conceits; they get queerly
out of range of Max's taste. He is much better when—
in *Enoch Soames* or *Not That I Would Boast*—he sticks
closer to a real background. Yet this is not enough, with
Max, to produce one of his first-rate stories: the feeblest
of the *Seven Men* are the ones that are least fantastic.
Max's talent for impersonation, extraordinary in its
way, is almost exclusively literary—that is, he can give
you a poem, a play, a letter, a speech in Parliament, but
he is unable to give you people—the heroine of *Zuleika*,
for example—whose style can have no basis in reading.
When Zuleika begins to talk like a book, she has to
explain that she has picked up the habit from a certain
Mr. Beerbohm, "who once sat next to me at dinner."
The two short stories mentioned above are the virtuoso
pieces of a parodist, as is the best thing in *Mainly on the
Air,* a portrait of a sententious old fraud called T. Fen-

ning Dodsworth; and *Zuleika,* it seems to me, succeeds best when the comedy is verbal, when it arrives at its own kind of parody by exploiting a preciosity that is half burlesque.

There is another set of contrasts in Max's work which should probably be approached in another way. The alien in Max Beerbohm has, one guesses, adapted himself to England at some cost to his better intelligence, but he takes his revenge in indirect ways and at unexpected moments. He has learned the most perfect manners. "Before all things, from first to last," he wrote, or quoted, on the flyleaf of his first book, "I am utterly purposed that I will not offend." Yet his writing is full of hoaxes: he loves to disconcert the reader with bogus historical characters and invented literary references, as he is reported, in private life, to be addicted to such practical jokes as pasting indecent words into the text of John Drinkwater's poems and leaving the book on the night-table of his guest-room.

These irreverent pranks by an imp at the expense of a perfect little gentleman, like the dandiacal aberrations of the foreigner in Max who is bored with his bowler hat, contribute to the series of surprises that are so much more spontaneous in Max's work and so much more piquant, than the mechanical paradoxes of Chesterton or even, sometimes, than the systematic efforts of Shaw to "put the obvious in terms of the scandalous." And Max's digs that have a background of demureness leave, in some cases, real scars. It is true, as Mr. Kronenberger says, that Max Beerbohm, in his later years has been a little in danger of slipping into the role of the professional old fogy. Yet he has not been always a conservative, nor has he always been a gentle "trifler." It was no doubt an exaggeration for Bernard Shaw to say, in 1917, that Max was "the most savage Radical caricaturist since Gillray," and that *Zuleika* was "only his play, not his work." But the series of political cartoons, done during the Boer War and called *The Second Childhood of John Bull*, as well as many of his other drawings between then and the first World War, would go a long way to bear this out. Max gave at that time the impression of being something of a middle-class liberal. In any case, there was sometimes in his caricatures, less often in his writings, an unmistakable accent of anger. His impudence was by no means so childlike as his caricatures of himself, wide-eyed and wispy-limbed, seemed calculated to make one expect; but his animus was never derived from political or moral principle: it was simply an intense dislike of certain vulgarities, stupidities, impostures. What one feels is irrepressible contempt in his drawings of Sir Edward Carson, in his caricature of "Mr. Charles Whibley consoling Mr. Augustine Birrell for the loss of the Education Bill by a discourse on the uselessness of teaching anything whatsoever, sacred or profane, to children of the not aristocratic class," and its effect is none the less deadly because the dig appears to be humorous and made, as it were, in passing.

The series called *Tales of Three Nations*, done in 1923, in which Max cartoons the shifting relations, between Napoleon's time and our twenties, of Germany, France and England, shows a point of view quite free from nationalism and a consistent sympathy with the underdog. He was frightened, however, by the Russian Revolution, and it provoked some of his bitterest pictures. He seems always to have been biassed against Russia, and one suspects that here a British provincialism combined with some Baltic inheritance to produce an unreasonable prejudice. But, aside from the vagaries of the Russians, the turn that things were taking dismayed him. In *A Survey* (1921), he explained, in an epistle to Britannia, that he "used to laugh at the Court and at the persons around it; and this distressed you rather. I never laughed with you at Labour. Labour didn't seem to me quite important enough yet. But Labour is very important now, very strong indeed; as you have found. And I gathered, this year . . . that you thought me guilty of not the very best of taste in failing to bow my knee to your new Baal." In *Observations* (1925), his last volume of topical caricatures, he has a drawing of Civilization wedded to the hideous Industrial System: "You took me for better or wuss in younger and 'appier days, and there'll be no getting away for you from me, ever"; and another, of the Governing Classes booted, bewigged, epauletted and equipped with a silk hat and an umbrella, assailed by a demon-eared Communism brandishing a knife and a torch. It is really the whole modern world that Max Beerbohm despises and dreads; but he has never worked out a consistent line for dealing with contemporary problems. His point of view is instinctively that of the cultivated merchant class. He may admire the feudal nobility, but he is not necessarily sympathetic with them. He prizes the security and freedom of the old-fashioned middle-class gentleman, but he hates all the horrors and rigors, on the masters' side as well as the workers', which have eventually resulted from the system upon which these advantages were based. The difficulties of his position are disarmingly exposed in his essay on servants in *And Even Now*—it appears that he does not like to be waited on and would be glad to see domestic service abolished—in which he calls himself a Tory anarchist.

This is deplorable from the point of view of the man who thinks that "art is a weapon" on one side or other of the class war; but it has not prevented Max Beerbohm from being one of the great critics of his time. Max the critic has a personality somewhat different, though never quite distinct, from Max the storyteller and personal essayist. The writer that emerges, for example, in the two volumes of theatrical notices contributed to the *Saturday Review* has stripped himself, after the pieces of the first few months, of the coyness which Mr. Kronenberger rightly complains of as Max's worst vice. Max tells us that this weekly journalism, which his friends thought a waste of time, actually helped him to improve his writing. In the course of his twelve years of service, he had reduced the arabesques of his earlier style to the sobriety of his later prose; and one meets here, as in no other department of his work, the mind that gives a base to the whole: very flexible, very free from prejudice (he has dropped his undergraduate poses), but completely sure of itself (though he has sometimes to revise his first verdicts), very definite and firm in its judgments, and very direct and courageous in registering unpopular opinions. In its different way, this body of writing is as remarkable as the dramatic crticism of Max's predecessor Shaw—who suggested him to fill his own place on the basis of the young man's attacks on Shaw's *Plays Pleasant and Unpleasant*. Max's caricatures of contemporaries, which are a criticism of public life, also give us the tougher Beerbohm (though, for some reason, the forewords to the albums are sometimes pitched in his coyest lisp). But the field in which his critical faculty is happiest and most at home is that of literature, and here the parodies of *A Christmas Garland*—the most searching, except Proust's, of our time—have their place in a body of comment which has undoubtedly left a deeper imprint than the lightness of its tone ever promised.

It is now a long time, however, since Max Beerbohm

the literary critic has played his bright pocket-torch on the present. One gets the impression that Lytton Strachey has been the last contemporary writer in whom he has felt any real interest. One would like to know, by word or picture, what he thinks of T. S. Eliot, Virginia Woolf, Hemingway, Priestley, Maugham. The only ray of light that has reached me on Max's opinion of Joyce has been by way of an anecdote which, since it brings out the discrepancies of our subject, may furnish this piece with an appropriate close. One of the younger English writers had shown Max a copy of *Finnegans Wake*. The veteran of the *Yellow Book* period, who had defended in his earlier days some startling unconventional work, examined this outlandish production; then, "I don't think," he said, "he'll be knighted for that." Max himself *had* just been knighted.

May 1, 1948

THE ORIGINAL OF TOLSTOY'S NATASHA

THE PRINCIPAL MODEL for Natasha in Tolstoy's *War and Peace* was his sister-in-law, Tatyana Andreyvna Behrs. She was sixteen when Tolstoy married, a gay, attractive and spirited girl, who was already a great favorite with him. She lived much in the Tolstoy household at Yasnaya Polyana in the country, and her brother-in-law used to tell her that she was paying her way by sitting as a model for him. Later, when she married a young magistrate, she continued to visit the Tolstoys, bringing her family to stay with them in the summer. Her husband died in 1917, and she went to Yasnaya Polyana to live with Tolstoy's daughter Alexandra, on a small pension from the Soviet government. Here, at seventy-five, she set out to write her memoirs, but did not live to bring her story much beyond her marriage in 1867, at the age of twenty-one.

This chronicle has just been translated and brought out for the first time in English under the title *Tolstoy as I Knew Him* and signed with the author's married name, Tatyana A. Kuzminskaya. The original Russian title, here retained as subtitle, *My Life at Home and at Yasnaya Polyana*, describes the contents better, for the book is by no means all about the Tolstoys; it is an autobiography of Tatyana. As such, it is a rewarding document, though not infrequently a boring book. Tatyana-Natasha was writing as a very old lady, on the basis of diaries and letters that date from her remote girlhood. Most of her comments on the literary figures whom she saw at close quarters in her youth—Ostrovsky, Turgenev, Fet and her brother-in-law Leo himself—show no respect for famous names. They are simply the reactions of a woman to various men she has met. At one point, after taking poison over a love affair that was going wrong, she quickly changed her mind about dying when another of her suitors called—received him politely and, going to her mother, begged to be given an antidote. Exercising no sense of selection, she merely writes down all the things that moved her at the moment of their occurrence, in the terms in which they interested her then. None of them seems to have acquired—it is perhaps what one would expect of Natasha—any sort of new significance in the light of her later experience. It is as if the child's passionate "crushes," her vanity in being admired, had been simply relived in memory. Though almost all Tatyana tells you fits perfectly the character created by Tolstoy and though the book is full of other people's testimony to her vivacity and her beauty, the excitement of Natasha is not there. What Tatyana had was evidently overflowing life, not literary ability. She was unable to dramatize herself and what she gives you is a long and slow record of sisters and brothers and parents, uncles and aunts and cousins, nurses and maids and coachmen, protracted visits to country houses and social calls in Moscow (where her father was Court Physician and the Behrses lived in a house at the Kremlin). All the incidents, the most serious and crucial, as well as the most trivial and frivolous, are noted down in the same casual proportions that they had for the young girl at the time. The marriage of a servant, the remodelling of a house, an accident on a dangerous road, a saddle that comes loose at a hunt, a cat that jumps out of the arms of one of the actors in amateur theatricals, are presented on about the same level as the volatile flirtations and engagements, the continual birth of children (in those days people had one a year), and the long illnesses and premature deaths that even the best city doctors could not seem to do much to prevent.

But the most important episode of Tatyana's youth affords a significant insight, much more so than she is aware, into the society to which she belonged and which her brother-in-law so brilliantly depicted. It is an episode typical of their world and yet one for which Tolstoy presents no equivalent in *War and Peace*—a drama that raises a problem which he was only much later to treat. The Natasha of real life had her Anatole Kuragin, as in *War and Peace*—his real name was even Anatole; and her eventual marriage with Kuzminsky seems to have had something in common with Natasha's final acceptance of Pierre. But, in between, had occurred the most serious love affair of her life: her tragically frustrated engagement to Leo Tolstoy's older brother Sergei.

Sergei Tolstoy had been living for years with a gypsy woman named Marya Mikhailovna, by whom he had two children. He had inherited an estate, which he farmed, not far from Yasnaya Polyana, and he lived there with his uncultivated mistress, shutting himself off from social intercourse with the neighbors of his own class. He fell in love with Tatyana and she with him, and he thought he could manage to marry her without telling Marya Mikhailovna. But the news of what was afoot soon reached her, and when her gypsy parents were told, they threatened to sue Sergei and create a public scandal. She was having another baby, which made things very difficult for him. And there was also another difficulty. Two brothers, in Tsarist Russia, were forbid-

den to marry two sisters unless both ceremonies were performed at the same time—since as soon as one of the mar-
riages had taken place, the in-laws of both the bride and
the groom became technically their blood relations. This
in itself made the match between Sergei Tolstoy and
Tatyana rather a shady transaction: a compliant priest
had to be found. (This point is not explained by the
editors, with the result that the situation is partly unintelligible to the non-Russian reader.) Sergei began to
stay away from Yasnaya Polyana, and when Tatyana
grasped the situation, she broke the engagement off,
though her disappointment was bitter and the shock had
a serious effect on her health. The rest of Sergei's story
is not told by Tatyana, but one can find it in *The Tragedy of Tolstoy,* by Tolstoy's daughter Alexandra. Sergei
married Marya Mikhailovna and became more and more
unsocial. His wife and daughters did all the housework
and lived in terror of him. He made it impossible for
one of these daughters to see a young man of the local
gentry who was in love with her and wanted to marry
her, on the ground that he was not well enough educated; and presently another of the daughters, "homely,
small, almost a dwarf," ran away with a good-looking
cook, who opened a shop with her money, treated her
brutally and finally deserted her, leaving her with several children. She died during the Revolution, "alone
and unhappy in a faraway village." The third daughter
eloped with a Bashkir, who had been brought from the
steppes to make kumiss, a fermentation of mare's milk
which had been prescribed for her health. She returned the
next year, with an undergrown little boy, who had yellow Oriental skin and slanting Oriental eyes. Her father
let her live in the house, in a back room as far as possible
from his study, but would not see the child. They and
Marya Mikhailovna, left alone by Sergei's death, died

miserably after the Revolution, when their house, from which they had fled, was burned down and the estate sacked. After the elopement of the second daughter, Sergei had made haste to agree to the marriage of his only remaining child to her insufficiently educated nobleman.

Now, Tatyana could hardly have known at the time that her brother-in-law Leo, who had first accepted her match with Sergei, then applauded her breaking it off, had himself had a serf-girl for a mistress not long before he married her sister. His diaries show how much he had cared for this girl: "I am in love," he declares in one entry, "as I never was before in my life. I have no other thought. I suffer." He has moments of indifference, of revulsion even, but his affection for her seems steadily to grow stronger. "It is getting to be even frightening," he later writes, "how close to me she is. . . . It is not merely the feeling now of a rutting stag, but that of a husband and a wife." He had a son by her, who afterward became coachman for one of his legitimate sons. And in the meantime, by one of those gestures of what he liked to regard as uncompromising honesty that were often so admirably calculated to give pain to other people, he had shown his young wife this diary at a time when his former mistress still sometimes came to the house—with the result that the poor Countess, already of a jealous disposition, was visited by homicidal impulses when she found the woman scrubbing the floors, and even took to disguising herself as a peasant and waylaying her husband about the estate to see whether he were still susceptible to the blandishments of pretty serf-girls. Twenty-seven years after his marriage, Tolstoy tried to write about this love affair, combining it with the story of a similar complication, in which a neighbor, after marrying a jealous wife, had shot his peasant mistress.

Tolstoy, in one of his versions of this story, follows the real tragedy; in another, he has the landowner shoot himself. He could not bring himself to publish the piece—to which he gave the title *The Devil*—presumably because, when he showed it to his wife as late as 1909, she was upset by it and made a scene; and it did not appear until after his death.

This situation was evidently a common one. Tolstoy's father, at the age of sixteen, had had an affair with a peasant girl, an affair arranged by his parents themselves; and a son, who was the product of this union, had turned up from time to time to plague the legitimate children. Tolstoy tells of his "strange feeling of consternation when in after years this brother of mine, fallen into destitution and bearing a greater resemblance to my father than any of us, used to beg help of us and was thankful for the ten or fifteen rubles we used to give him." The memory of his own illegitimate family recurred to torment Leo. "I looked at my bare feet," he wrote in his diary of 1909, "and remembered Aksinya [his mistress]—that she is still alive and that they say Ermil is my son, and that I do not beg her forgiveness, have never done penitence, do not repent every hour, and dare to judge others."

D. S. Mirsky, in his *History of Russian Literature*, has truly described *War and Peace* as an "heroic idyll of the Russian nobility," and pointed out that, in spite of the horrors of war and the ineptitudes of civilization, "the general message . . . is one of beauty and satisfaction that the world should be so beautiful." He suggests, I believe correctly, that Tolstoy's penchant for the idyllic is "the opposite pole to his unceasing moral uneasiness." Certainly *War and Peace* is one of the greatest of novels as it is one of the most enchanting. If it is not, as I do not think it is, quite one of the very summits of literature, it is because this idyllic tendency does here get the better of the author at the expense of the conditions of life as he actually knew and lived it. There is in the book, for all its realism, a certain element of the idealization in which we are all disposed to indulge in imagining the lives of our ancestors. In the case of Tolstoy, who had hardly known either his grandparents or his parents, this temptation must have been very strong. In the novel, Prince André and Pierre have their struggles with the problem of the peasantry, but the main problem is expelling the invader, and neither Natasha nor any of the men has to face any human relationship as painful as those in which the real Tatyana and the real Sergei and Leo Tolstoy found themselves involved. The Levin of *Anna Karenina,* which followed *War and Peace,* has to deal in a more direct and drastic way with his relation to the estate he has inherited and with the humans who are part of the estate, as Tolstoy did with Yasnaya Polyana; and immediately after *Anna Karenina,* Tolstoy himself appears in the character of Levin, writing the eloquent *Confession* in which he declares the insufficiency, for the moral life of a man, of property, social position and a comfortable family life, as well as of philosophy and science and the enjoyment and practice of literature. And he later tries to satisfy his moral needs by bringing himself closer to the peasants, on whose work he has always lived and who have given him the leisure to write—eating the same food as they and wearing the same clothes, working the same hours in the fields and mastering their manual skills. It was disturbing, no doubt, to a sensitive man, even after the liberation of the serfs in 1861—which Tatyana, by the way, hardly mentions, so little was it evidently noticeable in the relations of her people with their laborers and servants—to feel that one owed one's education and one's chance to pursue serious interests, as well as one's luxuries and pleasures, to the maintenance of a breed of inferior beings. But to know that one's own blood was mixed with the blood of this breed and to have to watch, in one form or another, the humiliation of one's own children must have been even harder to bear, a constant source of helpless anguish. (A gypsy singer, of course, might represent a higher stratum than that of a simple serf, but the consequences of marrying one, in Sergei's case, turned out to be just about as disastrous as if she had been a serf. When his daughter who eloped with the cook went to her Uncle Leo and asked him to approve this union, on the ground that she was following his doctrine by trying to put herself on a plane with the peasant, he lectured the girl severely, telling her that "no marriage could be happy between people who stood on different levels of development and had no interests in common.")

The emotional effects of this dilemma are not anywhere presented directly either in *War and Peace* or in *Anna Karenina,* though the situation appears in both. In the former, it is idyllic, like everything else. The uncle at whose house the Rostovs spend the night after the hunt has a housekeeper who is also his mistress, but the whole thing is most amiable and comfortable, and when Natasha has done her peasant dance—Tatyana tells us that this incident was derived from a performance of her own—the rosy and plump and good-looking woman sheds a tear or two through her laughter as she perceives that "this slim graceful countess, brought up in velvet and silk, this being so alien to her . . . was able to understand everything about Anisya and Anisya's father and her aunt and her mother, and every Russian in the world." In *Anna Karenina,* a similar situation is presented in a more embarrassing light. When Levin

goes with his wife to visit his dying brother, he winces
at having her meet the latter's ex-prostitute mistress, with
whom he has been living in misery, and he notes, for a
fleeting moment, her "expression of eager curiosity" at
encountering "that dreadful woman, so incomprehensible to her." It is only later, with *Resurrection,* begun in
1889 and not finished and published till 1899, that Tolstoy comes to grips with this situation. In his youth, he
had had an affair with one of his aunt's maids, who had
been dismissed for this reason and had come later to a
bad end. In the novel, Prince Nekhlyudov finds himself sitting on a jury which has to pass judgment on a
girl whom he recognizes as a maid of his aunt's whom
he has seduced under similar circumstances and deserted
when she was pregnant. She has since become a prostitute and is now implicated in a sordid murder, of which
she is completely innocent. At the trial, there is a mis-
carriage of justice, due partly to the carelessness of the
Court but partly to Nekhlyudov's own cowardice, and
the girl is condemned to Siberia. Nekhlyudov now
brings all his influence to have the decision reversed and
makes a vow to expiate his guilt by following her into
exile and marrying her. He does get her sentence com-
muted, and he accompanies the convicts on their journey; but Maslova spares him the final test, for, understanding the undesirability of his spending the rest of
his life with her, she marries one of her fellow-prisoners.
Nekhlyudov, on the very last pages, happens to pick up
a copy of the *New Testament* which has been given him
by a travelling evangelist, and is converted to a creed like
Tolstoy's own. From that day, for Nekhlyudov, says the
author, a new life begins, and "what that new period
will come to, time alone will show."

So we never know what happened to Nekhlyudov. It
is impossible, from what we have been told of him, to

imagine him turning saint or even finding employment that would satisfy his hunger for righteousness. Yet *Resurrection,* though it ends in the air, is not unworthy of its predecessors, and certainly does not deserve the disparagement that it usually gets. It is the novel in which Tolstoy comes closest to the problems of his own life, the only one in which he really grapples with the tragedies of a class-society, as he had seen them at first hand, as he had helped to produce them himself—the only one that gets out into the open such episodes as Tatyana had locked away in her diary. We do know what happened to Tolstoy when he tried to lead a new life: his fanaticisms and his worldly relapses, his absurdities and his desperate death. The story he himself had been living could no more come out satisfactorily than Nekhlyudov's story could. After the period of his first gratification at re-creating his lost parents and in restoring at Yasnaya Polyana the patriarchal family life of which in the preceding generation the continuity had been broken, a malaise which had survived these distractions inescapably asserted itself and came to ache through the whole of his work.

We have seen a somewhat similar preoccupation in the literature of our own South, from the days when George W. Cable was forced to come to live in the North for his boldness in describing the half-colored branches of the prominent white families of New Orleans to the days when the continued anguish of Negro and white relations has inspired those stories of Faulkner's in which neither reader nor author is ever allowed a moment's relief or repose, because the subject admits of no resolution. In Russia, the black-and-white issue was not present to deepen the class distinctions, and it was possible for the landowners in Tolstoy's fiction to contemplate marrying their mistresses, as it was possible for Sergei Tolstoy to remain in serious doubt as to whether it was right for him to put away his gypsy and marry Tatyana. But the strains and the mutilations incurred through these social differences periodically made themselves felt among all those gay parties in country houses, all those balls in St. Petersburg and Moscow, all those jolly affectionate family scenes, all those gallantries of handsome cousins.

August 28, 1948

"THE MOST UNHAPPY MAN ON EARTH"

A NEW EDITION of Swift's *Journal to Stella*, edited by Harold Williams, has been brought out by the Oxford University Press. The editing of this series of personal letters, discovered and published after Swift's death, has presented special problems to scholars. Not only do "the crowded, minute handwriting, the constant practice of abbreviation, the frequent scorings and blottings, often," as Mr. Williams says, "leave the true reading open to difference of opinion"; but the cipher of Swift's "little language," the curious baby-talk that he had apparently invented for Stella in her childhood and into which he still lapses in the journal, written when she was thirty, has never completely been penetrated. Mr. Williams is not the first editor who has restudied the difficult texts of those letters—twenty-five out of sixty-five—of which the originals survive, and who has attempted to reproduce them accurately, instead of more or less freely rewriting them or improvising when in doubt, as was the habit of certain earlier editors. But he has done on the journal a more thorough job than any of his predecessors. Unless more original letters turn up, this must remain the definitive edition. No document needs annotation more, and Mr. Williams has explained everybody and everything to which Swift refers in his chronicle of his visit to London in 1710–13, so crowded with dinners and transactions and interviews with all sorts of people who were after all sorts of things. The introduction is exact and terse in its unravelling of a tangled subject; the index is of an unprecedented fullness.

It is only when one compares this edition with the earlier one included in the best complete set of Swift, that of the old Bohn's Standard Library, that one becomes aware of the handicaps under which scholarly texts of the classics now come into circulation. The Bohn edition of the *Journal,* which cost five shillings, was well-printed in one volume on excellent paper and in admirably compact form. The portraits, engraved instead of photographed, were not perhaps so faithful to the originals as they are in Mr. Williams' edition; but the Bohn edition contained one feature, a gratuitous enrichment of a popular-priced book, which today appears almost incredible. Instead of rather a dim photograph of one page of one of the letters, which is the best the Oxford Press can do, the old volume had as a frontispiece a most remarkable folded facsimile of all four pages of one, which reproduced the color of the faded ink and the color and texture and watermark of the paper, and which was even sealed with real red sealing wax and stamped with Swift's seal. This must have been done by hand—from 1897, when the volume first appeared, till as late as 1908—for every copy of a book that was going into the common currency of a series not unlike the Modern Library.

But the *Journal to Stella* is essential for anyone who wants to know Swift. I do not think there is any other great writer whose work, for its appreciation, demands, as Swift's does, a fairly close familiarity with the ins and outs of his life. The popularity of Gulliver's Travels beyond anything else that Swift wrote is due not to its superiority but simply to the fact that it is the only one of his works on any considerable scale which presents an imaginary picture detached from Swift's own career and the historical background of his time. Swift, with his narrower range, has—in his solitary intensity of passion, his intellectual rigor and strength, his nobility and self-willed idealism, his tragic self-dramatization—something in common with Dante. But Dante got his whole career, personal, political and moral, inside his imaginary picture; Swift, though he, too, got his story told, scattered it in pamphlets and poems, in historical and political essays, in prayers and practical jokes, in epigrams and lampoons, in his correspondence with public men and in his personal letters to Stella.

It is hard to agree with George Saintsbury that this journal is the first modern novel. It shows too little imagination and requires too many notes. Except for the babblings of the little language, themselves of a chilling monotony, what you get is a bare enough record of Swift's habits and business in England—such a diary as, one would think, could not have been very much different if he had kept it for himself alone. Yet here we follow him with something like intimacy for the better part of three years. We see him as he looked to himself; and we feel the unflagging energy of that dynamo of furious emotion, all directed toward power and pride, yet subjected to a discipline so iron that it was impossible for him to be betrayed by any of the ordinary threats or baits. His arrogance imposes itself on us as it did on his contemporaries, because it is backed not merely by brains but also by austere character. We see him arrive in London as the champion of the Irish clergy in their attempt to get their taxes reduced, and we see him effect this purpose and go on to become a public figure, as influential as a great official. We see him as the practical intellect, only half masked, behind the Tory Ministry, equipping it, in a masterly tract, with the arguments that gave it its case for putting an end to the War of the Spanish Succession. And finally, on the collapse of this Ministry, we see him—his patrons afraid of him, chafing against his virtuous tyranny and refusing him the preferment he aims at: a deanery or a canonry which would keep him in England—sent back to the safe distance of Dublin as Dean of St. Patrick's Cathedral. It is a pure drama of personality, not of ideas or political principles. Swift was not even a contemplative man whose observations on life are interesting. His comment, as in *Gulliver's Travels,* written after his return to Ireland, is, couched in impassive prose, primarily a blast of poetic scorn at the animal nature of man. There are in the journal few general reflections, and such as there are are brief, but they may stick in one's head unforgettably, as I find that certain passages have done with me from a reading of more than thirty years back—not because they display Swift's intelligence, but because they show the darkness of his pessimism and the rigidity of his moral nature. "Lord Radnor and I," he writes, "were walking in the Mall this evening; and Mr. Secretary [Henry St. John, later Lord Bolingbroke] met us and took a turn or two, and then stole away, and we both believed it was to pick up some wench; and tomorrow he will be at the cabinet with the Queen: so goes the world." Or "I am just now told that poor dear Lady Ashburnham, the Duke of Ormond's daughter, died yesterday at her country house; the poor creature was with child. She was my greatest favorite; and I am in excessive concern for her loss. I hardly knew a more valuable person on all accounts: you must have heard me tell of her. I am afraid to see the Duke and Duchess; she was naturally very healthy; I am afraid she has been thrown away for want of care. Pray condole with me; 'tis extremely moving. Her lord's a puppy, and I shall never think it worth my while to be troubled with him, now he has lost all that was valuable in his possession. Yet I think he used her pretty well. I hate life, when I think it exposed to such accidents, and to see so many thousand wretches burdening the earth while such as her die, makes me think God did never intend life for a blessing."

Even in reading the journal, however, one ought to have some acquaintance with Swift's political writing of this period. Mr. Williams has done his best to fill in the political background as well as the personal one. There have lately been two new discoveries of data that might seem to throw light on the origins of Swift and Stella and their relations to one another; but these give rise to two different hypotheses which would appear to be mutually exclusive. Swift and Stella had first known one another, when he was twenty-one and she eight, in the household of Sir William Temple, where Swift lived for ten years as secretary and where Stella grew up as, presumably, the daughter of Sir William's steward and of a woman in the service of his sister. Yet there were rumors that both Stella and Swift were Sir William's illegitimate children. It is surely not credible, in the case of Swift, that he knew himself to be Sir William's son, for his attitude toward Sir William in the journal seems that of a former dependent toward a mildly respected patron, from whose service he has been glad to escape. But it has recently turned out that Sir William Temple's father, Sir John, of whom Swift himself said that he "had been a fast friend to the family," was one of the five persons who authorized, in 1666, the appointment of Swift's supposed father as Steward of the King's Inns in Dublin; and the discoverer of this fact, Mr. Denis Johnston, has concluded, with the support of some other

facts, that the mother of Swift at that time had been having a love affair with Sir John, and that Swift, born in
1667 and later assigned to the household of Sir William,
was Sir John's illegitimate son. If Stella was Sir William's
daughter, Swift would then be her uncle, and this
would explain his affectionate relation to her which
never became that of lover. But another new piece of
evidence, first published and examined by Mr. Maxwell
B. Gold in his book *Swift's Marriage to Stella,* seems to
bear out the assertions of several persons close to Swift
that he did have a marriage ceremony performed a few
years after his return from England, though he never
consummated the marriage and never saw Stella without
someone else present. If he had known himself to be her
uncle, it seems unlikely that he would have done even
this.

The celebrated anecdote about Swift, first printed
by Sir Walter Scott, thus remains as mysterious as ever:
"Immediately subsequent to the [marriage] ceremony,
Swift's state of mind appears to have been dreadful. Del-
any [an intimate friend of Swift's], as I have learned
from a friend of his relict, being pressed to give his opinion on this strange union, said that about the time it took
place, he observed Swift to be extremely gloomy and
agitated, so much so that he went to Archbishop King to
mention his apprehensions. On entering the library,
Swift rushed out with a countenance of distraction, and
passed him without speaking. He found the Archbishop
in tears, and upon asking the reason he said, 'You have
just met the most unhappy man on earth—but on the
subject of his wretchedness you must never ask a question.'"

The disease of which Swift died and under which,
apparently, his reason gave way has been diagnosed var-
iously as a malady of the ear and as hardening of the

arteries of the brain. Krafft-Ebing, whose comment on the case of Swift has been developed by Mr. Gold, thought he suffered from "sexual anaesthesia." But we still have no real idea of what had turned so much of Swift's hunger for love and creative thought into a cold and cruel need to dominate. There is one atrocious entry in the journal in which he boasts to the woman he undoubtedly loved of having interceded with St. John "to hinder a man of his pardon, who is condemned for a rape. The under-secretary was willing to save him, upon an old notion that a woman cannot be ravished; but I told the secretary he could not pardon him without a favorable report from the judge; besides he was a fiddler, and consequently a rogue, and deserved hanging for something else; and so he shall swing. What; I must stand up for the honour of the fair sex? 'Tis true, the fellow had lain with her a hundred times before; but what care I for that? What! must a woman be ravished because she is a whore?" But even more shocking, perhaps, are the last words of the last entry, in reference to a letter of Stella's: "I mightily approve ppt's [Stella's] project of hanging the blind parson—when I read that passage upon Chester walls, as I was coming into town and just received the letter, I said aloud: 'Agreeable B-tch.'"

January 22, 1949

WILLIAM FAULKNER'S REPLY TO THE
CIVIL-RIGHTS PROGRAM

WILLIAM FAULKNER'S NEW NOVEL, *Intruder in the Dust,* is the story of a Negro with white blood who refuses to behave with the submissiveness demanded of his color in the South and has developed so rigid a pride that, even when wrongfully charged with the murder of a white man, he can hardly bring himself to stoop to defend himself against the enemy of his race. The narrative deals with the adventures of the handful of people in the community (the Jefferson, Mississippi, which is the locale of most of Faulkner's fiction) who, having come to respect Lucas' independence, interest themselves in his case and exert themselves to save him from lynching. These champions include a boy of sixteen, who had once been rescued by Lucas when he had fallen through the ice; the boy's uncle, a local lawyer, who has lived abroad and has, to some degree, been able to surmount provincial prejudices; and an old lady of the best local quality, who had grown up with the accused man's dead wife in the relation of mistress and maid. All the happenings are presented from the point of view of the boy. It is his loyalty to the old Negro that leads to the discovery of evidence that the crime has been committed by someone else; and his emergence, under the stimulus of events, out of boyhood into comparative maturity is as much the subject of the book as the predicament of the Negro. The real theme is the relation between the two.

The novel has the suspense and excitement that Faulkner can nearly always create and the disturbing emotional power that he can generate at his best. The earlier Faulkner of *Sanctuary* was often accused of misanthropy and despair, but the truth is that, from *Pylon* on, at any rate, one of the most striking features of his work, and one that sets it off from that of many of his American contemporaries, has been a kind of romantic morality that allows you the thrills of melodrama without making you ashamed, as a rule, of the values which have been invoked to produce them. I do not sympathize with the line of criticism which deplores Faulkner's obstinate persistence in submerging himself in the mentality of the community where he was born, for his chivalry, which constitutes his morality, is a part of his Southern heritage, and it appears in Faulkner's work as a force more humane and more positive than almost anything one can find in the work of even those writers of our more mechanized societies who have set out to defend human rights. *Intruder in the Dust* is one of the most ardent demonstrations of this reconditioned Southern chivalry; and the question that arises in connection with it is not whether it paints too hopeless a picture but, on the contrary, whether it is not too positive, too optimistic—whether the author has not yielded too much to the temptations of the novelist's power to summon for innocence in difficulties the equivalent of the United States Marines.

I shall return to this aspect of *Intruder in the Dust*. In the meantime, it ought to be said that, from the point of view of the writing, this is one of the more snarled-up of Faulkner's books. It is not so bad as *The Bear,* which has pages that are almost opaque. But in his attempt to record the perceptions—the instinctive sensations and the half-formed thoughts—of his adolescent boy, in aiming at prisms of prose which will concentrate the infrared as well as the ultra-violet, he leaves these rays sometimes still invisible, and only tosses into our hands some rather clumsy and badly cut polygons. It would require a good deal of very diligent work and very nice calculation always to turn out the combinations of words that would do what Faulkner wants them to do. His energy, his image-making genius get him where he wants to go about seventy per cent of the time, but when he misses it, he lands in a mess. One cannot object in principle to any of Faulkner's practices: to his shifting his syntax in the middle of a sentence, to his stringing long sequences of clauses together with practically no syntax at all, to his inserting in parenthesis in the middle of a scene (in one case, in the middle of a sentence) a long episode that took place at some other time, to his invention of the punctuation (( )) to indicate a parenthesis within a parenthesis or to his creation of non-dictionary words. He has, at one time or another, justified all these devices. But what is the excuse for writing "the old grunt and groan with some long familiar minor stiffness so used and accustomed as to be no longer even an ache and which if they were ever actually cured of it, they would be bereft and lost"?—a mismanagement of relatives quite common in the Faulkner of the latest books. One is willing to give the benefit of the doubt to "regurg," "abnegant," "dismatchment," "divinant," "perspicuant," until one runs into a dictionary word used out of its real meaning, as in "it's only men who burk at facts"—when one realizes that Faulkner is not merely coining but groping. It is true that his new way of writing has enabled him to render impressions more accurately than he did before: but the passages that become unintelligible on account of a confusion of pronouns or that have to be read twice for lack of proper punctuation are not really the results of an effort to express the hardly expressible but the casualties of an indolent taste and a negligent workmanship that did not appear to the same degree in the prose—for the most part so steady and clear as well as so tense and telling—of such a novel as *Light in August*.

One finds here both the vigor of a tradition and the signs of its current decay. For the writing of Faulkner, too, has a noble and ancient lineage. Though he echoed, in his earlier novels, Hemingway and Sherwood Anderson, he belongs, really, not to their school but to the full-dress post-Flaubert group of Conrad, Joyce and Proust, whom he has sometimes echoed since. To their kind of highly complex fiction he has brought the rich and lively resources, reappearing with amazing freshness, of English lyric verse and romantic prose (as distinguished from what we now call American). This is an advantage that the Southern writers sometimes have—a contact with the language of Shakespeare which, if they sidestep the oratorical Southern verbiage, they may get through their old-fashioned education. And Faulkner, it must be said, often succeeds as Shakespeare does—by plunging into the dramatic scene and flinging down the words and images that flow to the ends of his fingers. This book, like all his books, is full of passages that could not have been written if he had sat down and contemplated the object—as Flaubert is said to have done the cabbage garden by moonlight—instead of allowing himself to be possessed by it. Minor but admirable examples in *Intruder in the Dust* are the renderings of the impression on the white boy of the smell of a Negro cabin, with all its social implications, and of the effect of a little frame church that, though lacking a steeple and shabbily patched, speaks to him with the spirit of the Calvinism to which its Scotch-Irish congregation have erected a degenerate shrine. Though he sometimes loses his grasp of language, he has described so many things so well—got out of them so much human meaning! No other of our contemporary novelists, perhaps, can compete with him in this department—for most of the best of them were bred in a world that is based on abstract assumptions, and they cannot help sharing these; whereas, for Faulkner the Mississippian, everything that a man has made wears the aspect of the human agent, and its impact is that of a human meeting.

To be thus out of date, as a Southerner, in feeling and in language and in human relations, may prove, for a novelist, a source of strength. But the weaknesses of Faulkner, also, have their origin in the antiquated community he inhabits, for they result from his not having mastered—I speak of the design of his books as wholes as well as of that of his sentences and paragraphs—the discipline of the Joyces, Prousts and Conrads (though Proust had his solecisms and what the ancients called anacolutha). If you are going to do embroidery, you have to watch every stitch; if you are going to construct a machine, you have to test every part. The technique of the modern novel, with its ideal of technical efficiency, its specialization of means for ends, has grown up in the industrial age, and it has, after all, a good deal in common with the other manifestations of that age. In practicing it so far from such cities as produced the Flauberts, Joyces and Jameses, Faulkner's provinciality, stubbornly cherished and turned into an asset, inevitably tempts him to be slipshod and has apparently made it impossible for him to acquire complete expertness in an art that demands of the artist the closest attention and care.

But *Intruder in the Dust* does not come to us merely as a novel: it also involves a tract. The story is evidently supposed to take place sometime this year or last, and it seems to have been partly inspired by the crisis at the time of the recent war in the relations between whites and Negroes and by the recently proposed legislation for guaranteeing Negro rights. The book contains a kind of counterblast to the anti-lynching bill and to the civil-rights plank in the Democratic platform. The author's ideas on this subject are apparently conveyed, in their explicit form, by the intellectual uncle, who, more and more as the story goes on, gives vent to long disquisitions that seem to become so "editorial" in character that it is difficult to regard them merely as a part of the presentation of the furniture of the uncle's personality. The series may be pieced together as something in the nature of a public message delivered by the author himself. This message, however, suffers from the handicap of being very obscurely expressed. Faulkner, who has shown himself a master at making every possible type of Mississippian talk in his natural idiom, has chosen to couch the uncle's conversations with the boy in a literary prose like his own at its most complicated and non-colloquial—so that it is difficult to reduce what is said to definite propositions. I shall, however, make an attempt to do so.

The point of view, then, seems to be as follows (interpolated comment by the critic):

"The people named Sambo" [the uncle's way of designating the Negroes] have survived the ordeal of slavery and they may survive the ordeal of dictatorship. The capacity for endurance of the Negro is a recurrent theme of Faulkner's, and his respect for their humble persistence is unconsciously but strikingly contrasted here with his attitude toward "the coastal spew of Europe, which this country quarantined unrootable into the rootless ephemeral cities" [as if the Italians, Greeks, Hungarians, Poles, and Czechs had not shown as much tenacity as the Negroes, and as if the Southern Negroes had not been kept alive—that is, encouraged to persist—by the people who had an interest in employing them, just as the immigrants from Europe were].

The Southerners in the United States are the only "homogeneous people." (The New Englander, in his pure and respectable form, crowded back by the coastal spew of Europe, is no longer of real importance.) "We are defending not actually our politics or beliefs or even our way of life, but simply our homogeneity, from a federal government to which, in simple desperation, the rest of this country has had to surrender voluntarily more and more of its personal and private liberty in order to continue to afford the United States." The Negro is homogeneous, too, "except that part of him which is trying to escape not even into the best of the white race but into the second best." The saving remnant of Southerners, such as the characters in the story who rescue old Lucas Beauchamp, should combine with the non-second-rate Negro—the second-rate variety being, by the author's definition, the Negro who demands "not an automobile nor flash clothes nor his picture in the paper, but a little of music (his own), a hearth, not his child but any child [back to Uncle Tom and Uncle Remus!], a God, a heaven which a man may avail himself a little of at any time without having to wait to die [oh, dem golden slippers!], a little earth for his own sweat to fall on among his own green shoots and plants [no large-scale agriculture for Sambo!]." Let the white man give the Negro his rights, and the Negro teach the white man his endurance, and "together we would dominate the United States; we would present a front not only impregnable but not even to be threatened by a mass of people who no longer have anything in common save a frantic greed for money and a basic fear of a failure of national character which they hide from one another behind a loud lipservice to a flag." [The Mississippian may have hold of something here.]

Lucas-Sambo must be defended "from the North and East and West—the outlanders who will fling him decades back not merely into injustice but into grief and agony, and violence, too, by forcing on us laws based on the idea that man's injustice to man can be abolished overnight by police." Any other course of conduct toward the Negro will risk dividing the country. Attempts on the part of the people in other sections of the United States to strengthen the hand of the Negro amount to nothing more than "a paper alliance of theorists and fanatics and private and personal avengers plus a number of others" [including a good many Negroes] against "a concorded [i.e., solid] South," which is now full of "ignorant people" from other parts of the country, "who fear the color of any skin or shape of nose save their own." Such action will force the many Southerners "who do begrieve Lucas' shameful condition and would improve it" and will eventually abolish it, to ally themselves with all those objectionable elements "with whom we have no kinship whatever, in defense of a principle [the inalienable right to keep the Negro down] which we ourselves begrieve and abhor." They will thus be forced into "the position of the German after 1933, who had no other alternative between being either a Nazi or a Jew, or the present Russian (European, too, for that matter), who hasn't even that, but must be either a Communist or dead." So the Southerners must be allowed, on their own initiative, in their own way, with no intervention by others, to grant the Negro his citizenship. Otherwise—

Otherwise, what? I have been able, I think, up to now, to make Faulkner's argument clear by quoting or paraphrasing his own words, with the addition of a little punctuation; but here I must present you with a chunk of his text without any elucidation, for I cannot be sure what it means: Otherwise "Lucas' equality" cannot "be anything more than its own prisoner inside an impregnable barricade of the direct heirs of the victory of 1861–1865 which probably did more than even John Brown to stalemate Lucas' freedom which still seems to be in check going on a hundred years after Lee surrendered." But, the other side may object: The South will never get around to doing anything for the Negro. Your policy, the South retorts, is dangerous, in any case: it will give rise to "a people divided [Faulkner thus seems to take it for granted that if Washington tries to back the Negroes, it will arouse the whole South to resistance] at a time when history is still showing us that the anteroom to dissolution is division."

But is pressure from outside worth nothing? Has it had no moral effect on the South? It seems to me that this book itself, which rejects outside interference, is a conspicuous sign that it has. The champions of Lucas Beauchamp are shown as rather reluctant, as even, at moments, resentful, in recognizing his rectitude and his dignity, but they do rally to get him cleared. It is true that you have had already, in the title story of *Go Down, Moses,* the same liberal lawyer and decent old maid working together to do the Beauchamps a kindness when their grandson has been executed for murder; but in this new book these white folks of the best old stock come to the rescue of the Negro with a zeal that I do not remember to have seen displayed by the inhabitants of Yoknapatawpha County in any other of Faulkner's books. Young Charles and his young Negro pal are transformed into Boy Scouts. Miss Habersham proves herself a dear gallant old thoroughbred. The uncle is as ironic and delightful as the uncle of the boy next door in E. Nesbit's books about the Bastable children. When this wonderful posse is on the march, they have hair-breadth escapes but get all the breaks. And, in the end, the vulgar upstarts who wanted to see Lucas lynched get into their vulgar cars and turn tail and run away. There has been nothing so exhilarating in its way since the triumphs of the Communist-led workers in the early Soviet films; one is thrilled by the same kind of emotion that one got from some of the better dramatizations of the career of Abraham Lincoln.

This is a new note to come from the South; and it may really represent something more than Faulkner's own courageous and generous spirit, some new stirring of public conscience. In the meantime, in harping on this message, I do not want to divert attention from the genius that produced the book, which sustains, like its predecessors, the polymorphous polychromatic vitality, the poetic truth to experience, of Faulkner's Balzacian chronicle of Yoknapatawpha County. Old Lucas and certain other characters have, as I say, appeared in *Go Down, Moses,* to which *Intruder in the Dust* is, indeed, more or less of a sequel, and the later adventures of Lucas are more interesting if you know his past history as recounted in the earlier volume, and understand his role in the tangle of black-and-white relationships which Faulkner has presented there. This subject of the complicated consequences of the mixture of white with Negro blood has been explored by Faulkner with remarkable intelligence and subtlety and variety of dramatic imagination; and Lucas himself, the black man who embarrasses a set of white relatives by having in-

herited the strongest traits of a white ancestor common
to them all, is one of the author's most impressive creations. Even when the prose goes to pieces, the man and
his milieu live.

October 23, 1948

IN MEMORY OF OCTAVE MIRBEAU

"Dear me, how far from infinite the world is! Talking to my cousin today, I mentioned Octave Mirbeau's name. 'Why, Mirbeau,' she said, 'let me see—that's the son of the doctor at Remalard, the place where we have our estate. I remember that two or three times I lashed him over the head with my whip. He was an impudent little thing as a child—his great idea was to show his bravado by throwing himself under the feet of our horses when we or the Andlaus were out driving.'"

Edmond de Goncourt: Diary,
August 26, 1889

I SHOULD LIKE to take the occasion of the reprint of a very respectable translation by Alvah C. Bessie of Octave Mirbeau's novel, *Le Jardin des Supplices* to look back at a remarkable French writer whose reputation, after his death in 1917, almost immediately evaporated both abroad and in his own country. Mirbeau belonged so much to his period that I may perhaps be pardoned for explaining that I first read him, and almost completely through, at the time of the first World War, and that he will always remain for me an old companion of my experiences of those years. As such a companion, he had perhaps more value than he might have had in other conditions. In the first place, he is at his best when he is describing those wretched French villages, with their doll-bedecked rundown churches, their diseased and deformed inhabitants and their pervasive smell of manure, among which I was then living on more intimate terms than those of the tourist who stares at them from the train and is thrilled by their look of antiquity. It is enough for me to open certain books of Mirbeau to see again their gray walls embedded in mud. In the second place, his favorite theme, the persistence in modern society of predatory and destructive appetites at variance with civilized pretentions, was particularly acceptable then, at a time when it was actually reassuring to read someone who was not trying to convince you that only the Germans had ever been bloodthirsty, who had never even fooled himself with the assumption that our exploiting competitive world was a respectable and reliable affair. And though I saw Mirbeau's faults even then, my opinion of him will always be colored by a certain special affection.

His compatriots, as we trace him through their criticism and journals, seem to have become toward him colder and colder. For Edmond de Goncourt, in the eighties, Mirbeau was a young colleague in the naturalistic movement, who was beginning to show distinguished abilities and who dedicated a novel to him. On André Gide, in the first years of this century, when Gide was an ally of the symbolists by no means enamored of naturalism, Mirbeau made a mixed impression. He responded to Mirbeau's warm indignations and admired some of his work, but complained that "the satirical spirit prevents his having any critical sense." By this time, it had become apparent that Mirbeau repudiated defiantly those versions of the French tradition that were in vogue at the turn of the century. He was not elegant and detached, like the Parnassians, not exquisite like the followers of Mallarmé, and he sometimes made heavy fun of the professional Parisian aesthetes. Nor would he attempt to adjust himself to the demands of a bourgeois audience. He scored against Paul Bourget, in his *Journal d'une Femme de Chambre,* by attributing to his servant-girl heroine a passion for the works of that fashionable novelist but making her conclude, after meeting him once, that, in the eyes of M. Bourget "people didn't begin to have souls below an income of a hundred thousand francs"; and he had none of the quiet discretion in running counter to accepted ideas that caused Anatole France to say of himself that the principal business of his life had been doing up dynamite in bonbon wrappers. He had not even the detachment of the naturalists. He was not only outspoken and tactless: he did not even value the classical *"bon sens français"*— behaved habitually, from the French point of view, intemperately, quixotically, absurdly. A Normand, he was in some ways quite close to the English, who figure in his books in a way that shows a special interest in them —that is, he was blunt, self-willed and not particularly intelligent at the same time that he was subject to moral passion and capable of profound insights and had the courage to give voice to both at the risk of being thought eccentric. In his character as publicist and journalist, in which he played for years a conspicuous role, he was vigorous and audacious. At the time of the Dreyfus case, he went on the stump in the provinces, rousing opinion in Dreyfus' defense; he forfeited by his very first article, in 1889, a job as a newspaper art critic by running down the academic painters and praising Manet and Cézanne; he loved to champion unrecognized writers like Maeterlinck and the seamstress Marguerite Audoux whose work had a lilylike innocence at the opposite pole from his own productions. In politics, he passed at an early stage from fire-breathing royalism to fire-breathing anarchism—the two attitudes having in common a violent hatred of politicians; and remained thereafter consistently pro-worker, anti-bourgeois and anti-clerical. He wrote a labor play, *Les Mauvais Bergers,* produced in 1897, with Sarah Bernhardt and Lucien Guitry, the long heroic speeches of which make very dull reading today, but which differs from most such dramas by its pessimism in regard to the workers' cause; and he created a scandal in 1908 by a play (written with Thadée Natanson), *Le Foyer,* that attacked the philanthropical workshops subsidized by the rich for the relief of the poor.

Nor did the literary cuisine of Mirbeau quite come up to the current French standards. He was always a conscientious workman: his books are never botched or sloppy; he has trained himself with earnest discipline to make the very best of his powers, and he can sometimes write with trenchant lucidity, if rarely with felicitous brilliance. But the seasoning is a little coarse; the ingredients are not well mixed. The flavor is sometimes flat; and there is even a kind of false taste that is calculated to horripilate the French. For example, Mirbeau had a passion for flowers, which he raised and of which he was a connoisseur, but his writing about them—of which there is a good deal in *Le Jardin des Supplices*—combines the botanical and the gaudy in a way that does not conduce to good literature. And his writing about love—exemplified, also, in this book—has similar characteristics. He thus scandalized the bourgeois public and often bored the men of letters, and when he died, his countrymen dropped him. I once talked about him with Jean Cocteau just after the last war. Cocteau expressed surprise that anybody at that late date should be reading Mirbeau at all. "That's a whole generation," he said, "that my generation has skipped." But he approved of

Sébastien Roch, one of Mirbeau's early books, which had made an impression on me, and suggested that a serious and chronic illness had caused a deterioration in his later work. If you consult the *Histoire de la Littérature Française Contemporaine* by René Lalou, published in 1922, you will find a discussion of Mirbeau, which is almost completely contemptuous and which takes it for granted that his novels are no longer of any interest. Though there are two or three brochures on Mirbeau in various journalistic series dealing with the writers of his period, there is, so far as I know, no reliable biography of him, and it is curiously difficult at the present time even to find out the main facts about his life.

Octave Mirbeau's fiction falls into two groups, quite distinct from one another and with a gap of a decade between them. His first three novels—*Le Calvaire, L'Abbé Jules* and *Sébastien Roch*—were written during the late eighties. All deal more or less with provincial life, and especially with personalities which have become distorted or stunted by not finding their true vocations or appropriate milieux. There is a good deal of original insight—contemporary with Freud's first researches—into the infantile causes of neurosis and the consequences of sexual repression. The first of these books is a study of an unstable young man from the country demoralized by a Parisian cocotte; the second, a strange and repellent tale, is a kind of imaginary memoir which a nephew has written of his uncle: a man of superior abilities, from a bourgeois village background, whose personality has been deformed by his mistake of entering the priesthood—a profession in which his intellectual arrogance, his intractable sensual appetites and his very gift of moral vision make him tragically out of

place. *L'Abbé Jules* has vivid flashes when the subject
is brought to life dramatically—as when the abbé, returning to his family, frustrated, embittered, forbidding,
and hardly condescending to talk to them, examines as
if astonished the quilt that they have handed him for a
carriage-robe; and both books have a clinical interest: Mirbeau, like Flaubert, was a doctor's son. But the third
novel, *Sébastien Roch,* is much better and was to remain
probably Mirbeau's best book. This is the story of a gifted
boy who is sent away from home to a Jesuit school,
where one of the priests seduces him, and who then
comes back to his little town, with his emotions in ago-
nized disorder and with no field for the exercise of his
talents. He tries to give himself an outlet by writing in
a diary and has an awkward love affair with a girl whom
he has known since childhood, and, finally, conscripted
for the Franco-Prussian War, is unheroically, ridicu-
lously killed. Everyone who has read this book knowing
James Joyce's *A Portrait of the Artist as a Young Man*
has been struck by parallels between them, in form as
well as in content. One would like to know whether
Joyce had read *Sébastien Roch.* It is not quite up to the
Portrait. It has elements of the romantic sentimentality
and of the dead mechanical caricature that impair the
soundness of all Mirbeau's work. But Mirbeau did his
most successful writing in his description of the Breton
countryside, and the anguish of adolescence has never
been more truthfully treated. If one compares these early
stories of Mirbeau with the fiction of his friend Guy de
Maupassant, who worked also in the naturalistic tradition, the advantage is not all with the latter. Maupassant has more skill and more style. But such a figure as the
conventional wife and mother of Maupassant's *Une Vie*
is simply the victim of a melodrama in which the villain is
the masculine sex. In *Le Calvaire,* the mother of the hero

is a somewhat similar case, but Mirbeau's psychological insight makes it impossible for him to deal in this one-sided pathos, and he shows us that the woman, from a "trauma" of her childhood, has a special predisposition to succumb to such a situation as that later created by her marriage. To the brilliant raconteur of *Boule de Suif,* the war of 1870, again, presents itself mainly in terms of the hatred between Germans and French, whereas with Mirbeau, when he touches on it, the patriotic antagonisms are undercut by a sense of what all men have in common.

Between *Sébastien Roch* of 1889 and *Le Jardin des Supplices* of 1899, Mirbeau published no more fiction; but the first two of his plays were performed, and in the years that immediately followed he wrote half a dozen others. These plays are less interesting than his fiction, but they occupy, in the history of the French theater, an almost unique place. When Bernard Shaw bestowed his accolade on the second-rate Eugène Brieux, accepting him as the great French practitioner of his own peculiar kind of drama, the comedy of social analysis, he might better have selected Mirbeau. Mirbeau's plays are, so far as I know, the only French work of merit that has anything in common with this English school. One of them, *Les Affaires sont les Affaires* (1903), enjoyed an immense success. It was admitted into the repertoire of the Comédie Française at a time when the Comédie produced almost no modern plays, and it continued to be done there for years, thus becoming the only work of Mirbeau's that has been endorsed as a classic, so that it is always well spoken of by such writers as M. Lalou. It is certainly Mirbeau's best play, though not so good as the best of his novels. It suffers from his characteristic fault of introducing incredible monstrosities, against a familiar realistic background, into a story that is meant to be plausible; but such a scene as the conversation between the business man and the ruined marquis is admirable in its confrontation, very similar to such scenes in Shaw, of the spokesmen of two social classes, who expound their opposing roles. And Mirbeau's one-acter *L'Epidémie,* in which a provincial town council declines to do anything about a typhoid epidemic that is killing off the local garrison, till they hear that a bourgeois has died of it, is closer to English satire than to the irony of Anatole France. "Typhoid fever," declares in a quavering voice the oldest member of the council, "is a national institution. Let us not lay impious hands upon our old French institutions"; and, "Let us not," seconds the doctor, "present foreign countries with the deplorable spectacle of a French army beating an ignoble retreat before a few problematical microbes."

Sébastien Roch, the Abbé Jules and the hero of *Le Calvaire* are all subject to a waking delirium—day-dreams in which sexual images are mixed nightmarishly with images of horror—of which Mirbeau sometimes gives descriptions almost as elaborate and solid as his accounts of actual events. The key to most of these fantasies is to be found in Mirbeau's perception that inescapable sexual repression or neurotic emotional impotence may result in sadistic impulses. Now, in the fiction of his second period, he ceases to try to present us with difficult cases of real human beings: it is as if he had allowed these fantasies to take possession of his imagination and to impose themselves upon him as generalized pictures of life. At their soundest, these later novels arrive through distortion at satire; at their worst, they are artistically meaningless, a mere procession of obsessive grotesques.

The first of these books, *Le Jardin des Supplices,* is an epitome of Mirbeau's whole vision after his shift to phantasmagoric mythology from naturalistic observation, and it states the Grand Guignol philosophy which he tries to derive from this vision. The story opens in the noxious atmosphere of corrupt Parisian politics under the Third Republic. A scoundrelly Cabinet Minister, whose future is a toss-up between jail and advancement, is blackmailed by one of his jackals and buys him off by sending him away to Ceylon on a scientific expedition financed by government funds. The object of this expedition is to study marine biology in the Indian Ocean —"to discover the primordial cell," as his chief rather vaguely explains to him, "the protoplasmic initium of organized life, or something of the kind." The lesser scoundrel (who tells the story), pretending to be a great biologist, embarks for the East and meets on the ship a beautiful young English lady named Clara, the daughter of an opium-dealer, who is returning to her home in Canton. She gives the impression of great virtue and dignity, and the impostor falls deeply in love with her. He has retained, unlike his chief, some remnants of moral feeling, and all the idealism of which he is capable comes to life under the influence of his passion. He grows ashamed of his bogus role, of his debauched and dishonest past—cannot bear that he should be deceiving a being whom he so much respects, and one day makes a clean breast to Clara of all the disgraceful truth. To his astonishment, she shows at once, and for the first time in their acquaintance, a vivid interest in him. She had paid no attention to him when she had thought he was a serious scientist, but the idea of his vileness pleases her. She is, it turns out, more corrupt than he: more positively perverse and more formidable. She goes to bed with him immediately in her cabin, and he becomes her abject slave. Instead of getting off at Ceylon, he goes on with Clara to China.

The second half of the novel is devoted to a detailed account of their visit to a Chinese prison. This prison has a magnificent garden, in which the convicts are tortured. The Frenchman is shocked and revolted, but he recognizes in what he sees simply a franker and more elegant version of the kind of thing that is going on, in a disguised and hypocritical way, in the Europe he has left behind. It is in vain that, trying to shut out the garden, he summons his familiar Paris. In a moment of revelation, he identifies these executioners with "all the men and all the women whom I have loved or imagined I loved, little indifferent frivolous souls, on whom is spreading now the ineffacable red stain," with "the judges, the soldiers, the priests, who everywhere in the churches, the barracks and the temples of justice, are busy at the work of death," and with "the man as individual and the man as mob," and with "the animal, the plant, the element, all nature, in fact, which, urged by the cosmic forces of love, rushes toward murder, in the hope of thus finding beyond life a satisfaction of life's furious desires, which devour it and which gush from it in spurts of dirty froth." Clara, however, is enjoying herself. Among the gorgeous flowers which are a feature of the garden and which seem to grow out of its putrescence and blood, she becomes hysterically excited and later, when they leave the garden, collapses in a fit of convulsions. When she comes to, she seems calmed and purged, and declares that she will never return there, but her Chinese maid assures her lover that she will be back on the next visitor's day. The traveller, though he has given up his mission, has, after all, from one point of view, discovered the secret of life.

It will be seen that Le Jardin des Supplices has, in conception, its Swiftian strength. The trouble is that, though the scenes in the garden sometimes verge on a true tragic irony, Mirbeau, where a Swift or a Dante would have kept them under severe control, indulges himself, like his Clara, a little too much in horror. The same kind of wrong exploitation of a promising satirical idea—which Swift, again, would have handled better—appears in the second of these later books, *Le Journal d'une Femme de Chambre*. Here Mirbeau set out to expose the meanness and sordidness of the French bourgeoisie by showing how they look to a servant who goes from one of their households to another. But the book is full of scandalous episodes that are not merely repulsive but also completely unreal. The whole effect is turbid and boring. Almost the only memorable thing in the book is the chapter that describes the humiliations to which women looking for jobs are subjected in employment agencies, and this suffers, like so much else in the later Mirbeau, from systematic exaggeration. The moral of *Le Jardin des Supplices* is repeated by the unlikely conclusion, in which Mirbeau has the victimized *femme de chambre* marry a brutal coachman whose attraction for her is partly due to her believing him to have committed an atrocious murder.

If one has read the contemporary accounts of Mirbeau during the years when he was writing these books, it is quite easy to diagnose the reason—aside from his overindulgence in the salacious aspects of his subjects— that they do not succeed as satires or as what he called some of his plays, *"moralités."* There is much testimony on the part of those who knew Mirbeau at this period that, however one might like him, his conversation made one uncomfortable, because it consisted so largely of the hair-raisingly implausible stories he would tell about every kind of public figure and about all the people he knew. He was not merely trying to be funny; nor were his stories merely exercises in the expected professional malice of the Parisian literary man. What made his talk disconcerting was that he had evidently fabricated these scandals yet believed them to be actual happenings. (He was, also, it seems, untruthful in his ordinary relations with people.) And his books produce the same effect. In Swift, one feels almost to the end, no matter to what lengths he goes, a sound basis in common sense: he is perfectly well aware that human beings are not really Yahoos and that the poor cannot eat their babies. But Octave Mirbeau does not seem to know when or how much he is deforming reality. The truth is that these stories are a little mad. For all their careful planning and deliberate execution, they represent psychological hypertrophies that are destroying a true sense of the world and preventing the development of the artist. Even the texture of the writing is coarser than that of the early novels. If Mirbeau began by anticipating Freud in the case histories of his early fiction, he took later, in a retrogression, to concocting the kind of nightmare that Freud found it profitable to analyze.

Much the best of Mirbeau's later books is the last thing he published, *Dingo,* which appeared in 1913, four years before his death; but, containing no scandalous material, it has never been translated into English and has attained less celebrity than *Le Jardin des Supplices* and *Le Journal d'une Femme de Chambre. Dingo,* which is told by the author as if in his own character and which sounds as if it were based on a real experience, is the story of an Australian wild dog that has been sent as a puppy to France and grows up in a small French town: perhaps the most debased and revolting of all Mirbeau's dreadful towns. The animal, more wolf than dog, is handsome, remarkably intelligent and devoted to his master and the family; but as soon as he grows out of puppyhood, he begins killing sheep, fowl and game at a rate that makes him a menace. In all this, however, we are made to see, with a subtlety rare in the later Mirbeau, how the master, without at first quite admitting it even to himself, is deriving a certain satisfaction from these crimes against his neighbors, whom he has gradually come to loathe for their self-righteous pusillanimity and cruelty. On one occasion, when he has gone to visit a family of old friends, whom he supposes himself to like, he vicariously betrays his real scorn of them by doing nothing to prevent the dog from slaughtering their pet sheep, which he associates with their feeble personalities. This dog, at least, is frankly a hunter and loyal to those who have cared for him as well as to a family cat with which he has been brought up. But he becomes more and more of a problem. The master is forced to leave the village; he goes to live in Paris, but here Dingo one day leaps at the throat of a man who is trying to steal him and gives rise to disquieting doubts. Then they travel abroad, but wherever they go, they get into some kind of trouble, and the owner is finally obliged to settle down in the country, at the edge of a large forest, in which the dog is free to roam and where he sometimes disappears for days. While they are living there, the master's wife breaks her ribs in a runaway, and the dog, understanding what has happened, keeps watch day and night in her room, resisting attempts to turn him out and refusing to take any food. He wastes away and dies.

This makes a much better book than my summary may suggest. *Dingo* and *Sébastien Roch* are Mirbeau's most successful novels. He loved animals, and in his later phase sometimes wrote about them more satisfactorily than he did about human beings. André Gide is quite correct in singling out the episode of the fight between the hedgehog and the viper as one of the only interesting things in *Les Vingt et un Jours d'un Neurasthénique,* another of Mirbeau's books of this period, the Arabian Nights of a nerve sanitarium, which in general represents an even less appetizing combination of dreariness with abnormality than *Le Journal d'une Femme de Chambre.* In *Dingo,* the dog and the cat are splendidly depicted and analyzed, and the humans are more human than usual. The book has an emotional effect, creates a disturbing suspense. Animal stories were rather fashionable in the early nineteen hundreds, but this is one of the most unconventional and one of the most remarkable, and almost achieves the plane of Tolstoy's wonderful horse story, *Kholstomer.* (Mirbeau, who greatly admired Tolstoy, is said to have had the dubious reciprocal honor of being regarded by the latter, in his later years, as the most important living French novelist.) Yet, like everything else of Mirbeau's, it misses the highest level. Dingo's depredations are on too enormous a scale. His virtues—he loves the poor and makes a point of cheering up the unhappy— a little too sentimental (the Ernest Seton Thompson touch); for Mirbeau has his great sentimentalities to compensate for his chronic ferocities. And the master's inexhaustible complacence, and the immunity that both he and the dog enjoy in connection with Dingo's killings, become rather improbable, too. The element of fantasy gets in again, and it impairs the interest of the record of what was evidently a real animal.

And now what about Mirbeau today, when the ferocity of modern man has demonstrated itself on a scale that even he had not imagined? Already at the time of the first World War, a book like *Le Jardin des Supplices* seemed definitely out of date. Mirbeau did have hold of a terrible truth; and yet, reading the book, as I did, in a military hospital behind the lines, one realized that the impression made by human pain as a part of one's daily routine was different from anything felt by a prosperous pre-war civilian writing at his ease about it (I have not been able to learn whether Mirbeau actually served in the war of 1870). There was too much Parisian upholstery, too much conventional literature, about *Le Jardin des Supplices*. The characters of Ernest Hemingway, with their bad nerves and their ugly conduct, reflected the cruelty of the time more effectively than Mirbeau's enormities and his rhetorical paroxysms. Brett of *The Sun Also Rises* is the Clara of the later generation, and a more convincing creation. Since then, the indiscriminate bombings of London and Berlin, the death-houses of Dachau and Belsen, the annihilation of Hiroshima, have made Mirbeau and Hemingway both seem somewhat obsolete. Is anyone troubled at present by the idea that human beings are torturing or murdering each other? Don't the bugaboo books of the later Mirbeau, with their mélange of human sympathy and sadism, look today like the slightly cracked fairy-tales of a not ungenial old romantic who was still naïve enough not to take such things for granted?

April 2, 1949

A REVIVAL OF RONALD FIRBANK

NEW DIRECTIONS has brought out an "Omnibus" of five of Ronald Firbank's novels: *Valmouth, The Artificial Princess, The Flower Beneath the Foot, Prancing Nigger* and *Concerning the Eccentricities of Cardinal Pirelli*—with an introduction by Osbert Sitwell, a revised and expanded version of a memoir which has already twice been printed in other volumes. It is a good thing to have Firbank revived. Just before this collection appeared, I had been reading those of his novels that I had not read when they first came out, and these had led me to reread those that I had read. A conviction had been gradually growing on me that he was one of the finest English writers of his period and one of those most likely to become a classic. In England he has been appreciated much better than over here. In America, he was introduced in the twenties by Mr. Carl Van Vechten, but, while Firbank was alive, only three of his ten books were ever published in the United States, and although these had a certain vogue, they figured mainly among the accessories of what was then called "sophistication" and were, I think, more or less confused, through no fault of Mr. Van Vechten's, with Mr. Van Vechten's own novels, which may have been influenced by Firbank but which were not on the same plane of artistic seriousness. Since Firbank's death in 1926, he has hardly been read over here. In England, he has always had a definite position. A collected edition of his work was brought out in a limited edition in 1929, with an essay by Arthur Waley and the memoir by Osbert Sitwell, and the next year a short biography by Ifan Kyrle Fletcher, with reminiscences by Sitwell and others. Both these were imported by Brentano's but aroused little interest in America. E. M. Forster, Cyril Connolly and Evelyn Waugh have all recognized Firbank's genius and written about him.

The story of Firbank himself is as strange and as entertaining, as full of surprising anomalies, as the queer cases presented in his novels. Ronald Firbank's paternal great-grandfather—I rely on Mr. Fletcher's memoir—had been a North of England coal-miner, who could not read or write. The grandfather got himself some schooling, left the mines to do railroad work and had become, by 1866, one of the biggest railroad contractors in England: a self-made man of the ruggedest mold, who would not accept foreign contracts because foreigners did not pay in English gold and who, when offered a loan free of interest, declined it with the remark: "I values at nowt what I gets for nowt." On discovering, in the stable of his eldest son, a fine hunter among the carthorses, he looked at it sourly and said: "Eh, lad!—that won't pull a load o' muck!" This son inherited the business, went into Parliament and was knighted. Mr. Fletcher conveys the impression that Sir Thomas was rather a stuffed shirt. He married the daughter of an Irish clergyman, and their second son was Arthur Annesley Ronald Firbank.

The boy had already from childhood the tendency to catarrh from which he was always to suffer and which finally caused his death. His mother, who had set Sir Thomas to collecting French furniture and porcelain, cultivated the son's sensibilities, coddled him and was always adored by him. (There are a number of striking resemblances between Firbank's personality and Proust's.) Ronald did not last a year at a public school, but he was later sent to France, where he lived in a château and studied French, with the idea of entering the diplomatic service. He published, in 1905, a little book containing two items: one a fairy-tale called *Odette d'Antrevernes,* which exhaled a sickly perfume of the nineties, the other —*A Study in Temperament*—a satirical conversation piece, in which he had found already his characteristic vein. The next year he went to Cambridge but he did not finish.

By this time—rich, shy and fastidious—he had managed to transform himself into something like a nostalgic caricature of the aesthetes of the Beardsley-Wilde period, whose productions, together with those of the *fin de siècle* French poets, provided his chief literary food. He surrounded himself with cut flowers, offered his visitors hothouse peaches, haunted the Russian ballet, wore Chinese and Egyptian rings. When people came to see him, he would sometimes carry on conversations looking out the window with his back turned toward his guests; and even with special friends, he was likely, after a witty beginning, to lapse into incoherent mumbling or to be seized by a *fou rire* which made it impossible for him to finish some anecdote or to go on reading aloud one of his stories. (Proust is said to have behaved in the same way.) When you talked to him, writes one of his college-mates, he was always "writhing about and admiring his hands" like "the portraits of society women by Boldini." On one occasion, when Firbank had been brought to meet some friend of a friend, he refused—no doubt imitating Wilde, who sometimes made similar objections—on the ground that the man was too ugly.

At first glance, you might get the impression that Ronald Firbank had come a very long way from his grandfather, the railroad contractor. Yet the role that Ronald played was deceptive. He had not quite left the old man behind. Though he expressed himself often like a school-girl in a high-pitched slithering voice, though he fidgetted and giggled and drooped, he had sharp powers of observation and a very shrewd sense of values. He was also more practical than people thought. His friends, who had supposed him incapable of travelling from London to Oxford, were surprised when he made journeys without mishap to such faraway places as Haiti and when they learned that he had put down singlehanded a mutiny on the boat on which he had made a trip down the Nile; and they would presently become aware, as he asked them to witness deeds and other legal documents, that he was well able to take care of his business interests. The point was that he was not a weak character but in some ways a very strong one. Harold Nicolson, who evidently had Firbank in mind in the story called *Lambert Orme* in *Some People*—though he transposed Firbank's writings and his later career into somewhat different terms—has dramatized the contrast in Firbank of fortitude and serious purpose with apparent frivolity and softness; but it is characteristic of the difference between Firbank and Nicolson that the latter, always grasping at accepted values, inexpugnably official-minded, should have made Lambert Orme prove his mettle as an officer in the first World War, whereas Firbank had shown his toughness, not by distinguishing himself in the war, but by refusing, as far as possible, to recognize it. It required a good deal of self-confidence to repudiate the public school code, to play the aesthete at that period and to that degree. The preciosity of Firbank's books seems so conscious and calculated that one

sometimes suspects him, in fact, of deliberately over-
playing this role. V. B. Holland, who knew him at
Cambridge, reports that, "seeing him once clad in a
sweater and football shorts, I asked him what on earth he
had been doing: 'Oh, football,' he replied. 'Rugger or
Soccer?' 'Oh, I don't remember'—and a laugh. 'Well,
was the ball round or egg-shaped?' 'Oh, I was never near
enough to it to see that!'" When the war came, he professed frank loathing of everything connected with it,
said he had always found the Germans "most polite."
He was called up again and again for medical examina-
tions and questionings by the military authorities, and
was finally rejected as physically unfit for service. When,
by mistake, he was then called up again, he threatened
to sue the War Office for libel and elicited an apology
from it. He protested against the war by shutting himself
up at Oxford for a period of two years, during which, according to legend, he spoke to nobody but his cleaning
woman and the guard on the London train. And for the
first time he applied himself to serious writing.

The exhilaration of reading about Firbank is that
which we derive from the spectacle—first, perhaps, made
popular by Lord Dundreary in that old play *Our American Cousin*—of the apparently silly ass who is really
superbly clever, of the sissy who ends by scoring off the
world which has been making fun of him. The anecdotes about Ronald Firbank are as amusing as the things
in his novels—especially his ostensibly irrelevant remarks,
which so often bewildered his companions but left
them uneasily wondering whether they didn't mean
more than they seemed to. When one of his friends had
said, "Good night, Firbank," as he put Ronald into a
taxi, "the taxi moved off, but before I had had time to
move, there was a violent rattling and banging and the

taxi stopped. Firbank leaned out of the window and called to me. 'I wish,' he said, 'you wouldn't call me Firbank; it gives me a sense of goloshes.'" When Sacheverell Sitwell complimented him on his latest novel, *Caprice*, he turned his head away and remarked in a choking voice, "I can't bear calceolarias. Can you?" The technique of his writing is similar. One may have thought, when one first looked at his books in the twenties, that they were foamy improvisations which could be skimmed up in rapid reading. Yet when one tried to run through them, one found oneself pricked by something that queerly impressed; one was aware of artistic seriousness, even if one did not linger to find out what the writer was up to. When one returns to them today, one realizes that Ronald Firbank was one of the writers of his time who took most trouble over their work and who were most singlemindedly devoted to literature. The memoirs of him testify to this. His books are not foolish trifles, scribbled down to get through the boredoms of a languid and luxurious life. They are extremely intellectual, and composed with the closest attention: dense textures of indirection that always disguise point. They have to be read with care, and they can be read again and again, because Firbank has loaded every rift with ore. The effect of his writing is light, but it differs from the flimsier work of the nineties, which, at first sight, it may resemble, in the tension behind it of the effort to find the felicitous or the witty phrase which will render the essence of something. The little dyed twirls of plume and the often fresh sprays of flowers, the half-stifled flutters of laughter and the *fusées* of jewelly fire, have been twisted and tempered in a mind that is capable of concentration. It is a glancing mind but rarely wobbles. Only in the dangling participles with which he sometimes begins his sentences and in a lack of continuity of movement of which I shall speak later does he betray a certain weakness of syntax. But phrase by phrase, sentence by sentence, paragraph by paragraph, chapter by chapter, the workmanship is not merely exact but of a quality for which the craftsman must gratuitously tax himself. It has recently been learned that Beardsley was the child of two generations of jewellers who were also goldsmiths, and, once one knows this, it is quite easy to recognize the influence of the family trade in his clear two-dimensional patterns with their tendril-like ramifications and their delicate scrollings of pin-point lines, in their wreaths and rosettes, their festoons and crests. Perhaps, in a less obvious way, the inheritance of Firbank from old Joseph counts for something here, too. Mr. Fletcher asserts that the grandfather was something of an engineering genius and that his work shows a passion for perfection. Certainly the work of the grandson—decadent though its subject matter usually is—never fails to live up to the slogan, "I values at nowt what I gets for nowt."

This work of the grandson is also in an old and strong English tradition: it belongs to the school of comedy that had its first great practitioner in Ben Jonson, that was exploited in its purest form by Congreve and the other Restoration dramatists, and that persists through a variety of modifications in Peacock, Gilbert and Aldous Huxley. The true products of this school are at the opposite pole from the hearty and hilarious English humor (though in some writers the two are combined). It is polished and coldly reasoned and rarely admits any kind of idealism. It is occupied with worldly values and if it ever turns its attention to general ideas, it makes mock of them all indiscriminately. Though it sometimes introduces a moralist who is supposed to act as a touchstone in showing up the faults of the other characters, it usu-

ally verges on cynicism, and it is always non-romantic
and non-sentimental. There is nothing, so far as I know,
quite like this English comic tradition in the literature
of any other country. Distinguished, unscrupulous, hard;
carved, gilded and decorative; planned logically and
executed deliberately; of good quality, designed for long
wear; intellectual but never intelligent—no people could
have developed it but the English. You may feel, when
you first approach Firbank, that his talent is too effemi-
inate to claim ancestry from this masculine line; and it
is true that a number of his books are occupied almost
exclusively with women, and that his writing is full of
trailed dots, coy italics and little cries. Yet these latter, always calculated, are really a part of his subject: the man-
nerisms that go with the habits of his special group
and time. You may think that this effete preciosity has
little in common with the brutality and elegance of
Love for Love and *The Way of the World*. Yet the fact
that Ronald Firbank is dealing with a later and less lusty
phase of the same society as Congreve should not keep
us from appreciating that his formal panels are no less
finely painted.

Ronald Firbank wrote one play, *The Princess Zoubaroff*, and it affords a useful opportunity to compare his
methods and point of view with those of Restoration
comedy. The men and women in Wycherley and Congreve are all engaged in chasing one another: they lack
sentiment but have vigorous appetites. The men and
women in Firbank, for the most part, have neither sentiment nor keen desires. To them marriage means as little
as it does to the characters of Congreve; but the alternative is not a succession of more or less piquant adulteries:
it is likely to be an adolescent falling-back on members
of their own sexes. Eric and Enid, in *The Princess Zoubaroff*, have been married hardly a week and Enid is still

answering congratulatory letters when they visit, at a villa near Florence, another young married couple. Both the husbands and the wives have gone to school together, and they immediately renew old relationships. Enid, who has married to escape from her family and has found marriage disappointing, is perfectly willing for Eric to go away with the husband of her friend on a trip to the Engadine. At the end of the first act, the young woman who has been married the longer conveys to her friend with ominous distaste, "as though she were sickening for the Plague," an intimation that she is going to have a baby. In the next act, the two ladies, with others of the English colony, are recruited by a Russian princess for a sort of Lesbian convent, while the baby is left in the hands of a nurse. The husbands have now been away a long time, and the young women take in with apathy the report of a mountain-climbing accident which may mean that both have been killed. But in the third act the men drift back. They are received without excitement and are themselves very much relieved when they see the wives go off to the Princess's convent. The Scotch nurse at this point gives notice, and the father is left with the baby, whose name he does not even know. His only idea about it is to send it at once to the right kind of school.

This skeleton will bring out the difference between Congreve's men and women and Firbank's. The difference in their literary methods corresponds to the difference in subject. Where the speeches in Congreve are set-pieces, where the scenes have the give-and-take of an energetic well-played game, the dialogue in Firbank is all vague innuendos, gasps and murmurs, light caresses, small digs. Yet as writing it is no less consummate—and much finer than that of Wilde when he is working in the Congreve tradition. Not that Firbank's fluttering

absurdities are more skillful than Wilde's ringingly
turned epigrams; but there is always in the comedies of
Wilde an element of conventional theater—of melodrama or simple farce—though in this he is of course
running true to the tone of his late-Victorian time. *Lady
Windemere's Fan* has passages that might almost have
been written by Pinero; *The Importance of Being
Ernest* is still not far from *Charley's Aunt*. Firbank's
comedy belongs to a society that is as non-moral as the
Restoration and quite detached from the middle-class
standards that still make themselves felt in Wilde.

One finds also in Firbank, however, besides this dur-
able old English tradition, a certain influence from
modern France—notably, I should say, from *Histoire
Contemporaine,* Anatole France's Bergeret series. One
seems to find the Anatole France formulas both in Firbank's tricks of style and in his presentation of episodes.
In the latter connection, Firbank seems also to have reproduced France's faults—for the weakness of his narratives, like the weakness of France's, is a lack of
continuous development. One chapter does not lead to
another, but each makes a little vignette which, significant and finished though it is, does not always fall into
place as part of a coherent scheme.

The point of view in these comedies of Firbank,
though they derive from an ancient tradition, is unconventional and very personal. Evelyn Waugh, in his appreciation of Firbank, has explained his own indebtedness to him, and a comparison of these two writers
brings out Firbank's peculiar strength. For Evelyn Waugh
belongs to the category of social satirists who "castigate
the vices" of their time by referring them to old-
fashioned virtues which they imagine to have flourished
in a previous age. It is possible for a writer of this kind

to describe the most fantastic occurrences and the most outrageous behavior, and yet not to antagonize the public, to enjoy, even, a wide popularity, because he reassures the reader by implying an irreproachable standard of stability and respectability. It is the technique of Horace's Augustan odes—a technique which Ronald Firbank could not exploit. He had no real place in English life. He could not invoke old Joseph. His own career and that of his grandfather had not a moment in common. In only one of his novels—*Inclinations*—does Firbank make sound English values assert themselves to the confusion of international decadence. Here a girl from a good county family goes to Greece with a Lesbian novelist, persists in remaining unconscious of the nature of her companion's interest in her, breaks the older lady's heart by running away with an Italian count, returns to her family in England with a baby but without her husband, who is supposed to be looking after his estate but who is suspected of having deserted her, and finally, when family and friends have become completely convinced that the rascally foreigner has let her down, scores again when he duly appears and proves to be not an adventurer but an excellent fellow of limited intelligence and simple tastes like her own. It is a pity that this most satisfactory of Firbank's early books has not been included in this omnibus rather than *The Artificial Princess,* which, good though it is in its way, was Firbank's first longish story, written rather under the influence of Beardsley's *Under the Hill* and not published during Firbank's lifetime. The three novels that followed *The Artificial Princess—Vainglory, Inclinations* and *Caprice*—are all attempts, most successful in spite of their apparent fanciness, to depict English life and character. Ronald Firbank has caught certain aspects of these as perhaps no one else has done—particularly the English habit of pretending to disregard what is uppermost in people's minds and always talking about something else. In Firbank's next novel, *Valmouth*, he is dealing still with the English scene but has found his own vein of fantasy, and develops in terms of high caricature the theme of the English capacity for carrying on unperturbedly in the presence of the scandalous or the catastrophic.

Thereafter, he abandons England, and we get *The Princess Zoubaroff* (Florence), *Santal* (Algiers), *The Flower Beneath the Foot* (an imaginary European kingdom), *Prancing Nigger* (the West Indies), and *Concerning the Eccentricities of Cardinal Pirelli* (Spain), in which, though the English still figure, they become less and less conspicuous. Yet, free to go where he pleases, with no British conventions to hamper him, Ronald Firbank is not, even now, at ease in his chosen role of well-heeled international drifter. He obviously delights in the humors of *The Princess Zoubaroff*, but this shimmering and chiming comedy leaves a lasting and a disquieting impression. It is really an understatement of the same theme that D. H. Lawrence became violent and shrill about: the biologically sinister phenomenon of a slackening of the interest in mating on the part of the privileged classes of Europe.

Firbank's next book, *Santal*, a very short one, has attracted less attention than any other of his mature writings, but I do not agree with his critics, Mr. Waley and Mr. Forster, that it is altogether without merit. This is his most nearly realistic story, and the only one that is not a comedy. It is Firbank's most direct approach to the personal situation which is reflected by all his work, for it is the story of the religious vocation of an orphaned Arab named Cherif, who, discovering that he has no close ties with the relatives who have taken him in and is incapable of sharing their prosaic interests, sets out on a pilgrimage to a holy man who is supposed to live in the mountains. He finds nothing, his water gives out, and he is left in the barren wilderness reading the Koran and dying of thirst. There were few of Ronald Firbank's contemporaries who could have equalled the writing of such a passage as that which works up to the sentence: "Beneath the pitiless sun all signs of life had vanished, and in the deep of noon the hills looked to ache with light." But Firbank here was under the handicap of having himself been a poor little rich boy, so that it was difficult for him to manage a hero who was supposed to be a poor little poor boy. He could have known little of physical discomforts, and, though he is admirable at describing the landscape, he is unable to conjure up the sensations of a boy riding for days in the desert. Firbank said that, when he was writing *Santal*, he found that the subject bored him and that, reacting from it, his imagination flew to the other extreme and presented him with the luxurious aristocrats of *The Flower Beneath the Foot*, which he could hardly wait to begin. Yet this next book, so funny in its exquisite way, so squirming with court scandal, deals with a similar subject: Laura de Nazianzi, niece of the Mistress of the Robes, "more piquant perhaps than pretty," whose large gray eyes "surveyed the world with a pensive critical glance," is in love with young Prince Yousef of the Kingdom of Pisuerga, whose face, though "handsome to tears," had, "even when he had been a child, lacked innocence," and he apparently returns her love; but for reasons of state he drops her and marries an English princess. Laura enters a convent, and the last turn of the screw for her is that she finds the nuns too much distracted by the excitement of the royal wedding to attend to their religious duties. Laura watches the wedding procession, beating her hands on the broken glass that bristles from the convent wall.

Yet, eventually, we are told, Laura became a saint. This turning to religion from the life of the world is a theme in all Firbank's later books. If you should read *The Flower Beneath the Foot* without knowing Firbank's work well, you might think this was all a joke, that he was merely being silly and witty, as he was in *The Princess Zoubaroff*, about the fashionable aspects of religion. But that was not the case. "I believe that in his early youth," writes one of his friends, Lord Berners, "he had thought of taking Holy Orders. But more than once he had said to me, 'The Church of Rome wouldn't have me and so I laugh at them.'" (He had, however, become a Catholic at Cambridge in 1908.) He strikes one as having nothing to fall back on save his capacity for self-dependence and the discipline imposed by his writing. Art was his only sainthood. He was solitary and must have been lonely, though when someone suggested this, he replied, "I can buy companionship." Though he loves all the gossip of the world he frequents, it is mainly for what he can make of it; and though his work is full of naughty jokes that combine in a startling way a pansy archness with a brutal coarseness, one feels that his interest in sex is also mainly an aesthetic one. From the discrepancies he found in himself—pathetically stunted functions entangled with admirably developed talents, childish inadequacies in personal relations alongside a mature grasp of moral values—he never seems to have had any relief except through the demoralizing comedy and the grotesque pathos of his novels. These novels, in one way or another, like the limericks of Edward Lear, almost always present the eccentric at odds with established society—though established society in Firbank may be itself unconventional and the eccentric, like Laura de Nazianzi, an honest and natural person. The heroines of the early novels—the touching Mrs. Shamefoot of *Vainglory*, who, married to an important public figure and not at all amused by her social set, has concentrated all her longings on having her existence commemorated by a stained-glass window in the local cathedral; Miss Sinquier of *Caprice*, the daughter of a rural dean, who steals the family silver, sells it and blows the money all in, in London—with the aid of hangers-on picked up at the Cafe Royal—on producing *Romeo and Juliet* with herself in the title role, only to be killed after the opening night as the result of catching her foot in a mousetrap and falling through a trapdoor in the stage—these are figures of an incredible drollery; but there is something behind them that is not quite funny. Even the Lesbian lady of *Inclinations*, whose frustration is represented by a chapter consisting solely of the exclamation "Mabel!" printed eight times, elicits a certain sympathy. Later on, more and more, the eccentrics become saints. Even Miami of *Prancing Nigger*, who has removed her family from the country to the city and watched the rest of them go to pieces there and who loses her country lover at sea, is last seen as a pious pilgrim on her way to a miraculous shrine. And in the figure of Cardinal Pirelli, Firbank bent all his resources to the creation of his noblest eccentric who is at the same time his strangest saint. The Cardinal, who, having already a dubious reputation, has baptized, out of pity for a childless woman, one of the pups of her favorite dog, comes to present an ecclesiastical problem and soon finds himself shadowed by a Vatican spy who is trying to get something on him. The Cardinal plans a flight from Spain, but on the eve of departure has a fatal stroke in circumstances of the most outrageous scandal. "Now," writes Firbank, "that the ache of life, with its fevers, passions, doubts, its routine, vulgarity, and boredom, was over, his serene, unclouded face was a marvelment to behold. Very great distinction and sweetness was visible there, together with much nobility, and love, all magnified and commingled." (Note here the ache of life that recalls the ache of the hills in the passage quoted from *Santal*.)

Lord Berners, in an account of Firbank's death, says that he was told by a man who lived on the opposite side of a courtyard from Firbank's apartment in Rome, that he had sometimes been wakened at night by the sound of his neighbor's immoderate laughter. Just as his conversation and his reading to friends would sometimes be broken off by paroxysms of mirth that were likely to end in coughing, so even when he was writing alone this uncontrollable laughter would sometimes put an end to his work. So he had been diverted from the sad little story of Cherif to the hilarious but even more harrowing comedy of *The Flower Beneath the Foot*. Ronald Firbank was the poet of the *fou rire*. That is the key to the whole of his work. There is anguish behind it all—and the more ridiculous it is, the better he is expressing this anguish. *The Eccentricities of Cardinal Pirelli* is at once his most preposterous book and the one that has most moral meaning; it combines his most perverse story with his purest and most beautiful writing. He has here expressed his ideal conception, quite heretical but not irresponsible, not lacking in serious intention, of what a Catholic priest might be, and this has enabled him, for the first time, through art, fully to accommodate his imperfections, to triumph over his disabilities. It may be that the dead Cardinal's serenity had been won by him, too, for a moment in the few weeks of life that were left him.

For Firbank himself was to die just after he had finished this novel. On his last visit to England, he told his friends that he had wanted to write a certain number of books, that he had now written them and that he would probably write no more. He was just on the verge of forty and was worrying about his wrinkles. His lungs and heart were in very bad condition, and he had been virtually condemned by the doctor. In Rome he came down with some kind of "chill." He was alone in a rented apartment, where he would not let his friends come to see him, because, he said, the wallpaper was too hideous. He had even sent away his nurse, in the belief that he was getting well. When Ronald Firbank died, Lord Berners was his only friend in Rome. He knew nothing of Firbank's family—his mother had died not long before but he had a sister living—and found the name of his solicitor by chance on a crumpled piece of paper. Not knowing that Firbank was a Catholic, he had him buried in the Protestant Cemetery, curiously but not incongruously, not far from Shelley and Keats. When Osbert Sitwell went to visit the grave, all trace of it had disappeared. The sexton explained that the body had been moved to a Catholic cemetery. Thus, as Sitwell remarks, there was even about Firbank's burial "an inconsequential as well as a tragic element."

December 10, 1949

PAUL ROSENFELD: THREE PHASES

THE DEATH of Paul Rosenfeld has left me not only shocked at the unexpected loss of a friend, but with a feeling of dismay and disgust at the waste of talent in the United States. Paul, when I first knew him—in 1922, I think—was one of the most exciting critics of the "American Renaissance." I had read, while in the army in France, an essay on Sibelius in the *New Republic*, which had had upon me the exhilarating effect that wartime reading sometimes does; and later, when I was back in New York, a longer study on Richard Strauss, a great musical hero of the time, which brought into the writing itself something of the Straussian brilliance but probed with a very sure hand what was specious and vulgar in Strauss. It was the first really searching criticism that I had ever seen of this composer, and both these essays amazed me. They had a kind of fullness of tone, a richness of vocabulary and imagery, and a freedom of the cultural world that were quite different from the schoolmasterish criticism which had become the norm in the United States. *Musical Portraits,* in 1920, the first book that collected these pieces, seemed at the time absolutely dazzling. Paul told me, when I knew him later, that the point when he had felt his maturity was the moment when he had realized with pride that he could turn out as good an article as Huneker; but actually he much surpassed Huneker, who, useful though he was in his role, always remained a rather harried journalist, trying to produce a maximum of copy in order to get money to go abroad. Paul was a serious writer who was working from New York as a base. One had always had the impression that Huneker came in through the back door at Scribner's in a day when the arts were compelled to give precedence to money and gentility, and that there had been something in Bernard Shaw's prophecy that, if he stayed in the United States, he would never be anything but a "clever slummocker"; and one now heard depressing reports that he was old, poor and ill in Brooklyn. But Paul Rosenfeld seemed the spirit of a new and more fortunate age, whose cosmopolitanism was not self-conscious and which did not have to be on the defensive for its catholic interest in art and life. The portraits of Paul's first book dramatized modern music as no criticism had done before; they brought into range a whole fascinating world, united though international, of personality, poetics, texture, mood. Paul Rosenfeld at that time enjoyed a prestige of the same kind as Mencken's and Brooks's, though it was not so widely felt as the former's.

He had inherited a comfortable income, and he built himself at Westport, Connecticut, a small and attractive house, where he lived alone with his work and entertained his friends. The first time I ever saw him, I had not yet met him. It was in Paris sometime in the summer of 1921, and I was dining alone one night in a favorite Italian restaurant, very clean and rather austere—I remember it as always quiet and filled with a clear twilight—to which I had been taken first by somebody during the war and to which I liked to return, ordering almost always the same meal that I had had when I went there first: ravioli and Asti Spumante. A party of three sat down at the table just across from mine, and though I had never seen any of them before, I recognized them soon as Paul Rosenfeld, Sherwood Anderson and Anderson's wife, the sculptress, Tennessee Mitchell. I had heard in New York that Paul was taking the Andersons to Europe, where Anderson had never been, and I observed the party with interest and heard snatches of their conversation. Tennessee Mitchell had the aspect and the manner of a raw-boned prairie woman, and I was touched by Paul's obvious effort to approximate for her benefit to a modestly folksy manner. I was reminded of the incident later when I read in Sherwood Anderson's memoirs that he had sat in the Tuileries one day— he is here apostrophizing himself—with "the tears running from your eyes, because you thought everything around you so beautiful." It was all very typical of the period, and so are my first memories of Paul after I got to know him in New York. I spent a weekend with him once at Westport—sometime in 1922—and read him an article I had just written about T. S. Eliot's *Waste Land* on the occasion of its getting the *Dial* prize. In·the city I had been leading at that time rather a frenetic life, and I remember what a relief it was to talk about art with Paul in an atmosphere completely free from the messy dissipation and emotion that were characteristic of the twenties, and for once to get a good night's sleep in a house where everything was quiet and simple. I had that night a delightful dream, which still comes back to me quite distinctly, of little figures that were really alive though much less than life-size, dancing with slow grace to an exquisite Mozartian music which filled me with peace and joy. It was an antidote to the stridencies of the jazz age, which Paul's spirit had managed to exorcise. He loathed jazz in all its raw forms and could only accept it transmuted by the style of a Stravinsky or a Copland.

With his fair reddish hair and mustache, his pink cheeks and his limpid brown eyes, his clothes which always followed with dignity the Brooks-cut college model, his presence, short though he was, had a certain authority and distinction. It was something that made Anderson call him the well-dressed man of American prose. He had a knack of turning pretty little speeches and he was also genuinely considerate in a way that was rare in that era, but he could be forthright when the occasion demanded, and, though naturally candid and warm, he would retire—which always amused me—at a suspicion of imposture or imposition, into a skeptical and ironic reserve. He was, I think, the only man I have known of whom it could truly be said that he possessed a Heinesque wit, and I always thought it a pity that his humor, which contributed so much to the pleasure of being with him, should have figured so little in his essays. (Since writing this, however, I have been looking into one of his later books, *An Hour with American Music,* and I see that it is full of *wit.* It was the humor of exaggeration, to which he sometimes gave rein in his talk, that rarely appeared in his work.)

When I got to know Paul better, we sometimes compared notes about our childhood and education. He had gone to school on the Hudson and had afterwards graduated from Yale, and the latter institution, though he seemed to feel a certain respect for it, had rather oppressed him at the time he had been there; but he had been fortunate in being able to escape to spend his summer vacations in Europe. When he had once found out, he told me, that there existed somewhere else an artistic and social and intellectual world larger and more exciting than anything he had known in America, and that he could always go back to it later, he found that he could endure New Haven, to which he was so ill-adapted, without fears of suffocation. He had grown up in uptown New York in a German-Jewish household, and he had never belonged to any church or been trained in any religion; but he had got from his parents a grounding in the classical German culture, musical and literary. When he went to Europe in summer, he loved to visit a German uncle, who was something of a *bon vivant*. His parents had both died when he was young, and his only close relative was a sister. He never married and, so far as I could see, had no real desire to marry, enjoying the bachelor's life which his moderate means made possible.

His strongest tie was undoubtedly with Stieglitz, toward whom he stood in something like a filial relation; and the group around Stieglitz became for him both family and church. The only traditionally and specifically Jewish trait that ever came, in my intercourse with Paul, as something alien that blocked understanding between us was the quality of his piety toward Stieglitz, whom he accepted and revered as a prophet, unquestioningly obedient to his guidance in the spirit that has been sometimes exemplified by the disciples of Freud and Schoenberg; and his range as a writer on the plastic arts was limited by the exclusiveness of his interest in the work of the Stieglitz group. It was difficult, if not impossible, to persuade him to pay attention to any contemporary American painter who was not a protégé of Stieglitz', and if Stieglitz had excommunicated a refractory or competitive disciple, Paul Rosenfeld, following the official directive, would condemn him, not merely as an artist but as a reprobate who had somehow committed an unpardonable moral treason. He had the tone of the old-fashioned brother whose sister has fallen to shame, or the member of a Communist sect reacting to the name of a heretic.

For the rest, his affectionate and generous nature had to spend itself mainly in the sympathy that he brought to the troubles of his friends and in the tireless encouragement of talent. His judgment here was usually shrewd, his insight often profound; he was tactful and unobtrusive in helping people who needed help, and he did not want thanks in return. His taking the Andersons to Europe is an example that happens to be known of the kind of thing he liked to do, and one has heard of his providing, at a critical time, resources for a now famous composer; but he undoubtedly did more for more people than anyone will ever know. It has remained in my mind that he was present at the deathbed of Randolph Bourne, desperately feeding him with oxygen in the effort to keep him alive. Bourne had been one of the most remarkable of the group that founded the *Seven Arts*. As a hunchback, he was unfit for the services and thus free to repudiate the war as an able-bodied writer could hardly have done so roundly; and the intellectual light and the moral passion, the mastery of self-expression, that led people to forget his deformity as soon as he began to talk, made his friends of that era feel that he was keeping alive spiritual values that might otherwise have gone by the board. "When he died," Paul wrote, "we knew that perhaps the strongest mind of the entire younger generation in America had gone. . . . We see the size of him plainly in the bitter moments in which we realize how vacant the scene has become in the many fields to which he brought the light of his own clear nature!"

II

Paul later sold his house at Westport and took a little corner apartment in an old and elevatorless house on the west side of Irving Place. There, however, he continued to flourish. He liked to give evening parties which were none the less agreeable for their rather old-fashioned character. What was unusual in the dry twenties was that there was very little liquor served: a highball or two or a little punch; and poets read their poetry and composers played their music. One met Ornstein, Milhaud, Varése; Cummings, Hart Crane and Marianne Moore; the Stieglitzes and all their group; the Stettheimers, Mumford, Kreymborg. One of the images that remains with me most vividly is the bespectacled figure of Copland, at that period gray-faced and lean, long-nosed and rather unearthly, bending above the keyboard as he chanted in a high, cold and passionate voice a poem of Ezra Pound's—*An Immorality*—for which he had written a setting.

In those days I saw a good deal of Paul in a business as well as in a friendly way, for I was working first on *Vanity Fair,* then on the *New Republic,* and Paul wrote a good deal for both. He grew rather stout at this time, and his style betrayed a tendency toward floridity. He felt afterwards, he told me, that his writing, like so many other things during the Boom, had, to its detriment, become somewhat overinflated. My impression is that when people say they do not like Paul Rosenfeld's style, they are thinking of characteristics that only became really rampant in some of his work of this period, and that they have no real acquaintance with his criticism either before or after. As an editor, I had sometimes to struggle with him over the locutions and vocabulary of his essays, and I am fully aware of his faults. He had spent so much time in Europe and he read so much French and German that he could never quite keep his English distinct from his other languages, and habitually wrote *ignore* as if it meant the same thing as *ignorer* and *genial* as if it meant possessing genius. He had also a way of placing adverbs that used to set my teeth on edge, as did some of these adverbs themselves, such as *doubtlessly* and *oftentimes*. There were moments when he *did* overwrite, working himself up into a state of exaltation with romantic Germanic abstractions that sounded a little ridiculous in English. But, going back to his essays today, one is not much bothered by this or even necessarily conscious of it. One finds a body of musical criticism that covers the modern field more completely than one had remembered and that stands up, both as writing and as interpretation, so solidly as to make quite unimportant these minor idiosyncrasies and slips.

There is of course an objection to Paul's writing which is based on disapproval on principle of the romantic and impressionistic school that he enthusiastically represented. In the serious literary journals, a new tone had just been set in the twenties by T. S. Eliot's *The Sacred Wood*, which was spare and terse in style, analytical and logical in treatment. Paul Rosenfeld, who lacked the intellectual instruments for dealing with literary ideas (though he was expert at dealing with musical ones), was somewhat less satisfactory—except when writing of certain kinds of poetry that had something in common with music—on the subject of literature than he was on music and painting; but it was very unjust that this fashion should have prejudiced against him the editors of the kind of magazine on which he most depended for a market. The same tendency appeared in the musical world; and the critics—though less, I think, the composers—complained of his lack of scholarship on the technical side of music. To this a writer who is not a musician can only reply that it seems to him that the moment the critic departs from the technical analysis of a score, he is writing impressionistic criticism; and that Berlioz in his essays on Beethoven's symphonies and Debussy when he is putting on record such an opinion as that Edvard Grieg was a bonbon stuffed with snow are just as much impressionistic critics as Paul Rosenfeld ever was. Berlioz and Debussy, of course, were a great deal more literary and programmatic than the generation of Schoenberg and Stravinsky have liked to be thought to be; but I believe that Paul was right in insisting that every valid work of art owes its power to giving expression to some specific human experience and connecting it with some human ideal. For musicians it must of course be profitable to read the kind of score-by-score study that has been made by Albert Berger, for example, of the development of Aaron Copland; but, as a layman who merely listens to music, I do not see that it is easy to dismiss the interpretations given by Paul of the emotional and social content of the more "abstract" modern composers: Schoenberg and Stravinsky, Bartók and Hindemith. It is just here, where the composer invites it least, that Paul's insight most proves his genius.

All those years we talked much of such matters. The kind of writing I did myself aimed at something rather different from his, and he horrified me once by saying that his idea of good prose was something that was laid on like a thick coat of paint; but we had in common a fundamental attitude and invoked a common cultural tradition, which it is easiest to call humanistic. Among the few things that I really look back upon with anything like nostalgia in the confusion and waste of the twenties are such conversations as those with Paul when we would sit in his corner room, beneath his little collection of Hartleys and O'Keeffes and Marins, surrounded by his shelves full of Nietzsche and Wagner, Strindberg, Shaw and Ibsen, Tolstoy and Dostoevsky, Flaubert, Claudel and Proust, Henry James and Poe, and the English poets that he had read at Yale, or walk

back and forth at night between my place and his. He
liked New York, was a thorough New Yorker, and—except for a few weeks in the summer, when he would
visit the Stieglitzes at Lake George and, as Georgia
O'Keeffe once told me, take the same walk every afternoon, or for an occasional out-of-town lecture or concert—he rarely ventured to leave the city. He did visit
the Andersons in Virginia, and once got as far as New
Mexico—when Georgia O'Keeffe was there—and even
saw an Indian corn dance; but it was difficult to make
him take an interest in any but the most self-consciously
aesthetic aspects of American cultural life. I tried again
and again to get him to read such writers as Ring Lardner and Mark Twain, but I never had the least success.
When I finally resorted to the device of giving him
Huckleberry Finn as a Christmas present, he obstinately
refused to open it, having learned that Henry James
had characterized Mark Twain as a writer for immature
minds. I told Paul once later on, when the first liveliness
of the twenties was spent, that he would not have lived
very differently if he had been the leading music critic
of Frankfort, Dresden or Munich; but he protested at
once against this. He could never be so free, he said, in
Germany—or anywhere else except New York.

III

The depression was disastrous for Paul. His income
dwindled almost to nothing; and he was forced to give
up Irving Place, moving first to a small apartment on
Eleventh Street just off Fifth Avenue, then later to a
much less accessible one in the far reaches of West Eleventh Street. The *Dial* suspended publication in 1929;
the *New Republic* was in the hands of an editor of
whom it might almost be said, as the Nazis said of them-

selves, that when he heard the word *culture* he reached
for his gun. Paul, for the first time in his life, was
obliged to resort to real hackwork: little odd jobs and
reviews, for which he was not well paid. He developed
diabetes and grew thin; and something, I got the impression, went wrong with his personal affairs—though
of this I never heard him speak. The staffs and the principal contributors of the *Dial* and the *New Republic*,
both non-commercial affairs financed by rich patrons,
had been groups of serious writers who had had lunches
and dinners together, where plans and current events
were discussed, and who had been part of Paul's social
life as well as a stimulus to his work. But now, when
endowments were drying up, there was a movement
toward the political Left, and such groupings and common undertakings as the New York "intellectuals" (so
called now rather than "writers" or "artists") continued
to go in for in the thirties, were mostly oriented in the
direction of Communism. Paul intensely disliked all
this, and though one of the great merits of his criticism
had been its sure sense of musical personalities as the
reflections of their national and social backgrounds, he
would indignantly deny at this time that art had anything to do with history. When I argued such questions
with him, I found that "the Artist" meant for him a
being unique and god-like, and that Paul would not
admit for a minute that a philosopher or a scientist or a
statesman could achieve an equal creative importance.
On one occasion he was somehow persuaded to attend an
election rally held by the Communists in Cooper Union,
at which there were to be speeches by writers who had
announced that they would vote for the Communists
and who paid their homage to Communism as a literary
restorative and bracer in the vein of the new convert
to evangelism or the patent medicine testimonial; but,

seated in a conspicuous place in one of the front rows, he attracted unfavorable attention by pointedly refusing to rise when the *International* was sung.

I was deep in Left activities myself, but I always continued to see him and occasionally went to concerts with him. If you dined with him in his apartment, he cooked and served the dinner; and the difficulty was, if you ate out with him in one of the Greenwich Village restaurants, ever to pay back his hospitality, as he invariably snatched the check and insisted on settling it himself. Even now that he had no regular platform, he continued to go to concerts and make notes on his impressions of the music and put them away in his files; and he continued to look for new talent and to acquire new protégés—though he sometimes had fits of gloom in which he would declare that American music was an abomination of desolation. He was sharply unsympathetic with the new tendency of American composers to abandon the abstruse researches into which they had been led by Schoenberg, the high seasoning and classicizing and virtuosity of abbreviation characteristic of Stravinsky and others, and to try to produce a music that could be heard and enjoyed by bigger audiences than those of the Composers' League. He was shocked, almost personally hurt, when Americans whose work he had thought promising did anything for the radio or Hollywood or published popular books. He expressed his views on this general subject in his essay on Kurt Weill and *Gebrauchsmusik*, in which he asserted that all music was useful, since "all works of musical art express essences and ideas and thus, with their symbols of the inner truth of life, provide the best of bases of social relationships," and that there was of course no reason why composers who "deeply felt the spirit and symbols of social rituals" should not provide these rituals with music—so long as the music provided "conveyed an individual interpretation of the meanings of the ritual" and not merely "general and conventional symbols and a sort of collective expression." He concluded: "Let us by all means have *Gebrauchsmusik*. But let it be the work of artists, not of 'revolutionary' academicians." It will be seen that these considered and formulated views were less severe than his instinctive attitude toward the practice of American composers; and I guessed that this attitude was due to his lately having felt himself a little out of things as well as to disappointment at any evidence that other artists cared anything for popular success.

But it worried me to feel, as time went on, that he was beginning to lose his self-confidence. He had put a good deal of work into the writing of what I gathered from his descriptions was a kind of symphonic novel based on a visit he had made to Rome, but he had decided that his whole conception was vitiated by some moral falsity and he withheld it from publication—which seemed to me a morbid symptom. A healthy writer either knows what he is doing or doesn't discover his error till after he has published the book. The persecution of the Jews by Hitler came later to weigh upon Paul and to become overpoweringly identified with the difficulties he was facing at fifty. The times had not brought to fulfillment that creative and enlightened era of which the sun had seemed to be rising in the days when the *Seven Arts* was founded: totalitarian states and class pressures were closing down on the artistic élite. The independent American journalism that had flared up for a while in the twenties had given way to the streamlined commercial kind, and the non-commercial magazines were composed for the most part by this time of second-rate academic papers and the commentaries of Talmudic Marxists. Even the *New Yorker*, more lib-

eral and literate than most of the new magazines, and in
its own way quite independent, was unable to find a
place for Paul: it, too, had a conventional style, which
sometimes ran to insipidity through the solicitous care
of the editors to eliminate anything unexpected in the
way that their writers expressed themselves. It was primarily a humorous weekly and had a department that
exploited the absurdities that appeared in other papers,
so that they had to be on their guard against writing
that might be thought ridiculous. It was one of the
most cruel blows of Paul Rosenfeld's later years that the
New Yorker would not print his articles after asking
him, as he assumed, to act as their regular art critic.
Paul's prose, as I knew, had its blemishes, but at its best
it would have been hopelessly refractory to the *New
Yorker* processing mill. There was at that time not a
single periodical which would print the work of a writer
simply because he knew his subject and wrote about it
well. Paul sometimes showed signs of a fear that he had
been made the victim of a boycott; and at others was too
ready to blame himself. He said to me once that his
inheritance from his grandmother had unfitted him to
struggle with the world; that he had thrown up his first
and only job—as a reporter on a New York paper—
when, finding that the work embarrassed him, he had
reflected that he did not need a job to live. Certainly he
was unfitted for putting himself over or making terms
with editors and publishers; no one ever had less sense of
business. He never could understand that writing was a
commodity like any other, which, from the moment one
lacked a patron, had to be sold in a hard-boiled way; and
the world came more and more to divide itself for him
into two classes, black and white: the negative forces of
darkness that were closing down to crush him and the

few pure children of light who survived and could heal and save.

I was distressed by him in these latter days and used to wonder how the circumstances had been combined to undermine so able a man, with the shift in economic conditions, by way of his very virtues even more than by way of his weaknesses. Certainly it was unwise of Paul to have depended as much as he did on the writing of musical criticism. Since he was himself not a musician but a writer, he should not have tied up his talent with the reporting of contemporary concerts. It is impossible for a master of words completely to express himself by merely rendering the effects of some other art; and I have never really understood why Paul did not tackle some bigger subject—a history of American music or a biography of some composer—which would have got him an advance from a publisher and supplied him with a sustaining interest. One might have said the same thing about Huneker; but it is no great comfort to realize that Paul Rosenfeld, in an age which prided itself on its emergence from the Philistinism of Huneker's, should have burned out in much the same way and been left in the same neglect. The burning-out and the public indifference seem somehow to work together. They are an old and depressing story in the American intellectual world.

When I got back to New York from Europe in the autumn of 1945, I spent with Paul a wonderful evening, which, though I may have seen him once or twice afterwards, has left me with a last lively impression that I am extremely glad to have. He was in very much better spirits than he had been during the years of the war. He had received from a foundation a substantial grant to do a book of literary studies; and it seemed to cheer him up to hear talk about Europe again, now that the war was over and the arts might be expected to revive. I told him about my enthusiasm for Benjamin Britten's opera, *Peter Grimes*, which I had heard that summer in London. And both of us were glad to find someone to whom one could express oneself freely about the current state of letters and art. He was angry over his treatment at the hands of one of the highbrow quarterlies, the editor of which had first asked him to be a member of the advisory board and had then refused to print his articles, keeping them, however, for months without letting him know about them. I had had with this same magazine an almost equally annoying experience; and I managed to make Paul laugh by describing to him an essay in which this pedantic editor, in the course of a rigorous analysis of Macbeth's "Out, out, brief candle" speech, conducted in the rigorous spirit of the new "methodological" criticism, had said something like, "We cannot know why Shakespeare has chosen for death the curious adjective *dusty*, but the epithet has a quaint appropriateness that can be felt but hardly explained." We rapidly became so exhilarated, abounding so, as Henry James would say, in our own old sense, affirming our convictions so heartily and making such hilarious fun of the more tiresome of our contemporaries, that we went on till what was for Paul a late hour, walking the autumn streets and stopping off for coffee and beer at Childs' and the Lafayette, almost as if we had been back in the twenties, with the new era of American art just beginning to burst into life between Macdougal Street and Irving Place. Less than a year later, Paul died of a heart attack as he was coming out of a movie, to which he had gone alone.

And now, despite the miseries of his later years, he remains for me, looking back, one of the only sound features of a landscape that is strewn with distortions and wrecks: a being organically moral on whom one could always rely, with a passion for creative art extinguishable only with life. It has worried me to reflect that the rise in morale I thought I had noted in him when I talked to him last was not, after all, to lead to anything, and to remember how unhappy and insecure, how unrewarded, he was at the end. There are tragedies of untimely death which—coming at the end of a man's work or breaking off his career at a crisis—represent a kind of fulfillment. But one can find no justice in Paul's. His death had no dramatic appropriateness; nor was it preceded, I fear, by any very steady serenity. It had been obvious, in view of the interest that had been stimulated in American music, partly through Paul's own efforts, and of the quantity of books about music that were now getting into type, that it was time for a reprinting of Paul's criticism; and the suggestion had been made to two publishers that an omnibus be brought out. But he had not had even this gratification. One can only reassure oneself by remembering that the work he had done was of the kind that pays for itself, because it is done for love, in the desire to give life away, and because it brings, in the doing, elevation and liberation of spirit. To have had thirty years of such work is not the least enviable of destinies; and Paul's best writing bears on every page his triumph and his justification.

1947

INDEX

An asterisk indicates a reference to an author whose work is mentioned without his being named.